THE
NEW
LIFETIME
READING PLAN

FOURTH EDITION

THE
NEW
LIFETIME
READING PLAN

FOURTH EDITION

CLIFTON FADIMAN AND JOHN S. MAJOR

HarperCollins*Publishers*

HarperCollins books may be purchased for educational, business, or sales promotional use. For information, please write to: Special Markets Department, HarperCollins Publishers, Inc., 10 East 53rd Street, New York, New York 10022.

FOURTH EDITION

Designed by Ruth Lee

Library of Congress Cataloging-in-Publication Data
Fadiman, Clifton, 1904–
    The new lifetime reading plan / Clifton Fadiman and John S. Major.—
4th ed.
        p.   cm.
    Includes bibliographical references (p.   ) and index.
    ISBN 0–06–270208–4
    1. Best books. 2. Books and reading. I. Major, John S. 1942– . II. Title.
Z1035.F29   1997
011'.7—dc21   97-2975

97 98 99 00 01 ❖/RRD 10 9 8 7 6 5 4

CONTENTS

PART TWO

PART FOUR

CONTENTS

CONTENTS

PREFACE

The Lifetime Reading Plan was first published in 1960; the second and third editions, with revisions and amplifications, appeared in 1978 and 1986. Those editions, in the distinctive voice of Clifton Fadiman, distilled and shared the reflections of a lifetime dedicated to reading. With this fourth edition of the Plan, Mr. Fadiman for the first time has a co-author; and I feel greatly honored to have been asked to join him in this enterprise. I will say more below about how we divided the work of preparing this edition.

Readers familiar with earlier editions of *The Lifetime Reading Plan* will notice several significant changes in this new version. The changes begin on the title page—the book is now *The New Lifetime Reading Plan*, to emphasize that this edition has been very substantially revised and enlarged. The most pervasive, and most significant, change is that the material recommended for reading has been broadened to include works from the literatures of the whole world. As recently as a decade ago it was reasonable to construct a program of guided reading that included only works in the Western tradition, while acknowledging that a time might come when a shrinking world, and improvements in various communications media, would make familiarity with all of the world's literary traditions a requirement for the well-educated and well-read person.

That time has come sooner than one might have expected. For an American in the last decade of the twentieth century, the "global village" is a reality, the world having been shrunk by jet aircraft, by communications satellites, by instantaneous television news from everywhere, and by the Internet, to the extent that, in a sense, nothing is foreign to anyone's experience. Moreover, the United States, from its origins a nation of immigrants, has been enriched anew in recent years by fresh arrivals from all over the world, one consequence of this being that as a people, our cultural roots have become more diverse than ever before. Because our country is now more profoundly multicultural than ever, and also because it is to everyone's personal advantage to cast as wide a net as possible in harvesting the world's cultural riches, the works suggested in *The New Lifetime Reading Plan* now include Lady Murasaki along with Miss Austen, Tanizaki cheek-by-jowl with Faulkner, Ssu-ma Ch'ien as well as Thucydides. We think that these additions to the Plan will enhance both your pleasure and your sense of achievement as a reader.

The inclusion in this edition of such works as the Koran—the fundamental scripture of Islam—and the Zen scripture *The Platform Sutra of the Sixth Patriarch* raises the question of why the Bible is not listed here as well. The reason is simple. We assume that nearly every reader of this book will own a Bible and be at least somewhat accustomed to reading it; and there is nothing we might try to say about it that would not seem presumptuous.

A number of authors represented in earlier editions of the Plan have now been dropped, as having not stood the test of time as well as one might earlier have expected. These include George Santayana, John Dewey, and André Malraux (the latter demoted to a supplementary list of twentieth-century authors). Dropped, too, are several larger works of synthesis, such as the Durants's *Story of Civilization*. With the expansion of the book to include the non-Western world, we quickly realized that it would be better to drop that category of work, and to restrict our recommendations to what Robert Hutchens of the University of Chicago termed "original communications"—books that retain the capacity to speak directly to us across gulfs of time and space. In addition to some two dozen writers from the non-Western world, a few new authors from the Western tradition appear here for the first time, including W. H. Auden, Charlotte Brontë, Emily Dickinson, Anthony Trollope, and Edith Wharton.

Also appearing here for the first time are a handful of scientists, from Galileo to Thomas Kuhn. Science is a somewhat difficult category to accommodate adequately in the Plan, for several reasons. Scientific writing is frequently highly technical, making demands of knowledge that most readers cannot meet. Scientists have often, in addition, not been very good writers, nor has the culture of science necessarily encouraged an agreeable literary style; so many scientific works give little pleasure to the nonspecialist reader. It is also true that books have usually not been the medium of choice for original communications in the sciences; most often scientific discoveries have been described in short papers presented at learned meetings or published in professional journals or, more commonly today, distributed as "preprints" on the Internet. But there have been exceptions to these patterns, and we present several of the most interesting of them here.

Still another change in this edition of the Plan is in the arrangement of material. In earlier editions, the readings were arranged topically, under such headings as Narratives, Plays, and Poetry, being grouped within those categories by original language. With the addition of non-Western works to the Plan, that arrangement began to seem more confusing than helpful. In this edition, works, regardless of genre or original language, are arranged in simple chronological order by the birthdates of their authors. (Dates are given in the culturally neutral form "Before Common Era" [B.C.E.] and "Common Era" [C.E.] in place of the specifically Western and Christian designations B.C. and A.D.) We have divided the body of the book into five parts that represent nothing but broad spans of time. They have no general worldwide significance—Heian Period Japan is not equivalent to medieval Europe in any meaningful way—but they might encourage you to look for particular contrasts and similarities in works from widely different places but of roughly the same age. Dividing the contents of the book into smaller parts will also, we hope, make the prospect of reading through all of these works seem less daunting than it might otherwise.

A device that has been retained from earlier editions is the practice of including in our discussions cross-references from one author to others. These take the form of numbers in brackets; for example, talking of Thucydides, Fadiman says, "He is the first historian to grasp the inner life of power politics. Hobbes [43], Machiavelli [34], and Marx [82] are, each in a different way, his sons." These cross-references are not intended to make you turn immediately to the authors mentioned, or to try to follow a zigzag path of reading as one cross-reference leads to another. Rather their purpose is to get your attention, to make you pause for a moment to consider that the authors of these original communications have, over years and centuries, carried on a Great Conversation with each other; we can listen in. And even in cases where no direct communication could be expected, there is often resonance; like calls to like, which is why the essay on Confucius contains a cross-reference to Plato.

Following the main entries for the Plan, I have added a new section called Going Further. This lists, with very brief comments, selected works of 100 additional authors from the twentieth century, writers that you are likely to find to your taste if the books recommended and discussed at greater length have pleased and interested you. The Bibliography and Suggestions for Further Reading of previous editions have now been combined into a single Bibliography, which I have revised and updated as necessary.

Most of the entries in this edition have been carried forward from the third edition, with revisions ranging from minor to extensive. Clifton Fadiman has written new essays for some of the new Western authors included in this edition. I have written all of the essays describing the non-Western materials, as well as those for a handful of the newly included Western authors. Mr. Fadiman and I are very closely in accord in our literary opinions and judgments; we would hardly have undertaken this joint project otherwise. Nevertheless we have decided to sign each essay with the initials of its author; part of the value of this book should derive from the freedom of its authors to be opinionated, and we did not want to strive for an artificial homogeneity either of style or of judgment.

All of these changes have but one purpose, which is to make the Plan available and useful to a new generation of readers.

J.S.M.

A PRELIMINARY TALK WITH THE READER

The books here discussed may take you fifty years to finish. They can of course be read in a much shorter time. The point is that they are intended to occupy an important part of a whole life. Many happen to be more entertaining than the latest bestseller, but it is not on the entertainment level that they are most profitably read. What they offer is of larger dimensions. It is rather like what is offered by loving and marrying, rearing children, carving out a career, creating a home. They can be a major experience, a source of continuous internal growth. Hence *lifetime*. These books are life companions. Once part of you, they work in and on and with you until you die. They should not be read in a hurry, any more than friends are made in a hurry. This list is not something to be "got through." It is a mine of such richness of assay as to last a lifetime.

The aim is simple. The Plan is designed to fill our minds, slowly, gradually, under no compulsion, with what some of the greatest writers have thought, felt, and imagined. Even after we have shared these thoughts, feelings, and images, we will still have much to learn: We all die uneducated. But at least we will not feel quite so lost, so bewildered. We will have disenthralled ourselves from the merely contemporary. We will understand something—not much, but something—of our position in space and time. We will know how we have emerged from our long human history. We will know how we got the ideas by which, unconsciously, we live. Just as important, we will have acquired models of high thought and feeling.

I do not wish to claim too much for *The New Lifetime Reading Plan*. It is not magic. It does not automatically make you or me an educated man or woman. It offers no solution to life's ultimate mysteries. It will not make you happy—such claims are advanced by the manufacturers of toothpastes, motorcars, and deodorants, not by Plato, Dickens, and Hemingway. It will merely help to change your interior life into something a little more interesting, as a love affair does, or some task calling upon your deepest energies.

Like many others, I have been reading these books, off and on, for most of my long life. One thing I've found out is that it's easy enough to say they enlarge you, but rather difficult to prove it to younger readers. Perhaps it's better to say that they act like a developing fluid on film. That is, they bring into consciousness what you didn't know you knew. Even more than tools of self-enhancement, they are tools of self-discovery. This notion is not mine. You will find it in Plato, who, as with many other matters, thought of it first. Socrates called himself a midwife of ideas. A great book is often such a midwife, delivering to the light what has been coiled like an embryo in the dark depths of the brain.

For whom is this Reading Plan meant? Not for the highly educated or even (not always the same thing) the very well read. They would find nothing new in what we have to say. The titles here listed would be perfectly familiar to them. Indeed, they could add many more, and legitimately quarrel with some of our choices.

In general the Plan is meant for readers from eighteen to eighty plus, who are curious to see what their minds can master in the course of their remaining lifetime, but who have not met more than ten percent, let us say, of the writers listed. It is meant for college graduates who were exposed to many of these books during the undergraduate years but who successfully resisted their influence. It is meant for the college graduate—his or her name is legion—to whom most of these writers are hardly even names. It is meant for the high school graduate who might well have profited from a college education but did not have the chance to do so. It is intended for that great and growing army of intelligent men and women who in their middle years are penetrated by a vague, uncomfortable sense that the mere solution of the daily problems of living is not enough, that somewhere, some other worlds of thought and feeling are calling out for exploration. It is intended for the eager young man or woman of modest means (many of these books can be bought for little money) for whom the thrills of business competition or homemaking, while valid, are inadequate. It is intended for the retired elderly who have found that growing roses or looking at television does not leave them mentally exhausted. It is intended for teachers (college teachers, too, in some cases) who would like to deepen and extend their knowledge and sensitivity, and so deepen and extend the nonmaterial rewards of their noble vocation.

C.F.

(The above is an edited and shortened version of the original *A Preliminary Talk* . . . , which appeared in earlier editions. My work on this new edition has been greatly facilitated by the help of my invaluable assistant, Anne Marcus.)

PART ONE

I

ANONYMOUS

ca. 2000 B.C.E. (Scribe Sin-Leqi-Unninni, ca. 700 B.C.E.)

The Epic of Gilgamesh

The *Epic of Gilgamesh* is without doubt the world's oldest surviving narrative poem, and one of the founding works of Western literature. It has not yet become widely known among general readers because the poem had been lost for many centuries prior to its rediscovery in the nineteenth century (and so played no role in Western literature from the Greeks to the Victorians), and because until recently its translators have tended not to work with the general reader in mind. With several excellent and accessible translations now available, there is no longer any reason to remain unacquainted with this remarkable glimpse into the mind of highest antiquity.

The epic relates a number of myths that attached themselves to the reputation of Gilgamesh, who seems to have been an actual king of the Sumerian city-state of Uruk around 2700 B.C.E. Scattered passages of the earliest version of the epic, in Sumerian, have been dated to around 2000 B.C.E.; the fullest known text, in Babylonian, was written by a scribe named Sin-Leqi-Unninni on tablets deposited in the library of King Ashurbanipal around 700 B.C.E. These and other tablets containing parts of various versions of the epic began turning up in archaeological excavations in Iraq and nearby countries in the nineteenth century; the scholarly work of assembling and collating the texts took many years, with some loose ends still stirring controversy in academic circles. The epic was evidently once much longer than the version that now exists. Its poetic style shows strong traces of oral origins; it is sometimes laconic,

3

often formulaic, even incantatory, and with a strong narrative pulse.

The epic as we now have it opens with a description of the physical strength and beauty, and the political power, of King Gilgamesh, but then quickly shifts perspective to tell how the people of Uruk feared and resented his arrogance and arbitrary exercise of power. To teach Gilgamesh humility, the gods created Enkidu, a hairy, wild man of the desert, to be Gilgamesh's rival and alter-ego. Gilgamesh sends a temple girl, Shamhat, into the wilderness to seduce Enkidu and so tame him. She does so, and brings him back to Uruk. When he arrives, he and Gilgamesh wrestle each other fiercely but soon realize that neither can overcome the other. Thereafter they become sworn brothers, and decide to embark on an adventure: to find and slay the terrible monster Humbaba. After they do so, the jealous goddess Inanna sends down the Bull of Heaven to destroy Uruk. Gilgamesh and Enkidu succeed in killing the bull also, but at the cost of Enkidu's life. Gilgamesh, disconsolate, goes on a journey to visit the keeper of the Underworld, Utnapishtim; the latter tells him the story of the great world-engulfing Flood, teaches him to accept the lesson of mortality, and allows him to return to Uruk.

It will be obvious to anyone raised in the traditions of Judaism, Christianity, or Islam that the *Epic of Gilgamesh* contains many parallels with the oldest books of the Hebrew Bible: The urbane, handsome Gilgamesh and the wild, hairy Enkidu recall Jacob and Esau, as Enkidu and Shamhat resemble Sampson and Delilah; the havoc wrought by the Bull of Heaven brings to mind the discord created by the casting of the Golden Calf during the years in the Wilderness (and Moses destroys the calf just as Gilgamesh kills the bull). The flood described by Utnapishtim sounds just like the flood of Noah. And so on. One might think at first that these themes in *Gilgamesh* are echoes of the Bible, but in fact the situation is just the reverse: one of the things that is most fascinating about the *Epic of Gilgamesh* is that it is *a precursor* of the Bible (though with no hint of Biblical monotheism). However one feels about the divine inspiration of the Bible itself, it is apparent from *Gilgamesh* that several key themes of the Hebrew Bible were couched in terms of symbols that had already been current in Mesopotamia for over a thousand years before the Bible began to be written.

Such weighty considerations aside, the *Epic of Gilgamesh* is well worth reading as a story of love and friendship, of adventure and danger and grief, and of a proud man's humbling encounter with mortality. The epic is now available in several fine English versions; I particularly like the verse translations by Danny P. Jackson and by David Ferry.

J.S.M.

2

HOMER
ca. 800 B.C.E.

The Iliad

The *Iliad* and the *Odyssey* are two long, ancient Greek narrative poems called epics. They are the first as well as the greatest epics of our civilization. Every time we refer to a siren or Achilles's heel or compare a lovely woman to Helen of Troy we are borrowing from these poems that are perhaps three thousand years old.

I say perhaps. We do not know when Homer lived—maybe between 800 and 700 B.C.E., maybe earlier. As a matter of fact we do not even know *whether* he lived. We do not know whether the stories were written by one man named Homer; or, as the old joke has it, by another fellow of the same name; or by a syndicate; or even, as Samuel Butler thought in the case of the *Odyssey*, by a woman. These questions are for scholars. The poems are for us.

Originally, it is supposed, they were listened to rather than read. Homer, whomever he or she was or they were, recited them.

The *Iliad* tells the story of some fifty days of the last of the ten years' siege of Troy (or Ilium) by a number of tribes we loosely call Greeks. This siege resulted in the capture and firing of Troy's "topless towers," which we know to have actually existed. To find out how Troy was taken, see Virgil's *Aeneid* [20].

The *Iliad* is probably the most magnificent story ever told about man's prime idiocy: war. The human center is Achilles. The main line of the narrative traces his anger, his sulkiness, his savagery, and the final assertion of his better nature. He is the first hero in Western literature; and ever since, when we talk of heroic qualities, Achilles is somewhere in the back of our minds, even though we may think we have never heard of him.

You can look at the *Iliad* through a diminishing glass. Then it becomes the story of a trivial scuffle, marked by small jealousies and treacheries, fought by long-dead semibarbarians who had hardly advanced beyond the sticks-and-stones era. The wars of The *Iliad*, compared with our splendid planetary slaughters, are petty stuff.

Strangely enough, when you actually start to read the *Iliad* the lens of this diminishing glass changes and becomes a magnifier. The scale of the war becomes unimportant; the scale of the men and the gods enlarges. The essential quality of the *Iliad* is nobility. Nobility is a virtue connected with magnitude; there are no small nobilities. General Eisenhower's *Crusade in Europe* was a useful book, portraying the largest single military and naval exploit in all history. Yet, compared with the *Iliad* recounting a local struggle of little historical importance, it lacks magnitude. This is no reproach to General Eisenhower. He was no Homer.

And there never has been another Homer. If a reading of the *Iliad* and the *Odyssey* does nothing else for us, it makes us reflect on the difference between art and science. There has been "progress" in the latter; there is none in the former. All imaginative artists, but only if they are great enough, seem contemporaries. That is the way to read them.

C.F.

3
HOMER
ca. 800 B.C.E.

The Odyssey

The *Odyssey* is a kind of sequel to the *Iliad*. It tells what happened to the Greek heroes after the sack of Troy. More especially it follows the fortunes of one of them: Odysseus, King of
Ithaca, also known as Ulysses. It describes what happened to
him during his ten years' long voyage home; the search of his
son Telemachus for his father—a theme repeated in hundreds
of novels since, such as Joyce's *Ulysses* [110]; the arrogant woo-
ing by the suitors of his patient wife, Penelope, during his
absence; Odysseus's return; and his bloody revenge on his enemies. The story is well known even to those who have never
read it. Like the Bible, it is less a book than part of the permanent furniture of our minds.

When we take up the *Odyssey* after the *Iliad* we step into a
different world. Even its sound is different. That of the *Iliad* is
clangorous with the clash of arms; that of the *Odyssey*, mur-
murous or thunderous with the myriad-mooded sea.

But the difference is more basic. The *Iliad* is tragic. It
announces a theme repeated in Western literature ever since,
and one that obsesses our own private minds: the limitations of
even the noblest spirits in the face of a world seemingly gov-
erned by unchangeable Fate. But the *Odyssey* is not tragic. It
stresses not our limitations but our possibilities. Its theme is
not courage in the face of death, but intelligence in the face of
hardship. It announces another of the great themes: the power
of intelligence, a theme to which we moderns readily respond.
Though Odysseus is brave enough, his heroism is of the mind.
He is not outsized in passion, like Achilles, but of human
dimensions, like us.

The tone of the *Odyssey* corresponds to this more homely
conception of man. While full of fairy-tale episodes, it

impresses us as does a realistic novel; indeed it is the first of all realistic novels, as it is the first of adventure stories, and still perhaps the best.

It is in this spirit that we may read it today, as a narrative of adventures that happened to an unusual man whose mind never stopped working. The mood of the *Odyssey* is more relaxed than that of the *Iliad.* And so should ours be as we read it.

C.F.

4
CONFUCIUS
551–479 B.C.E.

The Analects

For many people in the modern West, the most difficult step in reading and appreciating the *Analects* is to get beyond the stereotyped image of Confucius himself as a quaint oriental gentleman speaking in fortune-cookie aphorisms. His name was not Confucius, of course; that was bestowed on him by Jesuit missionaries in the seventeenth century, a time when, for Europeans, every respectable philosopher needed a Latin name. (*Confucius* is a Latinized form of K'ung-fu-tzu [*pinyin* Kongfuzi]'—meaning 'Great Master K'ung.')

His family name was K'ung, his personal name Ch'iu [Qiu]; he came from an old and respected family of the lower nobility, the class that in the medieval West would be called knights or *chevaliers*. He grew up as an expert archer and charioteer, a man of vigorous action as well as exquisite manners. He lived in a time of great social and political change, when the old

---

'There are two systems for spelling Chinese words in English in common use. I use the older Wade-Giles system in this book, because I think most American readers are more comfortable with it; but I also give the newer *pinyin* spelling in square brackets after the first use of each Chinese term. — J.S.M.

Chou [Zhou] Dynasty was losing its grip and the country was breaking apart into mutually hostile smaller states. His military skills were becoming obsolete; massive infantry armies and new weapons had doomed the old style of chivalrous small-scale warfare (not unlike that described by Homer [2]).

Confucius needed a new profession, and he tried, as did many others like him, to make his way as a freelance political advisor, drawing on his knowledge of history and the precedents found in ancient documents to help rulers survive in their newly danger-ous age. His fondest hope was to become prime minister of a state and use that position to restore the standards that he thought marked the founding of the Chou Dynasty, five hundred years earlier. He briefly held an official post in his home state of Lu, but never succeeded in convincing a ruler to apply his advice in a sys-tematic way. Though for a hundred generations of East Asians, Confucius has been the paradigm of a teacher and a sage, and though he has been one of the most influential philosophers in history, by his own criteria he was a failure. He died beloved by his disciples, but a disappointed man.

Confucius believed that the key to good government and social harmony was a proper adherence to natural hierarchies: 'Let the father be a father, and the son a son.' From the obedi-ence and deference owed by a child to a parent, and the corre-sponding protection and education given by the parent to the child, he thought, every other social relationship could be deduced: ruler and minister, husband and wife, elder and younger, even friend and friend (because each would defer to the other). He had an optimistic view of human nature, but believed that education was essential to develop that nature to its full potential. And, like Socrates (as described by Plato [12]), he understood that a recognition of one's own ignorance is the foundation of learning.

Though a man of deeply conservative views, Confucius opposed hereditary privilege in favor of a meritocracy—proba-bly his greatest gift to Chinese history, and to the world. His ideal was the *gentleman*, but he imbued that word with special

9

meaning: A gentleman, for him, was anyone whose actions, education and deportment marked him as such, while a lout whose father happened to be an aristocrat was no gentleman at all. Confucius also opposed written codes of law, which he saw as an invitation to deceit and evasiveness; he favored instead the rule of *li*, a word that has no English equivalent but which embraces, in part, the concepts of etiquette, decorum, ritual, and common law. This unwritten social code was to be put into action in a government run by the natural meritocracy of the virtuous (and it is interesting to compare this class with the ruling elite in Plato's *Republic*).

If Confucius wrote anything during his lifetime, it does not survive; the *Analects*, a collection of his conversations, lessons, and miscellaneous sayings, began to be compiled by his disciples shortly after his death, and was added to over a period of several generations. The book has no continuous narrative thread, and there are occasional passages that are obscure or confusing. Some of the teachings will seem self-evident, even banal; this is perhaps because they have so often proved to be true over a period of twenty-five centuries. Some readers will be bothered by Confucius's conservatism, and especially his unquestioning embrace of a patriarchal system that relegated women to an inferior status; reflect that the same charge could be leveled at every great thinker of the ancient world.

The *Analects* is a fairly short book, worth reading and re-reading; it is the record of a lively and generous mind.

J.S.M.

5

AESCHYLUS
525–456/5 B.C.E.

The Oresteia

(Ancient Greek tragedy is so different from the plays we are familiar with that the beginning reader will do well first to

study some standard book on the subject; or to consult the relevant chapters in a history of Greek literature; or at least to read carefully the notes and introductions usually accompanying the translation. You might also look up the myths associated with the names of the chief personages in the recommended play. See the Bibliography for some suggestions for further reading.

Classic Greek drama was written in verse, usually in an elevated and formal style. It was presented in the open air at the yearly festival at Athens in honor of the god Dionysus. That means the plays were part of a religious ceremony, attended, as a civic duty, by all or most of the citizens. The plays were given as trilogies, followed by a shorter play of a comic nature, and the dramatists competed with one another for the laurel of victory. Aeschylus's Oresteia is the only complete surviving trilogy.

It is hard for us to visualize these ancient Greek sunlit productions. They incorporated music, dance, and choral song, and doubtless words were declaimed or chanted in a manner quite dissimilar to our modern realistic convention. As the plots were usually reworkings of famous legends, they offered no suspense; everyone knew the story in advance. Two features, among others, that seem strange to us were the Chorus, which acted as a kind of commentary on the action, and the Messenger, who recounted offstage events, particularly if they were of a violent kind. As we approach Greek drama we must try to keep in mind that it is religious in origin and partly so in effect; and that its language and action are not in our sense "realistic.")

Though he did not "invent" Greek tragedy, Aeschylus is generally considered its earliest leading practitioner and so the ancestor of all Western tragic drama. He lived through the great days of the growth of the Athenian democracy and himself helped in its ascendancy, for he fought at Marathon and perhaps at Salamis. Born in Eleusis, near Athens, he spent most of his life in and around Athens, dying in Gela, Sicily, from the effects, says an improbable story, of a tortoise dropped by an eagle on his bald head. Of his ninety plays, seven survive.

Best of these is the trilogy known from its central character as the *Oresteia*. Its theme is one frequently encountered in Greek legend, family blood-guilt and its expiation. The *Agamemnon* is a play about murder, the murder of the returned hero Agamemnon by his faithless wife, Clytemnestra. The *Choephoroe (Libation-Bearers)* is a play about revenge, the revenge taken on Clytemnestra by Orestes, Agamemnon's son. The *Eumenides (Furies)* is a play about purification: the tormenting of Orestes by the Furies and his final exoneration by a tribunal of Athenian judges and the goddess Athena. The entire trilogy is a study in the complex operations of destiny, heredity, and pride, which produce a tragic knot untied by the advent of a higher conception of law and order.

As the word for Homer [2] is noble so the word for Aeschylus is grand. He cannot be read as modern plays are read. His language is exalted and difficult; it struggles magnificently to express profound ideas about guilt and sin, ideas that have become part of the world of imaginative literature right up to our own day with O'Neill [115] and Faulkner [118]. Aeschylus is much more akin to the author of the Book of Job than to even the best of our contemporary dramatists. He must be approached in that spirit.

C.F.

6

SOPHOCLES
496–406 B.C.E.

Oedipus Rex, Oedipus at Colonus, Antigone

Sophocles was born in what we would call a suburb of Athens, of upper-class family. He held high office; he was a constant victor in the dramatic competitions; he developed in various ways the relatively primitive techniques of Aeschylus [5]; he lived long and, it appears, happily; and he was one of the greatest ornaments of the Periclean Age. Of his more than one hundred twenty plays, we possess seven. But these suffice to place him among the few great dramatists of all time.

Formulas are treacherous. But it is not entirely untrue to say that the beginning reader may best see Aeschylus as a dramatic theologian, obsessed with God and his stern edicts. Sophocles may be seen as a dramatic artist, concerned with human suffering. Euripides [7] may be seen as a playwright-critic, using the legends as a vehicle for ideas current in his skeptical and disillusioned era.

The three recommended plays of Sophocles are all about the same family, that of King Oedipus, but they were not written as a trilogy. The order of their composition is *Antigone, Oedipus Rex, Oedipus at Colonus.* (The last, written by a very old man of undiminished powers, was produced in 401 B.C.E. after Sophocles's death.) If you wish, you may read them in the order of the chronology suggested by their action: *Oedipus Rex, Oedipus at Colonus, Antigone.* Together they are often called the Oedipus Cycle or the Theban Plays.

In his *Poetics,* Aristotle [13] tells us that Sophocles said he portrayed people as they ought to be, Euripides portrayed them as they are. He might have added that Aeschylus portrayed people as demigods driven by single outsize passions. Sophocles is particularly noted for the lyrical beauty of his choruses.

Aristotle considers *Oedipus Rex* the ideal play, admiring it especially for its plot and construction. Today we might stress other qualities. There is no doubt, however, that it is the most influential Greek tragedy in existence, the one most often revived, the one most universally studied. Its basic myth, that of a man who killed his father and married his mother, suggested to Freud [98] the name for the Oedipus complex. (Max Beerbohm called the Oedipuses "a tense and peculiar family.")

After reading *Oedipus Rex*, you may find yourself asking two profound questions that continue to be asked down to our own day: First, Is man free or bound? Second, If the intelligence brings tragedy, to what degree is it good? Technically the effect of the play depends in large part on the masterly use of dramatic irony—the device whereby the audience is in possession of crucial facts hidden from the protagonist.

Oedipus at Colonus is a difficult play, even for the learned reader. Unlike *Oedipus Rex*, it is not well knit; its interest does not lie in its plot. Perhaps it should be approached as a kind of miracle or mystery play, a study of a man more heavily burdened with guilt and knowledge than is normal, whose life is at last vindicated and given meaning by both the gods and the city of Athens. In the end Oedipus becomes a kind of transcendent hero, like King Arthur, and, also like him, comes to a mysterious end.

The *Antigone* is psychologically the most complex of the three plays. It has been viewed as a study of the conflicting claims of convention and a higher law of conduct, or, differently phrased, of the state and the individual. It is also one of the many Greek plays about hubris, or excessive pride—in this case, the pride of Creon—and the ruin that attends such immoderacy of feeling. You will encounter this notion again in Herodotus [8]. Before you start the *Antigone,* keep in mind that to the ancient Greeks the proper burial of the dead was a matter of overwhelming importance. Also you must accept the Greek idea (or at least Antigone's idea) that a husband or child is replaceable, a brother never.

In the Oedipus Cycle, Sophocles deals with the downfall of greatness. But he is inspired as much by the greatness as by the downfall. We might say that the special Sophoclean emotion comes from the tension between his sad recognition of man's tragic fate and his admiration for man's wondrous powers.

C.F.

7
EURIPIDES
484–406 B.C.E.

Alcestis, Medea, Hippolytus, The Trojan Women, Electra, The Bacchae

Though possibly fewer than fifteen years junior to Sophocles [6], Euripides inherited a different Greek world, torn by intellectual doubt and civil strife. His work seems to reflect the change. In Sophocles's sense of tragedy, there is a certain grave serenity; not so with Euripides.

He was born at Salamis, where the famous naval battle was fought. He appears to have led a retired, perhaps even an embittered life. One story has him living alone in a cave by the sea. Of his possibly ninety-two plays, nineteen survive, if *Rhesus* is genuine. Though they were popular, he won the prize, according to one account, only five times to Sophocles's eighteen.

Of the three great Attic tragedians, Euripides is the most interesting in the sense that his mental world is least alien to our own. A son of the all-questioning Sophists, swayed by the irony of Socrates, he, like us, felt the uncertainty of all moral and religious values. His later career contemporary with the suicidal Peloponnesian War, he, too, lived in a crisis period marked by fear, pessimism, and political confusion. The development of his genius was irregular and his thought is not consistent, but we can say that his outlook was rationalistic, skeptical, and, even if not in the exalted Sophoclean pattern, tragic. He would understand without difficulty certain existentialist and vanguard writers of today.

His plays are generally, though not always, marked by theatricality, even an operatic luridness; by exaggerated coincidence; by the employment of a knot-resolving "god from the machine"; by dialogue that is often debate and oration rather than impassioned speech; by a mixture of tones (Is *Alcestis* a serious or a comic play?); by unconventional, even radical ideas—*The Trojan Women* empties war of its glory, the *Medea* can be taken as a feminist tract, other plays portray the gods as either delusive or unlovely; by a remarkable talent for the depiction of women—the portraits of Phaedra and Medea are miracles of feminine psychology; and finally by a pervading interest, not in the relations between human beings and some supernal force, but in the weaknesses and passions of our own natures. As a psychologist and vendor of ideas, Euripides is the ancestor of Ibsen [89] and Shaw [99].

And yet he eludes formulas. His plays at times seem to be the broken record of a search for certainties that were never found. He can write realistic, even down-to-earth dialogue but also choruses and speeches of rare beauty. Plutarch tells us that certain Athenians, taken prisoner at Syracuse, were freed because they recited so enchantingly some passages from Euripides. He seems often to be a skeptic, almost a village atheist; yet in his masterpiece, his last play, the *Bacchae,* he delves profoundly and with strange sympathy into humanity's recurrent need for irrationality, even for frenzy. Euripides is not of a piece. Perhaps therein lies part of his fascination for a time that, like ours, specializes in damaged souls.

I have suggested six plays. They are arranged in the probable order of their composition or at least representation. But many others repay study, among them *Heracles*, *Hecuba* and *Andromache.*

As you read Euripides, see whether you can understand why Aristotle [13] called him "the most tragic of the poets."

C.F.

8

HERODOTUS
ca. 484–ca. 425 B.C.E.

The Histories

Of Herodotus we know mainly that he was born of good family in Halicarnassus, a city in Asia Minor, originally a Greek colony, but under Persian control for half his life. We know also that he traveled widely throughout the entire Mediterranean world, presumably amassing the materials that went into his *Histories,* a word that in the original Greek means inquiries or investigations. His work was famous during his lifetime and has never ceased to be so.

Herodotus states his purpose: to preserve "from decay the remembrance of what men have done" and to prevent "the great and wonderful actions of the Greeks and the Barbarians from losing their due meed of glory." The latter part of his book fulfills his purpose. It gives us as full and objective an account of the titanic struggle between Persia and Greece as was possible for this pioneer historian. With these "actions" we associate such glorious names as Marathon, Thermopylae, and Salamis, battles in a war in possible consequence of which we are today a part of Western rather than Asiatic culture.

But the earlier portions of the book, while all leading up to this grand climax, are really a kind of universal cultural history, mingling fact, anecdote, and myth, of the entire known world during the time immediately preceding and contemporary with Herodotus's own period.

In a manner sometimes confusing, sometimes enchanting, he mixes journalism, geography, ethnography, anthropology, fables, travelers' tales, and marketplace philosophy and moralizing. Though he writes in prose and about real rather than legendary events, he is nearer to Homer [2, 3] and to art than to the modern historian and so-called scientific history. The later Roman critic Quintilian said he was "pleasant, lucid, diffuse." All three adjectives are precise.

Hence the beginning reader should not seek in him a clear and, by present-day standards, correct account of the Greek–Persian Wars. He should be read, at least at first, in great long gulps, almost carelessly. He should be read for the stories, the digressions, the character descriptions, the fantastic oddments of information about the manners and customs of dozens of ancient peoples. And he should be read for the pleasure of meeting Herodotus himself—sometimes gullible, sometimes skeptical, always humane, humorous, curious, and civilized. Don't worry overmuch about who is who and what is where. The absorption of specific facts is less important than immersing yourself in the broad, full, buoyant Herodotean river of narrative. The Greek critic Longinus, who said of him "He takes you along and turns hearing into sight," gives us our cue—just to go along and see things.

C.F.

9

THUCYDIDES
ca. 470/460–ca. 400 B.C.E.

The History of the Peloponnesian War

Called by Macaulay "the greatest historian that ever lived," Thucydides belonged to a highly placed Athenian family and saw Athens at its height under Pericles. He was himself involved as a general in the war he chronicled. In 424 B.C.E., as a consequence of his failure to relieve the Thracian town of Amphipolis, he was removed from his command and banished, enduring twenty years of exile before being pardoned. In his history he refers to this crucial episode with brief, cold, third-person detachment. During these twenty years he traveled about in Sparta and elsewhere seeking and verifying the facts that form the material of his book. A tradition states that he was assassinated, perhaps in 400 B.C.E.

Never finished (it breaks off in 411 B.C.E.) but somehow a satisfying whole, his history records the great Greek Civil War between the imperial forces of Athens and the coalition headed by Sparta. The emphasis is almost entirely on the second half of the war, of which in his mature years Thucydides was a contemporary. This phase began in 431 B.C.E. and ended in 404 B.C.E. with the defeat of Athens, perhaps the most hopeful civilization the world has ever known and to whose purely intellectual eminence we have never since attained. Thucydides knew he had a great tragic subject. He devoted to it limited but magnificent talents of whose worth he was quite aware. With calm confidence he states that his work will remain "a possession for all times." So far he has not been proved wrong.

Though Thucydides and Herodotus [8] are partially contemporary, they have little else in common. Unlike Herodotus, Thucydides does his best to be what we now call a scientific historian. He believes the proper ordering of sufficient facts plus the exercise of a powerful mind can explain historical processes. He rejects entirely all fuzzy explanations, such as Herodotus's childlike notion of an avenging Nemesis, ever alert to punish arrogance like that of the Persians. He scorns omens, oracles, and prophecies; he does not need the gods. He analyzes the motives, rarely idealistic, that impel leaders and so precipitate great events. He supplements his extraordinary psychological insight with notable understanding, considering his time, of the demographic and economic forces that underlay the Peloponnesian War.

Where Herodotus is gossipy and digressive, Thucydides is austere and unified. He is not a cultural historian, but a politico-military one. He is skeptical, charmless—and, let us admit, difficult. He cannot be read except with one's full attention and is one of those writers who yield more with each rereading. Finally, he is the first historian to grasp the inner life of power politics. Hobbes [43], Machiavelli [34], and Marx [82] are, each in a different way, his sons.

Despite his severity and aristocratic denial of emotion, he grips the serious reader. Of the forty speeches he puts into the mouths of his historical personages, at least one, Pericles's Funeral Oration (Book II), is a supremely great dramatic monologue. Masterpieces also, though of differing kinds, are his accounts of the plague at Athens (Book II), the Melian dialogue (Book V), and the terrible Sicilian expedition (Books VI and VII) that signaled the end of Athenian dominance.

C.F.

10
SUN-TZU
ca. 450–ca. 380 B.C.E.

The Art of War

Very little is known about the life of Sun-tzu [Sunzi], except that he is a real Chinese historical figure, a younger near-contemporary of Confucius [4]. His name was Sun Wu (the honorific suffix *-tzu* simply means 'Master'), and the brief testimony of early historical records suggests that he had a successful career as a general and military planner in one or more of the kingdoms of the Warring States Period into which China dissolved in the waning centuries of the Chou [Zhou] Dynasty. Some time after his death, probably in the early to mid-fourth century B.C.E., his disciples wrote down what they remembered of his teachings. *The Art of War* is a more unified and doctrinally coherent book than the *Analects*, which suggests to some scholars that it was written down over a shorter period of time and by a group of people personally well-versed in Sun-tzu's teachings. In any case, the book attributed to Sun-tzu set the standard for all subsequent Chinese writings on military matters.

It is in some ways strange that *The Art of War* has been so highly esteemed, and so much imitated, as it has been throughout the history of traditional China. From pre-Confucian times, and even more so under the influence of Confucius and his school, Chinese social philosophy has downplayed the political role of warfare, and has insisted that military matters had to be kept firmly under the control of a civilian bureaucracy; little praise or honor was accorded to personal military prowess. (A famous Chinese proverb says "Do not take good iron to make a nail, do not take a good man to make a soldier.") On reading *The Art of War*, one sees that the apparent paradox resolves itself; it becomes clear that Sun-tzu was more a philosopher than a strategist, one who taught that the best victory is attained without a battle. Sun-tzu was a realist who recognized that warfare sometimes could not be avoided, and then must be pursued with the utmost vigor to a successful conclusion; his special talent lay in teaching rulers how to deploy their forces to maximum advantage. But he never glorifies warfare; his voice is that of a mature man dealing with the world as it is, not of a glory-seeking adolescent hero. Sun-tzu would not have had much use for Achilles (Homer [2]).

For Sun-tzu, the overall goal of the military strategist is plain: to maximize the effectiveness of whatever forces a ruler might have at his command. If the force be inherently great, choose a suitable target and a sufficient reason for attack, and crush the enemy with a single blow. If the force be weak and inadequate, find ways to elude, deceive, ambush, and exhaust the enemy so as to even the odds. Like Machiavelli [34], Sun-tzu did not trouble himself about the legality or morality of his methods; espionage, sabotage, and deceit were all fair play. It was, he insisted, best not to fight at all; if it became necessary for a state to fight, its ruler had no moral obligation greater than preserving the state's existence through victory.

Sun-tzu's forthright approach to power—his willingness to engage in no-holds-barred combat, his consistent and close attention to detail (such as "devise contingency plans on terrain vulnerable to ambush"), and the clarity of his style—has led in recent years to a new vogue for *The Art of War*, as a handbook of business management. The book itself and many derivative works have made their way onto the bookshelves of boardroom strategists, merger-and-acquisitions lawyers, personnel managers, and other modern warriors whose careers, like those of ancient Chinese kings, are fraught with danger and uncertainty.

Samuel B. Griffith's translation of *The Art of War* was for many years the standard version; it is still reliable. I prefer, however, the recent excellent translations by Roger Ames and by Ralph Sawyer, both of which incorporate up-to-date scholarship on the text.

J.S.M.

11
ARISTOPHANES
448–388 B.C.E.

Lysistrata, The Clouds, The Birds

We mentioned above, in the introduction to Aeschylus [5] and other Greek playwrights, that at the festivals of Dionysus a tragic trilogy was customarily followed by the performance of a comedy. This was not for any reason so trivial as to lighten the mood of the playgoers before they headed home. Rather, because tragedy and comedy alike were viewed as inseparable aspects of the human condition, it was considered necessary and appropriate to enact both at what was after all a solemn religious occasion. But it is also true that the rites of Dionysus allowed normal bounds of decorum and propriety to be set aside temporarily; the comedies performed during the festival played into that disruption of the normal social rules. Comedy was (and is) "transgressive," to use a critical term now much in vogue. In his plays Aristophanes hurled barbs of humor that still strike our funnybones today; even if we no longer recognize many of his topical references, we can at least imagine the discomfort of the targets skewered by his wit.

Eleven of the comedies of Aristophanes survive, the only substantial remaining body of early Greek comic plays. He was acknowledged a master of the form in his lifetime, and his reputation has remained high ever since, in part for reasons that unfortunately will not be accessible to most of us. He is, I am told, a brilliant stylist in Greek verse; he was also an accomplished parodist, capable of imitating and burlesquing the styles of Euripides [7] and Aeschylus [5]. These are matters that largely get lost in translation. But those of us who do not read Greek can still appreciate much of Aristophanes's humor. His basic comedic technique was to set up an absurd situation and then make his characters carry the situation through to its furthest extremes; this is a device that is employed constantly in movie and television comedies today. *The Clouds* is a satire on Socrates and other contemporary philosophers, who are made to seem as airheaded as the clouds among which they dwell. *The Birds* sets up a fantastic avian utopia when the world's birds decide to free themselves from the snares and arrows of humans; they beat their wings to prevent the smoke of sacrificial fires from rising to Olympus until they are granted their own realm—where they quickly show themselves to be as pompous, vain and fatuous as the humans they are trying to escape. *Lysistrata*, perhaps now the most famous of Aristophanes's comedies, has the women of Athens go on strike against their husbands, refusing all sexual favors until the men call off a war that they are planning. Here we see Aristophanes as a man of principle; a contemporary of Thucydides [9], he risked unpopularity or worse by opposing the Peloponnesian War, and indeed any military ventures that might compromise the republican simplicity of his beloved Athens.

Comedy fails if it is not funny, but as anyone who has ever had anything to do with the theater will affirm, it is also a very serious matter. As Freud [98] has pointed out, humor allows us to confront, and then deflect, taboos that can disturb us deeply at an unconscious level. Comedy has long had a role in bringing unpleasant realities into the light of day, as witness the privileged position granted to court jesters by rulers from Chinese emperors to Ottoman sultans to Burgundian dukes. Aristophanes used his plays to puncture pomposity, ridicule impropriety, and protest against jingoism and warmongering. He was certainly not the first writer to understand the social power of comedy, but he is one of the earliest that we know about, and still one of the greatest.

J.S.M.

12
PLATO
428–348 B.C.E.

Selected Works

Plato is less an author than a world of thought. He is probably one of the half-dozen most influential minds in Western civilization. Alfred North Whitehead has said that all Western philosophy consists of a series of footnotes to Plato, an exaggeration (or minimization), but not entirely untrue. The beginning reader cannot hope to explore the entire Platonic world, nor should he attempt it. The readings suggested below enable us to make his acquaintance and that of his master Socrates. And that is all.

A wealthy Athenian who lived through his city-state's great and also declining days, Plato experienced one supremely crucial event in his long life: his meeting with Socrates. (Compare Boswell and Johnson [59].) He had many talents, and was drawn, for example, toward both poetry and politics; but Socrates determined him to a life of thought, undertaken on many fronts.

The result of this life of thought was a series of "dialogues," long and short, some very beautiful, some dull, and most of them spotlighting his master Socrates. The "Socratic method" was part of the atmosphere of the period. Socrates questioned all things, and particularly the meanings men attached to abstract and important words, such as justice, love, and courage. The questioning was real; the truth was finally approached only through the play of minds, that give-and-take we call "dialectic." This mode of thought is exemplified and perfected in the dialogues. They are not mere exercises in mental agility (except occasionally) but works of art in which all the resources of a poetic and dramatic imagination are called into play. The reader of Plato, no less than the reader of Shakespeare, is reading an artist.

You should keep in mind three central Platonic notions: The first is that, as Socrates says, "a life without inquiry is not worth living." That lies at the heart of everything Plato wrote. The second notion is that virtue is knowledge; the sufficiently wise person will also be sufficiently good. The third notion has to do with the kinds of knowledge most worth having. Plato believed in "Ideas," invisible, intangible archetypes or prototypes of things and actions and qualities. These latter, as we know them on earth through the distorting veil of the senses, are but faint reflections of the heavenly Ideas. We call this mode of apprehending the universe Idealism; and Plato is its father.

His philosophy, however, is not a consistent whole, and in many respects it changed as he grew older and lost faith in humanity's ability to govern itself wisely. I suggest therefore that the dialogues be read, not as systematic expositions of dogma, but as the intellectual dramas they are, full of humor, wit, mental play, unforgettable extended similes called myths, and particularly full of one of history's most fascinating characters, the ugly, charming, mock-modest Socrates.

It might be best to begin with the *Apology,* in which Socrates defends himself against the charges of atheism and corrupting the youth. As we know, his defense was a failure—he was executed, by self-administered poison, in 399 B.C.E. The dialogue has, however, been a success for almost twenty-four hundred years.

Follow that with the *Crito.* Here Socrates gives us his reasons for refusing to escape from prison. Then perhaps the *Protagoras,* in many ways the most sheerly brilliant of the dialogues, and the perfect exemplification of Plato using all his talents. Some may wish to try the *Meno,* recording Plato's famous doctrine of recollection. Then comes the *Symposium,* practically a drama in its movement and structure. This deals with love in all its phases, including that accepted Greek passion, love between males. It deals also with drunkenness, as well as with more exalted matters.

After this perhaps the *Phaedo.* The sections on immortality may be skimmed or skipped, but the last few pages, describing Socrates's noble death, are required reading. Many good judges have felt them to be the finest short piece of narrative ever written. Finally, absorb as much as you can of Plato's most ambitious and rather difficult work, the *Republic,* which outlines his highly conservative ideal state and is the ancestor of all the Utopias and Dystopias—see Huxley [117] and Orwell [123]—that have since appeared.

So many of our notions and ways of thought go back to Plato (including some fantastic and even harmful ones) that knowing nothing of him means knowing less about one's self. To discover Plato is not merely to discover a masterly intellect. It is to come face to face, if you are an inheritor of the Western tradition, with much of the hitherto unsuspected content of your own mind.

C.F.

13
ARISTOTLE
384–322 B.C.E.

Ethics, Politics, Poetics

Aristotle tells us that education is accompanied by pain. An education in Aristotle himself certainly involves, if not pain, at least difficulty. Unlike his master, Plato [12], he is charmless. Furthermore, the fact that we do not possess his original works but only what has come down to us as probably students' notes, does not make for readability. You are warned not to expect from Aristotle the pleasure Plato offers, except that pleasure which comes from following the operations of a supreme brain.

Aristotle's intellect was one of the most comprehensive, perhaps *the* most comprehensive, on record. He wrote on everything, from marine life to metaphysics. While it is unwise to say that all these writings (many of merely antiquarian value today) can be related under a single system, it is true that Aristotle was a systematizer in the sense that Plato was not. He believed in the collectability and relatability of all knowledge. He spent his life collecting and relating. Our idea of an encyclopedia, a most fruitful notion, goes back to him.

Today we would say he was of upper-middle-class origin. At seventeen or eighteen he left his small native town of Stagira for Athens. Here for twenty years he studied at Plato's Academy. The influence of Plato is marked in his work (often by disagreement or development), but we know nothing about the personal relations between the two greatest philosophers of antiquity.

After Plato's death Aristotle sojourned for five years in Asia Minor and Lesbos, possibly engaged in biological research, for his mental bent was scientific and investigative, rather than artistic and speculative. In 343/2 B.C.E. he went to Macedon to tutor the future Alexander the Great. There is no evidence, despite all the sentimental romancing, that he greatly influenced Alexander's mind. The one great Alexandrian idea, that of a world imperium, is not Aristotelian.

In 335/4 B.C.E. Aristotle returned to Athens; organized his own school, the Lyceum; taught, wrote, investigated. In 323 B.C.E., perhaps because of his suspect connections with the Macedonian party, he found it expedient to exile himself from Athens. A year or so later the mere man Aristotle died in Chalcis, in Euboea. His influence, however, though it has had great downward swoops, has never died.

We cannot comment here on his crucial pioneering in logic—he is credited with inventing the syllogism—or in scientific method or in the biological and cosmological sciences or in esthetics. His *Poetics,* an analysis of classic Greek tragedy, has had a profound and continuing effect on literary criticism. In general we may say that his whole approach to life is more earthbound than Plato's, less utopian, certainly more geared to the actual nature and abilities of the ordinary man or woman.

This is borne out by a reading of the *Ethics* and the *Politics*.

The *Ethics* tries to answer the basic question, What is the Good? It involves an inquiry into happiness and the conditions that attend it; and into virtuous actions, thought of as means between two extremes of conduct. The "Golden Mean" is an Aristotelian catchword.

Ethics is a part of politics, for to Aristotle (and the Greek citizen in general) the individual cannot be thought of fruitfully except as a social and political animal. The *Politics* deals specifically with men in association. Much of our twenty-four hundred years of speculation as to the best form of government, whether ideal or contingent upon circumstances, traces back to ideas found in the *Politics*. This is not to say that Aristotle gives us universal political "truths"—for example, his views on slavery (as on women) are conditioned by his era. But his classification of the forms of government; his sense of the state as a *development*, not an imposed system; and his notion that the state must have a moral aim beyond that of a mere freezing of power: all this makes him alive and pertinent today.

The serious reader (and for Aristotle no other kind is possible) can handle all of the *Ethics*. Take it slowly. You might concentrate on Books I, II, III, VI, and X. Of the *Politics,* possibly the first and third of the eight books are the easiest of access.

C.F.

14

MENCIUS

ca. 400–320 B.C.E.

The Book of Mencius

Mencius was the second great philosopher of the Confucian school, exceeded in importance and historical reputation only by Confucius [4] himself. Mencius—his Chinese name was Meng-tzu [Mengzi]—was the disciple of a disciple's disciple, placing him doctrinally in a direct line of descent from the

Master in a society where the relationship between teacher and pupil was almost as important as that between father and son. The prestige and moral authority that Mencius enjoyed as a spiritual heir of Confucius helps to explain how he survived insulting a king to his face; the incident is described in the famous opening passage of the *Book of Mencius.*

Mencius, who like others of his class made his living as a wandering philosopher offering advice to the rulers of China's warring states, visited King Hui of the state of Liang. The king received him graciously, remarking that since Mencius had taken the trouble to come such a long way, he must have brought something that would profit his kingdom. Mencius responded with a wholly un-Confucian vehemence, verging on rudeness: "My teachings are concerned solely with benevolence and righteousness," he thundered. "How can there be any talk of 'profit?'" What are we to make of this response?

Mencius lived in an era that seemed to mock Confucius's hope of restoring the virtuous rule of the early Chou Dynasty. States repeatedly went to war against others, and the losers were annexed by the winners; treaties were made and broken with impunity; thrones were usurped and kings put to death by their courtiers or even by their own sons; prowess on the battlefield was the surest route to preferment at court; and codes of law began to replace the old aristocratic unwritten rules of conduct. Under these circumstances, Mencius devoted his career to an inquiry into human nature: Is human nature fundamentally good? If it is, what accounts for evil in the world?

Mencius's answer is that human nature is good but malleable. People can easily be led astray; hence the emphasis Mencius, like all Confucianists, placed on education, and particularly on moral education—an emphasis still honored throughout East Asia today. Beyond that, Mencius stressed the importance of virtuous leadership in creating a just society. The ancient Chinese political theory of the "Mandate of Heaven" held that the benevolent moral force of the cosmos itself would resonate so strongly with the moral character of a supremely virtuous man as to make him not only a natural ruler, but also one invulnerable to challenge. The founder of a dynasty would hand this tradition of virtuous rule down to his descendants, and with it the protection of Heaven that virtue conferred. But if the ruler ceased to be virtuous, Heaven would withdraw its Mandate, and a virtuous rebel would rise to found a new ruling house.

How, asks Mencius, does one know if a ruler has the Mandate? Like responds to like, he points out; if a ruler is virtuous, his goodness shining throughout the world will resonate with the goodness of human nature itself. People will flock from everywhere to live under the rule of such a monarch. Or, conversely, they will flee by night to escape the rule of a bad king, or, in extreme circumstances, rise in rebellion against a tyrant. Is it regicide to execute an evil king? No, answers Mencius, because he has already lost the Mandate; he ceased to be a king before he was deposed.

This explains Mencius's answer to King Hui of Liang: Only by basing his reign on benevolence and righteousness can the king show that he possesses Heaven's Mandate. If he perfects benevolent rule, people everywhere will long to be his subjects. That would surely benefit the king and his domain; but, as Mencius emphasizes, to concentrate on that outcome, rather than on the way to achieve it, would be to accomplish nothing.

The teachings of Mencius helped shape the ethical basis of monarchy in China for two millennia. Of course, no emperor ever felt able to rely only on Mencian "benevolence and righteousness" to the exclusion of armies and law codes, tax-collectors and constables, but the principle that people, being basically good, respond positively to virtuous rule was deeply embedded in Chinese political theory.

I should also note that the intensely social and communitarian views of the Confucian school did not go unchallenged; in addition to the *Analects* and the *Book of Mencius* you might also want to read the basic texts of Taoism, namely the *Tao Te Ching* [*Daodejing*] and the *Chuang-tsu* [*Zhuangzi*]. The first posits a monarchical absolutism based on the ruler's attunement to the *Tao*, or universal force; the second takes a stance of radical relativism, and argues for self-preservation through nonentanglement in the affairs of the world.

The *Book of Mencius*, like most other early Chinese philosophical works, was compiled by several hands rather than written personally by its nominal author. But it is accessible and coherent, and worth reading in its entirety. There is, moreover, an important reason for modern Americans to read Mencius: He is a distant ancestor of our own Revolution. In the seventeenth century, European Jesuit missionaries in China sent back glowing reports of the virtue and moderation of Chinese imperial rule, hoping to show that the Chinese were highly civilized and therefore presumably amenable to Christian conversion. The Jesuit letters were read avidly by Leibniz, Voltaire [53], and other leaders of the Enlightenment; Voltaire especially used an idealized vision of China as a platform from which to criticize the European rulers of his day. From his writings, and other sources, the Mencian idea that people have the right to rebel against a wicked monarch entered the political climate of the late eighteenth century. In the Declaration of Independence [60] Thomas Jefferson does not quite say that King George III has lost the Mandate of Heaven; but the resemblances between our founding political documents and the collected sayings of an ancient Chinese philosopher are nevertheless not accidental.

J.S.M.

15

Attributed to VALMIKI

ca. 300 B.C.E.

The Ramayana

Like almost all ancient Indian literature, The *Ramayana* is shrouded in mystery. We have the poem itself, a masterpiece of narrative verse on an epic scale; we know of its enormous influence, through translations into dozens of languages, on the literature, dance, and art of South and Southeast Asia. But when, where and by whom this brilliant work was written are questions that will never be answered satisfactorily. Of Valmiki, its nominal author, nothing whatsoever is known. At most one can surmise that the poem was composed over a long period of time by storytellers and wandering bards who shaped historical events and legends from the early centuries of the Aryan invasion of northern India (around 1200 B.C.E.) into what gradually became a single narrative. The *Ramayana* seems to have been written down in Sanskrit around 300 B.C.E. The text acquired some stability in written form, though it continued to evolve as it was translated into other languages and literary forms. It is one of the earliest works of Indian literature to be written in the *sloka* form, which consists of four lines of eight syllables each (or, more precisely, two double lines of sixteen syllables each) and admits of a variety of rhyme schemes and metric patterns. The *sloka* became the principal stanza form for classical Sanskrit verse; see, for example, Kālidāsa [23].

The *Ramayana* is a long narrative that combines a romantic tale of love and loyalty with warfare, adventure, and miraculous powers of good and evil. At the beginning of the tale, the noble King Rama wins the hand of Sita by being the only contestant in an archery match able to bend the bow of the god Siva (this motif recalls the archery contest in the *Odyssey* [3] in which Odysseus defeats the suitors of Penelope; the motif is found in very similar form in the *Mahabharata* [16]). Soon Rama is treacherously deprived of his kingdom and forced to live in the wilderness with Queen Sita and his loyal friend Laksmana. In Rama's absence, Laksmana is distracted from his task of guarding Sita by a mesmerizing golden deer that leads him into the forest. The deer, it transpires, has been conjured up by the evil monster Ravanna, king of the enslaved land of Lanka, precisely to get Sita alone. Ravanna tries to seduce her, but is repulsed; finally he simply kidnaps her and carries her off to Lanka. Much of the tale is devoted to the efforts of Rama and Laksmana to rescue Sita, which they finally do with the aid of the Monkey King Hanuman and an army of monkey warriors; Rama then reclaims his own throne. The story ends on a tragic note. When Rama brings Sita home to his royal city, the people reject her, because they doubt she preserved her chastity in captivity. She is forced to live once again in the forest, where she gives birth to Rama's heirs; when at last Rama comes to find her, she vanishes into the earth. The tale is Homeric in scope but utterly un-Homeric in mood, though the enchanted lands and grotesque monsters of the *Ramayana* have something in common with those of the *Odyssey*.

The *Ramayana* is a wonderful tale to read for its romance and adventure. It should also be an important part of one's personal Lifetime Reading Plan because its influence on the literature of a large part of the world would be impossible to exaggerate; this is part of the world literary canon. Just as Greek theater drew on a body of stories about gods and heroes that every Greek knew (see our introduction to Aeschylus [5]), so the various adventures and travails of Rama, Sita, Laksmana, Hanuman and the other characters of the *Ramayana*, along with the tales and characters of the equally important *Mahabharata*, form an inexhaustible source of stories for South and Southeast Asian drama, narrative dance, shadow-puppet theater, and simple folk tales. Their influence has spread more widely than one might expect; for example, the heroic trickster Monkey King of the Chinese novel *Journey to the West* [36] is Hanuman in another guise. Moreover, today as in the past, for millions of Indians Rama and Sita are not only completely real historical figures but also manifestations of the divine—literally a god and goddess. Just a few years ago a Hindu mob in the grip of neo-nationalist fervor spent several days razing a mosque that had been built on the site of the supposed birthplace of Lord Rama at Ayodhya; this is living literature with a vengeance.

The complete *Ramayana* is very long, and contains elements (such as lengthy recitations of the participants in various battle scenes) that are not much to our taste today. But there are several very good abridged translations that can be read with great pleasure; see the Bibliography for specific suggestions.

J.S.M.

16
Attributed to VYASA
ca. 200 B.C.E.

The Mahabharata

Like the *Ramayana* [15], the *Mahabharata* came together gradually over the course of the first millennium B.C.E. from oral tales of warfare and intrigue in the early days of the Aryan conquest of India. It is written in a variety of verse forms, including a sort of metrical prose, but it is primarily in *slokas* (for which see the *Ramayana*). One of several claimants to the title of "world's longest poem" (the true champion is probably the Kirghiz national epic, *Manas*), the *Mahabharata* began to assume written form around 200 B.C.E. Two centuries or so later it swallowed whole the *Bhagavad Gita*, which does indeed fit into the narrative of the *Mahabharata* but which previously had had an independent existence as a written text, and which usually is treated as a separate work, a practice that we follow here (see the next entry [17]).

Like the *Iliad* [2], the *Mahabharata* is an epic tale of war. It is narrated by the priest Vaisampayana, a disciple of the play's nominal author, Vyasa. That Vyasa's historical existence is doubtful is unimportant. He is presented in the epic itself as being of the lineage of its heroes, and as having the literary role of acting as a witness to the events of the epic, and thus of a guarantor of the authenticity of Vaisampayana's narrative. The epic is long and immensely complicated; the following summary of the plot is an oversimplification. It concerns two sets of cousins: the seven Pandava brothers, sons of King

Pandu, and the hundred Kaurava brothers, sons of King Dhritarastra. The cousins should have been friends and allies, but they become estranged by an escalating series of insults and rivalries (including a famous episode in which Arjuna, noblest of the Pandavas, wins the hand of Princess Draupati in an archery contest that recalls the *Ramayana*'s story of how Rama wins the hand of Sita). Finally the Kauravas, consumed by an almost demonic greed and rage, conspire to cheat the Pandavas of their birthright, and even of their princess, by engaging them in a crooked game of dice. With the last fatal cast of the dice, Bhima, the strongest and fiercest of the Pandavas, vows to "split open the body and devour the guts" of the leader of the Kauravas; war is the only possible outcome.

The war itself is recounted in a long series of set pieces, interrupted by numerous digressions—this is a *very* long poem. (An Indian proverb says "If you can't find something in the *Mahabharata*, it can't be found anywhere.") There is great slaughter among the armies of both sides, but, like Homer, Vyasa (or whoever wrote the *Mahabharata*) is uninterested in the fate of common soldiers. The poem keeps attention focused on the aristocratic principal players, and on the attributes they represent: Arjuna, a prince of supreme elegance and lofty moral principles—he resembles the Trojan Hector, except that his side wins; Bhima, as strong as Ajax and as filled with reckless rage as Achilles; Draupati, as implacable as Medea (see Euripides [7]) in seeking revenge for the wrongs done to her; Dhritarastra, grieving like Priam for the deaths of his sons; and many other stirring characters. The *Mahabharata* presents drama on a scale more archetypal than human; like the *Ramayana* it has proven to be an inexhaustible source of scripts for performance versions of all kinds (see, for example, Kālidāsa's *Sakuntala* [23]).

It is possible to read the *Mahabharata* in an unabridged English translation, but you will be happier with one of several excellent abridgments. The best of these are in prose; the decision of most translators not to try to reproduce the rhythms of the original verse is probably a wise one, though one regrets losing that dimension of the work. The most remarkable modern *Mahabharata* is the 9-hour performance version written by Jean-Claude Carrière for Peter Brook's theatrical company. Both on stage and on the printed page, Carrière's heroically long play succeeds in making the ancient Indian epic sing anew to our own time.

J.S.M.

17
ANONYMOUS
ca. 200 B.C.E.

The Bhagavad Gita

The *Bhagavad Gita* is set in the opening moments of the war between the Pandavas and the Kauravas recounted in the *Mahabharata* [16], and in fact the *Bhagavad Gita* is now embedded in the *Mahabharata*, an integral part of the larger work. But it seems clear that the *Gita* was written separately from, and later than, the rest of the *Mahabharata*; where the longer poem is an epic of dynastic warfare, the *Gita* is fundamentally a work of philosophy. And yet the philosophy of the *Bhagavad Gita* is the key to understanding the *Mahabharata* as a whole.

As the two opposing armies take the field, Arjuna, greatest of the Pandavas, calls upon the god Krishna to help him and his brothers. Krishna declines to take sides, but neither will he remain aloof from the battle; he says that he will fight on one side, and his own army will help the other side. He offers Arjuna the choice, and Arjuna wisely chooses Krishna alone rather than his innumerable horde of troops; Krishna becomes Arjuna's charioteer. As the battle is about to begin, Arjuna loses his nerve. He cannot, he tells Krishna, bear to think of killing the Kauravas, who are his uncles and cousins; he would rather die than dishonor himself in an ignoble battle.

Time stands still on the battlefield as Krishna instructs Arjuna in his duty. As the dialogue unfolds between hero and god, Krishna reminds Arjuna that the world itself is but an illusion; moreover even in the realm of what seems to be, there is no distinction between past, present and future. Arjuna's role is to fulfill his *dharma*, the path of duty laid out for him by fate. The responsibility for the coming death in battle of the Kauravas is not his; "even without you," says Krishna, "all these warriors arrayed in hostile ranks will cease to exist. They are already killed by me. Be just my instrument, the archer at my side!" Arjuna asks Krishna to reveal himself in his full divine glory; when his request is granted, he is overcome by awe and accepts his fate—the battle can commence.

The *Bhagavad Gita* is a short work, one that can be read in an hour or two but which repays many rereadings. I think you will agree with me that it is a work of almost hair-raising power and magnificence. This is a view that has been shared by many people in the West. The *Gita* was one of the first works of Indian classical literature to be translated into English when the British East India Company consolidated its colonial control of India. Emerson [69] admired the *Gita*; Thoreau [80] had a copy with him at Walden Pond and read it with enthusiasm. Perhaps the most famous Western quotation of the *Bhagavad Gita* was also the most apt: When Robert Oppenheimer observed the Trinity Test, the world's first explosion of an atomic device, he quoted the divine Krishna: "Now I am become Death, destroyer of worlds."

There are many English translations of the *Bhagavad Gita*; the version by the late Barbara Stoler Miller is, in my view, far superior to most others.

J.S.M.

18
SSU-MA CH'IEN
145–86 B.C.E.

Records of the Grand Historian

In early China, beginning well before the time of Confucius [4], royal governments included officials known by a title that we translate into English as Grand Historian. This official's duties involved not only preserving official documents and keeping a chronicle of the king's acts, but also responsibility for observing, interpreting, and recording portents and omens, everything from flocks of birds behaving strangely to a comet in the sky. Any of these could be warnings that Heaven was displeased with the ruler's stewardship of his realm. The position required special skills ranging from record-keeping to astrology, and so the office of Grand Historian was often handed down from father to son. In the second century B.C.E. two Grand Historians, Ssu-ma T'an [Sima Tan] and his more famous son Ssu-ma Ch'ien [Sima Qian], compiled a work that is one of the greatest histories every written.

China was unified in 221 B.C.E. by the famous First Emperor, Ch'in Shih-Huang-Ti [Qin Shihuangdi], whose tomb guarded by thousands of terra-cotta soldiers is one of the wonders of the ancient world. In an effort to suppress seditious independent thinking and to bring all knowledge under his own control, the emperor tried with some success to burn all privately owned books. When the imperial library was also burned in the rebellion that soon ended the emperor's repressive regime, China was in danger of losing its literary heritage. Under the succeeding Han Dynasty, teams of scholars were put to work to reconstruct the lost books from memory. As part of the same impulse to recover the past, Grand Historian Ssu-ma T'an was given the task of compiling a complete and systematic history of the world (i.e. China and its environs) from the beginning of time. Upon his death in 110 B.C.E., his son inherited both his office and the principal authorship of the great work that the father had begun, the *Shih chi* [*Shiji*]— a title that can be translated either as *The Historical Records* or *Records of the Grand Historian*.

The *Shih chi* is a massive work of 130 substantial chapters; it has never been translated in its entirety into a Western language. It consists of twelve chapters of narrative history, from the (mythical) Yellow Emperor, founder of Chinese civilization, up to the second century B.C.E.; ten chapters of dynastic tables and genealogies; eight treatises on such subjects as ritual, music, calendrical astronomy, water resources, and the agricultural economy; thirty chapters on the great royal and aristocratic families of the Chou era and the Warring States Period prior to the unification of China; and seventy chapters of biographies (some individual, some collective) of prominent people of all walks of life, from statesmen and generals to bandits and court jesters.

In its sheer scope the *Shih chi* is a remarkable work. Even more remarkable, perhaps, is how interesting, even entertaining, it is to read today. This is in part because Ssu-ma Ch'ien was a superb prose stylist in Classical Chinese (which has encouraged the literary efforts of his translators), and in part because his attitude toward the writing of history still strikes us as so modern. With Thucydides [9], he was one of the fathers of scientific history; he was careful to use only those earlier chronicles and historical documents that he thought were demonstrably accurate. He searched for old archives in the former capitals of defunct warring states; for recent history, he had access to, and quoted frequently from, documents in the Han imperial library.

His efforts to record the past conscientiously have stood the test of time. At the beginning of the twentieth century certain scholars applying modern Western critical methods proclaimed their "discovery" that the kings of the ancient Shang Dynasty (ca. 1500–1050 B.C.E.) named by Ssu-ma Ch'ien had never existed at all. Within a few years, however, archaeological excavations vindicated the ancient historian; the evidence showed that his genealogy of the Shang kings was entirely correct. It is quite amazing that Ssu-ma Ch'ien could have written about rulers a thousand years before his own time with such accuracy.

The *Shih chi* was completed under circumstances of heroic moral fortitude. Ssu-ma Ch'ien's monarch, Emperor Wu of the Han Dynasty, was one of China's greatest emperors, vigorous, far-sighted, and martial; he vastly extended the territory under Chinese rule. He was also a tyrant who reacted ferociously to any suggestion of disloyalty, as Ssu-ma Ch'ien learned to his sorrow. A certain general was punished for suffering a disastrous defeat on the northern frontier; Ssu-ma Ch'ien spoke up in the general's defense. For this temerity, he was condemned to be castrated. The expected outcome of this sentence was that he would commit suicide to spare himself a humiliating fate, but in a moving letter to a friend, he explained that he was willing to live on as a eunuch in order to bring his great work to completion. History is in his debt, not only for his own work, but because the *Shih chi* became the model for twenty-four subsequent official dynastic histories—each new dynasty considered it a sacred duty to write a history of its predecessor; so even did the Republic of China, which overthrew the monarchy in 1911. This continuous historical record from the second century B.C.E. to the twentieth century is unmatched by any other culture in the world.

For the modern reader, Burton Watson's *Records of the Grand Historian of China* is overwhelmingly the best translation of the *Shih chi*. I recommend that you read, in Volume I of Watson's translation, *Shih chi* chapters 6 ("Basic Annals of the First Emperor of Ch'in"), 68 ("Biography of Lord Shang"), and 87 ("Biography of Li Ssu"); and in Volume II, chapters 30 ("Treatise on the Balanced Standard" [i.e., money and taxation]), 110 ("Account of the Hsiung-nu"), 118 ("Biographies of the Kings of Huai-nan and Heng-shan"), 121 ("Biographies of the Confucian Scholars"), 124 ("Biographies of the Wandering Knights"), and 129 ("Biographies of the Money-makers"). I think that once you start you will want to read this book from cover to cover.

J.S.M.

19
LUCRETIUS
ca. 100–ca. 50 B.C.E.

Of the Nature of Things

Of Lucretius we know virtually nothing. A tradition states that he was driven mad by a love potion and that he ended his own life. This note of violence is at least not contradicted by the vein of passionate intensity running through his great and strange poem, *De Rerum Natura*.

We do not today cast our explanations of the physical and moral world into hexameters. But in classic times poetry was often the vehicle of instruction and propaganda. Lucretius's poem is such a vehicle.

His temperament was original, his thought less so. As he proudly avers, he borrowed his system from the Greek Epicurus (341–270 B.C.E.), who in turn derived parts of his theory from two earlier Greek thinkers, Democritus (fl. 5th century B.C.E.) and Leucippus (ca. 460–370 B.C.E.). The Epicurean philosophy has little in common with our modern use of the phrase. Acknowledging pleasure (or, more accurately, the absence of pain) as the highest good, it rests its ethics on the evidence of the senses. But the pleasures Epicurus recommends are those flowing from plain living and high thinking.

Denying the existence of any supernatural influence on men's lives, Epicurus holds that the world and all things in it are the consequence of the meeting and joining of refined but quite material atoms. Lucretius expounds this materialism systematically, explaining everything from optics to ethics in terms of atoms. He empties the world of God; his gods are do-nothing creatures living in the "interspaces," caring nothing about men. In effect he is an atheist. He attributes the origin and behavior of all things to the movement of the atoms composing them. Free will is saved by the idea of the "swerve" of some atoms, a break in the general determinism. To Lucretius, the soul dies with the body. He exhorts the human race to live without the fear born of superstition. *Of the Nature of Things* is pioneer rationalist propaganda.

The "atomic theory" of Lucretius was less absurd than many other early Greek explanations of the universe, but in all truth it has little resemblance to our modern atomic theory, and too much should not be made of the anticipation. On the other hand, Lucretius foreshadows much of our own thought in the fields of anthropology, sociology, and evolution. Like Euripides [7], he would have been quite at home in our century.

As we should expect, his poem is knotty and difficult, for physics and cosmology do not translate easily into verse. It is remarkable that he should have succeeded as well as he did. While there are many opaque stretches, they are worth struggling through in order to come upon the frequent passages of intense eloquence and beauty. These flow from Lucretius's ability, unmatched until we meet Dante, to hold in his head a complete vision of things and to body it forth in concrete, sometimes unforgettable images.

In Virgil's [20] famous line, "Happy is he who knows the causes of things," the reference is probably to Lucretius. It is Lucretius's passion for knowing causes, his stubborn refusal to be fobbed off with myth and superstition, together with his uneven but powerful art, that commend him to our modern temper. No matter how wrong he was in detail, it was a titanic achievement to build a universe out of nothing but matter and space.

C.F.

20
VIRGIL
70–19 B.C.E.

The Aeneid

The poet called by Tennyson "wielder of the stateliest measure ever moulded by the lips of man" used that measure to celebrate Rome's high destiny, yet was no Roman but a Gaul. He was born near Mantua, situated in what was then called Cisalpine Gaul. His quiet life was marked by study in Rome and by years of contemplation and composition at his Mantuan farm and later on at his residences in Campania. His relatively brief life span may point to the fragile physique of which we have other evidence. The great Maecenas, minister of the greater Emperor Augustus, was his patron, as he was that of Virgil's friend, the poet Horace.

Labor on his masterwork occupied his entire last decade. He felt the *Aeneid* to be unfinished and, dying, ordered its destruction. This was prevented by Augustus, however, whose gesture seems odd to us in an age when heads of state are not only proudly ignorant of literature but in some cases not even particularly literate.

Homer [2,3] may be said to have begun European literature, Virgil to have begun one of its subdivisions, the literature of nationalism. The *Aeneid* was written with a deliberate purpose: to dramatize, through the manipulation of legend, the glory and destiny of that Rome which had reached its high point in Virgil's own Augustan Era. The *Aeneid* is no more an "artificial" epic than is the *Iliad*. But it is a more self-conscious one. Writing it, Virgil felt he was performing a religious and political duty. Aeneas is called "pious," by which is meant that he was not merely orthodox in religious observance but faithful to the idea of Roman supremacy. The *Aeneid*'s political center of gravity may be located in the famous lines of Book VI, in which the spirit of Anchises is showing forth to his son the glorious future of Rome: "Romans, these are your arts: to bear dominion over the nations, to impose peace, to spare the conquered and subdue the proud."

Because this nationalist (but not at all chauvinist) ideal is one of the keys to Virgil's mind, the reader should be aware of it. But for us it is not the important thing. The *Aeneid* today is a story, a gallery of characters, and a work of art.

Its story is part of us. We may not have read Virgil, but nonetheless a bell rings if mention is made of Dido or the death of Laocoön or the Harpies or the Trojan Horse. The personages of the *Aeneid,* particularly the unhappy Dido and the fiery Turnus, have also remained fresh for two thousand years. Its art, hard to summarize, is not always immediately felt. It is based on a delicate, almost infallible sense of what words can do when carefully, often strangely, combined and juxtaposed and subdued to a powerful rhythm. It is this that has made Virgil among the most quoted of all poets. And back of the story, the characters, the art, there vibrates Virgil's own curious sense of life's melancholy, rather than its tragedy, his famous *lacrimae rerum*. The Virgilian sadness continues to move us though the Rome he sang has long been dust.

Keep in mind that the *Iliad* and The *Odyssey* influenced Virgil decisively. Indeed the *Aeneid*'s first six books are a kind of *Odyssey*, the last six a kind of *Iliad*, and Homeric references are legion. But Virgil is not as open as Homer. He requires more effort of the attention, he does not have Homer's outdoor vigor, and for his master's simplicity and directness he substitutes effects of great subtlety, many, though not all, lost even in the finest translation.

C.F.

21

MARCUS AURELIUS
121–180

Meditations

Marcus Aurelius Antoninus, ruler of the Roman Empire from 161 to his death, is the outstanding example in Western history of Plato's [12] Philosopher-King. His reign was far from ideal, being marked by wars against the barbarian Germans, by severe economic troubles, by plague, and by the persecution of Christians. It will be remembered not because Marcus was a good emperor (though he was), but because, during the last ten years of his life, by the light of a campfire, resting by the remote Danube after a wearisome day of marching or battle, he set down in Greek his *Meditations*, addressed only to himself but by good fortune now the property of us all.

The charm, the sweetness, the melancholy, the elevation of The *Meditations* are his own. The moral doctrines are those of the popular philosophy of the time, Stoicism, as systematically expounded by the Greek slave (later freed) Epictetus (ca. 55–ca. 135). Its ethical content is roughly summed up in Epictetus's two commandments: Endure and Abstain. Stoicism passed through many modifications, but in general it preached a quiet and unmoved acceptance of circumstance. It assumed a beneficent order of Nature. Humanity's whole duty was to discover how it might live in harmony with this order, and then to do so. Stress was laid on tranquillity of mind (many of our modern inspirational nostrums are merely cheapenings of Stoicism); on service to one's fellows; and on a cosmopolitan, all-embracing social sense that is a precursor of the fully developed Christian idea of the brotherhood of man. Stoicism's watchwords are Duty, Imperturbability, Will. Its tendency is puritanical, ascetic, quietistic, sometimes even escapist. Though a philosophy peculiarly suited to a time of troubles, its influence has never ceased during almost the whole of two thousand years. It seems to call out to people irrespective of their time and place—see, for example, Thoreau [80].

We find it at its most appealing in the *Meditations*. This is an easy book to read. We seem to be eavesdropping on the soliloquy of a man almost painfully attached to virtue, with a firm sense of his responsibility, less to his empire than to the Stoic ideal of the perfect man, untouched by passion, generous by nature rather than by calculation, impervious to both ill and good fortune. Says Marcus, in one of the saddest sentences of a book shadowed throughout by melancholy, "Even in a palace life may be lived well."

Through the years the Golden Book of Marcus Aurelius, as it has been called, has been read by vast numbers of ordinary men and women. They have thought of it not as a classic but as a wellspring of consolation and inspiration. It is one of the few books that seem to have helped men and women directly and immediately to live better, to bear with greater dignity and fortitude the burden of being merely human. Aristotle [13] we study. Marcus Aurelius we take to our hearts.

C.F.

PART TWO

22

SAINT AUGUSTINE
354–430

The Confessions

Autobiography would seem to be the easiest of all literary forms, for what could be simpler than to talk of one's own life? Yet though this Plan abounds in great poems and novels, great autobiographies are fewer. Of all the autobiographies ever written, perhaps the most powerful and influential in the Western tradition is the *Confessions* of Saint Augustine.

Compared with Marcus Aurelius [21], Augustine reveals a deeper, if less attractive, mind. The profundity of Augustine's intellect can be felt only by those willing to spend some time in the vast and obscure forest of his works, particularly his masterpiece, *The City of God*. But its intensity, its obsession with God, and its tortured concern with sin and salvation can be felt by anyone who reads at least the first nine books of the *Confessions*.

This Roman citizen, born in North Africa, who became the bishop of Hippo, is probably the most effective defender the Church has had in its long history. Yet, as he tells us, he came to Catholicism only in his thirty-second year, after he had tasted the delights of the flesh (including thirteen years with a mistress who bore him a son). His plea to God is familiar: "Give me chastity and continence, but not yet." The great change occurred after he had also dabbled in the heresy of Manichaeism and had sampled the classical doctrines of Platonism [12] and Skepticism and Neoplatonism. Readers of the *Confessions* will note the many influences, especially that of his revered mother Monica, that led him at last to his true vocation. His conversion in the garden, as described in the twelfth chapter of Book VIII, marks one of the pivotal moments in the history of Christianity as well as a crucial instance of the mystical experience.

There is a great deal of theology and Christian apologetics and biblical exegesis in the *Confessions,* notably in the last four books, dealing with memory, time, the nature of temptation, and the proper expounding of the Scriptures. But the power of the book is exerted even on the nonbeliever. The *Confessions* was originally written to bring men to the truth. For us it is rather a masterpiece of self-revelation, the first unsparing account of how a real man was led, step by step, from the City of Man to the City of God. To the psychologist, to the student of what William James [95] called the varieties of religious experience, it is endlessly interesting. But beyond this, it grips us because we cannot shut our ears to the terrible humanness of Augustine's voice. He is trying desperately to tell us the truth, about the events not only of his external life, but of his soul. The *Confessions* is the classic spiritual autobiography. In all our literature there is nothing quite like it.

C.F.

23
KĀLIDĀSA
ca. 400

The Cloud Messenger and *Sakuntala*

Kālidāsa is sometimes described as "the Shakespeare of India"; certainly he is universally regarded as the most accomplished stylist in the Sanskrit language in all of Indian literature. It may seem odd, then, that almost nothing is known about him. One must remember, however, that a fundamental precept of the Brahmanic religions, including Hinduism and Buddhism, is that the world and everything in it is purely illusory; under those circumstances, in traditional India, it apparently did not strike people as important to devise a system of numbering years consecutively to keep track of things like people's life-times. Kālidāsa perhaps lived around our year 400, perhaps a century later.

Tradition holds that he was of humble origins, and achieved fame and an appointment at a minor royal court entirely through his brilliance as a writer. He is said to have been a pro-lific writer as well, but only a few of his works survive—three or four long poems, and three plays. This Plan recommends that you read his two most celebrated works.

The Cloud Messenger (*Meghadūta*) is a poetic monologue in 210 stanzas; if one were to place it approximately in a genre of European verse, one could call it a pastorale. The conceit of the poem is that a young nobleman in the guise of a *yaksa* (a minor nature deity) for some unspecified offense has been exiled to a remote mountain. He misses his beautiful young bride, and imagines that she is pining for him as well at their palace in the Himalayan foothill city of Alaka. Seeing a passing cloud on the mountaintop, he asks it to float to Alaka and deliver a message of love and comfort to his wife. This gives the poet, in the voice of the young yaksa, a chance to describe the rivers and mountains, towns and cities that the cloud will pass on its way to deliver the message; the poem is a sort of travelogue in the form of a love letter. The tone of the poem, and the highly formal structure of the verse itself, is elevated and refined; the fanciful mission entrusted to the cloud mes-senger seems paradoxically all the more passionate for that air of elegant restraint.

Sakuntala and the Ring of Recognition, usually called simply *Sakuntala*, is a play that one might classify as a heroic romance. Like so much of Indian theater, its plot is derived from one of the many subplots of the *Mahabharata* [16]. Briefly, it concerns a king's love for a beautiful maiden, Sakuntala, daughter of a nymph and a sage-king. She has been raised in the forest, in total innocence, by an ascetic priest. One day, while out hunt-ing, King Dusyanta spies Sakuntala, and immediately falls in love with her; they become lovers, and she becomes pregnant by him. But duty calls, and he must return to his capital; before he does, he gives her a ring by which he will always recognize her. Later she travels to his court, but loses the ring along the way; when she arrives, he thinks she looks vaguely familiar, but he can't place her. Eventually, after many difficulties, the ring is recovered and the lovers reunited, to the satisfaction of all.

In one way at least the comparison of Kālidāsa and Shakespeare [39] is apt: Both were masters of writing in character, from the most royal and refined monarchs to the most bawdy and vulgar clowns. Kālidāsa in fact had an advantage over Shakespeare, because he had two languages at his disposal; in his plays, the most aristocratic characters speak classical Sanskrit, while the rest speak vernacular Prakrit. (It is as if in the plays of Molière the principal male characters spoke Latin, and everyone else spoke French.) I would suggest another Shakespearean comparison as well. The principal tension in *Sakuntala* is between duty and passion, between socially prescribed modes of behavior and spontaneous love. Shakespeare explored the same themes in *The Tempest*; it is an interesting exercise to read the two plays in close succession.

Sakuntala was first translated into English by Sir William Jones, a pioneer Western scholar of Sanskrit and the father of modern scientific linguistics; his translation was greatly admired by Goethe [62]. There have since been other excellent translations of the works of Kālidāsa, who deserves to become much better known in the West.

J.S.M.

24

Revealed to MUHAMMAD
completed 650

The Koran

Western Arabia during the early centuries of the Common Era was a prosperous part of the larger Semitic world, a land where the caravan trade from Yemen to the Levant created a cosmopolitan and lively society. Jews and Christians were a part of the local community, and the Torah and the New Testament were well known. Many, perhaps most, people in that part of the world considered themselves descendants of Abraham through his son Ishmael. Into that community, in the city of Mecca, Muhammad was born around the year 570. The first forty years of his life were unremarkable; he married a prosperous widow and was a respectable member of Mecca's mercantile class.

In 610 Muhammad began to preach what he described as messages given to him by God; he had, he said, been selected to warn the people that God's final revelation was at hand. He was a charismatic preacher who gathered many followers but also made enemies; the latter plotted to murder him in 622, but he was warned of the plot and fled to the nearby city of Medina. There he founded a theocratic state in accordance with the word of God as it had been revealed to him; the year 622 of the Common Era is the Year One of the Islamic calendar.

The Koran consists of 114 chapters, or *suras*, which in the written version of the holy book are printed simply in order of length, the longest first and the shortest at the end. There is no narrative thread in the Koran and no obvious connections linking each *sura* to the next; these features derive from the original oral nature of the text. (In fact *Al-Qur'an* means "the recitation," and in the Muslim world reciting the Koran is an important act of faith and religious witness.) The written text was not finalized until around 650, some twenty years after Muhammad's death in 632; it was compiled from memory and included all the material that, by consensus of the community, was considered to have been genuinely revealed to Muhammad by God.

From the point of view of a non-Muslim Western reader, the Koran seems remarkable at first glance for the degree to which it is part of the Jewish and Christian Biblical heritage. It is full of familiar figures; Abraham, Moses, David, Jesus, John the Baptist and many others are represented as prophets and messengers of God. A closer look shows that this familiar world is seen through a radically different lens in the Koran; all of the Biblical stories, all of the prophets and patriarchs, are presented as precursors leading up to the Koran itself, the Word of God as recited by Muhammad; the Koran presents itself as the "seal of prophesy," the final revelation of God's word on earth.

Accordingly, much of the Koran is devoted to telling the faithful exactly how they are to live in a state of *islam*, "submission," to God. These instructions for the regulation of a theocratic community are distilled in the Five Pillars of Islam, which are

1. The profession of faith: "There is no God but God, and Muhammad is his Prophet." (The word translated as "prophet" in this formula really has a stronger meaning: "One who warns of God.") Islam is a religion of uncompromising monotheism; God is absolute, omniscient, and omnipotent— nothing whatsoever happens on Earth or in the Heavens but by the will of God.
2. Prayer five times each day, according to prescribed rituals.
3. Fasting from dawn to dark during the month of Ramadan each year.
4. Giving alms to the poor.
5. At least once in one's lifetime, making a pilgrimage to Mecca, but only if one is in good health and has sufficient financial means to make the pilgrimage without impoverishing one's family.

These rules, supplemented by many more both in the Koran and in later compendia of religious law, mark off the Muslim community from all others; the Koran promises the protection of God to those who submit to his will, and damnation to all who reject it. The Koran thus creates a religious community that is inherently militant and evangelistic, while at the same time urging upon the faithful attitudes of moderation, tolerance, and a dedication to justice. The history of the Islamic world provides many examples of fanaticism, and equally many examples of enlightened tolerance; like all scripture, the Koran can be used to justify many things.

Some years ago I was privileged to talk with a very high official of our government, and I asked him (because the Middle East was very much in the news at the time) how many members of the presidential cabinet knew enough about Islam to name the Five Pillars of the faith. "That's easy," he replied. "Not one." At a time when one of every five people in the world is a Muslim, and the Islamic world contributes a disproportionate share of our government's foreign policy concerns, it seems to me a matter of simple good citizenship to know something about Islam. That is one good reason to read the Koran; others are the beauty of its majestically poetic language, and the fascinatingly refracted vision that it projects of the Biblical traditions at the heart of Euro-American mainstream culture.

J.S.M.

25
HUI-NENG
638–713

The Platform Sutra of the Sixth Patriarch

Buddhism arose in northern India in the sixth century B.C.E. through the life and teachings of Siddhartha Gautama. A prince of a small kingdom in the Himalayan foothills, he was shocked by the suffering that he saw everywhere in the world, and he went on a retreat to meditate for many days, sheltered by a great tree, searching for the cause of that suffering. At last he entered a state of pure understanding, thereby becoming the Buddha or "enlightened one"; and he began to preach a new doctrine on the basis of that enlightenment.

Gautama grew up in the Brahmanic religious world of ancient India, and he shared its assumptions (which we have already encountered in the *Bhagavad Gita* [17]): The world has no concrete reality, but is fundamentally illusory; each person is born and reborn many times, and carries from one birth to the next a burden of *karma* derived from good or ill done in previous lives; each person must follow his or her own *dharma*, or path of duty in the world. Building on this tradition, the Buddha formulated his new understanding in the Four Noble Truths: All life is suffering; suffering proceeds from desire; desire can be overcome; the means to overcoming desire is the Noble Eightfold Path (right intentions, right thoughts, right actions, etc.). The key insight here is that it is desire itself that keeps a person bound to the wheel of karma; the illusory world exerts such a pull on the ego that people seek rebirth, even though that inevitably only mires them in a new lifetime of suffering. Fortunately, the Buddha taught, it is possible to end that cycle of desire, and to reach a state of *nirvana*, extinction of the soul in pure enlightenment.

Buddhism spread widely in India, Southeast Asia, and Central Asia in the centuries after Gautama's death. It reached China in the first century C.E., and spread from there to Korea and Japan. Over the centuries Buddhism branched into many different schools and sects, and accumulated many scriptures (*sutras*, all at least nominally the teachings of the Buddha himself). The main branch of Buddhism that became popular in China was Mahayana, or "Greater Vehicle," Buddhism, which promised believers that saints, called Bodhisattvas, would reward their faith by helping them to break free of the wheel of karma and be reborn in paradise (a far cry from the austere nirvana of Gautama's original conception). Mahayana sects became extremely popular and encouraged many acts of devotion, from building temples and making holy religious images to copying and recopying the sutras.

A radical challenge to this form of Buddhism was mounted in the late fifth or early sixth century C.E. with the founding of a new school called Ch'an [Chan], the "meditation" school of Buddhism; most of us know the word better in its Japanese pronunciation, Zen. Founded by an obscure and semilegendary monk named Bodhidharma, the Ch'an school taught that salvation should be sought not in acts of religious merit, nor in the intervention of Bodhisattvas, but through an intense regime of meditation that would empty the mind of doctrine, scriptures, desires, distractions, and all attachment to the world, thus preparing the way for a wordless leap into enlightenment.

Bodhidharma's new sect suffered its own schisms and competing claims to leadership; it was finally united again by a most unlikely man. Hui-neng was an illiterate woodcutter from southern China who became a Ch'an monk, and soon showed a genius both for expounding the doctrine of the school and for imposing discipline on its monastic practices; he came to be accepted by all of the Ch'an subschools as the Sixth Patriarch in a line from Bodhidharma himself. *The Platform Sutra of the Sixth Patriarch* is a record of Hui-neng's life and work.

The book's title is odd; it is the only Buddhist text called a sutra that is openly and obviously not a record of the teachings of Gautama Buddha. The *Platform Sutra* consists of three main parts: an autobiography of Hui-neng, a long sermon, and a set of miscellaneous sayings, anecdotes, and teachings. Even more curious is the autobiography itself; Hui-neng is described as having been illiterate, and the autobiography is supposedly "as told to" a monk named Shen-hui. But it is really a fabrication, written long after Hui-neng's lifetime, possibly based on factual traditions handed down about him but including a great deal of hopeful confabulation as well. Hui-neng's sermon also was certainly transmitted orally for a long time before it was written down.

The most famous teaching recorded in the *Platform Sutra*, though, is probably the work of Hui-neng himself. A rival had written a poem:

The body is a tree of perfect wisdom,
The mind is the stand of a bright mirror.
At all times diligently wipe it clean;
Do not allow it to become dusty.

Hui-neng wrote in reply:

Truly perfect wisdom has no tree,
Nor has the bright mirror a stand.
Buddha-nature is forever clear and pure.
Where would there be any dust?

Hui-neng argues for a wordless discipline, transmitted by "silent precepts" from master to novice, to replace the sutras; tear them up, he shouts, get rid of them, they are only impediments to enlightenment. Of course this raises a problem that has haunted Ch'an (Zen) ever since—the *Platform Sutra* is only the first book in a huge library of Zen scriptures, this in a sect that says "destroy the scriptures" and teaches that enlightenment can come only from wordless discipline. The Chinese Taoist classic, the *Tao Te Ching*, says "The Tao that can be called Tao is not the universal Tao; words that can be spoken are not universal words." Zen encapsulates this nicely: "Those who know do not say, those who say do not know." Yet of the writing of books about Zen there is no end.

The *Platform Sutra* is fairly short, and it is not difficult to read. Unlike the sutras of mainstream Buddhism, it contains few unfamiliar terms and concepts (but if you want to see what these mainstream scriptures are like, try the *Diamond Sutra* and the *Lotus Sutra*). Even making allowances for pious legend-mongering, it paints a portrait of a remarkable individual, the woodcutter monk Hui-neng; it also allows one to gain an understanding of a religious faith and discipline that has been enormously influential in East Asian religion, literature and art for well over a thousand years, and which has in recent years made its mark in the Western world as well.

J.S.M.

26
FIRDAUSI
ca. 940–1020

Shah Nameh

Firdausi, the pen name of a man of obscure origins named
Abul Kasim Mansur, is generally regarded as the greatest poet
in the history of the Persian language. He is said to have been
born into a modest land-owning family in the city of Khurasan,
where he managed somehow to acquire a good education that
included not only the usual Islamic arts and sciences but also,
less usually, ancient Persian history and literature. He made
his way to the court of Shah Mahmud of Gazni and accepted a
commission to complete a long poem on Persian history (the
previous holder of the commission had died shortly after
beginning the poem).

The finished poem, the *Shah Nameh* or "Book of Kings,"
is composed of nearly 60,000 rhyming couplets and tells the
story of the Persian throne from the earliest days to the coming of Islam. Much of the poem is simply a recapitulation
of history, from the rise of the prophet Zoroaster (founder of
the pre-Islamic religion of Persia) and the glorious reigns
of the empire-builders Cyrus and Darius, to the wars with
Greece and the rise and fall of Persian royal dynasties; it ends
with the collapse of the Sasanid Kingdom in the mid-seventh
century.

But if we think of Firdausi as an historian, we find that he
fits no mold that we've encountered thus far in this Plan. His
history resembles neither the majestic sobriety of Thucydides
[9], nor the cheerful credulousness of Herodotus [8], nor the
systematic organization of Ssu-ma Ch'ien [18]. More than any
of these, Firdausi resembles Homer [2,3]; he is historian as
bard. His strength is in pure narrative; he has an eye for the
telling detail and the illuminating anecdote, and the elegance
of his poetry (apparent to some degree even through the

screen of translation) carries the work through occasional dry spells in the action. One thing that makes Firdausi's poetic history so interesting is his willingness to go beyond what most modern critics would call history proper and into the realm of legend to deal at length with the exploits of Persia's great culture-hero, Rustam. Rustam is a perfect prince, eloquent and elegant, but also a warrior of imposing strength and bravery; he is a sort of latter-day Persian reincarnation of Gilgamesh [1] with some of the attributes of Hercules, polished by the manners of a highly cultivated and refined court. He is the true hero of the *Shah Nameh*, an ideal to be emulated by future Persian kings.

Firdausi dedicated the *Shah Nameh* to his patron Shah Mahmud, but was sorely disappointed by the meager payment he received when he presented his work to the throne. Incensed, he wrote a devastating poetical satire on the tight-fisted monarch and then fled the court, spending much of his life as a traveling versifier before retiring to the family farm in his old age.

It would be impossible to exaggerate the importance of Firdausi's work in Persian literature. He set the standard for all poets who came after him, in the concision and the tight rhyme schemes of his couplets, in the highly rhythmic cadence of his verse, and in his poem's dramatic narrative scope. The *Shah Nameh* acquired the status of a Persian national epic, and until very recent times many quite ordinary people were capable of reciting long passages from it. By glorifying Persia's pre-Islamic past, Firdausi undoubtedly contributed to Persia's strong commitment to its own national culture in the face of Islamic universalism.

Finally, the *Shah Nameh* for centuries has served painters of miniatures in the Persian style as a source of stories, such as the exploits of Rustam and his knights, that they could illustrate. The finest of many illustrated editions of the *Shah Nameh*, commissioned by Shah Tahmasp in the early sixteenth century and now in the collection of the Metropolitan Museum of Art in New York, is one of the great masterpieces of world art. If you have access to a large urban library or museum research library, ask to see its copy (such a library almost certainly will have one, but as part of its special and rare book collection, not in general circulation) of the facsimile edition of this so-called Houghton Shah Nameh. This luxurious book, titled *A King's Book of Kings* and published by the Metropolitan Museum in 1972, comes as close as possible to reproducing the look and feel of the magnificent original. If you are able to see a copy of this facsimile after you've read the *Shah Nameh* yourself, it will give you a sense of the almost reverent esteem accorded Firdausi's great work in his native land.

J.S.M.

27
SEI SHŌNAGON
ca. 965–1035

The Pillow-Book

We know almost nothing about the life of Sei Shōnagon, one of the most brilliant writers that Japan has ever produced. The dates of birth and death conventionally given for her are guesses, based on an assumption that she was in her thirties when she was active as a writer and on a tradition that she died under difficult circumstances at an advanced age. She was born into the aristocratic Kiyowara clan, may have married an official named Tachibana no Norimitsu, and may have borne him a son. Even her personal name is not known for certain; Shōnagon was only her title as an imperial lady-in-waiting. The sole mention of her in the writings of her contemporaries is an uncomplimentary remark by Lady Murasaki [28], who disliked Sei Shōnagon's arrogance. Like most people, she would quickly have slipped into the obscurity of the past, save for her one stunning achievement: For a few years, exactly a thousand years ago (as of this writing), she kept a "pillow book" of random jottings about her life as a court lady that has enthralled and entertained readers ever since.

Sei Shōnagon lived during the Heian Period (795–1085), a very remarkable era of Japanese history. Blessed with a thriving agricultural economy, enriched by cultural influences from China and Korea, secure both from external attack and internal strife, the Japanese developed during that time an aristocratic society as refined and luxurious as any in history. In the beautiful city of Heian-kyō (now Kyoto), filled with villas, palaces and temples, emperors reigned but did not rule much, surrounded and flattered by an aristocracy that devoted itself to Buddhism and aesthetics. Persuaded by their faith that life on earth is both illusory and ephemeral, these aristocratic men and women made their time here as beautiful as possible; fashion, art, poetry, and many other aesthetic pursuits flourished. Eventually this way of life came to an end, overwhelmed by the rise of a provincial warrior class—the samurai who would dominate Japan for the next eight centuries.

While the Heian Period lasted, women enjoyed a degree of personal independence quite unusual in the history of traditional societies, and which they would lose under the rule of the samurai. They could and did inherit, own, and bequeath property. It was common for a man to marry into the family of his wife, and to be dominated by his father-in-law. Premarital and extramarital sex was winked at; men and women alike were free to pursue love affairs as long as they were discreet and considerate of the sensibilities of others. Men monopolized the administration of both government and private estates and were supposed to practice such martial arts as archery and swordsmanship. Women had little to do except to beautify their lives through the elegant arts.

It is thus perhaps not surprising that Heian literature was

created primarily by women. Men were expected to read and write Classical Chinese, the language of learning and religion (as Latin was in medieval Europe), while women usually wrote only in Japanese. Thus it fell to women to write the diaries, poetry, and fiction that laid the foundation for vernacular Japanese literature. In the constellation of Heian writers, Sei Shōnagon shines with particular brilliance.

Serving as a lady-in-waiting to Empress Sadako during the 990s, she was perfectly placed to observe and record events at court, and to comment upon them. The "pillow book" in which she wrote at night probably consisted of loose leaves of paper; much later, the leaves were copied in essentially random order, leading to the topical and chronological disarray of the book as we now have it. The book has no beginning, no end, and no plot; it can be tiring to read straight through, but is endlessly entertaining for browsing. It is famous for its many lists, such as "Things That Give an Unclean Feeling" ("A rat's nest"; "The containers used for oil") or "Rare Things" ("A servant who does not speak badly about his master"), and for Sei Shōnagon's pronouncements on matters of style and etiquette: "Nothing can be worse than allowing the driver of one's ox-carriage to be poorly dressed"; "I cannot stand a woman who wears sleeves of unequal width."

The Pillow-Book owes its enduring fame to the personality of its author, who was refined, demanding, censorious, sophisticated, witty, outspoken, and very accomplished. She was an egotist and a snob, admired by some of her contemporaries but probably not much liked. Part of the fascination of reading Sei Shōnagon's book is the realization of how badly one would fare if somehow one were to come under her critical eye. Her saving grace is that she was as unsparing of herself as she was of others; she had no illusions.

J.S.M.

28

LADY MURASAKI

ca. 976–1015

The Tale of Genji

Few people would argue with the assertion that *The Tale of Genji* is Japan's greatest work of literature. Some literary historians describe it as the world's first psychological novel; many critics regard it as one of the half-dozen or so finest novels in world literature. Like most of the best literature of the Heian period, it was written by an aristocratic lady about whom not very much is known. As with her slightly older contemporary Sei Shōnagon [27], even her real name has disappeared into the darkness of time. She is known to us as Murasaki Shikibu, but that is merely to call her "Lady Murasaki" after the name of the principal female character of her novel. She served as a lady-in-waiting to Empress Jōtō-mon-in, and kept a diary while she was at court in the years 1007–1010. (Her diary lacks the scathing honesty of Sei Shōnagon's, but reveals an altogether sweeter and more likable person.)

She was of course of proper aristocratic birth, and seems to have been given by her father an unusually good education even by the fairly liberal standards that prevailed for women at the time. She apparently knew Classical Chinese as well as Japanese, and at court had to take some pains to hide that fact, lest she seem too masculine. From this we can infer an early interest in literature and a talent for language that make the achievement of her great novel seem somewhat more explicable, if no less stunning.

The Tale of Genji depicts the aristocratic life of Heian Japan—the setting is two or three generations before Lady Murasaki's own time—through the life of Prince Genji, every Heian lady's dream of what a courtier should be. He is a master of every art from painting and calligraphy to incense-blending and origami; he can compose a stylish *waka* five-line poem as easily as he can breathe. He has an exquisite fashion sense;

his comportment is invariably elegant; his gifts to his ladyfriends are always in perfect taste. Interestingly he is not, at least from our point of view, very imposing physically; illustrated-scroll editions of the novel produced not long after it was written show him as pale and slightly pudgy. Genji is not so much a perfect hero as a perfect aesthete. Much of the novel is devoted to his numerous love affairs. Affairs, more or less clandestine, were very much the norm for that society, but what truly distinguishes Genji as a lover is his kindness and thoughtfulness; he is never cruel, and he treats his ex-lovers with great kindness and courtesy. Rather shockingly from our point of view, his one great love is his young bride Murasaki, whom he adopted as a ward when she was a young child, raised to be a suitably elegant companion to a courtier like himself, and married when she came of age. And it is only toward Murasaki that he behaves unforgivably: When he supplants her in her role as principal wife by making a socially advantageous marriage with a princess, she dies of a broken heart.

The whole atmosphere of *Genji* is suffused with beauty and refinement, but also with a sense of sadness and impending loss, a feeling that beauty is all the more beautiful for one's realization that it will soon fade. The sensibility of the novel, and the society it depicts, reflects the Buddhist conviction that the world we so crave is an illusion held together by desire. It gives us a glimpse of a rarefied and remote age; many readers find it hard, at first, to tune themselves to the pace and sensibility of the novel.

Murasaki wrote the *Genji* in installments, as a private entertainment for herself and her lady friends; one can imagine that the life of a court lady was often tedious, and the appearance of a fresh chapter of the tale of the Shining Prince would have been most welcome. One gets the sense also that Murasaki eventually grew tired of her novel, or at least of the obligation to keep producing new chapters of it. Violating all of our notions of a well-wrought plot, Genji dies three-quarters of the way through the book, and one imagines that, like Sir Arthur

Conan Doyle many centuries later sending Sherlock Holmes over the Reichenbach Falls, Murasaki decided to end her labors by killing off her hero. But like Sir Arthur, she wasn't allowed to get away with it; the novel resumes after Genji's death with the life and loves of his son Kaoru, and with a deepening sense that the characters of the book have lived through a golden age that will never return again.

I know very well that when you pick up the *Genji* for the first time, it will seem like a dauntingly big book; when you begin to read it, it may strike you as slow-paced and exotic to the point of seeming alien. Nevertheless, persist. Like Proust's *Remembrance of Things Past* [105], this is a very big book that truly repays multiple readings; at some point the strangeness will transform itself into wonder. The refinement and psychological acuity of Murasaki's prose will draw you into a world of the imagination that is one of the world's great artistic achievements.

A word on translations: The version by Arthur Waley (published in 1925–33) was for many years one's only choice, and it still is a pleasure to read; it is a classic in its own right. Even so, I prefer the newer version by Edward Seidensticker (1976), which is as smooth and readable as Waley's (though perhaps lacking some of Waley's Bloomsbury literary panache), and is much truer to Murasaki's text. Waley allowed himself editorial liberties that seem slightly presumptuous in dealing with a masterpiece of the rank of *The Tale of Genji*, while Seidensticker trusts Murasaki to speak for herself.

J.S.M.

29
OMAR KHAYYAM
1048–?

The Rubaiyat

I remember being told some years ago by an Iranian friend how surprised he was to learn that Omar Khayyam is known in the West entirely as a poet. He assured me that Omar Khayyam is remembered throughout the Islamic world, and particularly in his homeland of Persia (now Iran), as a great mathematician and astronomer. His verses, while esteemed, are seen as no more than any highly educated man of his time might have composed, and indeed was expected to be able to compose extemporaneously whenever the occasion arose. (The same talent was demanded of medieval Japanese courtiers; see Sei Shōnagon [27] and Murasaki Shikibu [28].) The story of how Omar Khayyam came to be a great poet in English is a fascinating one.

Start with the poetry itself. A *rubai* (plural *rubaiyat*) is a short poem, comprising a pair of couplets of which the first, second and fourth lines must rhyme. Most Western readers assume, for lack of any reason to the contrary, that "Rubaiyat" is the name of a long poem by Omar Khayyam; but the word itself could easily be translated as "Verses" or "Quatrains." The decision of Edward FitzGerald, who published his translation of the poem in 1859, to leave the title in Persian, can be seen as a deliberate choice emphasizing the "exotic" nature of the original work. Moreover, while hundreds of Omar Khayyam's *rubaiyat* have survived, in traditional Persian collections they are simply a large body of short poems, with no overall narrative or discursive structure. FitzGerald's great stroke of genius as a translator was to arrange Omar Khayyam's verses to produce a long, continuous poem, giving it an aesthetic and philosophical weight that was at best only implicit in the original scattered quatrains.

What we have, then, in the *Rubaiyat of Omar Khayyam* as translated by Edward FitzGerald (and retranslated a number of times since, sometimes more accurately but never more pleasingly) is a unique hybrid, a brilliant English poem created from Persian elements. It has evoked for generations of English readers a place that is perhaps more Persian than Persia, an exotic land of wine and roses that existed more for poets than for ordinary folk. FitzGerald's *Rubaiyat of Omar*

Khayyam (as opposed to the original collections of Omar Khayyam's *rubaiyat*) is, in fact, a prime example of what the Palestinian critic Edward Said has denounced as "Orientalism," the use of art and literature to create an exotic, romantic, and (he claims) fundamentally false image of Asian cultures, substituting European fantasies for real lands where people live and die, prosper and suffer, like anyone else. Said's charge is true to an uncomfortable degree, but it is not the whole story. Complicating the issue is the fact that Persian poets like Omar Khayyam themselves used verse to evoke an exotic, perfumed, mystical realm of the imagination; that quality is preserved, but not created, in translation.

The *Rubaiyat of Omar Khayyam* is, I suspect, not much read these days, but almost everyone can still quote from it the lines "A loaf of bread, a jug of wine, and Thou" (which is not quite accurate as a quote from FitzGerald's translation, though close enough). But isn't there something wrong with that picture? One firm principle of Islam is that alcohol is strictly prohibited to believers (see the Koran [24]); so what is Omar Khayyam doing invoking the pleasures of wine? The answer is that Islam (except in the ferocious fundamentalist form that is all too common in our own time) has generally made allowances for human frailty; alcohol is prohibited, but some people might nevertheless take a drink—and the fate of their souls is, as always, entirely in the hands of the only and omnipotent God. Indeed in the traditional Islamic world there was a long and tolerant association of wine and poetry; the Ottoman sultans strictly regulated coffee-houses as hotbeds of political dissent, but allowed taverns to open unmolested, as the haunts of harmless poets. (There was also a pious fiction that poets might use wine as a metaphor for the intoxication of romantic, or even of divine, love, without actually taking a sip of the stuff themselves.) And so wine and love and roses are used by Omar Khayyam to make a profound statement: that life is indeed full of pleasures, to be enjoyed to the full; but if one loves life, so one should not shrink from death—the one and the other alike are in the hands of God.

The *Rubaiyat of Omar Khayyam* is a sort of miracle, a collaboration between a gifted poet and a brilliant translator, bridging great chasms of time and cultural distance. The Persian mathematician and the Victorian Orientalist have together produced a book of verses that sing as sweetly in our own time as ever.

J.S.M.

30
DANTE ALIGHIERI
1265–1321

The Divine Comedy

Like his era, the life of Dante was disordered, but his masterpiece is the most ordered long poem in existence. During his lifetime his native Florence, and indeed much of Italy, was divided by factional strife. In this struggle Dante, as propagandist and government official, played his part. It was not a successful part, for in 1302 he was banished. To the day of his death, almost twenty years later, he wandered through the courts and great houses of Italy, eating the bitter bread of exile.

To our modern view his emotional life seems no less unbalanced. He tells us that when he was nine he first saw the little girl, Beatrice; and then nine years later saw her again. That is the extent of his relationship with the woman who was to be the prime mover of his imagination and whom, in the last canto of the *Paradiso,* the third part of *The Divine Comedy,* he was to place beside God.

Dante called his poem a *comedy* (the adjective *divine* was added by later commentators) because it began in Hell, that is, with disaster, and ended in Heaven, that is, with happiness. To the beginning reader it at first seems almost impenetrable. To daunt us, there is first its theology, derived from the great thinker Thomas Aquinas (1224/5–1274). There is its complex system of virtues and vices, in part stemming from Aristotle [13]. There is the fact that, as Dante tells us, the poem is written on four levels of meaning. There is its constant use of allegory and symbol, not a mere device with Dante, but part of the structure of his thought. And, finally, the poem is stuffed with contemporary references, for Dante was one of the few great writers who constantly worked with what today we would call the materials of journalism.

Despite these and many more impediments, Dante can still move the nonscholarly reader. Perhaps it is best, as T. S. Eliot [116] advises in his famous essay, to plunge directly into the poem and to pay little or no attention to the possible symbolic meanings. Its grand design can be understood at once. This is a narrative, like Bunyan's *Pilgrim's Progress* [48], of human life as it is lived on earth—even though Dante has chosen to make our earthly states vivid by imagining a Hell, a Purgatory, and a Paradise. We, too, live partly in a state of misery, or Hell. We, too, are punished for our sins and may atone for them, as do the inhabitants of Purgatory. And we, too, Dante fervently believed, may, by the exercise of reason—personified in Dante's guide Virgil [20]—and faith, become candidates for that state of felicity described in the *Paradiso*. Dante's moral intensity, though exercised on the life of his time and within the framework of the then-dominant scholastic philosophy, breaks through to the sensitive reader of our own century. Dante is as realistic, as true to human nature, as any modern novelist—and far more unsparingly so.

Furthermore, the poem is open to us *as* a poem. The greatest poetic imaginations are not cloudy, but hard and precise. Concision and precision are of the essence of Dante's imagination. He is continually creating not merely vivid pictures, but the only vivid picture that will fully convey his meaning. These we can all see and feel, even in translation: Dante is a great painter. Similarly we can all sense the powerful, ordered, symmetrical structure of the poem: Dante is a great architect.

One last word. I would qualify Eliot's advice to this extent:

no harm, and much good, will result from a reading of the introduction to your edition, for Dante's poem and his life and time are inextricably interwoven. Furthermore, most editions contain notes explaining the major references. A good way of trying Dante is to read a canto (there are one hundred in all) without paying any attention to the notes. Then reread it, using the notes. Do not expect to understand everything—eminent scholars are still quarreling over Dante's meanings. You will understand enough to make your reading worth the effort. A good modern translation is that of Allen Mandelbaum, in an edition that gives the translation and the original Italian on facing pages.

C.F.

31
LUO KUAN-CHUNG
ca. 1330–1400

The Romance of the Three Kingdoms

The Han Dynasty of China, founded in 206 B.C.E., was roughly contemporary with, and controlled an area even larger than, the Roman Empire. (Interestingly, China and Rome flourished on opposite ends of Eurasia in almost total ignorance of each other, an ignorance energetically promoted by the Central Asian oasis kingdoms that grew rich as intermediaries in the silk trade between the two.) Like Rome, the Han Dynasty eventually and inevitably declined and fell; after decades of corruption, factionalism, and popular rebellion, the dynasty collapsed in 220 C.E. But the succession to the Mandate of Heaven (see Mencius [14]) was unclear, and instead of one new dynasty arising to rule a revived and reunited China, the empire split into three competing kingdoms.

The Three Kingdoms Period, as it is called, lasted for only forty-five years—the kingdoms collapsed in 265, leading to an even longer and more chaotic period of disunion—but those years of turmoil and warfare left a disproportionate and indelible imprint on the Chinese imagination ever afterwards. The history of those competing realms—the Kingdom of Wei in the north, the Kingdom of Wu in the southeast, and the Kingdom of Shu Han in the west—was in due course formally recorded in a dynastic history, one of the series of histories modeled on Ssu-ma Ch'ien's *Records of the Grand Historian* [18]. But it seemed that the tone of a sober official history was not up to the task of conveying the stories of the heroes and villains, assaults and narrow escapes and clever stratagems, that flowed from those tumultuous times. (The Chinese title of the novel means "Supplementary Narratives to the History of the Three Kingdoms," implying that it contains all the good stories left out of the official version.) Over the centuries storytellers and writers of popular dramas and operas mined the semilegendary tales of the Three Kingdoms for new material with which to entertain their audiences. (This process is not unlike what happened in South Asia with the *Mahabharata* [16]; we'll see it at work again with *Journey to the West* [36].) Gradually these stories were collected, and by around 1250 an early version of *The Romance of the Three Kingdoms* had probably come into being. The novel as we now have it was written a century later by a scholar named Luo Kuan-chung [Luo Guanzhong]; the oldest known printed copy dates only from the mid-sixteenth century.

Why does the Three Kingdoms Period loom so large in Chinese imaginative literature? Partly for the reason that the dynastic struggles of medieval England were so attractive to Shakespeare [39]: There happened to be, during that period of history, an unusual collection of powerful and compelling individuals, people whose personalities resonate throughout the ages. Just as Richard III and Prince Hal and Falstaff populate the English imagination, so do the heroes of the Three Kingdoms animate the literature of China. In the *Romance* we find a marvelous cast of characters: Begin with Ts'ao Ts'ao [Cao Cao], the greatest of the Han generals, who finally rebelled and founded the Kingdom of Wei; he is excoriated as the paradigm of a traitor and villain (in Peking Opera his robes and armor are always black, and he has the most ferocious face make-up of any opera character). Then his adversary Liu Pei [Liu Bei], a surviving offshoot of the imperial family of Han, who tries to revive his family's fortunes in the Kingdom of Shu Han. He survives in large part with the aid of his loyal general Chu-ko Liang [Zhuge Liang], the model of loyalty and courage, the opposite (and constant opponent) of Ts'ao Ts'ao. Chu-ko Liang is the chief hero of the tale, and he is celebrated especially for his cleverness and unflappability. In one characteristic episode, when his army has nearly run out of arrows, he arranges to be resupplied by the enemy by setting up a row of straw dummies, which are promptly riddled with arrows that his troops can reuse. Also in the fray are general Kuan Chung [Guan Zhong], huge and fearless, who was formally enshrined as China's God of War in the sixteenth century; Chang Fei [Zhang Fei], a younger, more dashing, and more romantic military commander, and the Brothers of the Peach Orchard, a group of bandits turned patriotic knights. These are, it is important to understand, real historical figures, and they fight real historical battles; but their stories have been much embroidered along the way to inclusion in this book.

Not only does the Three Kingdoms Period offer a wonderful cast of characters, however; it also, at least in the popular imagination, saw a return to the (mostly legendary) chivalry and military rectitude of a much earlier era. In the episodes of the *Romance*, battles are fought in earnest, but there is also an element of sport in the fighting; heroes brag and enemies taunt each other, brothers-in-arms support each other to the death, generals fight ferociously, die bravely, celebrate hugely, and in general live on the edge, larger than life. The *Romance* has, in other words, the appeal that military "boys' books" always have, of letting their (mostly male) readers fantasize about warfare as a combination blood sport, male-bonding ritual, and fraternity party.

For that reason, and despite the (to us) remote exoticism of its setting, *The Romance of the Three Kingdoms* can still be read and enjoyed today as a surprisingly modern adventure tale and, as the ultimate boys' book writer Rudyard Kipling might have said, a cracking good yarn. Fortunately it can now be read in the superb new translation by Moss Roberts; his work has made all other translations obsolete—don't settle for any other.

J.S.M.

32
GEOFFREY CHAUCER
1342–1400

The Canterbury Tales

As Dante's great poem is called *The Divine Comedy* [30], so Chaucer's has often been called the Human Comedy. It is a fair distinction. Dante loved God; Chaucer loved human beings, including the imperfect and even sinful ones. Dante fixed his eye on those paths leading to perdition, purification, and felicity; Chaucer fixed his on the crowded highway of actual daily life. Both wrote of journeys. Dante's is a journey through three symbolic universes. But Chaucer takes thirty-odd Englishmen and Englishwomen of the fourteenth century on a real journey, on a real English road, starting at a real inn at Southwark, then just outside of London, and ending at the real town of Canterbury. Though Chaucer was greatly influenced by Dante, the two supreme poets of the European Middle Ages could not have been more unlike in temperament.

Their careers, too, though parallel in some respects, turned out differently. Like Dante, Chaucer was a civil servant. Serving under three kings he held various posts, many quite important, such as economic envoy, Controller of Customs, Clerk of the King's Works, Justice of the Peace, and others. He seems to have met with one or two brief periods of disfavor, but on the whole his life was lived close to the centers of English power. He rose steadily in the world, and all the evidence suggests a successful career, marked by lively contacts with the stir and bustle of his day, and sufficiently relaxed to allow time for the composition of a great number of works in both verse and prose.

He lacks Dante's depth, bitterness, intensity, vast scholarship, and complexity of imagination. Instead he offers more ingratiating if less overwhelming talents: broad humanity, humor, a quick but tolerant eye for the weaknesses of human nature, an unmatched gift for storytelling, a musical gift of a lower order than Dante's but nonetheless superb, and most of all a certain open-air candor that makes us at once eager to claim him as a friend.

As the Prologue indicates, *The Canterbury Tales* was originally conceived as perhaps one hundred twenty narratives of all kinds, held together by the ingenious device of having a band of pilgrims, bound for Thomas Becket's shrine, tell stories to while away the tedium of travel. Chaucer completed twenty-one of these, with three left unfinished or interrupted. Several are dull exercises in sermonizing and are well skipped. The Prologue, of course, must be read; it is perhaps the most delightful portrait gallery in all literature. The tales most generally admired are the ones told by the Knight, the Miller, the Prioress, the Nun's Priest, the Pardoner, the Wife of Bath (Chaucer's greatest single character, and comparable to Shakespeare's supreme achievements in comic portraiture), the Clerk, the Merchant, the Squire, and the Canon's Yeoman. I suggest you also read the various prologues, epilogues, and conversations that link the stories. Many readers prefer them to the Tales themselves.

Chaucer is a perfect yarn spinner, the founder of English realism, and an entrancing human being. He is also full of interesting information. He paints an immortal picture of Catholic medieval England, with all the warts left in, in colors as fresh and lively as though applied only yesterday. He can be read without any scholarly apparatus at all, though most editions supply a handful of notes explaining those customs and manners peculiar to his day. His book is an open book, like the *Odyssey* [3]and unlike *The Divine Comedy*. He makes you feel that a clear-eyed man of the world has taken you by the arm to tell you about the men and women of his time and, lo, they turn out to be oddly like the men and women of ours. There are no mysteries in Chaucer. Even when he is allegorical, he is plain and forthright.

If you are lucky enough to have an exceptional feeling for English words, you may find it quite possible to read a good deal of Chaucer in the original Middle English—at any rate the Prologue. But most of us need a translation, either a sound prose version (I like Lumiansky's) or the verse renderings by Coghill or Wright.

C.F.

33

ANONYMOUS

ca. 1500

The Thousand and One Nights

The story behind the stories is well known: Shahryar, the tyrant-king of Samarkand, demands a new virgin bride every night; every morning, the unfortunate bride of the night before is put to death. When Scheherezade is chosen for the office of bride-for-a-night, she beguiles Shahryar by telling him a story; she is so persuasive a storyteller that he cannot bear to have her killed, but calls her to his bed again the following night. And the next night and the next, until a thousand nights and a night have passed, and Shahryar has lost his taste for new brides, and for murder; he and Scheherezade live happily ever after.

All of that, of course, is fiction, simply a framing narrative for a large and diverse collection of tales. Shahryar is a figure of legend, and so far as anyone knows there never was a Scheherezade. Who wrote the stories, and when, is quite mysterious: Many of them seem to be of Indian origin, others Persian, but all of them are written in Arabic (hence the book's alternative title, *The Arabian Nights*), suggesting that the tales were compiled from diverse sources, possibly over a long period of time, by an Arabian literary antiquarian, or more than one. The earliest collections of these stories seem not to have taken the figure "one thousand and one" to mean anything more than "a large number," but the unknown editors of the definitive Arabic edition of the collection that was completed around 1500 were careful to adhere scrupulously to the framing story of Scheherezade by including exactly 1,001 stories.

The compilers of *The Thousand and One Nights* seem to have cast a wide net, searching throughout the Islamic world for material to include. The collected stories then spread beyond the sphere of Arabic literature to become part of world literature with surprising speed. Individual tales apparently became known in Europe (probably via the lively Mediterranean trade of the Ottoman Empire) in the sixteenth century. The first full translation, by Abbé Antoine Galland (into French) appeared in 1704–17. Galland's translation quickly became famous (it was almost certainly known to Swift [52], for example); such stock figures from the tales as Sinbad and Ali Baba entered the narrative vocabulary of European literature, and helped to define the West's image of Arabia and the Islamic world. Many other translations into European languages followed, most notably Sir Richard Burton's sixteen-volume unexpurgated version in 1885–88.

The word "unexpurgated" is important in understanding the full significance and appeal of *The Thousand and One Nights*. Almost all of us will remember tales like "Ali Baba and the Forty Thieves" from our childhoods, and indeed heavily cleaned-up and abridged editions of the tales have been produced as children's books for decades. But the originals are not at all like the Disneyfied versions made for children; some are

laced with very bawdy humor, others are frankly and seduc-
tively erotic, still others are swashbuckling tales of derring-do,
with details that are not for the squeamish. (We are familiar
with similarly prettified stories in Western literature; the children's books sold under the title *Grimm's Fairy Tales* have little to do with the earthy and sometimes quite horrifying
German folk tales actually collected by the Brothers Grimm.)

The Thousand and One Nights is one of the world's all-time
great bestsellers, whether in the original Arabic or in any of
dozens of translations, and deservedly so. Its tales can charm a
modern reader as they are supposed to have seduced Shahryar.
They appeal by their strong narrative force, by the sophisticated way in which they have been turned from oral storyteller's tales to well-crafted written stories, and by the sense of
magic and wonder that pervades them. The stories in the collection support each other; the total is greater than the sum of
the parts. But it is important to read them in a translation that
is accurate and not bowdlerized; see the Bibliography for our
suggestions.

J.S.M.

34
NICCOLO MACHIAVELLI
1469–1527

The Prince

Machiavelli is commonly linked with Hobbes [43] as one of the
two great early modern "realistic" theorists of political power.
They would have understood each other, yet they diverge in
some ways. Hobbes is by far the greater theorist. Indeed
Machiavelli is hardly a theorist at all; he is an observer, an ana-
lyst, and an instructor. Hobbes lays down a doctrine of "legiti-
macy"; Machiavelli is interested only in expediency. Finally
Hobbes is an absolutist. But Machiavelli (in his *Discourses on
Livy*, a profounder but less influential book than *The Prince*)

prefers republicanism, and anticipates several of the devices of modern parliamentary democracy. Yet the two may profitably be read in association. Together they help to explain the careers of such antimoralists as Richelieu, Napoleon, Lenin, Mussolini, Hitler, and Stalin. Also they help to explain the continuous though prettily disguised power struggle that goes on in all democracies, including our own.

Machiavelli was a practical politician. Under the Florentine Republic he held office for fourteen years, serving efficiently as diplomat and army organizer. In *The Prince* he incorporated the concrete insights he had gained during his observation of the Italian city-states and the emergent nations of Western Europe, particularly France. When in 1512 the Medicis regained power in Florence, Machiavelli lost his. Unjustly imprisoned and even tortured, he was exiled, and retired to his farm. There—compare Thucydides [9]—he employed his time in writing. He achieved some reputation as a historian, playwright, and all-round humanist man of letters. But it is as the author of *The Prince,* by which he hoped to regain political favor, that he is best known.

His reputation, an odd one, has given us the adjective "Machiavellian." During the Elizabethan era "Old Nick" was a term referring as much to his first name as to the Devil. Iago and a dozen other Italianate Elizabethan villains are in part the consequence of a popular misconception of Machiavelli. He became known as a godless and cynical defender of force and fraud in statecraft.

All Machiavelli did was to cry out that the emperor had no clothes on. He told the truth about power as he saw it in actual operation, and if the truth was not pretty, he is hardly to be blamed for that. He himself seems to have been a reasonably virtuous man, no hater of humanity, neither devilish nor neurotic.

Also it should be remembered that *The Prince* is a description of political means, not political ends. What Machiavelli seems really to have wanted (see his Chapter 26) was a united Italy, free of Spanish and French domination. Cavour and the nineteenth-century unifiers of Italy owe much to him; from a certain aspect he may even be considered a liberal. Yet there is no denying that his ideal Prince (he admired the ineffable Cesare Borgia) must separate himself from all considerations of morality, unless those considerations are themselves expedient. As for his view of the relationship between religion and the state: "All armed prophets have conquered and unarmed ones failed." The Ayatollah Khomeini would have grinned approvingly.

The Prince is a manual. It tells the ambitious leader how to gain, maintain, and centralize power. Once this power is established there is nothing, in Machiavelli's view, to prevent the state from developing just and free institutions. What is involved here, of course, is the whole question of means and ends, and Machiavelli does not resolve the problem.

Because the politics of European nationalism have been in part guided by this icy, terrifyingly intelligent book of instruction, it is well worth reading.

C.F.

35
FRANÇOIS RABELAIS
1483–1553

Gargantua and Pantagruel

This book, while it contains plenty of narrative, has no clear plot, is virtually formless, and eludes classification. It takes its place near the beginning of French literature, but the French novel does not descend from it. Nothing descends from it. Though it has had imitators, it stands by itself. It is a wild, sane, wonderful, exasperating, sometimes tedious extravaganza. Although it is open to a dozen interpretations, one thing at least can be said of it: It is the work of a supreme genius of language whose vitality and power of verbal invention are matched only by Shakespeare and Joyce.

About Rabelais's life we know little. He was a monk, a doctor, personal physician to the important Cardinal du Bellay, an editor, and of course a writer. At various times his books got him into trouble with the authorities. The more bigoted Catholics of his time attacked him; so did the Calvinists, whose bigotry one cannot qualify in any way. Still, despite his satiric view of the churchly obscurantism of his period, there is nothing to prove he was not a good, though hardly straitlaced, Catholic. Anatole France said that Rabelais "believed in God five days out of seven, which is a good deal." Fair enough.

The five books of *Gargantua and Pantagruel* (the fifth may not be entirely genuine) deal with two giants. The first book tells us about Gargantua, his birth, education, farcical war adventures, and the Abbey of Thélème he helped to build, whose only rule was: Do as you wish. The other four books are concerned with Gargantua's son, Pantagruel, that son's boon companion, the rascally, earthy, Falstaffian Panurge, and their wars, travels, quests for wisdom.

The tone varies. It is serious (we have still to catch up with Rabelais's ideas on education), mock-serious, satirical, fantastic, always exuberant. However, even at his wildest, Rabelais evidences two well-blended strains: one proceeding from his humanist conviction that all men desire knowledge and that all knowledge is a joyous and attainable thing (the book is, among other things, an encyclopedia); the other flowing from his personal conviction that "laughter is the essence of mankind."

Of all the writers we have met or shall meet he is the one most unreservedly in love with life. Even when attacking the abuses of his day, he does so in high, almost manic spirits. He would not know a neurosis if he saw one, and most of our gloomy modern novels he would destroy with a guffaw. He is a kind of happy Swift [52], or perhaps a Whitman [85] with an intellect. His characteristic gesture is the embrace. He can love both God and drunkenness. His laughter is so free and healthy that only the prudish will be offended by his vast coarseness, his delight in the eternal comedy of the human body.

Pantagruelism he defines as "a certain jollity of mind, pickled in the scorn of fortune." To enjoy him you must be a bit of a Pantagruelist yourself. His is a book you must give, or at least lend, yourself to, not bothering to ponder every morsel of his gargantuan erudition, and perhaps not trying to read more than a dozen pages at a time.

It is said that Rabelais left the following will: "I owe much. I possess nothing. I give the rest to the poor."

One final suggestion: Read any good modern translation—Cohen's or Putnam's or Le Clercq's. Avoid the famous Urquhart-Motteux version—a classic, but not Rabelais.

C.F.

36

Attributed to WU CH'ENG-EN
1500–1582

Journey to the West

Journey to the West was for most of the time since its publication attributed to "Anonymous," and only recently have literary scholars shown that its likely author was Wu Ch'eng-en [Wu Cheng'en]. Why would the author of one of the world's best picaresque novels hide his identity? The answer to that is found in Wu's own identity, as a proper Confucian gentleman-scholar and a poet of some repute. In the literary world of traditional China, people with a good classical education were expected to devote themselves to respectable literary forms like poetry and essays, and to engage in scholarly study of classical texts; they were most emphatically *not* supposed to do anything as frivolous as writing fiction. Not, of course, that there was no market for fiction; many of these same sober and conventional scholars would enjoy a good read in the privacy of their own homes. But they would not want it to be known that they actually *wrote* the stuff. So Wu Ch'eng-en launched his masterpiece into the world quietly.

In any case it might be more accurate to say that Wu assembled his novel as much as he wrote it; the episodic stories that make up *Journey to the West* had already been part of Chinese popular literature for hundreds of years by the time Wu finished his own treatment of them. They had been common as storyteller's tales in marketplaces all over China, and in the plots of many operas and puppet-plays. The characters of the tales are among the best-known and best-loved in all of Chinese literature: Stories of the sweet-tempered and rather unworldly pilgrim-priest Hsüan-tsang [Xuanzang]; his doughty traveling-companion Sun Wu-k'ung [Sun Wukong] the Monkey King; and their friends and helpers, the oafish but good-hearted Pigsy and the fish-spirit Sandy, have for centuries been as much part of a Chinese childhood as the characters from Mother Goose have been in the West. What Wu Ch'eng-en did was to take the diverse and scattered tales about these characters and weave them into a long and carefully structured narrative.

The novel's story is based on a real journey by a real priest, one that for some reason then acted as a magnet for tall tales over the years. The Chinese Buddhist priest Hsüan-tsang (602–664) traveled from China to India, with the emperor's blessing, to try to find scriptures that were still unknown to Chinese Buddhism and better editions of familiar ones. The journey was successful, and Hsüan-tsang returned to great acclaim. He undoubtedly contributed to the growth in both sophistication and popularity of Buddhism during the glorious T'ang Dynasty (for more on T'ang Buddhism, see also Huineng [25]).

But in *Journey to the West*, Hsüan-tsang's travels are not much more than a peg on which to hang story after story of magical powers, fierce monsters, and the triumph of good over evil. (Chinese commentators, though, have traditionally interpreted the story as an allegory of the difficult journey to Buddhist enlightenment.) The real hero of the tale is Monkey, who is quite certainly a literary cousin of the heroic Hanuman, king of the monkeys in the *Ramayana* [15]. Tales of the Monkey King seem to have arrived in China from India with the introduction of Buddhism in the first century C.E., but in germinal form, later to be much embroidered and elaborated by Chinese storytellers.

In the opening chapters of *Journey to the West*, the monkey Sun Wu-k'ung is born when a huge stone magically splits open and the young monkey emerges into the world. Monkey, energetic and curious, immediately begins to make mischief. In his early adventures he steals a magical iron cudgel from the Dragon King at the bottom of the ocean, insults the Jade Emperor of Heaven, and installs himself as King of the Monkeys in the land of Fruit and Flower Mountain. But soon Hsüan-tsang (in the story usually called by his Buddhist name, Tripitaka) leaves on his journey to India, and Kuan-yin, the goddess of mercy, assigns Monkey the task of helping him on his way. The main part of the book consists of dozens of episodes of Hsüan-tsang being attacked, bewitched, led into trackless deserts, or otherwise finding himself in dire straits, always to be rescued from his predicament by Monkey and his companions. It is all marvelous fun, and it continues to enchant: A Chinese television series of episodes from *Journey to the West* produced in the 1980s became an enormous popular success.

Wu Ch'eng-en's novel clearly is grounded in an oral tradition, and it really demands the kind of leisurely presentation that oral narration imposes on a story. It doesn't necessarily lend itself to the kind of straight-through assault that is the modern approach to reading a book. I would recommend that you start with Arthur Waley's wonderfully translated and greatly condensed version, published under the title *Monkey*; later on spend some time at least browsing in Anthony Yu's masterful complete translation, published as *Journey to the West* by the University of Chicago Press.

J.S.M.

37

MICHEL EYQUEM DE MONTAIGNE
1533–1592

Selected Essays

Many names on our list are far greater than Montaigne's. But the view of life he represents is so deeply rooted in many of us that, while more powerful minds retain interest only for scholars, he will continue to capture the attention of the average intelligent reader. He appeals to that part of us more fascinated by the questions than by the answers.

Montaigne, one of the pioneers of modern French prose, was of good merchant-family stock. On his mother's side he was partly Jewish. Apparently there was sufficient money in the family to permit him on his thirty-eighth birthday to semi-retire to his round tower on the family property. In a period when educational experimentation was generally popular, his own education was unusual. Until he was six he spoke only Latin. He tells us that he was awakened each morning by "the sound of a musical instrument," an anticipation of our clock radios. He studied law, occupied a magistrate's seat in the Bordeaux parliament, served in various capacities under three French kings, and during his later years wasted some of his genius on a job, the mayoralty of Bordeaux, fit only for mediocrity. His real life is preserved in his *Essays*. Of these there are 107, if we include the book-length *Apology for Raymond Sebond*. As far as we can determine, they were written, and rewritten, from his thirty-ninth year, after he had withdrawn to a life of tranquil study and contemplation, to the year of his death.

As he says in his preliminary word to the reader, they were composed not for fame, favor, or fortune, but merely to portray himself, in all candor and indiscretion. For this purpose he invented a new form of literature, as important in its way as the internal combustion engine, and far more pleasant. The

French word *essai* means literally a trial or attempt. Each essay is a trial of the content of his mind, an attempt to find out what is there so that, though he may know nothing else, he may at least know himself.

Montaigne's essays are not like those we find in our better magazines today. They are formless, they rarely stick to the announced subject, and they are chock-full of classical quotations; for Montaigne, in addition to being a man of practical affairs, was a learned humanist. The modern reader may at first find these obstacles irritating.

However, if the evidence of four centuries of survival is any indication, you will eventually be won over by Montaigne's charm, wisdom, humor, style, and mental slant. He began as a Stoic (see Marcus Aurelius [21]) but soon developed a generally skeptical, though never cynical or negative, view of mankind. He was interested in everything, convinced of nothing. His motto was "What do I know?" His emblem was a pair of balances. He remained a good Catholic, because he was born one, and died in the odor of sanctity. But the tendency of his extremely influential writings has been to encourage the growth of free thought. In his characteristic gesture of suspended judgment, dogmatists will find little pleasure.

Montaigne's charm inheres in his style, that of the frankest, freest conversation, "simple and unaffected, the same in writing as on the tongue." He is particularly candid on matters of sex, and those of us who are used to the naive obsessions of some modern novelists may find it interesting to see what a grown-up man has to say on the subject. Montaigne is not only the first informal essayist but incomparably the best. His art is always concealed. The man he gives you is never an improved version submitted for public approval, but always and forever himself. He writes as if he were continually enjoying himself, his weaknesses and oddities and stupidities no less than his virtues.

You may wander about almost at will in Montaigne. He should be read as he wrote, unsystematically. However, time has winnowed out certain of the essays as superior or more important. For the nearest thing to a reasoned defense of his skeptical position, see the rather long-drawn-out *Apology for Raymond Sebond*. In addition you might tick off the following, whose very titles will give you a good foretaste of Montaigne.

From Book 1: That intention is judge of our actions; Of idleness; Of liars; That the taste of good and evil depends in large part on the opinion we have of them; That to philosophize is to learn to die; Of the power of the imagination; Of custom, and not easily changing an accepted law; Of the education of children; Of friendship; Of moderation; Of cannibals; Of solitude; Of the inequality that is between us; Of ancient customs; Of Democritus and Heraclitus; Of vain subtleties; Of age.

From Book 2: Of the inconsistency of our actions; Of drunkenness; Of practice; Of the affection of fathers for their children; Of books; Of presumption; Of a monstrous child; Of the resemblance of children to fathers.

From Book 3: Of the useful and the honorable; Of three kinds of association; On some verses of Virgil; Of the art of discussion; Of vanity; Of experience.

Try to get a modern translation, such as Trechmann's or, better, either Donald Frame's or M. A. Screech's. Avoid Cotton's version; it is an antique.

C.F.

38

MIGUEL DE CERVANTES SAAVEDRA
1547–1616

Don Quixote

Don Quixote is one of the few books on our list that may profitably be read in an abridged (but, please, not a bowdlerized or children's) version. Walter Starkie has done a good job along this line. However, if you use, as I suggest, a complete translation, do some skipping. Whenever (or almost whenever) you come to a goatherd or a shepherdess, some drivel lies ahead. Skip all the interpolated pastoral yarns that pleased Cervantes's audience but bore us stiff. Skip every bit of verse you meet; Cervantes is one of the world's worst poets. Finally, use *only* a modern translation—Cohen's or Starkie's or, best of all, Putnam's. Post-finally, do not be put off by an occasional tedious passage or chapter in Part 1. Persist to Part 2. It is by far the greater. Even the finest writers sometimes have to educate themselves through the medium of their own creation, and apparently that is what happened to this poor, maimed ex-soldier Cervantes. From writing about Don Quixote and Sancho Panza he learned how great they really were. Ten years elapsed between the publication of the two parts, and those ten years made a difference in Cervantes's genius.

These warnings are needed because, like *Paradise Lost* [45] and *The Divine Comedy* [30], *Don Quixote* is one of those books more reverenced than read, more lauded than enjoyed. It has had its ups and downs. Perhaps it reached its peak of popularity in the eighteenth century—you will see how much it meant to Laurence Sterne [58], for example. It is not so widely read in our time. Still, the fact remains that, after the Bible, it is one of the half-dozen books in the world most widely translated and studied. And for this there must be good reasons.

There are.

Of these reasons Cervantes himself suggests the simplest. He remarks, in the second chapter of Part 2, "No sooner do [people] see any lean hack than they cry out: 'There goes Rosinante.'" In other words, his book is crowded with immediately recognizable human types, and in this case a nonhuman type. The whole world understands at once what we mean when we call someone quixotic or say that he tilts at windmills. There are really only a few literary characters we think of as permanently alive. Hamlet [39] is one, Don Quixote surely another.

The second reason is no less simple. *Don Quixote*, once you allow for its leisurely tempo, is one of the best adventure stories ever written, perhaps the best after the *Odyssey*. That is what makes it a classic for the young. When you reread it years later you perceive that it is also a great adventure story of the mind, for some of its most exciting events occur during the conversations between the knight and his loquacious squire, two of the best talkers who ever used their vocal cords creatively.

The third reason sounds simple but is not so.

Don Quixote is a supremely humorous novel. A familiar anecdote tells us that when King Philip III of Spain noticed a man reading beside the road and laughing so much that the tears were rolling down his cheeks, he said, "That man is either crazy or he is reading *Don Quixote*." Some readers laugh aloud, others grin, some smile externally, others internally. And some read it with a curious emotion mingling delight and sorrow. Cervantes's humor is hard to define because it is not a "character trait" in him; it is the man himself, hence a mystery. The best clue to his humor is Walter Starkie's remark. He calls Cervantes a humorist, "which meant that he could see more than one thing at a time."

This brings us to the deepest of all the reasons for *Don Quixote*'s greatness—the fact that, though it is not obscure, its meanings seem to change with each generation, indeed with each reader, and none of these meanings is trivial.

We all know that Cervantes started out to write a satire on chivalric romances. Or so he seems to say. Don Quixote himself, the lean, grizzled Knight of the Sorrowful Countenance, began his life as a figure of fun. So did his earthy, stocky, proverb-crammed squire, Sancho Panza. Yet, by the end of the book, both have become something else, as well as more like each other, as the critic Salvador de Madariaga remarks. Together they seem to sum up, roughly, the warring elements in all of us: our defiance of society and our acceptance of it; our love of the heroic and our suspicion of it; our passion for creating worlds of the imagination and our rueful compromise with the *status quo.*

And so we come to the *Don Quixote* "problem," as fascinating as the *Hamlet* "problem." Is this book a burlesque of chivalry? Or is it the most persuasive of pleas for the chivalric attitude, apart from any specific time or institution? Is it a satire on dreamers? Or is it a defense of dreaming? Is it a symbol of the tragic soul and history of Spain? If so, why does it speak so clearly to men of all nations and races? Is it the author's spiritual autobiography? A study of insanity? Or of a higher sanity? Or is it, couched in terms of picaresque incident, a dramatized treatise on illusion and reality, akin to the plays of Pirandello? Finally—just to indicate how complex interpretation may become—is Don Quixote, as Mark Van Doren thinks, a kind of actor, who chooses his role because by so doing he can absorb life and reflect on it in a way denied to the single, unvarying personality?

I leave you to the golden book that Macaulay thought "the best novel in the world, beyond comparison."

C.F.

PART THREE

39
WILLIAM SHAKESPEARE
1564–1616

Complete Works

Enjoying Shakespeare is a little like conquering Everest: much depends on the approach. Let's clear away a few common misconceptions.

1. He was a man, not a demigod. He was not "myriad-minded," even though Coleridge [65] said he was. He does not "out-top knowledge," even though Matthew Arnold said he does. He was not infallible—merely a genius, one of many the human race has produced. He was also a practicing theater craftsman, a busy actor, and a shrewd, increasingly prosperous businessman. A genius may live a quite conventional life, and Shakespeare (unless you are terribly shocked at his leaving his young wife and children for some years) seems to have done so.

2. He is our greatest English poet and dramatist. But he is not always great. He often wrote too quickly, with his eye not on posterity but on a deadline. Some of his comic characters have lost all power to amuse, and it is best to admit it. His puns and wordplay are frequently tedious. He can be obscure rather than profound.

3. He is not a great original thinker. Few poets are—that is not their business. Those who seek ideas that have changed the world should not go to Shakespeare; they will be disappointed.

4. Finally, we all (including this writer) feel we "know" Shakespeare, when what we probably know is merely what we are supposed to think about him. Hard though it is, we must try to clear our minds of the formulas inherited from the average high school or college English class. Approaching the

plays as "classics" is less fruitful than approaching them with
the fresh expectancy with which we attend the opening performance of a new play.

This brief note therefore does not at all suggest what to
look for. Even if you are not looking for anything in
Shakespeare you will find something.

Read, do not study him. And of course reread him, for the
simple approach I have advised will disclose only a part of a
complex artist. Many men have spent almost their entire lives
on Shakespeare and felt no regret.

To read all of Shakespeare is well worth, let us say, a half-
year out of the ordinary three score and ten. Yet few of us possess the necessary curiosity. Judgments vary, but of the thirty-
seven plays the following dozen may be recommended as
minimum reading, to be done not as a block but in the course of
your lifetime: *The Merchant of Venice, Romeo and Juliet, Henry
IV (Parts I and 2), Hamlet, Troilus and Cressida, Measure for
Measure, King Lear, Macbeth, Antony and Cleopatra, Othello,*
and *The Tempest.*

Shakespeare also wrote a sonnet sequence, some of the poems
being clearly addressed to a young man, others to an unidentified
"Dark Lady." Though the whole forms a kind of loose progression, the sonnets may be read singly with perfect satisfaction.
Some of the more famous: numbers 18, 29, 30, 33, 55, 60, 63, 64,
65, 66, 71, 73, 94, 98, 106, 107, 116, 129, 130, 144, and 146.

C.F.

40

JOHN DONNE
1573–1631

Selected Works

Had the Lifetime Reading Plan been compiled in 1900, Donne
and Blake [63] might have been omitted. The shift in emphasis

is more than a matter of fashion, though both men do happen to be fashionable in literary circles. It is a matter of taste; but taste, when it mirrors a real change in our view of ourselves, can be a profound thing.

Neglected for some generations after his death, Donne impresses us today because he speaks to our condition, as Milton [45] does not. In another fifty years or so this may no longer be true. At the moment, however, Donne seems to us a great writer, not merely because he has so powerfully influenced modern poetry, but because his voice is that of a modern man. It is no accident that in 1940 Hemingway [119] should have drawn the title of his novel *For Whom the Bell Tolls* from one of Donne's *Devotions,* published in 1624.

Born of a Roman Catholic family, Donne was on his mother's side related to the martyr Sir Thomas More. Some years at Oxford and Cambridge were followed by the study of law, by a period of worldly and amorous adventure in London, by foreign service, and by a marriage—injudicious from the practical viewpoint—with the highborn niece of his employer, Sir Thomas Egerton. Donne's career prospects darkened and for a decade the young couple endured discouragement and poverty. At forty-two, after much serious reflection, Donne forsook the family faith and took orders in the Anglican church. He rose until he became Dean of St. Paul's in London, and the most famous preacher of his time. The daring young spark of the earlier love poems was now a God-tormented man, assailed by visions of death and the indignities of illness. He rejected "the mistress of my youth, Poetry" in favor of "the wife of mine age, Divinity." His obsession with mortality grew with the years. Today you may visit the crypt in St. Paul's and see Donne's statue, sculpted during his lifetime, wrapped in a winding sheet. As his last hour neared he contemplated from his bedside a painting of himself in a shroud, his eyes closed as if death had already touched him.

Donne's *Devotions* and *Sermons* are quite unlike conventional religious literature. They are works of art, combining an almost frightening spiritual intensity with cunning elaboration of rhythm and metaphor. The *Devotions* are addressed to himself. The sermons were delivered before large audiences, often before the king. No Sunday pieties, they were designed deliberately to work upon the emotions. They can still do so, with their art if not their doctrine.

Donne's poetry is at once highly sensuous (often highly sensual), uncompromisingly intellectual, and startlingly personal. By the use of metaphor, sometimes complex, sometimes brutally direct, Donne merges sense and intellect in a manner to which our own taste seems keenly receptive. At his worst his figures of speech are the ingenious conceits that annoyed the forthright Dr. Johnson [59]. At his best they seem identical with the thought itself.

His love poetry bypasses not only all the Elizabethan conventions, but all the standard sentiments that had been the staple of erotic verse up to his day. "For God's sake hold your tongue, and let me love." A man who begins a poem that way is imitating no one. He is not writing exercises. He is a real man speaking, and his voice is in the room. Donne can be shocking, outrageous, tender, learned, colloquial, fantastic, passionate, reverent, despairing; and sometimes he is several of these in a single love poem. It is his awareness of the complexity of emotion that recommends him to our unsimple time. And what is true of his love poetry is also true of his devotional verse, which often seems to have an erotic tinge: It is the work of the whole man, including the physical man. Two often-quoted lines condense a great deal of John Donne:

> Love's mysteries in souls do grow,
> But yet the body is his book.

We may, very roughly, liken Donne's poetry to El Greco's painting. As El Greco distorts line, so Donne distorts language, not out of any lust for experiment, but to achieve calculated effects of emphasis, intensity, and directness obtainable in no other way. Just as El Greco's colors at first seem harsh and unnatural, so Donne's rhythms are broken, rough, the agitated reflection of emotions themselves broken and rough. The spiritual pain and tension that we feel in El Greco we feel also in Donne. His faith was not serene; it was shadowed with anxieties, perplexities, contradictions that seem to anticipate the climate of our own sorely beset time.

Donne produced much writing of interest mainly to the scholar. For the beginning reader, who may be familiar with only a few anthology pieces, I might suggest: the *Songs and Sonnets,* the *Elegies,* the *First and Second Anniversaries,* the *Holy Sonnets,* the *Devotions Upon Emergent Occasions,* and perhaps a few of the *Sermons.* At first this "angel speaking out of a cloud" may seem far-fetched and needlessly difficult. But, behind his odd metaphors (often drawn from the trades and sciences) and his seeming extravagances of style lie sound reasons. Careful reading will soon make these reasons apparent, and his personal idiom will become less and less alien as it becomes more and more fascinating.

C.F.

41
ANONYMOUS
published 1618

The Plum in the Golden Vase (Chin P'ing Mei)

The *Chin P'ing Mei* [*Jin ping mei*] is a famously, even scandalously, erotic novel. It has been banned in China for much of the time since its publication in the early seventeenth century, though that has seldom stopped it from being circulated surreptitiously. Its reputation as a "dirty book" has assured it a stormy career in the West as well; for many years the only widely available translation had all of the sexy parts in Latin, shrouded, as the translator explained (borrowing a phrase from Edward Gibbon), "in the decent obscurity of a learned language." (There was a time when the existence of similar passages in the works of Ovid and other Classical authors spurred schoolboys on to feats of Latin erudition that they seldom matched in the classroom.)

If the *Chin P'ing Mei* were only an erotic novel, though, it would not be of all that much interest; the sexually explicit passages are far tamer than one will find in any commonplace bodice-ripper in our own time. What makes this a great novel, indeed a classic of world literature, is that it is a brilliant social satire and critique, a devastating portrayal of sixteenth-century China in the grip of decadence, cynicism, and excess. David Roy, the most recent and best translator of the *Chin P'ing Mei*, likens the book to Dickens's *Bleak House* [77] in the power of its indictment of a whole society. (The events of the novel are set in the period 1122–1127, the waning years of the Northern Sung Dynasty, but that was simply protective coloration for the anonymous author; readers in the time the book was written would have recognized the society it describes as their own.)

The novel depicts life in the household of Hsi-men Ch'ing [Ximen Qing], a merchant in a provincial city of China: his business dealings, his amorous intrigues, his ill-gotten gains, and finally his death, the disintegration of his household, and the thwarting of his schemes. The novel, in 100 chapters, is enormously long and dense, with numerous plot twists and narrative byways; it has been compared to the works of Joyce [110] and Nabokov [122]. But whatever the book's complexity Hsi-men Ch'ing remains its focal figure, and he is one of the most marvelous scoundrels in all of world literature. He is sexually insatiable, and this lust is symbolic of his more general greed for money, power, and pleasure. His six wives and concubines are not merely companions and playthings: One joins his household after he conspires with her to poison her husband; another is the seduced former wife of his neighbor and sworn brother. Just as he stops at nothing in assembling his harem, so he is contemptuous of ordinary morality in his business dealings; his philosophy of life is to grab what he can when he can, and devil take the hindmost.

The concept of a charming literary villain is not so shocking to us nowadays, but to a traditional Confucian Chinese readership Hsi-men Ch'ing was not merely titillating, he was profoundly threatening. Two of the founding principles of Confucian morality are that human nature is by nature good, and that social order proceeds from the benevolent influence of the ruler radiating throughout the realm (see Mencius [14]). The author of the *Chin P'ing Mei*—and it is no wonder that he took pains to preserve his anonymity—is telling his readers that human nature is, on the contrary, immoral and opportunistic, and that in contemporary society there is no sign of transforming, benevolent virtue diffusing outwards from the throne. In its own time, then, the *Chin P'ing Mei* was a work of social criticism verging on sedition. Today that impact has become somewhat blunted, but the fascinating tale of greed, folly and retribution remains for us to enjoy. We will also notice that in its psychologically authentic characters, its multilayered plot, and its focus on the affairs of a single wealthy household, this novel points directly ahead to *Dream of the Red Chamber* [56], the greatest of all works of traditional Chinese fiction.

The *Chin P'ing Mei* is, though, a very long novel, with an involved story and an enormous cast of characters with (to most Americans) very unfamiliar-sounding names. It is not difficult to read, but it is difficult to get started reading. You might want to wait to read this until you have already flexed your literary muscles on a couple of other very long novels— say, *Don Quixote* [38] and *The Tale of Genji* [28]. Choose the best possible translation, too; Clement Edgerton's four-volume version is good; David Roy's translation, of which only the first of a projected five volumes has been published as of this writing, is truly brilliant.

J.S.M.

42

GALILEO GALILEI

1574–1642

Dialogue Concerning the Two Chief World Systems

Galileo is the sort of man who gives the Renaissance its good reputation. Born into a good bourgeois family in Pisa, he studied mathematics, made a career as a scholar, and lived a happy, even somewhat self-indulgent, life. If his only accomplishment had been to make his seminal discoveries in astronomy and what we would now call astrophysics, he would rank high on any list of all-time great scientists. But his scientific work encompasses far more than that. As a military engineer, he demonstrated that the path of a projectile follows the mathematical curve called a parabola (paving the way, for good or ill, for modern artillery and the ballistic missile). He was an experimental physicist of true genius, who discovered that all falling bodies (leaving aside questions of friction or air resistance) accelerate at the same rate, independently of their weight, and who showed that a pendulum of a given length and weight takes a uniform amount of time to complete a swing, regardless of the swing's amplitude. These discoveries—which had enormous consequences for the further development of physics and engineering—not only went against the conventional wisdom of Galileo's time, but they seem to contradict common sense itself. Galileo's stubborn willingness to pursue his experiments and to state his findings whether or not people initially found them plausible served him well the first time he turned a telescope to the heavens.

It was typical of Galileo to wonder what stars and planets might look like through a telescope; it was typical of him, too, that when he needed a telescope he made one himself. In 1609 he looked through his new instrument at the night sky, and was nearly bowled over by what he saw: the Milky Way, not a tenuous river of light stretching across the sky, but a continuous band of an uncountable number of stars; the Moon pockmarked with craters and with craggy mountains and (it seemed) flat, tranquil seas; Venus, not a shining sphere, but a crescent like that of the moon, because, as Galileo quickly realized, it was in orbit around the sun; four small satellites circling around Jupiter; strange knobby bulges on each side of Saturn (his telescope was not sharp enough to resolve the rings of Saturn). This was the sky as no one had ever seen it before.

Galileo rushed to spread the news of his observations, in a small book that he called *Sidereus Nuncius* (The Starry Messenger; there is a nice translation by Albert van Helden). Published in 1610, it was an instant bestseller, printed and reprinted all over Europe; within five years it had even been translated into Chinese (by a Jesuit missionary). But while the world marveled, and savants rushed to acquire telescopes to see for themselves, Galileo began to ponder deeply the implications of his discoveries. He worked for twenty years to refine his opinions, and to present an unassailable case for his cosmological theory.

What Galileo realized as a result of his astronomical observations is that the view of the universe proposed by Copernicus in 1543 must be correct. Copernicus himself had not made that claim; he only said that to put the sun, rather than the Earth, in the center of the universe made for a simpler model, and made the mathematical calculations of orbital periods easier. He also deflected any criticism of his motives by delaying publication of his work until he was on his deathbed; if the work proved controversial, he wouldn't have to deal with the consequences. Copernicus's sun-centered model became widely known, but as long as it was considered "just a theory" it caused no particular controversy. People continued, on the whole, to believe in the old Aristotelian-Ptolemaic Earth-centered universe, a model that had not only tradition and common sense, but the sanction of the Church, behind it. In 1616 the Church authorities, sensing a threat, warned Galileo against teaching the Copernican system and issued an edict formally condemning it.

But Galileo was undeterred. Finally, in 1632, he published the work that rocked the foundations of classical learning and ensured his own place in the pantheon of scientific courage: *The Dialogue Concerning the Two Chief World Systems*. Using the dialogue form (familiar to Renaissance intellectuals through the rediscovered Greek classics, especially Plato [12]) for its persuasive power, he leads the reader step-by-step through his discoveries, and asking the reader to assent to innocuous-seeming conclusions on their basis. And then, at last, he says, "But notice that you yourself have now created the Copernical model." It is a rhetorical work of genius, and is as persuasive today as it was in 1632. How, one wonders, could anyone fail to be convinced by it?

But the Church authorities at Rome were not persuaded; rhetoric had no power against dogma. And so Galileo was called before the Inquisition and forced to recant his theory; aging, tired, and ill, he really had no choice. He was required to spend the rest of his life under house arrest in his beloved city of Florence. But his *Dialogue*, though burned by the Inquisition, continued to circulate; within a few years, the Copernican model of the universe was taken as an established fact in scholarly circles throughout Europe. And Galileo apparently knew that he would be vindicated; after he humbled himself before the Inquisition by affirming that the Earth lies unmoving at the center of the cosmos, he muttered under his breath, but loudly enough for witnesses to hear, "And yet—it does move."

Galileo's work led directly to that of Sir Isaac Newton just a few decades later. But while Newton's *Principia Mathematica* was written for an audience of specialists and is quite impenetrable to the lay reader, Galileo was writing for the general educated public. His *Dialogue* is a model of clarity; any serious reader can understand it. If you can find a copy, or can ask your library to get it on interlibrary loan, use Giorgio de Santillana's abridged-text version; he sharpens the dialogue by omitting some rhetorical byways, and his explanatory notes are excellent.

J.S.M.

43
THOMAS HOBBES
1588–1679

Leviathan

We read the philosophers not only because they are in themselves interesting, but because their ideas have consequences. The quarrel between the individual and the state as to the proper division of power is central to our time. Hobbes is important because he presents the first modern reasoned case for the state as the exclusive holder of power, so long as that state can offer protection to its citizens. Thus all of today's authoritarian regimes, whether Marxist or non-Marxist, may claim Hobbes as one of their earliest and greatest advocates.

Hobbes received a good classical education at Oxford. He later used his scholarship to prepare a translation of Thucydides [9] in whose work he saw a demonstration of the evils of democracy. For some time he made a living as a tutor in a noble family. In his middle years, apparently as a consequence of reading a proof in Euclid, he turned from the classics to science and philosophy. His political sympathies during the great English Parliamentary struggle were Royalist; for a short period he taught mathematics in Paris to the future Charles II. But his deeper loyalty was to power irrespective of party. Hence, after Cromwell's victory, he made submission to the Protector. During the Restoration, though attacked as an atheist, he managed to survive successfully enough to reach the age of ninety-one.

His fame rests on the *Leviathan*. Published in 1651, it was merely a systematic development of ideas he was already holding some years before the Civil War came to a head.

Hobbes's absolutist theory of the state rests on his anti-heroic conception of man's nature. He is a thoroughgoing mechanistic materialist. He does not deny God. But God is irrelevant to his thought. He believes in a proposition by no means self-evident—that all men are primarily interested in self-preservation. In a natural, lawless state this passion results in anarchy, and the life of man, in his most famous phrase, is "solitary, poor, nasty, brutish, and short."

To escape such an existence, man institutes a commonwealth or government, the great artificial construct Hobbes calls Leviathan. To secure peace, or, as we say today, "security," we must relinquish our right of private judgment as to what is good or evil, placing that right in the hands of a sovereign or assembly. Hobbes prefers a monarchy, but his logic would suggest no basic objection to a committee or party, as in the Communist Leviathan. In such a state, morality would flow from law rather than law from morality.

Most so-called realistic theories of politics find their source partly in Hobbes, though also in Machiavelli [34]. Our own democratic doctrine is anti-Hobbesian in its view of human nature. It rests on the notion of a division of powers (Hobbes thought the Civil War came about because power was divided among the king, the lords, and the House of Commons); on a system of checks and balances; and on a vague but so far workable theory of the general will expressed in representative form. To understand what really separates us from all authoritarian regimes, a reading of the *Leviathan* is most helpful.

Despite his iron doctrine, Hobbes himself seems to have been a pleasant and rather timid fellow.

He writes a crabbed, difficult prose. Save him for your more insistently intellectual moods. Read the Introduction and Parts 1 and 2 entire, if possible; Chapters 32, 33, 42, and 46 of Parts 3 and 4, in which he argues against the power claims of all established churches; and finally his Review and Conclusion.

C.F.

44
RENÉ DESCARTES
1596–1650

Discourse on Method

Descartes is often termed "the father of modern philosophy." Even if this were not so, he would still be well worth reading for the elegant precision of his prose and the mathematical clarity of his reasoning. These two qualities, more than his specific doctrines, have deeply influenced the French character.

Descartes's family was of the minor nobility and he never had to support himself. This was as it should be; we shall never know how much genius has been lost to the world by reason of the need to make a living. We willingly provide free board and lodging for lunatics, but recoil before the idea of doing so for first-class minds.

Descartes received a good Jesuit education. As his health was poor, his masters, intelligent men, allowed him to stay late in bed instead of compelling him to play the seventeenth-century equivalent of basketball. This slugabed habit he retained all his life. It was responsible for much calm, ordered thought.

Even as a young man Descartes had begun to distrust the foundations of everything he had been taught, except mathematics. This skepticism (which did not conflict, it appears, with conventional piety) was reinforced during his Paris and Poitiers years (1614–18) when he read Montaigne [37]. He finally abandoned study and set off on a career of mild military adventure and travel. He was resolved, he says, "no longer to seek any other science than the knowledge of myself, or of the great book of the world."

His great creative years, from 1629 to 1649, were spent mainly in Holland, at that time a general asylum for intelligence. His fame grew to such proportions that Queen Christina of Sweden invited (that is, commanded) him to visit her and teach her philosophy. In Sweden Descartes was forced to rise at 5:00 A.M. in cold weather in order to converse with the queen. A few months of such barbarism were enough to kill him. Had not this arrogant monarch caused his death just as directly as if she had shot him, the world might have had another twenty years of Descartes's mind.

However, he managed to do pretty well. Though the two talents were inextricably connected, Descartes was an even greater mathematician than philosopher. One morning, while lying in bed, he hit upon the idea of coordinate geometry, which married algebra to geometry. He also worked in physics, though with less distinction.

Descartes's doctrines, dualistic and materialist in tendency, are both interesting and influential. But it is as the creator of a new, or at any rate fresh, method of thought that his position was secured. He threw aside much, though not all, of scholastic reasoning and, as it were, started from scratch. He began by doubting everything. The progression of doubt, however, ended at the point where he found that he could not doubt the existence of his own thought. "I think, therefore I am" is the famous formula with which he begins. (In a somewhat different form, it is found in Augustine [22], too, but Descartes made it do work and Augustine didn't.) He then proceeds to build a system of thought, using four main principles you will find described in his *Discourse on Method.* "Cartesian doubt," however, describes not only a method but an attitude of mind, and this attitude was to influence profoundly post-Cartesian speculation, whether scientific or philosophical.

We read Descartes, then, as the first supremely great mind to receive its stimulus from the new physics and astronomy of Copernicus, Galileo [42], and others. He incorporates the outlook of the tremendous renaissance of science, partly contemporary with him, that was to reach a high point with Newton.

C.F.

45

JOHN MILTON
1608–1674

Paradise Lost, Lycidas, On the Morning of Christ's
Nativity, Sonnets, Areopagitica

Milton's life opened on a fair prospect and closed in darkness. At Christ's College, Cambridge, the delicate-featured boy was called, half in scorn, half in admiration, "The Lady of Christ's." He found his vocation early: poetry and classical scholarship. A period of reading and study at his father's country house (1632–38) was followed by a year or two of Continental travel. During this time he was a humanist not greatly different from other humanists of the Renaissance. Then came twenty years of stormy political and religious controversy. Some magnificent prose resulted, but little happiness—and many may think these years a waste of his genius. Championing the Parliamentary cause, hating "the bishops," he served as Latin secretary to Cromwell for over a decade, overlaying his original humanism with Puritan doctrine. From his forty-third year to his death he was blind; none of his three marriages turned out well; and with the Restoration all his political hopes and dreams were dashed. Nothing was left him but poetry and his personal Christianity, a kind of dissidence of dissent.

This was the man who wrote *Paradise Lost,* he and his widow receiving eighteen pounds for the effort of justifying the ways of God to men; who told us that poetry should be "simple, sensuous, and passionate," but did not always follow his own prescription; whose *Areopagitica* is the classic defense of free speech and who fiercely supported Cromwell's rigid Puritan theocracy; whose views on divorce were three hundred years ahead of his time and whose views on women were those of a dimwitted barbarian; who was a master of the language and yet may be said to have written English as if it were Latin or Greek.

The average reader, approaching this unhappy Samson, meets two obstacles. The first is Milton. The second is Miltonese.

It is hard to like John Milton. Suffering the penalty of charmlessness, of humorlessness, he has been less read than admired, less admired than merely accepted. The "God-gifted organ voice of England," as Tennyson called it, is a pretty intimidating voice as well. Milton was a man of the utmost courage; but it is not the kind of courage that kindles the imagination because it is not married to much humanity, and distills the smell of stubbornness. His pride was too magnificent for any alloy of mere conceit; yet we are made uncomfortable by his "elaborate assumption of the singing-robe," by his flat statement that he will pursue "things unattempted yet in prose or rhyme." He is a hard man to live with. Shakespeare [39], even Dante [30], had not only the uncommon but also the common touch. Milton lacked it. Making due allowance for Samuel Johnson's [59] Toryism, it is hard not to agree with his view of Milton: "an acrimonious and surly republican."

And the style is suited to the man. It has, as Milton proudly states, "no middle flight." It can be grand; it can be windy; it can be sublime; it can be pompous. It is never charming, restful, or easy, except in the minor poems and even then infrequently. It is difficult, odd in syntax and vocabulary, uncompromising in its elevation.

Perhaps I have persuaded you to skip Milton. That was not my intention. For all the mustiness of his theology and morality, for all his mannerism (though it was no mannerism to him), for all the negative magnetism of his personality, he remains a great artist in both verse and prose. With rocklike—he would say adamantine—grandeur he continues to impose himself even on our age, which laughs at grandeur, at the noble style, and at erudition.

It is worthwhile to make a special, even a painful effort of adjustment to read Milton. If he is a museum piece, he is a rare, precious one. If you cannot stomach his message in

Paradise Lost, at least read it for the gorgeous sound, the elaborate imagery, the portrait of Satan, that fallen god with whom Milton himself had so much in common. No one will ever again write like this. No one will ever again conceive such perfect, rolling periods as are to be found in his most eloquent prose.

When we step inside our first great Gothic cathedral, our feelings are mixed. It seems alien, it seems too complicated, it does not seem quite human. But gradually we accustom ourselves to what the builders had in mind. Little by little the structure and sweep and decoration and color become familiar. Soon two clear emotions begin to arise in us, different in nature, yet capable of blending: awe and esthetic pleasure. Milton is a little like that. He cannot inspire these emotions all the time, nor should one be too obstinate in seeking them continually. But they are there for you, if you read him in small doses, skipping when he is too wearisome or too exalted for our commoner clay.

C.F.

46
MOLIÈRE
January 15, 1622 [baptized]–1673

Selected Plays

Molière's real name was Jean-Baptiste Poquelin. The son of a prosperous Parisian upholsterer, he received a good Jesuit education, read for the law, and at twenty-one renounced security and upholstery for the chancy and unrespectable life of the stage. His company failed in Paris. He spent many years, perhaps thirteen, knocking about in provincial inn-yards, mounting farces, learning from the ground up the business both of the theater and of human nature. In 1658 his company reestablished itself in Paris under the patronage of the brother of Louis XIV. It was successful and so was Molière, operating as actor, manager, and writer of whatever seemed called for: farces, court entertainments, comedies.

In his personal life he was less fortunate. At forty he married Armande Béjart, who may have been the illegitimate daughter of his former mistress, and, some said, his own daughter, though there is little evidence for this contention. Half his age, Armande doubled his troubles, which were complicated by overwork, illness, and the many controversies brought on by Molière's satires on affectation, religious hypocrisy, and conventional prejudices. One night, while playing the title role in his own comedy *The Imaginary Invalid* he hemorrhaged on-stage, dying soon after.

There are at least two Molières. Unhappily they are often found in the same play. The first is the play-it-for-laughs commercial hack who knows all the tricks. Molière the gagman and knockabout farce-confector would have no trouble in Hollywood today. Indeed Hollywood, though it does not know it, is still using switches on comedy situations developed or, less often, invented by Molière.

The second Molière is the strange man who turned his own sad life into comedy: his illness into *The Imaginary Invalid;* his tragic marriage into *The School for Wives;* and, I think, his own bittersweet view of his society into *The Misanthrope.* Molière will never be a great favorite of the English-speaking world. His characters are conceived in the French classic tradition (when they are not even simpler reincarnations of the Italian commedia dell'arte). That is, they are not individuals, as Hamlet and Falstaff are, but walking and mainly talking incorporations of single passions or ideas. From our viewpoint his plays are lacking in action. Finally he has none of the richness or unexpectedness of our Shakespeare [39]. Molière is all logic and neatness.

Yet if we are willing to accept the French classic notion of a play as a kind of organized argument, constructed in accord with the rules of rhetoric, Molière is suddenly seen to be a master. We do not have to know much about the rules he followed (or quite often broke) to enjoy his thrusts at exaggerated conduct, his constant sense of the ridiculousness of human behavior, and the curious sadness that underlies much of his most hilarious comedy. "It's a strange business, making nice honest people laugh," says Dorante in *The Critique of the School for Wives*. Molière must have found it so.

For those who do not know French he offers only moderate enjoyment. Somehow in English he sometimes sounds what he was not—simpleminded. I rather like the translations by either Donald Frame, Richard Wilbur, or Morris Bishop. Try *The School for Wives, Tartuffe, The Misanthrope*, and *The Would-Be Gentleman*. There are four other equally major plays: *The Miser, Don Juan, The Imaginary Invalid*, and *The Learned Ladies*.

C.F.

47
BLAISE PASCAL
1623–1662

Thoughts (Pensées)

Pascal is a seeming oddity, for he possessed in the highest degree a number of traits not usually combined in a single personality. First and foremost, he is a scientific and mathematical genius. Second, he is a master of prose style; indeed he is often thought of as the norm of classic French prose. Third, he is an acute though unsystematic psychologist. Fourth, he is a God-thirsty, tormented soul, a kind of failed saint. To a freethinker such as Eric T. Bell, author of the fascinating *Men of Mathematics*, Pascal ruined his life by his preoccupation with religious controversy: "On the mathematical side Pascal is the greatest might-have-been in history." It is hard to make a sensible judgment. Pascal was Pascal. The man who in love and terror cried out for God, and the man who thought of the omnibus and invented the syringe are somehow indivisible.

At twelve, before he had been taught any mathematics, Pascal was proving Euclid for himself. At sixteen he had written a trail-blazing work on conic sections, of which we possess only fragmentary indications. At eighteen, he had invented the first calculating machine and so became one of the fathers of our Computer Age. At twenty-four he had demonstrated the barometer. He did classic work in hydrostatics, and most of us remember Pascal's Law from high school, provided we were lucky enough to attend a high school that offered physics. In mathematics he is famous, among other matters, for having discovered and shown the properties of a notable curve called the cycloid. For its beauty and also for its power to excite controversy, this has been termed the Helen of geometry.

His major contribution, not merely to science but to thought in general, is perhaps his work in the theory of probability, the glory of which he shares with another mathematician, Fermat. It is interesting to recall that the ascetic Pascal was stimulated to his great mathematical discoveries by a gamblers' dispute involving the throw of dice. The ramifications of probability theory, writes Bell, "are everywhere, from the quantum theory to epistemology."

As mathematician and physicist, Pascal will rank higher than he will as moralist and religious controversialist. Yet in these latter fields his influence has been considerable. Just as Montaigne [37], who both fascinated and repelled Pascal, stands for one mood of mankind, so Pascal stands for another. Montaigne lived at ease with skepticism; Pascal's heart and mind cried out for certainties. Montaigne contemplated the sad condition of man with interest, humor, and tolerance. Pascal, who had brilliant wit but no humor, regarded it with terror and despair, from which he was saved only by throwing himself on the breast of revealed religion.

His finest, but to us not most interesting prose, is contained in his *Provincial Letters,* which you will find in most editions that print the *Pensées.* These letters are masterpieces of polemic, directed against certain tendencies of the Jesuit order of Pascal's day, tendencies he and his associates of the Jansenist movement considered too tolerant of man's moral frailties. (Jansenism was a kind of puritanical sect within Catholicism, stressing predestination and asceticism, but also inspiring new and brilliant techniques in the education of children.) This controversy, which made Pascal a bestseller, is today of interest mainly to theologians and historians of religion.

The *Thoughts*, or *Pensées*, are in a somewhat different category. They consist of a series of scrappy, often unfinished notes, originally intended to serve as parts of a grand design, a reasoned defense of the Christian religion against the assaults or the lethargy of freethinkers. Into them Pascal put his painful sense of the inadequacy, even the absurdity of man, as measured against the immensity of the universe, the endless flow of eternity, and the omniscience and omnipotence of God. A great deal of modern antihumanist pessimism flows from Pascal. Those who reject man as the center of the universe, whether they are religionists or nihilists, find the *Pensées* to their taste. He represents one profound mood of mankind, that which finds man glorious in his powers yet in the end pitiful and incomprehensible to himself.

The nonscientific Pascal is preserved by his style and by his emotional intensity. As a psychologist of the soul his genius is measured by the fact that he can still move many who are quite unable to sympathize with his sometimes noble, sometimes merely frantic devotionalism. Two Pascalian sentences, or cries from the heart, are frequently quoted. The first is "The eternal silence of these infinite spaces terrifies me." The second is "Man is but a reed, the weakest thing in nature; but he is a thinking reed." Between them these two statements suggest moods common to all men and women, whether they be Christian, agnostic, atheist, or of some other creed.

C.F.

48

JOHN BUNYAN
1628–1688

Pilgrim's Progress

A hundred years ago anyone who spoke of a muckraker or a worldly-wise man or Vanity Fair or the slough of despond or the valley of humiliation would have known he or she was quoting from *Pilgrim's Progress.* For over two centuries, starting with the publication of the first part in 1678, this book was probably more widely read among English-speaking people than any other except the Bible. It cannot, of course, speak to us as powerfully today as it did to the plain, nonconformist folk of Bunyan's time, wrestling with their conviction of sin, fearful of Hell's flames, hoping devoutly for salvation. And yet, for all its revivalist theology and its faded Dissenter's devotionalism, it is still worth reading, not alone for its historical importance, but as a work of almost unconscious art.

We marvel that Christianity could have been founded by so few men, most of them obscure and unlettered. The miracle seems a little less baffling if we consider that these men may have been like John Bunyan. Recall his life: a poor tinker and ex-soldier, almost completely unschooled—indeed he tells us that at one point he had forgotten how to read and write; converted to the Puritan creed; arrested in 1660 as "a common upholder of several unlawful meetings and conventicles"; spending, except for a few weeks, the next twelve years in Bedford jail; refusing the conditions of release: "if you let me out today, I will preach again tomorrow!"; leaving behind him a wife and four children, one of them blind; spending his imprisonment in writing as well as in memorizing the Bible and John Foxe's *Book of Martyrs;* jailed again for six months in 1675, during which time he wrote the first part of *Pilgrim's Progress;* released once more, only to become one of the most popular preachers of his time.

Written in what is now quaint English, *Pilgrim's Progress* is a simple allegory for simple people, offering terribly simple answers to the dread question, What shall I do to be saved? It is whole cultures remote from Augustine [22] and Dante [30], whose books it in certain respects resembles. Its faith recognizes only a black-and-white ethic. It appeals to a ferocious piety (though Bunyan himself was kind and tolerant) discoverable today only in our intellectual backwoods. And its author, with his dreams and voices and visions and his skinless conscience, was, no doubt of it, a fanatic who would offer Freud [98] a perfect field day.

But it is a remarkable book all the same. It has swayed not only millions of God-fearing plain folk, but sophisticated intellects like Shaw [99]. Its prose is that of a born, surely not made, artist—muscular, hard as nails, powerful, even witty. Has a certain kind of business morality ever been more neatly described than by the comfortable Mr. By-ends? "Yet my great-grandfather was but a water-man, looking one way and rowing another; and I got most of my estate by the same occupation." And, if we cannot respond to the theology, it is hard not to respond to the strong rhythm and naked sincerity of that triumphant climax: "When the day that he must go hence was come, many accompanied him to the river side, into which as he went, he said, 'Death, where is thy sting?' and as he went down deeper he said, 'Grave, where is thy victory?' So he passed over, and all the trumpets sounded for him on the other side."

Of the writers, listed in this Plan, who had preceded him, Bunyan had read not a line. He merely quietly joined them.

C.F.

49

JOHN LOCKE
1632–1704

Second Treatise of Government

With the Restoration (1660) Locke's father, a Cromwell man, lost much of his fortune. This may have inclined his Oxford-trained son to balance his wide intellectual interests with various governmental and semigovernmental activities. As he had, among other things, studied medicine, he was able to serve as household physician, as well as personal secretary, to the first Earl of Shaftesbury. With the latter's fall from power in 1675, Locke removed to France for four years; returned to England under Shaftesbury again; following the latter's exile and death, sought refuge in Holland; and in 1689 was back in England, favorably received by the new regime of William and Mary. During these years he worked on his *Essay Concerning Human Understanding*, which appeared, together with the *Two Treatises of Civil Government*, in 1690. The latter, however, had been written twelve years before and are not, as has been thought, a defense of the Revolution of 1688, except by anticipation.

During the whole of the eighteenth century Locke's influence was marked. Through Voltaire [53] and Rousseau [57] he provided some of the ideas that sparked the French Revolution. Through Jefferson and other Founding Fathers [60, 61] he determined to a considerable extent the ideas that went into the Declaration of Independence and the Constitution. His views on religious toleration, education, and politics, though not in every instance original, did much to establish the mental climate of the Industrial Revolution and to promote the advance of democratic government.

His major work, the *Essay Concerning Human Understanding*, is generally supposed to have founded the British empirical school of philosophy. This school rejects the doctrine that ideas are innate and derives them rather from experience. If you have a special interest in the fascinating history of theories of knowledge, you might tackle the famous *Essay*.

For the rest of us it is useful to have at least a rough idea of Locke's *Second Treatise of Government*. Like Hobbes [43], he addresses himself to the central question, What is the basis of legitimate power? His answer, though on many points open to criticism, clears the way for the development of representative government, just as Hobbes's answer does for authoritarian government. Hobbes's idea of a "contract" centers in the relinquishment of an individual's power to an absolute or almost absolute sovereign or assembly. Locke's "social contract" is made between equals (that is, property-holding male equals) who "join in and make one society." Government is not divinely instituted; it is not absolute; and its authority is limited by notions familiar to us: the separation of powers, checks and balances, and the permanent retention by the individual of certain "inalienable rights." For Locke these latter include life, liberty, and property. Against a government that does not guarantee such rights, rebellion is legitimate.

While Locke's specific political doctrines are of great historical importance to us, it is perhaps the general tenor of his thought that, through the Founding Fathers, has continued to influence the American conception of government. Locke is optimistic, as we are. He is relatively undogmatic. He hates bigotry and absolutism. He conceives of society as open and experimental. He believes the state should aim to further the happiness of all its citizens. These may seem tame ideas today, but they were inflammatory in his time. And, though few people read Locke, his views continue to exert influence.

C.F.

50
MATSUO BASHŌ
1644–1694

The Narrow Road to the Deep North

Bashō is probably the only Japanese poet whose name is widely recognized in the West. He is associated, rightly, with *haiku,* the gemlike three-line, seventeen-syllable poetic form that, for many Western readers, seems to encapsulate the Japanese aesthetic sensibility. His best-known poem has been translated countless times:

furu ike ya	Ancient silent pond
kawazu tomikobu	Then a frog jumped right in
mizu no oto	Watersound: kerplunk

What is not so well known is that the haiku evolved relatively late in the history of Japanese verse, and that Bashō was one of its chief inventors.

From the late ninth century onward, Japanese poets abandoned long verse forms and wrote almost entirely in the form called *tanka* (or *waka*), the "short poem" of thirty-one syllables in five lines: 5–7–5–7–7. (This was the kind of poem that Genji [28] wrote to his ladyfriends with such facility, and in which they replied to him.) The tanka was and is a flexible and expressive poetic form, but also a limited one; it precludes any kind of narrative or even sustained emotional development. By the thirteenth century poets regularly tried to avoid its limitations by composing tanka in sequential, quasi-narrative cycles of as many as a hundred poems. This led in turn to *renga,* or linked verse, a kind of sequential poem of indefinite length, often composed collectively by two or more poets (and sometimes as a social amusement over cups of *sake*). To begin, someone would propose an initial triplet (5–7–5), which always included a seasonal reference; the next person would add the closing couplet (7–7), the next would contribute a new triplet, and so on, for as long as people wanted to continue. In the hands of truly skillful poets, this process could produce long poems of delightful complexity and wit, characterized by the kind of free-association that we would expect to find more on the psychoanalytic couch than in a poem.

And this explains how the haiku became a cornerstone of modern Japanese poetry. With linked verse having freed up the poetic triplet as the starting point of a long poem, it only required a poetic genius like Bashō to realize that the triplet could stand on its own. Bashō spent much of his life refining the haiku form, in particular experimenting with ways to integrate haiku into prose narrative. His favorite genre for doing so was the travel memoir, of which *The Narrow Road to the Deep North* is his finest and most famous work.

Bashō was born into a minor and somewhat impoverished samurai family, at a time when Japan's warrior aristocracy was making a painful adjustment to a long period of domestic peace and tranquillity, a time when abilities other than swordsmanship were needed to make a good career. As a young man he was appointed to a post as gentleman-companion to a young samurai from a much more exalted family, and the two spent their time mainly in studying and writing poetry. After his master's early death, Bashō left the family's service and began a lifelong precarious existence as a wandering poetry teacher and Zen lay brother. He eventually became famous and attracted a number of students who themselves became famous poets (as well as larger numbers of hangers-on seeking to bask in his limelight). But fame seems to have meant nothing to him except insofar as it assured him a warm welcome wherever he went. He apparently owned almost nothing, lived in temples or the most frugal of rented houses, and was never happier than when he was exploring the back roads of Japan on foot, trusting fate to provide him each day with a simple meal, a place to stay, and fellow poets with whom to exchange verses.

The Narrow Road to the Deep North records a six-month journey in 1689 that took him north from Tokyo (then called Edo), then west over the mountainous spine of Japan to the coast of the Japan Sea, then southwest and south over the mountains again, ending at the town of Ogaki (near modern Nagoya). This journey involved traveling on foot through country that even today is rugged and remote, and Bashō's travel account contains hints of some anxious days traversing narrow and uncertain roads. But the air of the book reflects mainly its author's cheerful and optimistic disposition, his love of new experience, and his conviction that things will work out all right in the end.

In my view *The Narrow Road* is an example of a very rare thing—a perfect book. I would not change a syllable of it. By the time he wrote it Bashō had completely mastered the art of combining prose and haiku verse into a seamless narrative of the utmost simplicity and economy of style. It is a very short book, far less than a page per day for his six-month journey. (Contrast this with the long-windedness of many travel writers today.) Everywhere he went, Bashō distilled his response in haiku verse. In untalented hands haiku are simply boring and insignificant little snippets of pseudoverse (and many people think of haiku the way they think of abstract painting: "Anyone could do that." Anyone can try, that is; the results are usually awful.) In the hands of Bashō and a few other masters, haiku are tiny marvels, each one a small flash of Zen enlightenment. *The Narrow Road* shows a genius at the height of his powers.

J.S.M.

51
DANIEL DEFOE
1660–1731

Robinson Crusoe

Robinson Crusoe is one of the most famous books in the world. Its publication, however, though successful, was a minor incident in its author's crowded, singular, and not entirely unspotted life. A butcher's son, Defoe traveled widely in his youth; was once captured by Algerian pirates; went bankrupt for seventeen thousand pounds—which he later paid off; supported William of Orange in 1688; served as pamphleteer, propagandist, and secret agent under four sovereigns; changed his allegiance without ever abandoning what we would today call a liberal political position; got into trouble through his partisan writings and was stood in the pillory, from which rather unliterary vantage point, with true middle-class enterprise, he managed to sell quite a few copies of a broadside entitled "Hymn to the Pillory"; saw the inside of a prison; wrote *Robinson*

Crusoe, the first of his novels, when he was almost sixty; in all composed over four hundred books and tracts, very few of which bore his name on the title page; and, according to one account, died hiding out from his creditors. He also married and engendered seven children.

Defoe was perhaps the first truly outstanding professional journalist (or hired hack, if you prefer) in England; the father of the English novel (try his *Moll Flanders,* if you haven't read it); and a master of the trick of making an invention seem so true that to most of us Robinson Crusoe (a figment, though suggested by a real episode) is a living person.

Robinson Crusoe is supposed to be a boys' book. However, like its greater cousin *Huckleberry Finn* [92], it is a boys' book only in that it satisfies perfectly those male dreams that happen to be most vivid in boyhood but continue to lead an underground life in most men until they die. Virtually every male dreams of being completely self-sufficient, as Crusoe is; of building a private kingdom of which he can be undisputed lord; of having that deliciously lonely eminence emphasized in time by the establishment of a benevolent colonial tyranny over a single slave (Friday); of accumulating wealth and power that can never be endangered or vulgarized by competition; of enjoying success through the wholesome primitive use of muscle and practical good sense, as against the effete and troublesome exercise of the intellect; of doing all this in an exotic setting quite remote from his dull daily habitat; and finally of living in a self-made Utopia without any of the puzzling responsibilities of a wife and children. (*Robinson Crusoe* and *Moby Dick* [83] are the two great novels that manage superbly without involving more than one sex. They have never been popular with women.)

Robinson Crusoe has no plot. Its hero, though a sturdy stick, is nonetheless a stick. On reflection, the book's smug mercantile morality seems offensive. All this matters not at all against the fact that it is a perfect daydream, a systematic and detailed wish-fulfillment. Its appeal is heightened in that the most romantic experiences are related in the baldest prose. Its utter lack of fanciness makes the daydream respectable. We believe it precisely because it is not "literature."

When we were young we could see only that it was entertaining. Now, rereading it, we can perhaps see why it is also, as books go, immortal.

C.F.

52
JONATHAN SWIFT
1667–1745

Gulliver's Travels

Thackeray [76] once said of Swift: "So great a man he seems to me, that thinking of him is like thinking of an empire falling." Swift's mind was not comprehensive, perhaps not even very subtle. But it was extremely powerful, it was the mirror of an extraordinary temperament, and so its frustration, decay, and final extinction do suggest the tragic dimensions of which Thackeray speaks.

Swift was an Anglo-Irishman, born in Dublin and dying there, as Dean of St. Patrick's Cathedral. Like his fellow countryman Shaw [99], he had a genius for exposing the vices and weaknesses of his age. Like Shaw, too, he was a master of the English language, so that today his prose can be read with pleasure even though much of what he wrote about is of interest only to scholars. But here ends the parallel. Shaw's was one of the most successfully managed careers in history, Swift's one of the least. Shaw died after bestriding his world like a colossus. Swift died much as he foresaw, "like a poisoned rat in a hole."

His century is often called the Age of Reason, and he was one of its chief ornaments. He did worship reason: *Gulliver* may be seen as a picture of the consequences of humanity's refusal to be reasonable. The irony is that this apostle of reason should also have been a man of volcanic, baffled passions; that the terrible fits of dizziness and, later, deafness from which he suffered beginning in his twentieth year led him at last to the loss of that reason he so much admired; that some enigmatic lack apparently precluded what we think of as a normal sex life; that his split allegiance (was he an Irishman or an Englishman?) helped to unbalance him; that his semiexile in Dublin for his last thirty-two years was a permanent cross to his spirit, even though the Irish loved him as their champion. This man should have been the intellect and conscience of England. But melancholy marked him for her own; ambition denied withered him; and so his life, whose inner secrets we shall probably never know, was what the world called, and he himself called, a failure. Pointing to a blighted tree, he once remarked that he, too, would die first "at the top," and so he did, a ruined monument to frustration.

He left behind him a great mass of poetry and prose. Much of it is in the form of political pamphleteering, for he was in large part a journalist and propagandist. Some of it is in the form of his strange letter-diary, addressed to his ward, and known as the *Journal to Stella*.

One small part of it is a masterpiece. When first published in 1726 *Gulliver* was an instant success "from the cabinet council to the nursery." It is one of those curious works to which we may apply Lewis Muniford's sentence: "The words are for children and the meanings are for men." In fact, however, though children have always taken to their hearts at least the first two books of *Gulliver* (Lilliput and Brobdingnag), Swift wrote it with a serious purpose—"to mend the world." *Gulliver* is so rich a book as to bear many interpretations, but I think we may say that Swift wanted to hold up a mirror that would show humanity its true and often repellent face; and by doing so to force us to abandon our illusions, forswear our lies, and more nearly approach that rationality from which his Yahoos are the terrible declension.

In addition *Gulliver* is a political allegory. Its hidden references mean less to us than they did to the Londoners of 1726. The best thing is to pay no attention to the transient satire that threads it. As readers have discovered over more than two and a half centuries, there is plenty left: irony that applies to the human race wherever and whenever found; a biting humor; delightful invention; and a prose style of utmost clarity and power.

Swift's essence you will find in the last book, describing the voyage to the land of the Houyhnhnms. Here the misanthropy flows not from meanness but from an idealism broken under the buffets of fortune. Somehow, despite his ferocity, it is impossible to think of Swift as malicious. His inner contradictions are sorrowfully hinted at in the Latin epitaph he wrote for himself. In St. Patrick's Cathedral he lies at peace at last in a place "where bitter indignation can no longer lacerate his heart."

C.F.

53
VOLTAIRE
1694–1778

Candide and other works

Voltaire died at eighty-four, the uncrowned king of intellectual Europe, the undisputed leader of the Age of Enlightenment, the most destructive of the many sappers of the foundations of the Old Regime destroyed by the French Revolution. As dramatist, poet, historian, tale teller, wit, correspondent, controversialist, and coruscating personality, he had achieved a formidable reputation. His productivity is unbelievable; he left behind him over fourteen thousand known letters and over two thousand books and pamphlets. Yet he is most easily remembered for an extended little bittersweet joke that he wrote in three days. All his tens of thousands of ironies fade before the irony of this one circumstance.

Voltaire—his name was possibly an anagram for his probable real name, François-Marie Arouet—handled his career, including his business affairs, with the capacity of a Shaw. But he made one error. He wrote *Candide*. By doing so he obscured the remainder of his vast production. So much else is brilliant and well worth reading—the *Philosophical Dictionary*, *Zadig*, *Micromégas*, *The Age of Louis XIV*, the *Letters Concerning the English Nation*. Yet *Candide* is what we read, for it is perfection.

Also it is so lucid as to need little commentary. It was partly inspired by one of the events it chronicles, the devastating Lisbon earthquake of 1755. Voltaire uses this—as well as all the other misfortunes of poor Candide, Dr. Pangloss, and their companions—to make fun of what he conceived to be the smug optimism of the famous philosopher Leibniz, caricatured in the figure of Pangloss. As philosophy *Candide* is oversimplified, indeed shallow, for Voltaire's intelligence was quick and comprehensive rather than deep. But as lightning narrative, flashing with wit, as a pitiless yet funny indictment of the follies and cruelties of mankind, it has not yet been surpassed.

Its form is a favorite one of Voltaire's century, that of the philosophical romance. *Gulliver's Travels* [52] belongs to this category, and a good modern example is Thornton Wilder's *The Bridge of San Luis Rey*. It anticipates also another of the forms later fiction was to assume, that of the development novel, tracing the education of a young man. We shall meet this form again when we discuss *The Red and the Black* [67], and we will see it extended and deepened in *The Magic Mountain* [107]. Candide's education of course was of a uniquely violent nature, so violent that one can hardly help sympathizing with his rather mournful conclusion that, in this far from the best of all possible worlds, the most sensible thing we can do is to "cultivate our garden."

The reader, however, must not be misled by this jewel of wicked irony into thinking that Voltaire was no more than a genius of mockery. Like Shaw he could not help being witty;

and like Shaw he was a very serious, courageous, and humane fighter for the liberation of the human mind.

C.F.

54
DAVID HUME
1711–1776

An Enquiry Concerning Human Understanding

In proportion to its population Scotland has probably produced more first-rate minds than any country in the world except ancient Greece. Of these minds David Hume is surely one.

Intended by nature for abstract reflection, Hume, after short tries, sensibly rejected both the law and a business career. He spent three years in France, wrote his *Treatise of Human Nature* (of whose first part the *Enquiry* is a development), and watched it fall "dead-born from the press." The first volume of his *Essays* (1741) brought him greater success. Following their publication he occupied a number of official posts and one unofficial one, that of tutor to a certified lunatic, who was however a peer. One foreign service job netted him almost a thousand pounds, and he increased this small fortune with the profits from his triumphant and highly partisan *History of England*. In 1769, a rich man, he retired to his new house in Edinburgh and became a sort of Dr. Johnson [59] to that brilliant little capital.

In his interesting *Autobiography* he describes himself as "a man of mild dispositions, of command of temper, and of an open, social, and cheerful humor, capable of attachment, but little susceptible of enmity; and of great moderation in all my passions. Even my love of literary fame, my ruling passion, never soured my temper, notwithstanding my frequent disappointments."

Hume developed Locke's antimetaphysical position and so helped to clear the way for British utilitarianism in the nineteenth century (see John Stuart Mill [72]). His *Enquiry*, clear but not easy reading, deals with the original sensations he calls *impressions*. "All probable reasoning is nothing but a species of sensation." He is, as the quotation would indicate, a skeptic. He sees no rational connection between cause and effect, causation in his system being equal to mere sequence.

This central skepticism he applies to the self, which he deems unknowable; to morality, which he separates from religion; and to religion, coming "from the incessant hopes and fears which actuate the human mind."

Hume's balance and commonsensical temperament would have rejected the great romantics of the century following his. Yet they might well justify their position by appealing to Hume's total skepticism with respect to the existence of rational belief.

His skepticism was not mere academic theory. He philosophized, he admitted, not because he was certain of establishing the truth, but because it gave him pleasure. Few philosophers have been so honest.

C.F.

55
HENRY FIELDING
1707–1754

Tom Jones

Like his fiction, Fielding was open, generous-hearted, full-blooded. Some of his character as a young man is doubtless reflected in Tom Jones himself, as perhaps the adult Fielding may be seen in the wonderful portrait of Squire Allworthy.

Well-connected, well-favored, well-educated, Fielding led the pleasantly unrestrained life of the upper-middle-class youth of his time, getting into the proper improper scrapes with girls. For some years he supported himself by writing successful, worthless plays. The best of the lot, *Tom Thumb*, was at least good enough, it is said, to make Swift [52] laugh for the second time in his life. This career as a playwright Fielding cheerfully abandoned when the Prime Minister, Walpole, engineered a government censorship act directed primarily at him, which incidentally stultified English drama up to the advent of Shaw. Fielding then turned to the law, journalism, and novel writing, mastering each in turn. Appointed Justice of the Peace in London, he fulfilled his duties conscientiously, even brilliantly, organizing a detective force that later developed into Scotland Yard, and being generally influential in softening the harsh justice of his day. Having abused his body hopelessly, he journeyed to Lisbon in search of health, and there died at the early age of forty-seven.

One episode of his vigorous, crowded life is typical. His first wife—she is the model for Sophia Western, the heroine of *Tom Jones*—he loved to distraction. Three years after her death he married her maid, and was condemned for doing so by every snob in England. He married her, however, because she was about to bear his child, and he wished to save her from disgrace. The word for Fielding is manly.

About his best novel little need be said. It lies open for your enjoyment. It has no depths to be plumbed. Its style, though a bit long-winded by our post-Hemingway standards, is transparent. The characters are lifelike and simple—we may have forgotten that in real life there actually are simple people. At one time its plot was greatly admired; Coleridge [65] foolishly declared it one of the three perfect plots in all literature, the others being those of Ben Jonson's *Alchemist* and Sophocles's *Oedipus Rex* [6]. Today the intrigue, turning on Tom's true paternity and maternity, though manipulated with masterly skill, seems rather mechanical.

What we cannot help responding to are the comic genius animating the long, crowded story; the quick-moving panorama of eighteenth-century life in town and country; the colorful procession of picaresque incidents; and especially the zest for and tolerance of human nature, which, as Fielding says, was all he had to offer on his bill of fare.

Fielding elevated the English novel to the high estate it has since enjoyed. His aim, he tells us, was to write comic epic poems in prose, in which the lives of recognizable men and women of all stations would be presented without fear or favor by means of an organized, controlled narrative. He once described himself as a "great, tattered bard"; and there *is* a little of Homer [2,3] in him.

Among the other attractions of *Tom Jones* are the essays that precede each section. These should not be skipped. Not only do they reflect a mind of great charm and health and sanity, but, together with the prefatory remarks to his other fictions (*Joseph Andrews, Amelia*), they comprise the first reasoned esthetic of the English novel.

C.F.

56
TS'AO HSÜEH-CH'IN
1715–1763

The Dream of the Red Chamber (also called The Story of the Stone)

The Dream of the Red Chamber is by common consent the greatest work of fiction ever written in Chinese. It is probably semiautobiographical, but it is also a great work of the imagination; it draws on its author's immensely learned command of earlier Chinese literature (including such novels as the *Chin P'ing Mei* [41]), but it goes beyond any work of literary creation that had ever been attempted in China. It is a huge, sprawling novel, spanning 120 chapters, introducing around 30 principal characters and more than 400 minor ones; it is a love story, a novel of manners, and perhaps a gentle social critique (though with nothing like the satirical bite of the *Chin P'ing Mei*). Most of all it is an elegy.

Ts'ao Hsüeh-ch'in [Cao Xueqin] certainly lived some of what he wrote about. He was born into a formerly wealthy family fallen on hard times. His grandfather Ts'ao Yin was a hereditary bondservant of the Ch'ing imperial family (by no means a lowly status), and had served as an imperial commissioner in Nanjing. But when Hsüeh-ch'in was in his early thirties, imperial favor was withdrawn, and the family moved to Beijing to live in slowly deepening poverty; deprived of his expected career in service to the imperial family, he devoted his life to writing his great novel. (Some of the stigma that had earlier attached to writing fiction had worn off by the eighteenth century; see Wu Ch'eng-en, [36]. Perhaps, too, faced with the collapse of his hopes, Ts'ao Hsüeh-ch'in simply didn't care very much whether his work was respectable or not.) The first eighty chapters circulated in manuscript form during his lifetime, but a complete edition of the book was not published until 1791–92; the last forty chapters seem to have been very heavily edited by the publisher, in part to omit any hint of dangerous criticism of the imperial family. The book's transcendent qualities immediately won it an admiring readership, and it has been treasured by readers ever since.

The Dream of the Red Chamber (also known by an alternative title, *The Story of the Stone*) describes the slow decline in wealth and power of a great family, the Chia [Jia] clan. The action takes place mainly in their elegant mansion and, especially, in its large, beautiful garden. The principal character is a young man, Chia Pao-yü [Jia Baoyu], who is assumed to be, in part, Ts'ao Hsüeh-ch'in himself. Raised by his strictly orthodox Confucian father for a life of public service, Pao-yü is happier and more at ease in the women's quarters of the mansion, where he finds romance and delicacy of feeling rather than his father's stern rectitude. He falls in love with his doomed, melancholy cousin, Lin Tai-yü [Lin Daiyu], but eventually marries a rival, Pao-ch'ai [Baochai]. Tai-yü dies of despair; Pao-yü loses his mind, eventually recovers, prepares himself for an official career but ultimately leaves the world behind to become a monk, assuring the collapse of the family fortunes. The plot of the novel is intricate, convoluted, and not always even consistent; in outline it might sound like soap opera. What saves it is its literary grace; the author's remarkable ability to observe and describe the intricate details of upper-class life in traditional China; and above all the psychological depth of the book's characters. Pao-yü and his cousins are not stock figures of melodrama, but rather fully realized human beings with whom the reader readily identifies, even across great gaps of time and culture.

The book's title deserves a moment's attention. The translation "Dream of the Red Chamber" became current in the 1920s, and is now so widely known as to have become standard; and it would be futile to try to change it. But it is worth knowing that *lou* doesn't really mean "chamber"; a *lou* is a multistoried building or tower, the sort of high pavilion (red-lacquered pillars, fancy roof bracketing) that would grace the garden of a wealthy traditional Chinese household. So *Hung lou meng* means something more like "Red Pavilion Dream," or better, "A Dream in a Red Pavilion." The title alerts us to the role the garden and its buildings will play in the story, and to the possibility that the whole story—life itself—might be (in Buddhist fashion) merely a dream.

It was probably to avoid using the misleading title "Dream of the Red Chamber" that David Hawkes used the alternate title *The Story of the Stone* for his complete translation of the novel. It is by far the best English version and should be used in preference to all others.

J.S.M.

57

JEAN-JACQUES ROUSSEAU
1712–1778

Confessions

Of all the great writers we have met, including Wordsworth [64] and Milton [45], Rousseau is the most irritating. His whole character offends any reasonable mind. Socially awkward; sexually ill-balanced; immoral; nauseatingly sentimental; mean and quarrelsome; a liar; the victim of a large number of unpleasant ills, from persecution delusions to bladder trouble; a defender of the rights of little children who states calmly that he abandoned his five illegitimate offspring to a foundling institution: that is Rousseau, or part of him. It is simply exasperating that this absurd fellow, who died half-cracked, should also have been one of the most powerful forces of his time, the virtual ancestor of the romantic movement in literature and art, and one of the major intellectual sources of the French Revolution. Even more annoying is the fact that this vagabond-valet-music teacher, whose formal education ended at about the age of twelve, should be a writer of such persuasion that, though his arguments have been refuted by many, his rhetoric still bewitches. The whole Rousseau case is highly irregular.

We have encountered the title *Confessions* once before, with Saint Augustine [22]. In one respect the two men are alike. Both had and recorded a decisive spiritual experience that changed the course of history. Saint Augustine's occurred in a garden, Rousseau's on the road to Vincennes, outside Paris. He was reading a paper as he walked along, on his way to visit the famous philosopher Diderot. He noticed an announcement. The Dijon Academy was offering a prize for the best essay on the subject "Has the progress of the arts and sciences contributed to the purification or the corruption of morals?"

"All at once," says Rousseau, "I felt myself dazzled by a thousand sparkling lights; crowds of vivid ideas thronged into my head with a force and confusion that threw me into unspeakable agitation; I felt my head whirling in a giddiness like that of intoxication." Out of this trance or vision or fit came his first work, the *Discourse on the Arts and Sciences*. It won the prize, it gained him European fame, and it led to his establishment as the most revolutionary writer of his time. In it and succeeding works he attacked progress as a corrupter of man's natural goodness. He assailed private property. He inveighed against the evil influence of educational discipline on a child's mind. He pointed out the constricting power of organized religion. In his crucial *Social Contract* he cried out against those political institutions so contrived that "man is born free and everywhere he is in chains."

It is easy to say that Rousseau was a misfit, that his championship of nature and of man's innate goodness sprang from his inability to adjust to the demands of organized society. That may be true. But what he said—it was not new, merely never before so irresistibly expressed—was what his century wanted to hear. This eccentric prophet, this wild "man without a skin," as Hume [54] called him, came at exactly the right time. And his power persists. Some of it, particularly in the field of education, has worked constructively. For Rousseau, unlike Voltaire [53], was a positive man; he meant his ideas to form the future.

Confessions is his masterpiece. One of its opening statements arrests attention at once, and has never ceased to do so: "I am commencing an undertaking, hitherto without precedent, and which will never find an imitator. I desire to set before my fellows the likeness of a man in all the truth of nature, and that man myself. . . If I am not better, at least I am different."

Rousseau lies, exaggerates, and often misunderstands himself. Yet, except for one thing, he makes good his boast. He was wrong in saying that his book would never find an imitator. It has found thousands. The whole literature of modern autobiography, when designedly confessional, stems from this one book. Renowned writings like those of Chateaubriand and Amiel stem from it; dubious self-revelations like those of Frank Harris stem from it; confessional magazines stem from it. But, in its eye-opening candor on the one hand and its remarkable free-flowing and often lyrical style on the other, it has never been equaled.

Rousseau is easy to read. You need no one's guidance to

help you make up your mind about him. However, just to confuse you a little, here are two judgments. The first is Romain Rolland's: "He opened into literature the riches of the subconscious, the secret movements of being, hitherto ignored and repressed." The second judgment is by Samuel Johnson [59]. To Boswell's question whether he considered Rousseau as bad a man as Voltaire, Johnson replied: "Why, Sir, it is difficult to settle the proportion of iniquity between them."

C.F.

58
LAURENCE STERNE
1713–1768

Tristram Shandy

Sterne is a rare bird, a bit gamy, and not to everyone's appetite. You may find yourself one of the many, including the most cultivated minds, who simply do not read Sterne with pleasure. But the Lifetime Reading Plan cannot well omit his book. It is original in two senses: Though indebted to Cervantes [38], Rabelais [35], and Swift [52], there is nothing quite like it; and it is the origin, or at least the foreshadowing, of much great modern fiction.

Sterne was himself something of an original. Born of an unsuccessful English army officer and an Irish mother, he was, following an irregular childhood, educated at Cambridge. He took holy orders, though of neither holiness nor orderliness did he ever possess a scrap. Family connections helped him to obtain a series of livings in Yorkshire. He settled down to the light duties of a typical worldly eighteenth-century parson, punctuated by "small, quiet attentions" to various ladies; a sentimental romance, recorded in his *Letters of Yorick to Eliza*; health-seeking trips to France and Italy, one of which produced his odd little travel book, *A Sentimental Journey;* and his death of pleurisy at fifty-five. His external life has no distinction. Everything that matters in it is to be found in *Tristram Shandy,* whose first two volumes burst upon a delighted (and also shocked) world in 1760.

If you can take *Tristram Shandy* at all, the first thing you will notice is that very little happens in it. Not till the fourth of its nine books does its hero even manage to get himself born. It seems one vast digression, pointed up by blank pages, whimsical punctuation, and a dozen other typographical tricks. Second, you will note that it is a weirdly disguised story about sexuality; in a sense it is one long smoking-room yarn. Sterne's interest in sex is not frank and vigorous, like Fielding's [55]. It is subtle, suggestive, enormously sophisticated, and some have called it sniggering. Certainly it is sly. Third, you will find a quality more highly prized by Sterne's generation than by ours. They called it sensibility or sentiment. To us it sounds like sentimentality, the exhibition of an emotion in excess of that normally required by a given situation.

Though *Tristram Shandy* seems a completely whimsical book, it is actually one of the few great novels written in accord with a psychological theory. Sterne was much influenced by John Locke's [49] *An Essay Concerning Human Understanding* with its doctrine of reason and knowledge as derived from sensory experience. *Tristram Shandy* dramatizes this theory, and in the course of the dramatization creates half a dozen living characters: My Uncle Toby, Mr. and Mrs. Shandy, Parson Yorick, Dr. Stop, the Widow Wadman.

Tristram Shandy, unlike most novels, is not about things that happen. As its full title, *The Life and Opinions of Tristram Shandy,* suggests, it is about thought, about the inner lives of its characters. It is a true psychological novel, perhaps the first. Hence its rejection of straight-line chronology, as well as its odd punctuation, which mirrors the wayward, associative, crisscrossing paths of our minds and memories. Thus it anticipates Joyce [110], Proust [105], Mann [107], and the modern psychological novel in general, with its flashbacks, abrupt transitions, zigzags, and serious attempts to reflect the pressures of the unconscious.

Sterne is more than a genius of the odd. He is the most modern, technically creative novelist produced by his century. If *Tristram Shandy* seems strange, it is not merely because Sterne is an eccentric, though he is and glories in so being. It is because the book is actually nearer to the realities of mental life than a conventional novel is. And that is something that takes getting used to, because we so rarely stop to look at ourselves in the acts of thinking, feeling, and remembering. Some awareness of all this may help you to enjoy Sterne's strange masterpiece.

C.F.

59

JAMES BOSWELL
1740–1795

The Life of Samuel Johnson

If Rousseau's was the first modern autobiography [57], Boswell's may claim to be the first modern biography. His *Life* is the best in the language, perhaps the best in any language. It was published seven years after the death of its subject, in 1791. Ever since, Samuel Johnson has been the most intimately known figure in English literature. But he is more than a literary character. Many who have never read a line of his essays or his *Lives of the Poets* or his grave, rather impressive poetry nevertheless claim him as a familiar friend. He will never cease to be quoted, often by people innocent of the source of the quotation.

This is all the consequence of a meeting in Davies's London bookshop on May 16, 1763, between the literary dictator of England, then fifty-three, and an eager, hero-worshipping Scot, then twenty-two. Sensing his own vocation, Boswell at once began to take notes of the great man's talk and habits and opinions. He continued this activity, with intermissions, up to Johnson's death in 1784. The result is a full-length portrait, complete with warts, of a stunning character; plus an equally lively picture of the swarming, noisy, brilliant literary and social life of the latter part of the eighteenth century, which boasted, in addition to Johnson, such colorful men as Burke, Garrick, Goldsmith, and Sir Joshua Reynolds; plus an unconscious revelation of Boswell himself, who has turned out to be perhaps the most interesting of them all.

Boswell was of good Scottish family. Trained in the law, he preferred other modes of experience: good conversation, liquor, wenching, travel, some abortive meddling in politics, and the company of any great man he could contrive to meet, including Voltaire [53] and Rousseau [57]. He was the prototypical groupie. Above all, however, he was a natural writer. He possessed most of the attributes of a supreme reporter. He wrote easily. He had a phenomenal memory. He knew how to take notes, written or mental. He wrote things down when he heard them. He had a nose for the striking, concrete detail. He loved gossip and scandal. And he generally happened to be around when something new was being done or being said.

But beyond this, he knew how to *create* news. Had Boswell never existed, Johnson would still have been a great personality. But we might never have known it. Boswell *made* Johnson talk. Not that he encountered any innate reluctance, but he forced Johnson into full flower, with the aid of naive or cunning questions, by irritating or flattering him, by caressing or exacerbating his prejudices, even by demeaning himself so as to permit Johnson to enjoy a recordable triumph over him. Johnson is a creation. And that is why Boswell is more than a superb reporter. He is an artist, just as surely as Rembrandt or Hals or any other first-rate portrait painter is one.

In the last fifty years or so our view of Boswell has changed radically. Back of this shift lies what Christopher Morley called "the most exciting adventure in English letters." In 1927 Lieutenant-Colonel Ralph Isham, a rich and persuasive connoisseur, bought from the owners of Malahide Castle in Ireland some of Boswell's papers that had been lying there untouched for generations. This discovery had been preceded by others of a similar nature and was at once followed by more. Finally there was amassed an enormous collection of eighteenth-century material, by or about Boswell and other contemporaries, which has given us radically new insights into the period. Of this material numerous volumes have been published. The first, *Boswell's London Journal 1762–1763*, is the most interesting to the general reader.

What we now see is a Boswell who is no longer merely the faithful recorder of Johnson's thunder. We have a fantastic fellow, an odd genius, with a little of Hamlet in him, a damaged soul, a divided mind, a shrewd fool, a libertine—and a far finer writer than we had ever thought him. The fact is, that though Johnson was a great man and Boswell was not, the disciple is beginning to overshadow the master. In his subtleties, his despairs, his divisions of mind, his violent alternations of emotion, he seems to make a special appeal to our time. Consequently his masterpiece gains a dimension.

C.F.

60

THOMAS JEFFERSON and others

Basic Documents in American History

edited by Richard B. Morris

This entry needs little commentary. Much as they have been modified, our basic political ideas are still to be found, classically expressed, in a very few documents: the Declaration of Independence, the Constitution, the Virginia Statute for Religious Freedom, the Gettysburg Address, and a few others. The Declaration and the Constitution, in particular, deserve to be read slowly, carefully, and with deliberate attention to every word and phrase; that is how they were written, and that is how their meanings will disclose themselves to you.

Many handy collections of our important state papers exist; Morris's is quite serviceable. He prints about fifty documents, from the Mayflower Compact to almost our own time. Most are of interest mainly to students of history. As examples of the use of the language they get progressively worse after Lincoln (whose speeches also richly repay careful reading), a fact from which you may draw any conclusion you prefer.

C.F.

61

HAMILTON, MADISON, and JAY

The Federalist Papers

1787

edited by Clinton Rossiter

The Federalist Papers, by Alexander Hamilton, James Madison, and John Jay, represents American political thought and expression at a peak of elegance and power it has never since attained. Conceived originally as journalistic letters intended to mobilize New York State public opinion in support of the proposed Federal Constitution of 1787, they are not merely historical documents but in many cases masterpieces of reasoning. In 1788 Jefferson wrote to Madison praising them as "the best commentary on the principles of government which was ever written." It is illuminating to study them in connection with your reading of Aristotle's *Politics* [13], Hobbes [43], Locke [49], Marx and Engels [82], Machiavelli [34], and Tocqueville [71]. Not all the Papers need to be read. A fairly thorough knowledge of this classic may be gained by a reading of numbers 1–51, 84, and 85.

C.F.

PART FOUR

62
JOHANN WOLFGANG VON GOETHE
1749–1832

Faust

Goethe is often called "the last Universal Man." He possessed the sort of nonspecialized mind that no longer exists, and the lack of which may be leading us to disaster. This colossus lived a long and superbly favored life. He loved plurally. He wrote, brilliantly or tediously, in every possible form. Creative artist, government administrator, scientific researcher, and theorist, he was fantastically versatile. He invented German literature, and then for half a century dominated it. Like his contemporary Napoleon, he was more a force of nature than a man.

Perhaps more than either he was a process. One key to Goethe is a pair of words: change (he might have said metamorphosis) and development. Although he felt both himself and nature to be wholes, his sense of himself, as well as of nature, was evolutionary. He outgrew women, ideas, experiences, only to incorporate what they had taught him into a new, larger, ever-growing Goethe. "I am like a snake," he said. "I slough my skin and start afresh." Perhaps we should speak of Goethe as we do of some great country, like the United States. At any moment he is the sum of a complex historical past and the potentialities of an incalculable future. In his lifelong emphasis on growth, change, striving, activity, and the conquest and understanding of the world Goethe was himself what we have come to call a Faustian man, typifying a major aspect of our modern Western life-feeling.

His dramatic masterpiece grew as Goethe himself did. As a small boy in his native Frankfurt he saw a puppet show based on the old folk-character Faust. From that day to a few months before his death, when he finished Part 2, *Faust* continued to develop in his mind and on his writing table. Part 1 was started in his early twenties and completed almost thirty years later. Neither part is really a play for the stage. Both are changing visions of life, written, as Goethe's own career was conceived, in many different tonalities and styles, from the obscene to the sublime.

Part 1 is the simpler and less profound of the two, and the easier of access. It is familiar to us partly because its legend has attracted so many writers and composers. The Faust–Margaret love story inspired Gounod's famous opera.

Part 1 deals with an individual soul, the seeker Faust: his intellectual disillusionments and ambitions; the temptations put in his way by the fascinating, all-denying Mephistopheles; his seduction of Margaret; and the promise of redemption through love. Part 2 deals with the "great world," not of the individual Faust but of Western humanity. It is really a kind of historical phantasmagoria, with the legendary Helen, whom we met in Homer [2,3], symbolizing the Western classical world and Faust himself symbolizing the modern or post-Renaissance Western world. Heaven, Hell, and Earth are the settings of *Faust* as they are of *The Divine Comedy* [30]. But Goethe is not as clear as Dante, and many of his meanings are still being quarreled over.

In translation Goethe, like Molière [46], is not entirely satisfactory reading. Yet some acquaintance, however superficial, must be made with this European titan who has influenced hundreds of writers, including the greatest moderns, such as Thomas Mann [107].

C.F.

63

WILLIAM BLAKE

1757–1827

Selected Works

Once, William Blake tells us, he walked to the end of the heath and touched the sky with his finger. At four he screamed upon perceiving God's head at the window. He saw angels in boughs and the prophet Ezekiel under a tree. His wife once remarked placidly, "I have very little of Mr. Blake's company. He is always in Paradise." Perhaps an exaggeration, but there is no doubt that Blake felt himself on all fours with spirits. He is the supreme type, at least in modern times, of the visionary poet.

Toward this strange, baffling man of streaky genius one has a choice of attitudes. You may put him down as a faker, though the sweetness and honesty of his whole life belie it. Some of his contemporaries, quite celebrated then, quite forgotten now, called him a harmless lunatic. A psychologist will talk of Blake's "eidetic vision," which is simply a specialized ability to project into the external world images we usually hold in our minds. Many children have this power, Joan of Arc may have had it, and rationalists cite it when trying to explain the visions of saints and even Jesus. Finally you can ponder Blake's sly and, from the viewpoint of the professional artist and poet, quite practical advice to his friends: "Work up imagination to the state of vision."

It doesn't matter. By the pragmatic test Blake is a success. His paintings, drawings, and engravings, though not of the highest order, are beautiful and moving. His finest verse, of which there is not a great deal, is original and unforgettable. His ideas, long mocked or neglected, appeal with increasing force to those who have lost faith in materialism's ability to bring happiness to the race.

Blake was that rare thing, a completely spontaneous human being. "A man without a mask," a friend called him. Living and dying in poverty, he was probably one of the most energetically joyful men of his time. He had some secret of ecstasy denied to most of us, and at times it stimulated odd behavior: He and his wife were once discovered in their little arbor, stark naked, reading *Paradise Lost* aloud. To the visitor he called out cheerily, "Come in! It's only Adam and Eve, you know."

In his rejection of most of the institutions of his time (as well as in his crankiness) he resembles other figures we shall meet, such as Thoreau [80], Nietzsche [97], and Lawrence [113]. His romanticism is a far deeper thing than that of the romantic poets who followed him—Wordsworth [64], Keats, Shelley. "Man is all imagination," he tells us. "God is man and exists in us and we in him." And again: "We are led to believe a lie when we see *with*, not *through*, the eye."

His scorn of what is called common sense led him to champion freedom of all kinds, in the religious, political, and sexual spheres. Calmly, in a memorable sentence, he anticipates Freud [98]: "Sooner murder an infant in its cradle than nurse unacted desires." For him "Exuberance is Beauty." Nonconformists of all stripes love to quote "Damn braces. Bless relaxes." He hated all those virtues arising out of measure and calculation: "The tigers of wrath are wiser than the horses of instruction."

Blake has the defect of his qualities. His interior world was so vivid that he often lost touch with the exterior world. He may wrap piercing truth in a cloud of frenzy. But the cloud is there; he can be a bad communicator. His private mythology is contained in the so-called *Prophetic Books*. Scholars keep on trying to unravel them. To most of us they will seem like delirium interrupted by gorgeous eloquence.

Blake's nature mingled high natural intelligence and piercing intuition. In his aphorisms and his best verse the two elements are held in balance. His poetry is not artless—Blake was an excellent craftsman with his pen as well as with his pencil and graver. But in the best sense it is childlike—that is, pure, flowing, simple in diction, wildly imaginative. T. S. Eliot's [116] severe and just judgment is really a tribute: "Dante [30] is a classic, and Blake only a poet of genius."

For all his extravagance and seeming mooniness, Blake must be seen as essentially a moralist, of the prophetic rather than the reflective order. His defense of imagination and instinct is religious in tone. Whether he writes about children or spirits, his concern is "to cleanse the doors of perception." His thought can be merely odd or ill-balanced: Blake shows that uncertain sense of proportion often possessed by self-educated geniuses. But just as frequently it goes straight to the heart of what is wrong with an industrial society disfigured by its "dark, Satanic mills." Yet there is no do-goodism in Blake. He is a hard-core rebel, like Shaw [99], and, like Shaw, a dangerous man.

Of his verse I suggest you read *Poetical Sketches, Songs of Innocence, Songs of Experience, The Everlasting Gospel* and the *Preface to Milton*. To get some notion of the principles by which Blake lived his quietly rebellious life, see *The Marriage of Heaven and Hell, All Religions Are One*, and *There Is No Natural Religion*. His ideas on art may be understood through his divertingly ill-tempered *Annotations to Sir Joshua Reynolds's Discourses*.

C.F.

64
WILLIAM WORDSWORTH
1770–1850

The Prelude, Selected Shorter Poems, Preface to the Lyrical Ballads (1800)

In a famous parody of one of Wordsworth's sonnets, the English humorist J. K Stephen wrote:

> Two Voices are there: one is of the deep;. . .
> And one is of an old halfwitted sheep
> Which bleats articulate monotony. . .
> And, Wordsworth, both are thine. . . .

My Wordsworth contains 937 closely printed pages. Of these, possibly 200 are in the voice of the deep. The remainder are bleatings. Wordsworth, who never understood how to cut things short, persisted to his eightieth year. Of these years only the first half were, from posterity's viewpoint, worth living. The last forty were of great interest to Wordsworth; of considerable interest to the three female acolytes who took care of him; and of some interest to literary scholars attracted by the problem of the decay of genius.

The main influence on Wordsworth was Wordsworth. I know of no major literary figure who was so continuously and so favorably impressed by himself. This highly successful love affair dried up in him the springs of self-criticism; and as he had no humor to start with, four-fifths of his work turned out to be a crashing bore.

Of the non-William-Wordsworthian influences, the most important was the English countryside, which he may almost be said to have invented. It touched something in him deep, pure, and unselfish, releasing some of his finest verse. The second influence was the superior intelligence of Coleridge [65]. Their friendship produced the epochal collaboration of the *Lyrical Ballads* (1798) and the no less epochal Preface to the edition of 1800. The third influence was Wordsworth's sister, Dorothy, a remarkable neurotic whose eyes and ears were far better than her brother's and whose alertness to the face of nature provided him with many insights for which he is usually given full credit. At this late date it would be prissy to deny that the relation between Dorothy and William was unconsciously incestuous, at least on Dorothy's part. This has no bearing whatsoever on the value of his work.

Minor influences were the French Revolution and Annette Vallon, a Frenchwoman who seems to have stimulated Wordsworth to something mildly approaching passion. At first the eager young poet was a partisan of the Revolution. Its excesses, plus his own deep quietistic bias, plus what seems to have been plain caution (compare Milton [45]) combined to change Wordsworth into a dull reactionary. The connection with Annette Vallon, resulting in an illegitimate daughter, he did his best to hide from posterity. His whole conduct in the affair (compare Fielding [55]) is unmanly, even callous. This again has nothing to do with the value of his work.

The odd thing is that, though Wordsworth's poetry and

manifestos really did help to liberate our emotions (see Mill [72]), his own emotions were limited in number and even in depth. He wrote beautifully about nature, children, the poor, common people. Our attitudes toward all these differ today from the attitudes of the neoclassic eighteenth century against which Wordsworth courageously rebelled; and this change we owe in part to a poet most of us do not read. Yet he himself never observed nature with the particularity of a Thoreau [80]. He does not seem to have understood children—the sonnet "On the Beach at Calais" is supremely lovely, but there is no real child involved (even though he is writing about his own daughter), merely an abstract, Wordsworthian idea of childhood. For all his influential theories about using "the real language of men," he does not seem to have had much idea of how humble folk really talked. And, except perhaps for the Annette Vallon affair, in which he conducted himself like a poltroon, he was incapable of a strong, passionate love for a woman.

And now that I have said all this, an open confession of my dislike of Wordsworth, I must make two obvious statements far more to the point. The first is that he wrote some great verse, though I think virtually all of it is contained in his long poetical autobiography, *The Prelude,* plus "Tintern Abbey," "Ode: Intimations of Immortality," "Michael," "Resolution and Independence," "Ode to Duty," and a scattering of superb sonnets and shorter lyrics.

The second statement is that he opened the eyes of poets and ordinary human beings to the possibilities of a fresh approach to nature, to the life of feeling, and to the English language. With Coleridge, he diverted the course of English and American poetry. He helped to release it from conventionality, stock epithets, city-pent emotions. His famous definition of poetry as "the spontaneous overflow of powerful feelings" arising from "emotion recollected in tranquillity" is limited and partial. But as a corrective to the petrifactions of the eighteenth century it was badly needed. For all its excesses, the romantic protest has proved valuable to the Western tradition.

It is probable that Wordsworth will become more important as a historical event than as a poet. But he is great enough in both categories to warrant some acquaintance. After all, this humorless, mentally and emotionally straitened egomaniac in a few short years did write verse that helped to "cleanse the doors of perception."

C.F.

65

SAMUEL TAYLOR COLERIDGE
1772–1834

The Ancient Mariner, Christabel, Kubla Khan, Biographia Literaria, Writings on Shakespeare

In a moment of self-forgetfulness Wordsworth called Coleridge "the most *wonderful* man" he had ever known. Shelley hailed him as this "hooded eagle among blinking owls." His good friend the essayist Charles Lamb spoke of him as "an Archangel a little damaged" and of his "hunger for eternity." The scholar George Saintsbury ranked Coleridge, as literary critic, with Aristotle [13] and Longinus. Mill [72] remarked, "The class of thinkers has scarcely yet arisen by whom he is to be judged," and many thoughtful students feel the statement, made over a century ago, still stands. Such judgments could be multiplied by the score.

They were made about the greatest might-have-been in English literature. For the fact is that Coleridge's reputation and influence are both far more imposing than his work. His mind, a Tuscarora for depth, a Pacific for vastness, was never quite able to pull itself together. Though the *Biographia Literaria* comes nearest to it, he wrote no single, complete prose masterpiece. Like Wordsworth's, much of his verse, though more intensely felt, is balderdash. Of the three poems by which as a poet he will live, only *The Ancient Mariner* is a finished whole. Often ranked as the finest Shakespearean critic who ever wrote, he never imposed order on his mass of essays, lectures, notes, and conversational remarks.

At no time in his incoherent life did Coleridge show any notable common sense. There are many men, often of the highest order of mind, who should be exempted from the pressures of normal living. Coleridge was one of them. He had no capacity for marriage, little for fatherhood, not much for earning his board and lodging. He tried soldiering, preaching, periodical journalism, lecturing, even foreign service under the governor of Malta. During his latter years he wasted part of what might have been productive energy in incessant and apparently uniquely brilliant monologues. ("The stimulus of conversation suspends the terror that haunts my mind.") Tortured by neuralgia and other ills, plus intense melancholy, he sought relief in laudanum and became an addict. For the last eighteen years of his life, withdrawn from his wife, he lived under the medical care of a kindly friend, James Gillman.

In a sense the "person from Porlock" who is said to have interrupted him as he was writing down the dream-dictated lines of *Kubla Khan* (modern scholarship is skeptical of this story) was a real-life reflection of his own inner disorder. He was continually interrupting himself. His mind was too active and associative for him to complete any project. His whole life is like a mass of notes, undigested, erratic, sometimes baffling, sometimes profound, rich in wonders.

The fruitful association with Wordsworth produced the *Lyrical Ballads*, to which Coleridge contributed his lone undisputed masterpiece, *The Rime of the Ancient Mariner*. Here, as also in the unfinished *Kubla Khan* and *Christabel*, he successfully compelled "that willing suspension of disbelief for the moment which constitutes poetic faith" and so contributed to the mainstream of romanticism. That magic, eerie note he never again quite sounded.

What fascinates in Coleridge is that, along with his genius

for the fairy tale (these poems, though not for children, belong to the literature of the fairy tale), he possessed a speculative mind of the rarest power. He wrote on metaphysics, politics, theology. Never reducing his insights to a system, he nonetheless remains a psychologist of most original gifts. And as a literary critic of the romantic school he has no peer in the language.

When you think of Coleridge you may quite naturally think also of Poe. Neither was able to manage practical life. Both had minds that worked as well in the area of ratiocination as in that of dreams. But there the parallel more or less ends. Poe's erudition was spotty, Coleridge's incredibly vast ("I have read everything"). Poe's mind was acute, Coleridge's brooding, penetrating, and hungry for vast unities. Poe was an interesting minor failure. Coleridge was a fascinating major failure. But he was so fascinating and so major that even as a failure he bulks larger than his admired friend Wordsworth, who finished work he never should have started and ended as poet laureate, while Coleridge died in poverty.

C.F.

66

JANE AUSTEN
1775–1817

Pride and Prejudice, Emma

By common consent Jane Austen is what Virginia Woolf [111] calls her: "the most perfect artist among women." True enough. But today we might well question Virginia Woolf's well-intentioned qualification. Jane Austen is simply a great artist. Some critics, usually male, emphasize her genius for small-scale but deadly accurate domestic comedy as feminine rather than masculine, or point to the circumstance that she lived right through all of the Napoleonic wars without mentioning them in her work. But in the very long run all of us, male and female, might agree that a profound insight into the perennial human comedy is more valuable than the most conscientious observation of historical events.

Miss Austen, as it somehow seems proper to call her, was the daughter of a rural rector, and one of a large family. Though her own circumstances were always modest, she was well connected with the middling-rich landed gentry of southern England, and it is their traits and worldly interests that she reflects in her novels. Though there is some evidence of a frustrated love affair, she never married. During all the years of her brief life she lived quietly with her family, writing her novels in the midst of the domestic come-and-go, for years on end not even boasting a room of her own. Her social life was pleasant, active, genteelly restricted. While her genius generally is a sufficiently bewildering phenomenon, it is particularly hard to figure out how she could have known so much about human life when she saw so little of it. But great artists, as Henry James [96] pointed out, need only a suggestion, a *donnée*, and they are off and running.

Among other qualities, Jane Austen had one many modern novelists lack: She knew her own mind. Her novels are not (like those, let us say, of Thomas Wolfe) experiments in self-discovery and self-education. She knew precisely what interested her—"those little matters," as Emma puts it, "on which the daily happiness of private life depends." She knew that the private lives of her special world turned not on high ideals, intense ambitions, or tragic despairs, but mainly on money, marriage (sometimes but not always complicated by love), and the preservation of a comfortable division between social classes. The activities of these limited people she viewed as a comedy, more or less as a highly intelligent, observant, articulate maiden aunt might view the goings-on of a large family. Jane Austen is sensible, rational in the eighteenth-century manner, ironical, humorous. She would think little of philosophers and perhaps not much of poets.

What gives Miss Austen her high rank, despite her

restricted subject matter, is the exquisite rightness of her art, the graceful neat forms of her stories, the matchless epigrammatic phrasing of her unremitting wit. She has little passion, no mystery, and she prefers to avert her face in a well-bred way from the tragedy that lies on the other side of the comedy she understands so well. She was born to delight readers, not to shake their souls.

There is no agreement as to her best book. *Pride and Prejudice* has perhaps had the most readers, but *Emma*, I think, is a more searching as well as a gayer story; so I have suggested these two. If you have read them, try *Mansfield Park* or *Persuasion* or *Sense and Sensibility*. They are all pure Miss Austen, a writer so charming that it seems clumsy to call her a classic.

C.F.

67

STENDHAL
1783–1842

The Red and the Black

One hundred years ago Stendhal (one of his more than 150 pseudonyms, his real name being Marie-Henri Beyle) would not have been listed among the major novelists of Europe. Fifty years later the situation would have changed: He would have been named among the first half-dozen novelists of France. Today the shift is even greater: Many rank him among the foremost novelists of any time and place. Stendhal lived partially in the future, and so he would have foreseen all this. Indeed he did foresee it. "I have drawn a lottery ticket," he wrote, "whose winning number is: to be read in 1935."

So, though most of Stendhal's stories are laid in Napoleonic and post-Napoleonic Europe, we would expect his feeling for life and his way of expressing it to be modern. And that is roughly what we do find. Some qualifications should be made, however. His plots seem to us to smack of opera. His dialogue is more formal than that to which our phonographic realists have accustomed us. And, in the case of his masterpiece *The Red and the Black*, the title refers to forces no longer operative—the Red standing for the uniform of Napoleon's soldiers, the Black for the cassock of the clergy. The hero, Julien Sorel, wears the black because in his day a poor youth with his special talents could advance himself only through the church, whereas Julien's heart and imagination belong to the Napoleonic era he thinks of as more glorious than his own. However, the deeper tensions in Julien are not peculiar to the France of his generation. They are part of our modern consciousness.

Stendhal's genius lay partly in prevision. His novels, particularly this one, anticipate many of the motifs and devices we are used to in contemporary fiction. That is one reason why he can be called the novelist's novelist. *The Red and the Black*, for example, is the first classic expression of the young-man-from-the-provinces theme—a theme on which all the books of Thomas Wolfe and dozens of other novels merely ring changes. Also it heads a long line of narratives whose subject is the dissatisfaction of the heroine with an empty society—see Carol Kennicott in Sinclair Lewis's *Main Street* and of course Emma Bovary [86]. Though George Eliot [84] dared to portray an intellectual, it is in *The Red and the Black* that we first get the type fully and closely studied. And so we can keep on identifying in Stendhal other anticipations of twentieth-century fiction: his systematic rather than intuitive use of psychology; his understanding of what is now called ambivalence; his extraordinary detachment from his characters; and especially his major preoccupation, which is with the outsider, the "being apart," who cannot become reconciled with an inferior or materialistic or merely boring society.

The reader will perceive all this only *after* reading *The Red and the Black*. While reading it you will be caught up in a fascinating love story, which somehow seems far more adult than any encountered in the Victorian novelists. Furthermore you will experience the sensation only the finest psychological novelists can give—that of actually, for a dozen hours or so, living inside the passionately intense, complex minds of a few invented persons who become realer to you than your own neighbors.

Final note: Many good judges rank *The Charterhouse of Parma* as equal to *The Red and the Black*. Try it.

C.F.

68

HONORÉ DE BALZAC
1799–1850

Père Goriot, Eugénie Grandet, Cousin Bette

Unlike Stendhal [67], of whom he was one of the few to show any early appreciation, Balzac today is not as widely read as he should be. Everyone admits his achievement, but no one is quite sure what it is. Does he rank among the greatest of novelists? The answer is not clear. Faults stand out that were not so apparent during his century: faults of taste especially; a weakness for melodrama, almost for detective-story melodrama; an incapacity to portray character as changing and developing; and, most important, certain defects of intelligence. Another trouble is that he never wrote a masterpiece. I recommend three titles, among his best known, but they do not represent him properly. Nor would any other three titles. To be overcome by Balzac you should read fifty or sixty of his novels; and life is too short. But for sheer energy as well as for the variety of his social portraiture, Balzac is perhaps unsurpassed.

Balzac was a Stendhalian Young Man from the Provinces. There is a famous scene at the end of *Père Goriot:* The ambitious young Rastignac looks down on the lights of Paris and cries "Between us henceforth the battle is joined." There was plenty of Rastignac in Balzac. Once as a young man he seized a pencil and, under a picture of the Little Corporal, wrote: "What Napoleon could not achieve with his sword I shall accomplish with my pen."

With this ideal of conquest always before him, Balzac lived like a madman and died exhausted at fifty-one, perhaps, as has been said, as the result of drinking fifty thousand cups of coffee. He engaged in frenzied financial operations for which he had no talent. He wasted time on one of the most absurd love affairs in literary history. He piled up huge debts. And always he wrote, wrote, wrote, through the night, incessantly for twenty years and more, sometimes from fourteen to eighteen hours a day. Only the scholars know exactly how many books he turned out, perhaps over 350 in all, with perhaps 100 making up what he called his "Human Comedy." Here is his description of this manic, comprehensive design: "The immeasurable scope of a plan which embraces not only a history and criticism of society, but also an analysis of its evils and an exposition of its principles, justifies me, so I believe, in giving my work the title. . . The Human Comedy." The implied comparison is, of course, with a man he resembled in virtually no way—Dante [30].

Balzac did not live to complete his vast picture of the French society of his day. *Le Père Goriot, Eugénie Grandet,* and *La Cousine Bette* are merely three bricks of this unfinished edifice. The first is a study in irrational passion, the unrequited love of a father for his two daughters, a kind of middleclass Lear minus Cordelia [39]. The second is a study in avarice. The third is a portrait of female vindictiveness. All three deal with monomanias, as do so many of Balzac's fictions.

These three novels, one drawn from the worldly life of Paris, the others picturing provincial manners, have what is found in all his work—force, vivid detail, a talent that makes him the father of a certain school of modern realism. Finally, they all expose Balzac's major obsession, which was money. He lived in a period, like our own, of money-making, money-losing, money-loving; a period in which the greatest sin was not treachery but bankruptcy. No other novelist before him understood the world of money as did Balzac. Thus he may be considered the ancestor of all our contemporary novelists of business and finance.

These are not inconsiderable qualities. To them we must add a demonic power of static characterization. Mme. Marneffe, Grandet, Gobseck, Goriot, César Birotteau—if not complex creations, these are solid ones. And when one looks at the mere formidable bulk of his work, so firm in its grasp of reality, so loaded with hard, vivid detail, so close to so many kinds of life, it is difficult not to take off one's hat to this flawed titan.

C.F.

69
RALPH WALDO EMERSON
1803–1882

Selected Works

Thoreau's influence over us has increased as his friend Emerson's has declined. Thoreau [80], reaping the reward of greater daring and a firmer grasp on rude fact, casts the longer shadow. Yet Emerson, for all his gassiness and repetitiousness, was, in the first place, one of the central American thinkers of his century; secondly, a formulator of certain attitudes that seem permanently American; and finally a writer, at his best, of remarkable force, wit, homely vividness, and freshness— surely one of the finest epigrammatists in English. For these reasons we read him. But beware of overlarge doses. At times he offers fine words in lieu of thoughts, and he never understood how to organize or compress large masses of material.

Emerson was the leader of the Concord transcendentalist school, which taught a curious hodgepodge of fashionable idealisms. After graduation from Harvard, he became a teacher, then a preacher. When he found that he "was not interested" in the rite of Communion, he left the ministry. He never ceased, however, to be both teacher and preacher, developing into a kind of benevolent pastor without portfolio, dispensing spiritual goods without benefit of theology and indeed without the support of any concrete idea of God. As itinerant lecturer and unsystematic sage, he purified the moral atmosphere of his restless, expansive era more effectively than did all the ordained ministers combined.

Emerson is the first important spokesman for those elements in the national character we vaguely term optimistic, idealistic, democratic, expansive, individualistic. He preached the self-reliance on which we pride ourselves. In *The American Scholar* he issued what the elder Holmes called "our intellectual Declaration of Independence," a note we have since continually and sometimes raucously sounded. Emerson stresses the newness, the freshness of the American viewpoint; he invites his countrymen to "enjoy an original relation to the universe"; he emphasizes what up to fairly recently was one of our proudest boasts, "the infinitude of the private man," the integrity of the individual mind.

Emerson believed the universe was good. Most Americans think so, too, though not always for Emerson's reasons. At any rate his emphasis on the power of the will, on inspiration, on an open-ended future, has always appealed to us. Sometimes we have vulgarized his affirmative doctrine. It is but a short series of missteps from Ralph Waldo Emerson to Billy Graham.

I suggest you read the short book called *Nature,* published in 1836, which contains most of Emerson's informal philosophy; *The American Scholar,* the essays "History" and "Self-Reliance"; the essays on Plato [12] and Montaigne [37] from *Representative Men;* the essay on Thoreau; and, best of all, *English Traits*, which, though written for its time, seems to me the most durable of all Emerson's work.

C.F.

70

NATHANIEL HAWTHORNE
1804–1864

The Scarlet Letter, Selected Tales

In any well-considered list of the dozen greatest American novels *The Scarlet Letter* would almost certainly appear. Yet one may wonder at first why this should be so. Its background is seventeenth-century Puritan New England. When Hawthorne wrote about it, the scene was already beginning to appear remote; today it might seem very far away indeed. Furthermore we are not quite sure that Hawthorne's picture of a sin-obsessed, guilt-ridden society offers even the interest attaching to historical accuracy. Most recent researches tend to show that the Puritans were a far more relaxed people than their brooding descendant conceived them to be. Finally, Hester's and Dimmesdale's adultery and expiation appear to have a forceful meaning only within the framework of a dogmatic Christian morality. Many of us, living in a post-Freud world, may read this book for the first time only to exclaim "What's he making all the fuss about?"

And yet, while we may smile away the Puritan ethic that suffuses it, we somehow cannot smile away the book itself. Its power to move us persists, even though we may admire it for qualities different from those that originally won Hawthorne his reputation. For us this is only incidentally a story of the bitter fruits of adultery. It is even more incidentally a historical picture of a bygone society. What we now seem to be reading is a profound parable of the human heart. It happens to be expressed in symbols that were particularly meaningful to Hawthorne and his time. But they are only symbols, and flexible ones at that, applicable to the human condition as it exists everywhere and at all times.

Take that moral which Hawthorne, toward the end of his

dark and beautiful romance, puts in a sentence: "Be true! Be true! Be true! Show freely to the world, if not your worst, yet some trait whereby the worst may be inferred!" Though couched in didactic phrases, is this not an indictment of repression, a plea for that purification of our souls that comes only from facing, not deceiving, ourselves? In the same way we feel that Chillingworth's dissolution is inevitable in any man in any society who tries to live by life-denying emotions. We feel also, as Hawthorne explicitly says, that love and hate begin to resemble each other when both depend too exclusively, too passionately on the possession of the loved or hated object.

In other words, we no longer read this as a book about how two young people were punished for committing adultery. We read it as the work of a moral psychologist who knows as much about our own hidden guilts and fears as he did about those of his tortured Puritans. I suggest that if we approach *The Scarlet Letter* in this light it ceases to be the faded classic suggested by its old-fashioned style and its, to us, excessive moralizing. We begin to see what the critic Mark Van Doren means when he tells us that Hawthorne's "one deathless virtue is that rare thing in any literature, an utterly serious imagination."

Hawthorne once wrote of his workroom: "This deserves to be called a haunted chamber, for thousands and thousands of visions have appeared to me in it." Much of our life we pass in the prosaic light of day. But a part of it even the most normal of us pass in a haunted chamber. Hawthorne is the classic historian of this haunted chamber.

I should add that it will repay you to read or reread, in addition to *The Scarlet Letter,* a few of Hawthorne's somber allegorical shorter tales, particularly "Young Goodman Brown. . . ," The Minister's Black Veil," "The Birthmark," and "Rappaccini's Daughter."

C.F.

71
ALEXIS DE TOCQUEVILLE
1805–1859

Democracy in America

Had this Lifetime Reading Plan been compiled eighty or ninety years ago, Tocqueville probably would not have been represented. From the appearance in 1835 of the first part of his masterpiece he has never ceased to be read and studied. But it has taken considerably more than a century to disclose him in his true proportions, as one of the few supreme sociological and political observers and theorists of the American experiment.

Tocqueville's family was of the lesser French nobility. Thus he preserved all his life a deep attachment to the virtues of conservatism and aristocracy. The inexorable logic of his mind compelled him to discern in democracy the wave of the future, while his roots in tradition helped him to measure the origins and dimensions of that wave with a certain useful and lucid detachment.

On May 11, 1831, the young Tocqueville, accompanied by a brilliant colleague named Beaumont, reached our shores. Their avowed purpose was to observe and report on the American penal system. The pair traveled seven thousand miles in our country and Canada. They sailed home on February 20, 1832. In the course of these pregnant nine months Tocqueville saw us during one of our most interesting and critical periods, that of the earlier phase of the Jacksonian Revolution. The outcome was the publication, in 1835 and 1840, of the two parts of his monumental work, *Democracy in America*. This, together with his briefer but no less seminal *The Old Régime and the French Revolution*, embodies the enduring Tocqueville. I might add that he wasted a certain amount of time from 1839 to 1848 serving as a member of the French Chamber of Deputies, and later held brief office as minister for foreign affairs.

Tocqueville may be described, very roughly, as a liberal aristocrat, a kind of Lafayette with brains. *Democracy in America* had a double purpose: to describe and analyze the democratic (which seems to have meant to him largely egalitarian) system in America; and to turn that observation and analysis into a guide for future political thought and action in Europe, particularly in his native land. Many good judges believe his book is still (and by far) the deepest, wisest, and most farseeing ever written about this country.

He made, of course, many errors of observation. Nor have all of his prophecies come true. Yet no thoughtful American can read his book today (and, by the way, it is a masterpiece of elegance and organization) without marveling at his sympathy, his understanding, his balance, and his prescience. Though in his time our modern capitalist structure was still only in embryo, he understood its future, its strengths, its weaknesses, and its capacities far better than did the later Marx [82]. More than a century and a half ago he warned us against "the possible tyranny of the majority." He outlined the mass age in which we live. But he also saw how our system could mitigate and control the perils of political and social conformity, and he recognized in it one of the broad paths his century and ours would largely follow.

His basic intuition is revealed in the statement "A new science of politics is needed for a new world." Such a new science, he felt, was developing, not always harmoniously, not without travail, in the United States. And he knew quite well what he was doing: "I have not undertaken to see differently from others, but to look further, and while they are busied for the morrow only, I have turned my thoughts to the whole future."

What probably interests us most, as we read Tocqueville, is the startling applicability of his insight to our present condition. He foresaw, while America was still largely an agricultural country, the attraction that business and industry would have for us all. He foresaw our materialism, but also our idealism.

He foresaw the inequities industry would bring in its train. And, most important, he foresaw our future power and, let us hope, our future greatness.

C.F.

72

JOHN STUART MILL
1806–1873

On Liberty, The Subjection of Women

Mill is the classic instance of the child prodigy who, despite an abnormal education, manages to live a good and useful life. You will find his story in his sober but extremely interesting *Autobiography*.

The elder Mill was a follower of Jeremy Bentham. Bentham's name is linked with utilitarianism, an unimaginative if well-intentioned doctrine that stressed utility and reason, two terms it never strictly defined. It taught that the object of social action was to bring about the greatest happiness for the greatest number, and tended to ignore the temperamental and psychic differences among human beings. Young John was brought up in the shadow of this doctrine, caricatured by Dickens [77] in his Gradgrind.

Educated entirely by his logic-factory of a father, Mill was reading Greek at three and starting a history of Roman government at eleven. At thirteen he was about as well educated as an English university graduate. This force-feeding saved him at least ten of the years most first-rate minds are compelled to waste in our own school system. But it had its drawbacks: "I never was a boy," confessed Mill. The morbid emphasis on reason produced a mental crisis in his twentieth year, from which he was saved partly by the youthful resilience of his own fine mind and partly by his reading. Wordsworth [64] in particular revealed to him the existence of a life of feeling. (This critical experience would appear to give the lie to W. H. Auden's [126] famous statement, ". . . for poetry makes nothing happen.")

His crisis, together with the influence of Mrs. Harriet Taylor, whom he met in 1830 and married twenty-one years later, led Mill to recognize the weaknesses of his father's iron calculus of pleasures and pains. He was to spend much of his life, as writer, Member of Parliament, and social reformer, in liberalizing and humanizing utilitarianism. Thus, working with other "philosophical radicals," he helped to create a climate of opinion that led to many of the reform movements of the last hundred years, from woman suffrage to the New Deal. His *The Subjection of Women* stands as a milestone in the history of the evolution of human freedom.

Mill thought that except for his *Logic* his essay *On Liberty* would outlast his other works. In its own unemotional, English way it is a masterpiece of lucid persuasion and humane feeling. Probably no finer plea has ever been written for the claims of the individual against the state. Mill stresses the need for creating a great diversity of temperaments. He urges the protection of minorities. He advocates the utmost possible freedom of thought and expression. He comes out for the encouragement of nonconformist, even eccentric thinkers. His central principle is still far from realization in our state-dominated era, and still worth realizing: "The sole end for which mankind are warranted, individually or collectively, in interfering with the liberty of action of any of their number, is self-protection."

Mill should be read as the representative of the purest liberal English thought of his century. His American brothers are Thoreau [80] and Emerson [69], though he lacks the radical daring of the first and the eloquence of the second.

C.F.

73
CHARLES DARWIN
1809–1882

The Voyage of the Beagle, The Origin of Species

But for the good luck of having been invited to participate in the round-the-world voyage of the survey ship *Beagle,* Charles Darwin might well have spent his life as a country parson, giving lackluster sermons, indulging his amateur passion for geology and natural history, and presenting obscure papers on his observations at meetings of the county's learned society. His powers of observation and deduction would have been keen even in such a humble setting; presented instead with the fossils of Argentina, the geology of the Andes, the finches of the Galapagos Islands, and much more, his genius took root, blossomed, and bore fruit. Darwin's powerful intellect and his uncompromising intellectual honesty led him down paths that he was reluctant to follow, finally making him one of the greatest scientific revolutionaries of all time.

Charles Darwin was born into a life of affluent comfort and high intellectual expectations. He was not expected ever to have to work for a living, but he was expected to be very bright and to use his intelligence well. His paternal grandfather was the poet and natural philosopher Erasmus Darwin; his maternal grandfather (and grandfather also of his future wife Emma Wedgewood) was Josiah Wedgewood, wealthy founder of the famous pottery works. Both were part of a large circle of friends and scientific associates that included Benjamin Franklin and Joseph Priestly. Young Charles, passionately interested in beetles and rocks but not particularly interested in a profession, spent an undistinguished college career at Edinburgh and Cambridge and took holy orders for want of anything better to do. He was just the sort of well-to-do young man likely to be placed, through family influence, in a comfortable country parsonage to live a bland and blameless life.

Fate intervened in 1831 in the form of Captain Robert FitzRoy, who was about to take the *Beagle* on a planned two years' voyage to survey the coasts of South America, and who needed an amiable young man, preferably a naturalist, to serve as his companion and messmate—basically to give him the intellectual companionship of someone of his own social class during what promised to be a long and tedious trip. Darwin was chosen, and chose to go, despite the vehement objections of his father; the voyage (which turned out to last five years, not two) changed his life.

He was ready to see the world's natural wonders with an open mind. He had read—devoured—Lyell's path-breaking *Principles of Geology*; he had participated in discussions at Cambridge speculating about the "transmutation" of species from their original Edenic forms; he was well aware of good reasons to think that fossils were something more than relics of Noah's Flood. On the *Beagle*'s voyage he showed the capacity for hard work that was to distinguish the rest of his life. Whenever the ship touched land Darwin was ashore collecting specimens, observing geological strata, riding on horseback for miles inland and for weeks at a time in search of new material. His own assistant was kept busy preparing bones, skins, rocks, and pressed plants, all of which Darwin shipped back to London by the ton.

Those eventful five years are recounted in Darwin's first popular book, *The Voyage of the Beagle*, a marvelous blend of scientific reporting and travel writing; the energy, curiosity, and sheer love of life that Darwin experienced during his formative voyage shines through on every page. It is a book to be read with pleasure by anyone who has the slightest interest either in the natural world or in world travel, and with pure delight by those who love both.

Darwin returned to England in 1836, and never set foot abroad again. He married his cousin Emma, started a family (touched by the characteristic Victorian tragedy of the death of a favorite child), settled in a big, comfortable house in Kent, and devoted himself with single-minded energy to the work of making sense of the great fabric of life. As early as 1837, his journals show, he was beginning to formulate a theory of evolution by natural selection. But time and again he would work on his theoretical material and then put it aside. He was often ill with mysterious maladies, which in retrospect surely look stress-related; he knew very well that his evolving theory of evolution posed a direct challenge to the Biblical doctrine of divine creation, and he agonized at the pain this would cause many people whose affection and good opinion he cherished— beginning with his beloved wife, whose religious views were far more conventional than his own. In the meantime he worked on his *Beagle* specimens, published an exhaustive scientific study of barnacles, and cultivated an acquaintance among dog breeders, horse trainers, and pigeon fanciers (raffish folk not ordinarily sought out by solid upper-middle-class people like the Darwins), looking for clues to natural selection in the artificial selection practiced by breeders of domestic animals.

In the end, an unexpected external pressure forced his hand. In 1858 he received from Alfred Russel Wallace, a naturalist and professional museum specimen collector living in the East Indies, a paper outlining a theory of evolution by natural selection—exactly what Darwin had been struggling toward for twenty years. Darwin wrote back asking that they present joint papers to the Linnaean Society, and Wallace graciously agreed. Evolution by natural selection was now out in the open, and the debate was on—a debate that continues to rage to the present day. (Wallace had neither Darwin's class advantages nor his scientific training; his theory of evolution came through intelligent insight, not deep scientific investigation. Still, Wallace's contribution deserves more acknowledgment than it usually gets. And his own book of scientific travel writing, *The Malay Archipelago*, is a gem, well worth reading alongside *The Voyage of the Beagle*.)

The initial papers by Darwin and Wallace were followed in 1859 by *On the Origin of Species by Natural Selection*, Darwin's full explication of his theory. It is not a particularly easy book to read, but it offers rewards to compensate for its difficulty. Darwin knew full well that his theory was not seamless; there were gaps in the fossil record, no one had ever observed the emergence of a new species through evolution (an impossible requirement, because it occurs over many generations), and, most crucially, the mechanisms of genetic inheritance were a complete mystery to Darwin and most of his contemporaries. (Gregor Mendel, the discoverer of the principles of genetics, had sent Darwin a copy of his paper describing his famous experiments, but Darwin either didn't read it or didn't appreciate its significance. Mendel's work, published in a very obscure journal, remained essentially unknown until the early twentieth century.) And so Darwin's strategy in *Origin* is to persuade by brute force, adducing a huge mass of solid evidence and overcoming objections, when the evidence does not suffice, by evoking analogies and plausible guesses. It relies more on brazenness than subtlety; yet at the same time the keenness of Darwin's insights—looking where others had looked before, and seeing what they had never seen—fills the book with intellectual excitement.

Darwin's theory did not take the world by storm; on the contrary, it was opposed immediately by many scientists as well as by the religious establishment, and it won general acceptance only gradually. But from the moment the *Origin* was published, opposition to Darwin's theory of evolution was, in a sense, a rear-guard action; it might take awhile, but Darwin had already won. To read *On the Origin of Species* is to observe a scientific revolution in progress, and to make the acquaintance of one of mankind's most powerful minds.

J.S.M.

74

NIKOLAI VASILIEVICH GOGOL
1809–1852

Dead Souls

This does not seem like a particularly appealing title. Actually the term refers, as you will discover, to Russian serfs who had died but were still carried, until the next census, on the tax rolls. The book is not as morbid as it sounds.

Gogol is not a particularly appealing figure either. His family heritage was a poor one; he had an unbalanced youth; he failed at the law, as a government clerk, as an actor, as a teacher. To the end of his short life he remained a virgin, and in his latter years religious mania clouded his mind. As a writer he enjoyed a number of triumphs, but at bottom he was appalled by the electrifying reaction to his books and plays. He wandered aimlessly over Europe and made a pointless pilgrimage to the Holy Land. During his last days he burned his manuscripts, so that we possess only a fragment of the second part of *Dead Souls,* which when completed was to show good victorious over evil. He died in what seems to have been delirium.

Yet this queer duck, who surely cannot be said to possess a powerful mind, virtually founded Russian prose and gave Russia a masterpiece that became a part of world literature. Speaking of Gogol's most famous short story, Dostoyevsky [87] said, "We all come out of 'The Overcoat.'" Compare Hemingway's remark [119] about *Huckleberry Finn* [92]. Gogol's untraditional genius apparently led him to break with the formalism and rigidity that marked much previous Russian writing, just as Mark Twain did in our own country. The giants who followed him benefited from this liberation.

I once wrote an Introduction to *Dead Souls* that the brilliant author of *Lolita* termed "ridiculous." I think Nabokov [122] must have felt queasy over my notion (shared by many) that *Dead Souls* is a great comic novel. He must surely have objected also to my other notion (also not uniquely held) that Gogol in one of his moods—for he did not have a coherent system even of prejudices—was in this book expressing a certain dissatisfaction with the Russian feudal system. But it is also true—this is Nabokov's emphasis—that *Dead Souls* is a demonic book, as well as a funny one. It does have a nightmare, almost a surrealist, tone. Usually likened to Dickens [77], Gogol is even more akin to Poe [75]. That *Dead Souls* can please me as well as Nabokov may have exasperated Nabokov, but furnishes at least some slight evidence of the variety of Gogol's appeal.

At any rate, this is a fascinating, almost madly vivid, loosely composed yarn about a great, bland rogue and his travels through what seems, to a mere American, a real, if heavily caricatured, early-nineteenth-century Russia. Its laughter is mingled with melancholy—the poet Pushkin, after listening to Gogol's reading of the first chapter, sighed, "Lord, how sad is our Russia."

I cannot command the original, but nonetheless dare to recommend one translation, and one only. It is by Bernard Guilbert Guerney. It just sounds right. The others have a stiffness foreign, I am told, to Gogol's spirit.

C.F.

75
EDGAR ALLAN POE
1809–1849

Short Stories and Other Works

Poe may not rank among the greatest writers, but he ranks among the unhappiest. He has become a symbol of unappreciated genius.

His life was made up of misfortunes, some caused by lack of understanding on the part of his contemporaries, and many caused by his own disastrous inheritance and weaknesses. The child of wandering actors, he was brought up as the ward of a prosperous merchant with whom he quarreled as soon as possible. His education, at the University of Virginia and West Point, was interrupted by his talent for delinquency. He married his thirteen-year-old cousin, and her early death may have been the deciding factor in his ruin. His first volumes of poems were not noticed. He was a capable journalist but mismanaged what might have turned into a successful career. He engaged in desperate, immature, incomplete love affairs. Drugs, alcohol, overwork, poverty became the staples of his life. He died in utter wretchedness. Of all the writers we have met or shall meet, surely he was the most miserable. Even the bitter Swift [52] for a time enjoyed the company and praise of his equals. Poe never did.

Poe's verse has always been popular, and in France it was for a time much more than that. Probably all that is worthwhile can be read in half an hour. The rest sounds thin and affected today, though Poe was better than "the jingle man" Emerson [69] called him.

But his tales, monologues, and some of his critical essays, despite infuriating faults of style, retain their interest. His mind was neither powerful nor balanced—but it *was* original, running creatively counter to the rather insipid thought of most of his American contemporaries. James Russell Lowell's famous estimate may not be too far from the truth: "Three fifths of him genius and two fifths sheer fudge."

What is most notable in Poe is that he either pioneered or originated half a dozen fields. With his three tales "The Murders in the Rue Morgue," "The Purloined Letter," and "The Gold Bug," he not only invented the detective story but practically exhausted its possibilities. The critic Howard Haycraft credits him with laying the form's complete foundation and then goes on to name ten elements of the modern detective story, all to be found in Poe. Similarly Poe blazed the trail leading to what is now called science fiction. His theories of "pure poetry" influenced the important French symbolist movement of the latter part of the nineteenth century, and so affected the great modern poet Yeats [103]. Poe defined and illustrated the tale of single effect. In his strange and morbid stories we find many anticipations of modern psychology, including the motif of the death wish and that of the split personality (see his remarkable "William Wilson"). Poe's prevailing moods of desolation and isolation set the tone for much writing of our own century. Finally, for all his faults, he was our country's first important literary critic, generally making his judgments on a broad base of first principles.

Many of today's critics see in American writing two major strains that sometimes intermingle. The first is optimistic, practical, democratic. The second is pessimistic, guilt-laden, aristocratic, and deeply involved with the heart's darker concerns. The latter tradition found its first notable figure in Poe, and that is why he is more than a mere writer of gruesome romantic tales.

C.F.

76
WILLIAM MAKEPEACE THACKERAY
1811–1863

Vanity Fair

Thackeray was a broken-nosed giant of a man, standing six feet four, yet without giving the impression of strength. Unlike Dickens [77], he was educated as a gentleman. His novels have a sophistication Dickens's lack, though they are greatly inferior in vitality.

In 1833 Thackeray lost virtually his entire inheritance of twenty thousand pounds. Despite his natural bent for writing, were it not for this misfortune he might never have been forced into the business of grinding out novels and essays to support his family. In 1840 his wife, following the birth of their child, lost her reason, and never regained it, though she survived her husband by thirty-one years. This tragedy contributed to the melancholy suffusing Thackeray's work, and also to his idealization of women, perhaps a mechanism by which he bought off the guilt feelings his wife's insanity would naturally arouse in him.

Thackeray might have been happier among the elegant rakes of the preceding century. But he did not have the temperament to flout his time as Emily Brontë [79B] did. She could do so because she lived outside the great world. Thackeray was very much in it, and so are his novels.

He seems to have given the Victorians just what they wanted, a mixture that both soothed and stimulated. His best book, *Vanity Fair* (the phrase is from Bunyan [48]), is really concerned with the rise, fall, and partial rise again of a woman out for the main chance. At no point, however, does Thackeray make her character explicit; he is a master at saving appearances. Furthermore he is careful to present in his dimwitted Amelia an exaggerated picture of the ideal Victorian female, and to pay his respects at regular intervals to those domestic virtues Queen Victoria had substituted for sterner ones.

But *Vanity Fair* rides two horses at the same time. Even while preserving an atmosphere of respectability and sentimentalism, it is delicately exposing human nature in all its weakness, egotism, capacity for self-delusion, and mean genius for compromise. In their secret hearts his readers knew that their England, like that of the Napoleonic period Thackeray was depicting, was a Vanity Fair, with much about it that was ignoble and canting. Thackeray appealed to their critical intelligence and yet at the same time managed to support their conventional prejudices.

In *Vanity Fair* the contradiction is covered over by his art, which is a kind of sleight of hand. How well, how gracefully he tells his story and manipulates what he calls his puppets! How pleasantly conversational is his tone! How easy to take is his irony, that of the tolerant, worldly-wise clubman—and how flattering to our own picture of ourselves as similarly charming

and superior raconteurs! And so, though our conventional prejudices are quite different from those of the Victorians, though
our novels are frank about sex while Thackeray is disingenu-
ous, nevertheless we can still enjoy *Vanity Fair.*

We can enjoy the panoramic picture of high life in England
and on the Continent around the time of Waterloo. We can
enjoy the well-controlled plot. But mainly we can still enjoy the
perfect symbol of Vanity Fair—Becky Sharp. Becky is of
course the ancestress of all the beautiful, immoral female
adventuresses (Scarlett O'Hara, for instance) who have since
enraptured readers. Because of Becky Sharp, Thackeray's masterpiece will never completely fade. She resolves one of the
simpler contradictions in our human nature. For men will
always (if possible) marry good women and secretly admire
bad ones. And women, knowing that one of their jobs is to
keep the race going, will always come out strongly for morality,
and tend to have a furtive feeling that somehow immorality
seems darned attractive. Thackeray, who had little depth but
much worldly wisdom, understood this division in our nature
and through Becky Sharp exploited it perfectly.

C.F.

77
CHARLES DICKENS
1812–1870

Pickwick Papers, David Copperfield, Great Expectations,
Hard Times, Our Mutual Friend, The Old Curiosity
Shop, Little Dorrit

The commentaries you have so far been reading average perhaps eight hundred words. In writing about Dickens the most
economical way to use about fifty or so of those words might
be as follows: The Artful Dodger, Fagin, Dick Swiveller, Flora
Finching, Sairey Gamp, Mr. Micawber, Sam Weller, Uriah
Heep, Mr. Dick, Bella Wilfer, Joe Gargery, Miss Havisham,

Pumblechook, Wemmick, Bumble, Pecksniff, Mrs. Nickleby, The Crummleses, Quilp, Podsnap, Toots, Rosa Dartle, Chadband, Miss Flite, Inspector Bucket, the Tite Barnacles, Mme. Defarge, the Veneerings. As soon as a Dickens reader recalls any of these names a mental curtain goes up and he sees and hears living, talking human beings.

With Tolstoy [88], Dickens is perhaps one of the two novelists who have been accepted by the whole world—and Dickens with the greater joy. Philosopher George Santayana, after listing all of Dickens's defects, such as his insensibility to religion, science, politics, and art, concludes that he is "one of the best friends mankind has ever had." That is true. And possibly just because Dickens has been so overwhelmingly popular, it is only in recent years that he has been assessed, not as a beloved household fixture, but as a novelist almost of the stature of Dostoyevsky [87], with whose passionate, troubled imagination he has much in common.

I assume that in your youth you read at least *David Copperfield* and were probably forced to read A *Tale of Two Cities,* one of his worst novels. When rereading him, I suggest you consider the following:

1. Dickens, though children love him, is not a writer only for children or the immature. He is enormously easy to read, yet is a serious artist. He is serious, even though one of his main methods of exposing life is that of high (or low) comedy. He is more than a creator of funny eccentrics. For example, see whether you can detect his constant and powerful use of symbolism, almost in the modern manner; the dust heaps in *Our Mutual Friend* furnish a good illustration.

2. Whatever the sentimentality in Dickens may have meant to his time, it is hogwash to us. An understanding of him as a whole will only be blocked if we try to be moved by his mechanical pathos, or indeed pay more than cursory attention to it. Everyone remembers Oscar Wilde's "One must have a heart of stone to read the death of little Nell without laughing."

3. If Dickens's characters are "caricatures," as some think, why do they stick in the mind and continue to move us so strongly?

4. Dickens was a passionate, unhappy man, who apparently never recovered from his miserable childhood (how many waifs and strays there are in his books!) and who failed signally as husband and father. His passion and unhappiness are subtly reflected in his novels, as is his sense of guilt. Thus as he aged his books grew in depth. Compare the light-heartedness in *Pickwick* (and yet there are those Fleet prison scenes) with the sense of suffering in *Little Dorrit* or the dark, brooding atmosphere of *The Mystery of Edwin Drood* left unfinished at his death. The notion of Dickens as a kind of jolly literary Kriss Kringle has stopped many readers from seeing all there is in him.

5. If Dickens is merely a "popular" novelist, why is he still read, whereas Scott, who was just as popular in his day, is not?

I am merely hinting that, as with Shakespeare [39], it is best to abandon most of the notions derived from our childhood and high school experience with Dickens. There's more in him than met the Victorian eye. It is there for us to find.

C.F.

78
ANTHONY TROLLOPE
1815–1882

The Warden, The Last Chronicle of Barset, The Eustace Diamonds, The Way We Live Now, Autobiography

Like many aspiring novelists toiling as waiters and taxi drivers in our own time, Anthony Trollope in his youth had to work in order to write. He was born into a marginal middle-class family presided over by an ineffectual father; there was enough money to send him to school, but not enough to allow him to be happy in the rigid public school social hierarchy. After leaving school he worked as a junior clerk in the Post Office Department. At work his energy and enterprise began to assert themselves; he was promoted to a better position in Ireland, and started writing in his spare time; his first novels—juvenile work compared with his later confident style—have Irish settings. He rose high enough in the postal administration to make a small but important contribution to the comforts of life: He was the father of the mailbox. (Before Trollope you had to go to the Post Office to mail a letter.)

And always, he wrote: Every day before breakfast, at the prodigious rate of a thousand words an hour. (Of the writers recommended in this Plan, perhaps only Balzac [68] wrote with more manic concentration.) In 1855 he had his first real popular and financial success with *The Warden*; by 1859 he was doing well enough as a writer to resign from the civil service and devote himself entirely to his writing career, with time out, briefly, for a fling at running for public office. He died in 1882, and his last novel (*Mr. Scarborough's Family*) was published posthumously a year later, the final volume in a very long shelf of books comprising the complete works of Anthony Trollope.

Most unfairly, it seems to have been precisely his popular success and his phenomenal productivity that deprived Trollope of a higher critical reputation for most of his lifetime, and for most of the time since. No one, sniffed highbrow critics, could write that many books, enjoyed by so many readers, and be any good. Most of Trollope's books have, I think, never gone out of print, and he has never lacked loyal readers; but it has only been within the past couple of decades that a critical reassessment of Trollope has finally elevated his work to the place it deserves in modern Western literature. Reading Trollope is like eating peanuts—you can't stop; but Trollope is not mental junk food, he's very, very good.

We recommend four of Trollope's novels; you'll want to read more. *The Warden* is the first of many novels that

Trollope set in the fictional cathedral town of Barset. It tells the bittersweet tale of a too-unworldly clergyman who only wants to do good, honorable work in running an old people's retirement home, and whose gentle life is upset by a rival clergyman more interested in doing well than in doing good. Read also *The Last Chronicle of Barset*, the final novel, as the title suggests, in this series of tales about the town, its clergy, and its country gentry. Then try *The Eustace Diamonds*, part of a series following the life of an aristocratic politician, Plantagenet Palliser (later Lord Omnium), and featuring especially his brilliant, ambitious wife; this one is an incisive study of the psychological impact of money on human relationships. *The Way We Live Now*, written when Trollope was sixty years old, is a darker and more cynical novel. It features one of Trollope's few unredeemed villains, the scheming financier Melmotte, along with a gaggle of people who fall for financial and marital schemes they should know enough to avoid; it is wonderful social satire. Finally, read the *Autobiography*, in which Trollope brings to his own eventful life the same acute psychological insight he applies to his fictional characters.

Let me share a personal habit: I love to read Trollope, and never more than when I travel. Try it. The Penguin editions especially are gratifyingly fat and yet compact, easy to read and yet long enough to last for the most grueling series of plane-rides to far-flung places. He makes a marvelous companion.

J.S.M.

79
THE BRONTË SISTERS

The three Brontë sisters and their brother, Branwell, a kind of forerunner of the Beat Generation, lived most of their short lives in their father's parsonage at Haworth in the North Riding of Yorkshire. For entertainment they depended largely on their own minds plus the stories they heard about the often violent behavior of the semiprimitive countryfolk of the neighborhood. None of the novels produced by the three sisters exhibits that solid acquaintance with real life that we feel at once in Fielding [55]. In their childhood and youth the Brontës invented imaginary kingdoms of extraordinary complication. Over the years they recorded the history and characters of these fantastic countries, playing with their literary fancies as other children play with toys.

Charlotte Brontë died just short of her thirty-ninth birthday; Emily died of tuberculosis at thirty. Anne died at twenty-nine, leaving behind two novels (*Agnes Grey* and *The Tenant of Wildfell Hall*) that are much inferior to those of her sisters. It is remarkable that in their brief and highly constrained lives, lived in the bosom of a distinctly odd family, the sisters were able to focus their imaginations to produce such an outpouring of fiction, including two novels that retain their power undiminished to the present day.

79A
CHARLOTTE BRONTË
1816–1855

Jane Eyre

A lady once asked Samuel Johnson [59] why in his Dictionary he had defined "pastern" as the "knee" of a horse. "Ignorance, madame, pure ignorance," he replied. Why, in earlier editions of this book, did I omit *Jane Eyre*? Carelessness, dear reader, pure carelessness. From my teenage reading I remembered *Jane Eyre* as an interesting but old-fashioned romantic novel slanted to female interests. And so, until recently, I did not bother to reread it and so correct a narrow-minded youthful judgment.

The jacket blurb on my copy calls *Jane Eyre* "one of the great love stories of all literature." This says what is most important to the general reader. The book is about passion, and the passion is so concentrated and powerful that it breaks free of the stiff, overwrought prose. Here the style cannot throttle the feeling. *Jane Eyre* would make a great opera. The book's value is not demeaned by the fact that it is best read at the age of twelve or thirteen, and better by girls than by boys. Teenage romanticism has today been overlaid by our ultrapermissive culture, but it has not been killed or even basically altered. Were this not so, *Jane Eyre* would long ago have ceased to be read.

Yet *Jane Eyre* is not so much about love itself as about Jane's need to be loved. Ditto for Rochester. It's curious how many modern novels, quite unromantic in tone, use this same theme. We can think of it, in modern jargon, as the expression, in a novelized dream, of the repressions Charlotte herself felt when she was approaching thirty.

Think of *Jane Eyre* also as a development novel: the emergence of the Ugly Duckling—a development, on the part of the Brontës, that took place largely in their imaginations. As Jane walks down the corridor of the third story of Thornfield Hall (before Rochester appears) she has visions of a larger life, of "a tale that was never ended—a tale my imagination created, and narrated continuously; quickened with all of incident, life, fire, feeling, that I desired and had not in my actual existence." Surely here Charlotte is talking about herself, and her sisters, too.

So much of this seemingly old-fashioned story seems peculiarly modern. For example, though Charlotte Brontë gives us nothing but genteel hints, Mrs. Rochester is a stunning portrait of a nymphomaniac. Similarly, the inexorable St. John Rivers is a study in repression, though Charlotte Brontë would not have put it that way. And Stephen King today attracts the fascinated and terrified reader with the same kind of appeal that Charlotte manipulates with her lunatic in the attic.

One of the strongest reasons for the novel's unkillability is the permanent attraction of the Byronic hero, and in particular the Byronic hero as "older man"—especially if he is in need of reform. The character Rochester is truly complex, a self-mocker and a mocker of others, who lives by and on irony. This creates his own misery, but he wants to conquer the ego that

eats his soul. He might very well have been created by any of
the novelists of our Age of Anxiety, Norman Mailer perhaps, or
Philip Roth.

Jane Eyre is among the first feminist novels ever written, in
its own indirect way a protest against the nineteenth century
idea that women "ought to confine themselves to making pud-
dings and knitting stockings, to playing on the piano and
embroidering bags." The book can also be seen as a forerunner
of thousands of rebellion-against-authority novels.

Of the dated style one may say that the story is so gripping
that the outworn words are no impediment. We are overcome
by Charlotte Brontë's passionate belief in her story—plus her
intelligence, which makes us forget the old-fashioned expression and the melodramatic action.

I recently came across this remark from Oscar Wilde:
"Owing to their imperfect education, the only works we have
had from women are works of genius." There's something to
this. When women have finally won their battle, as they will,
they will produce works as mediocre as those of most male
writers. Meanwhile, *Jane Eyre*'s impassioned *cri-du-coeur*
claims its rightful place in our Lifetime Reading Plan.

79B
EMILY BRONTË
1818–1848

Wuthering Heights

Like Jane Austen [66], Emily Brontë was a parson's daughter,
but there the resemblance ends. It is unsettling to pass from
one to the other. They do not belong to the same world. They
do not even seem to belong to the same sex. One is a master of
perfectly controlled domestic comedy. The other is a wild
demiurge of undomesticated tragedy. One excludes passion,
the other is all passion. Jane Austen knew her limited, highly
civilized world thoroughly; her novels grew out of needle-sharp

observation as well as native power of mind. Emily Brontë knew the Yorkshire moors, her own family, and little else, and we can hardly say what her single novel grew out of.

In many respects *Wuthering Heights* is an absurd book. It retains something of the daydream atmosphere of the Brontë sisters' Yorkshire childhood. But the daydream has become a nightmare. Its plot, turning on the devilish Heathcliff's revenge on all those who stood in the way of his passion for Catherine Earnshaw, is sheer melodrama. Its story-within-a-story method of narration is confusing. Its characters use a language unconnected with normal speech. And these characters, except for Heathcliff and Catherine, are drawn with no special skill.

And yet somehow people have found the book gripping. Not as a work of art, perhaps, but as a dream is gripping. Its primary quality is intensity. Despite all the old-fashioned machinery of the intrigue, we succumb to this intensity, or at least are made uneasy by it.

Emily Brontë is an original. She had, it is true, read a few of the romantic poets and Gothic romancers of her time, but *Wuthering Heights* owes little to them. It is also true that she may have received some real-life stimulus, when composing her novel, from the crazy love affair through which Branwell was passing at the time. But at bottom the origins of this strange book are untraceable. It was spewed up out of a volcanic, untrained, uncritical, but marvelous imagination. It had no true forebears. It has had no true successors.

C.F.

80

HENRY DAVID THOREAU
1817–1862

Walden, Civil Disobedience

Thoreau seems to have spent much of his life talking to himself; since his death he has been talking to millions. Perhaps, indeed, hundreds of millions, for the program of Gandhi (who influenced Martin Luther King) and at one time the politics of the British Labour Party were both profoundly affected by Thoreau's ideas. Now, far more than a century after his death, it is safe to say that *Walden* (with which we may group *Civil Disobedience*) is one of the most influential books not only of its century, but of ours. Today, defying everything our evolving technocultural society lives by, it speaks to us more urgently than ever. It and *Huckleberry Finn* [92] are probably the two *central* American statements in our literature. If I add that Thoreau's prose is as enjoyable, as crackling, as witty, as full of sap as any yet produced on this continent, I shall have listed the essential reasons for reading *Walden* and as many other of the major essays as you care to try.

Thoreau had no time to waste in making money. Early in life he decided to do not what society suggested for him, but what he himself wanted. At various times he earned his bare keep by schoolmastering, surveying, pencil-making, gardening, and manual labor. He also appointed himself to certain jobs such as inspector of snowstorms and rainstorms. He wrote tirelessly (this man was no idler—he worked harder than any fifty leading board chairmen), mainly at a vast journal, some of it still in manuscript. From his books and journalism he earned little. His first book was printed in an edition of one thousand copies, of which fewer than three hundred were sold. He remarked, "I have now a library of nearly nine hundred volumes, over seven hundred of which I wrote myself." He spent his life in occasional converse with Emerson [69] and the available Concord literati and transcendentalists; more often talking to hunters, trappers, farmers, and other plain folk who lived close to the natural world he loved; most often with himself, tramping the woods and fields around his home, noting, with two of the sharpest eyes that ever existed, the behavior of the earth, water, and air, of which our lives seemed to him extensions; and at all moments thinking.

He really lived the life Emerson so beautifully preached, of self-reliance, nonconformity, simplicity, plain living, and high thinking. Of external events there were few: a pallid, unsuccessful romance (there is no question that, though Thoreau was a great man, he was a defective male); the two crucial years at Walden Pond, where he built a house for twenty-eight dollars and fended almost completely for himself; the overnight jailing for a refusal to pay his poll tax to what he considered an immoral government; his brave public defense of John Brown.

Thoreau needs little commentary; he is an expert at explaining himself. But let there be no misunderstanding: This man is dangerous. He is not a revolutionary but something far more intense—a radical, almost in the sense that Jesus was. He does not, like Marx, want to overturn society. He would say that Marx's life-denying state is no better than any other life-denying state. He simply opposed *himself* to the whole trend of his time, as well as to that of ours, whose shape he foresaw. By withdrawal, he set his face against invention, the machine, motion, industry, progress, material things, associations, togetherness, cities, strong government. He said it all in one word: Simplify. But if that word were taken by all of us as literally as Thoreau himself took it, our civilization would be transformed overnight.

Knowing that "the mass of men lead lives of quiet desperation" (how often the phrase is quoted nowadays), he determined to live entirely by his own lights, in fact to *live* rather than to adjust, accumulate, join, reform, or compete. His private notion of living may not appeal to those of us who lack his genius for enjoying and interpreting nature; but the force of his general doctrine of the meaning of human life does not rest on the private notion.

It is a fair guess that this queer Yankee semihermit, this genuinely rugged individualist who distrusted the state and treated July 4 like any other day, may turn out to be, oddly enough, not only the most American of all our writers, but one of the most enduring.

C.F.

81

IVAN SERGEYEVICH TURGENEV
1818–1883

Fathers and Sons

Of the four great nineteenth-century Russian novelists, Turgenev seems to wear the least well. Perhaps that is because, as authorities tell us, his style is of such delicacy and evocativeness that no translation does it justice. Or it may be that some of his themes have lost their attractive power: the "superfluous men," the charming but effete Russian gentry of the 1840s and 1850s; the struggle, if the term is not too strong, between the dominating female and the weaker male; the pale beauty of early love, of frustrated love, of remembered love; and his recurrent motif, the mutations of failure.

Turgenev's mother was a witch out of a dreadful fairy tale. The terror and despair she inspired in her son never left his mind and crept into much of his work. His lifelong passion for the famous, ugly, but apparently fascinating singer Pauline Viardot-Garcia offered no compensation for his bruised spirit. He followed her about Europe like a dog, enjoyed (if he did) her ultimate favors only briefly, and obtained what happiness he could by living near her or at times with her and her husband. There is no doubt that she distorted his view of women; he seems either to fear them or to sentimentalize them.

Turgenev shuttled between his Russian estates and Western Europe for many years, and spent the last twenty or so mainly in Paris and Baden. He was an expatriate, rather like Joyce [110]. Like Joyce, he widened his own country's perspective by throwing open to it a view of cosmopolitan culture. Also like Joyce, this "Westernizer" continued to draw his central inspiration from his native land, no matter how distanced his external life became. Turgenev's political position, throughout the century that was preparing for 1917, was that of the unengaged, liberal, enlightened, humane skeptic. Hence his books, while at once winning the admiration of the cultivated, often failed to please either the reactionaries or the radicals.

Some of his shorter works (particularly many of the *Sportsman's Sketches)* are indeed beautiful. But probably his reputation will continue to rest mainly on *Fathers and Sons,* also translated as *Fathers and Children.* As its title suggests, it was intended to be a study of the conflict between the generations. The theme, in my opinion, has been more powerfully treated by other novelists, including Samuel Butler in *The Way of all Flesh.*

To us, however, *Fathers and Sons* appears more interesting as the first classic presentation of that element in the Russian character which surfaced in our time and which, let us hope, will become less aggressive as the Russians move toward a democratic culture. Turgenev lacks Dostoyevsky's intuitive, indeed terrifying grasp of the revolutionary-terrorist temperament [87]. Yet in Bazarov, the center of his masterpiece, he does give us a clear, almost Olympian picture of the mid-nineteenth-century *nihilist* (the word is Turgenev's invention). In Russia, as the years went by, the nihilist type was to assume a number of different forms: the terrorist, the anarchist, the atheist-materialist, the science worshiper, and at last the dedicated Communist. Though the book exhibits in relief most of Turgenev's other admirable qualities—particularly his economy and his un-Russian clarity of form—it will stand or fall, I think, with Bazarov.

C.F.

82

KARL MARX
1818–1883

FRIEDRICH ENGELS
1820–1895

The Communist Manifesto

Ideas have consequences. In no case can this be more clearly shown than in that of Karl Marx. He would perhaps have denied it. He would have said that, the victory of the proletariat being inevitable, his life and work were devoted merely to clarifying the issues and perhaps slightly accelerating the outcome of the struggle. Nevertheless, the history of the world since 1917 seems to have confirmed the judgment expressed in the first sentence of Isaiah Berlin's *Karl Marx: His Life and Environment*—"No thinker in the nineteenth century has had so direct, deliberate and powerful an influence upon mankind as Karl Marx." It is for that reason alone that a reading of *The Manifesto of the Communist Party* (for which his coworker Engels is partly responsible) is here suggested. Marx was a highly unpleasant person, and most of us reject his doctrines, but to have no acquaintance with him or them is to remain partially blind.

Up to 1849 Karl Marx, a German-Jewish middle-class intellectual, had spent most of his mature years in subversive journalism in Cologne, Paris, and Brussels. Forced to leave Prussian territory, he emigrated to England. The last thirty-four years of his life were spent there, mainly in the British Museum, which may claim to be the physical incubator of the Communist Revolution. Marx's life was uneventful; it has become eventful posthumously.

His major work is of course *Capital*. There is no sense in recommending that you read it, unless you are a very earnest student indeed. In addition to its impenetrable German style, its difficulties are formidable; and much of it has been rendered utter nonsense by the passage of time and the movement of Marx's revered history.

The Communist Manifesto, however, is quite readable. Indeed one might wish it had been less so. It is not a work of literature or even an example of ordered thought. It is propaganda, but epochal propaganda. Its original function was to supply a platform in 1847 for the Communist League, as it was then called. Its continuing function has been to supply propaganda for the entire communist movement, particularly as it developed after 1917. In clear, if deliberately rhetorical terms, it presents the main theses of classical communism: that any epoch as a whole is explainable only in terms of its modes of production and exchange; that the history of civilization is a history of class struggle; that now the stage has been reached in which the proletariat must emancipate itself from the bourgeoisie by means of a total overturn of society, and not merely a political revolution.

The Manifesto begins with one of the most famous sentences ever written: "A spectre is haunting Europe—the spectre of Communism." It concludes with three sentences no less famous: "The proletarians have nothing to lose but their chains. They have a world to win. Workingmen of all countries, unite."

The dissolution in our time of the USSR may seem to have demonstrated that Marx's concluding sentences are untrue. But there are millions of Chinese who are taught Communism as the only truth, and it is a disturbing fact that our free enterprise system is still opposed by many in what was once the Soviet Union. Unfortunately *The Communist Manifesto* must still be read as something more than an historical document. Its influence remains one of the iron realities of our era.

C.F.

83

HERMAN MELVILLE
1819–1891

Moby Dick, Bartleby the Scrivener

At twenty-five Melville had already had most of the experiences that were to supply him with the raw materials for his books. As a seaman he had served aboard the trader *St. Laurence,* the whaler *Acushnet,* the Australian bark *Lucy Ann,* and the frigate *United States.* He had sailed both the Atlantic and the South Seas. He had undergone "an indulgent captivity" of some four weeks with a cannibal tribe in the Marquesas.

His adventures had been preceded by an aimless, sketchy education and were to be followed by a little formal travel in Europe and the Holy Land. These external events—plus a brooding, powerful, and original genius—were enough to produce not only *Moby Dick* but almost a score of other works in prose and verse. One of these, *Billy Budd, Foretopman,* was published many years after his death, and is well worth reading. He wrote *Typee,* an account of his stay with the cannibals, when he was twenty-five. It had considerable success. Nothing he wrote thereafter received much popular welcome, and the latter half of his life was spent in obscurity and loneliness. *Moby Dick* (1851) was not precisely unnoticed, it is true, but it was not understood. Not until the Twenties of our century, about thirty years after Melville's death, was it resurrected by a few devoted scholars. Then Melville's reputation skyrocketed, and it has never since greatly diminished. *Moby Dick* is recognized everywhere as one of the world's great novels.

"I have written a wicked book and feel as spotless as the lamb," wrote Melville to his good friend Hawthorne [70]. An interesting sentence. Partly it is light irony. Partly it is a recognition of the fact that *Moby Dick*'s metaphysical and religious defiances would hardly please Melville's straitlaced family. And partly it is a fair description of the book. For, though the intention is of course not wicked, the novel *is* about evil, and it is hardly Christian in tone.

There are other narrative prose works of the imagination that can be read on two or more planes—for instance, *Gulliver's Travels* [52], *Alice's Adventures in Wonderland* [91], *Huckleberry Finn* [92], and *Don Quixote* [38]. *Moby Dick* belongs with them.

With a little judicious skipping, boys and girls can enjoy it as a thrilling sea story about a vengeful old man with an ivory leg pursuing his enemy, the White Whale, to their common death. Grownups of various degrees of sophistication can read it as a tempestuous work of art, filled with the deepest questionings and embodying a tragic sense of life that places it with the masterpieces of Dostoyevsky [87] and even, some think, Shakespeare [39]. And no one at all sensitive to our language can help being moved by its magnificent prose, like an organ with all the stops out.

Moby Dick is not a hard book. But it is not a transparent one either. We all feel that Ahab and the whale (and the other characters) mean more than themselves, but we may well differ over what those meanings may be. For some, Moby Dick symbolizes the malignancy of the whole universe, the baffling inexorability of Nature, that Nature from which we, if we are sensitive and energetic of mind, somehow feel ourselves estranged. That dark Nature is always in Ahab's consciousness. Indeed Moby Dick may be thought of, not only as a real whale, but as a monster thrashing about in the vast Pacific of Ahab's brain, to be exorcised only by his own self-destruction. *Moby Dick* is not a gloomy or morbid book, but you can hardly call it an argument for optimism.

Many years ago, writing about *Moby Dick*, I tried to summarize my sense of it. Now, rereading it for perhaps the fifth time, I find no reason to change my opinion: "*Moby Dick* is America's most unparochial great book, less delivered over to a time and place than the work of even our freest minds, Emerson [69] and Whitman [85]. It is conceived on a vast scale, it shakes hands with prairie seas and great distances, it invades with its conquistador prose 'the remotest secret drawers and lockers of the world.' It has towering faults of taste, it is often willful and obscure, but it will remain America's unarguable contribution to world literature, so multileveled is it, so wide-ranging in that nether world which is the defiant but secretly terror-stricken soul of man, alone, and appalled by his aloneness."

The long short story "Bartleby," published in a magazine two years after *Moby Dick*, could have been written only by the creator of that book. Even today, in a time more receptive to its dark atmosphere, perhaps Samuel Beckett [126] alone might find in Bartleby's inveterate passivity something congenial to his talent. But in 1853 (Poe [75] died in 1849) no American writer but Melville could have even imagined the tale's subject. Indeed it does not seem to have been understood at the time; several commentators thought it a humorous work.

With his quiet "I would prefer not to," Bartleby—"pallidly neat, pitiably respectable, incurably forlorn"—counters all attempts at human contact. Problem: How to spin fifty pages out of pure negation? Somehow Melville builds a haunting narrative around a being, otherwise sane and well conducted, who confronts life with an Everlasting Nay—and this at a period when all his countrymen were constructing a great nation with unprecedented energy and a positive passion for experience.

Using the modish phrase of our own day we may interpret "Bartleby" as a study, some generations before Freud [98], of the death wish. Or perhaps it belongs, like Conrad's masterly "The Secret Sharer" [100], to the rich literature of the doppelgänger—for are not poor Bartleby and his highly normal narrator eerily bound together? Or it may be a private allegory, hiding and revealing Melville's own loneliness, his remoteness from the roaring materialism of his day.

In any case, a story to trouble one's dreams.

C.F.

84

GEORGE ELIOT
1819–1880

The Mill on the Floss, Middlemarch

It may interest only historians of literature, but there does exist a kind of shadowy stock exchange on which the reputations of established writers fluctuate, though not wildly. During the last fifty years or so the stock of Shaw [99] and Wordsworth [64] may have slipped a few points. That of O'Neill [115],

Forster [108], Kafka [112], Donne [40], Boswell [59], and Tocqueville [71] has probably risen. With George Eliot the rise has been marked. In large part this is due to the advocacy of the formidable English critic F.R. Leavis as well as that of other scholars.

The common reader, recalling the high school infliction of *Silas Marner*—or possibly merely intimidated by the memory of the author's countenance, so suggestive of a sorrowful, though brainy, horse—still shies away from her. George Eliot is one of many writers handicapped by the existence of photographers and portrait painters.

In many ways, however, she is a most interesting figure. Born Mary Ann Evans, of a middle-class commercial family in Warwickshire (her father was a carpenter who rose to be estate agent), she early evidenced the passion for learning that was to mark her career. In her teens she was deeply and narrowly pious; but wide reading, plus conversations with minds less evangelically committed, soon stripped her of dogmatic faith. Her rejection of a conventional God and of Immortality was, however, balanced by her devotion to Duty, an abstraction that seems to have taken on for her some of the attributes of the Deity.

After her father's death she moved to London, engaging successfully in highly intellectual journalism and meeting some of the best minds of her time, including Herbert Spencer and John Stuart Mill [72]. In 1854 she decided the shape of her life. She formed a permanent, illegitimate but not covert connection with the learned journalist and biographer George Henry Lewes. Lewes's wife had already had two children by another man (ah, those proper Victorians), was mentally unbalanced, and was not living with Lewes at the time. The relationship between Eliot and Lewes, lasting till Lewes's death in 1878, was both happy and eminently respectable. A year and a half after Lewes died, Eliot married an American banker, John W. Cross, she being sixty to his forty. Obviously a strong-minded lady.

The strength of her mind is apparent not only in her courageous, laborious life but in her novels. To us they may seem
rather prosy, supersaturated with reflection and moralizing,
and, especially in *Romola,* smelling somewhat of the lamp. Yet
they quietly blazed wide trails without which the modern novel
would have been impeded in its evolution. D. H. Lawrence
[113] summed it up: "It was really George Eliot who started it
all. It was she who started putting action inside." Perhaps in
this respect Sterne [58] preceded her, but the eccentricity of
Tristram Shandy put it outside the mainstream of English fiction, whereas George Eliot navigated its very center. She
depicted the interior life of human beings, and particularly
their moral stresses and strains, in a way then quite new to fiction. She also deliberately departed from other conventions
such as the Dickensian happy ending and the standardized
conception of romance. Finally, she poured into her stories
something few previous novelists had possessed: the resources
of a first-class intellect. She included ideas in her view of life.
She even dared to portray intellectuals—a commonplace proceeding since Joyce [110] but one not to be found in Jane
Austen [66] or Fielding [55] or Dickens [77].

The partly autobiographical early chapters of *The Mill on
the Floss* recreate the special atmosphere of childhood with an
insight, tenderness, and charm unsurpassed until we reach
Huckleberry Finn [92]. The minor characters, particularly
Aunts Glegg and Pullet, are so solidly conceived that the passing of the society in which they are rooted has not diminished
their vitality. The struggle of poor Maggie to express her
genius for love in a world that is too much for her is still
poignant. And finally *The Mill on the Floss*, like all Eliot's fiction, is suffused with a moral seriousness—neither prissy nor
narrow, but rather the effluence of a large, powerful, ponder-
ing, humane mind. In current novels such moral seriousness is
rarely found. But a few hours with George Eliot may serve to
suggest that, for all her didacticism, this novel must always be
one of the staples of major fiction.

Middlemarch is today considered not only her masterpiece but one centrally located in the tradition of the English novel. In an essay written as long ago as 1919 Virginia Woolf [111] called it "one of the few English novels written for grownup people." In accord with the taste of its period it is intricately, even densely, plotted, tracing the careers of several pairs of lovers and spouses. One of its themes turns on the political and social controversy preceding the passage in 1832 of the first Reform Bill. We are more likely to respond to the broad picture of provincial society displayed on all levels, as well as to the sexual and intellectual frustrations of its heroine, Dorothea Brooke. As a study in unhappy marriage it made Victorian readers uncomfortable, and so thorough and compassionate is its psychology that it still moves us today.

Each great novel requires its own reading tempo. This one must be read slowly. It does not march. It unfolds.

C.F.

85

WALT WHITMAN
1819–1892

Selected Poems, *Democratic Vistas*, Preface to the first issue of *Leaves of Grass* (1855), *A Backward Glance O'er Travelled Roads*

I hear America singing. I celebrate myself. I loaf and invite my soul. I wear my hat as I please indoors or out. I find no sweeter fat than sticks to my own bones. I am the man, I suffered, I was there. Do I contradict myself? Very well then I contradict myself. Passage to India. I sound my barbaric yawp over the roofs of the world. A woman waits for me. When I give I give myself. The long brown path before me leading wherever I choose. The never-ending audacity of elected persons. Pioneers! o Pioneers! Out of the cradle endlessly rocking. When lilacs last in the dooryard bloomed. o Captain! My

Captain! Who touches this, touches a man. I think I could turn and live with animals. A great city is that which has the greatest men and women. The United States themselves are the greatest poem. The mania of owning things. These United States. To have great poets, there must be great audiences, too. Me imperturbe, standing at ease in nature. Powerful uneducated persons. Leaves of grass.

I have omitted the quotation marks around these lines and phrases because the marks hardly exist in our minds and memories. It is Whitman's language rather than his message that exerts power. He worked with all his soul to become a national bard, the voice of "the divine average," the Muse of Democracy. But we have no national bards; the average man or woman does not feel divine, nor wants to; democracy prefers to get along without a muse. Whitman loved his country and often wrote thrillingly about it, but it is probable that he never really understood it. He has penetrated not because he is accepted by the "powerful uneducated persons" he idealizes, but because he is a poet in the original sense, a maker, a coiner of wonderful new language.

His ideas, if you can call them that, he borrowed from many sources, including Emerson [69], who was among the first to hail his genius. His rhythms echo, among other books, the Bible. Nonetheless he is a true revolutionary in poetry. His free-swinging, cadenced, wavelike verse, his fresh (even if often absurd) manipulations of language, his boldness of vocabulary—all helped to liberate American poetry, and have had a profound effect abroad. There is no doubt also that his erotic candor was useful in the revolt against the genteel tradition.

The first three issues of *Leaves of Grass* (1855, 1856, 1860) contain ninety percent of his best work. After that he tended to repeat himself or to create poses rather than poetry. Whitman was a bit of a charlatan; if you want to be fancy you can say that he wore masks.

He was homosexual. His verse, and particularly his odd

notion of democracy, cannot be understood except in the light of his bias toward males.

He had an original temperament, a certain peasant shrewdness, but only a moderate amount of brains. He can excite us with his rhapsodic, prophetic note. He can move us with his musical threnodies. He can cause to pass before our eyes a series of wonderful tiny images of people and things in action. These are not small gifts. They are enough to make him the greatest of American poets.

On the other hand, he tries too hard to make a virtue of his deficiencies. He was poorly educated, his experience of life (despite the legends he busily circulated) seems to have been limited, and he depended too much on the resources of his own rich temperament and too little on the common stock of three thousand years of the Western tradition. This makes him parochial when he thinks he is being daringly American. It lends a certain hollowness to his boast that he is "non-literary and non-decorous."

Ignoring scales of values, he embraces and celebrates all creation—often with infectious passion, often absurdly. Everything in Whitman seems to be equal to everything else; everything becomes equally divine. Sometimes the reader, fatigued by so many unvarying hosannas, is inclined to agree with the poet Sidney Lanier, who said that Whitman argues that "because the Mississippi is long, therefore every American is God."

All these criticisms have been made often, and more severely. Yet he somehow remains. England and the Continent, anxious to believe that his barbaric yawp is the true voice of America (it satisfies their conventional romantic notion of us), appreciate him more widely than we do. But reasonably cultivated Americans, if not Whitman's beloved workers, also acknowledge his curious and thrilling spell. It is not because his is a truly native voice—Frost [106] is far more authentically American. It is rather because his chant is universal, almost Homeric [2,3], touching in us primitive feelings about death and nature and the gods who refuse to die in even the most civilized among us. Trail-breaking in form, Whitman seems to be preclassical, pre-Christian in feeling, though he thought of himself as the trumpeter of a new time.

In addition to the three important prose works suggested, the reader might tick off, for minimum reading, the following poems: his masterpiece, "Song of Myself"; "I Sing the Body Electric"; "Song of the Open Road"; "Crossing Brooklyn Ferry"; "Song of the Answerer"; "Song of the Broad-Axe"; "Out of the Cradle Endlessly Rocking"; "As I Ebbed with the Ocean of Life"; "When I Heard the Learn'd Astronomer"; "By the Bivouac's Fitful Flame"; "As Toilsome I Wandered Virginia's Woods"; "The Wound-Dresser"; "When Lilacs Last in the Dooryard Bloom'd"; "There Was a Child Went Forth"; "Proud Music of the Storm"; "Passage to India"; "Prayer of Columbus"; "A Noiseless Patient Spider"; and "Years of the Modern."

C.F.

86

GUSTAVE FLAUBERT
1821–1880

Madame Bovary

Before commenting on this novel, I wish to recommend the one translation that does it justice—that by Francis Steegmuller. It will serve to convince the reader that good reasons exist for its author's high reputation.

When *Madame Bovary* was first published, in serial form, Flaubert had to defend himself before the public prosecutor against charges that it was offensive to morality and religion. He won the case. But the excitement over *Madame Bovary*, though transferred from the moral to the literary plane, has never since quite died down. The novel has continued to agitate many readers, including other novelists and critics. I must at once admit that, while I admire it as an unquestioned masterpiece, I nevertheless find it a bit chilly in its superb detachment.

Unlike Balzac [68], Flaubert was the classic type of the pure and dedicated artist. The son of a Rouen surgeon, he pursued law studies in Paris briefly and unhappily; in 1844 suffered a nervous attack; then withdrew to a life of study and writing varied by intervals of travel and erotic experience. He was not by nature a happy man. His native melancholy was further underlined by the loss of loved ones, by the misunderstanding with which the world greeted much of his work, and by the self-torture that followed from his literary perfectionism.

"The Idea," he wrote, "exists only by virtue of its form." Form to Flaubert meant more than a frame or a pattern. It was a complex affair. A few of its many elements were "the perfect word" (*le mot juste*), cunningly contrived and varied rhythms, assonance, reverberant or echoing sequences of symbols, and a genuine architectural structure. Over *Madame Bovary* he spent five laborious years. Before his time, no novels in French had been so carefully written. Which is why I suggest Steegmuller's translation: The emotional tone and weight of *Madame Bovary* are created by the use of a special language, requiring the most careful carry-over into English.

Flaubert believed that the artist hovered somewhere above the moral universe, that he should not judge, explain, or teach but merely understand and perfectly record. Insofar as this novel is devoid of sentimentality, as it is of pity, Flaubert succeeded in his aim. Yet it conveys a message, if only a negative one; and that message we have already received in the pages of *Gulliver's Travels* [52]. Like Swift, Flaubert did not love the human race. *Madame Bovary*, for all its seeming detachment, seems to me a beautifully organized expression of misanthropy.

Whether or not this is true, no one can deny its influence. Most of the later novels that turn on the discrepancy between our ideal lives and the actual gray ones that we live owe much to Flaubert. Madame Bovary is the first Walter Mitty. She has given a name, *Bovarysme,* to her disease, a morbid passion for believing oneself other and better than one is. It is even possible that thousands of young men and women have rebelled against their environment, in daydream or in reality, not because they were spontaneous rebels, but because *Madame Bovary* infected them—just as young men committed suicide as a consequence of reading Goethe's *Sorrows of Young Werther* [62].

There are other sides to Flaubert than those revealed in what is by most critics considered his masterpiece. I recommend particularly a reading of *Three Tales,* of which one, "A Simple Heart," discloses an almost Christian compassion not elsewhere to be found in this great, unhappy writer.

C.F.

87

FEODOR MIKHAILOVICH DOSTOYEVSKY
1821–1881

Crime and Punishment, The Brothers Karamazov

Dostoyevsky's life and work are of a piece. Suffering, violence, emotional crises, and extravagance of conduct mark both. The terrible sincerity of his novels flows in part from the anxieties that clouded the author's whole career. It is well for the reader to know this. To read Dostoyevsky is to descend into an inferno.

Like Flaubert [86] he was the son of a physician. Again like Flaubert he was when young introduced to scenes of suffering, disease, and death, and never forgot them. In his fifteenth year his gentle mother died, and not long afterward, in 1839, his father was either murdered by his own serfs or, more probably, died of apoplexy. Dostoyevsky was left desolate and defenseless. Perhaps from this period stems the epileptic tendency that was to overshadow his whole life, if also perhaps to give him a certain visionary inspiration. In 1849 his connection with a group of dreamy young radicals caused his arrest. He was sentenced to death, but just before the firing squad was about to do its work, his punishment was commuted. This experience marked him deeply. He then spent four years in a Siberian convict camp, enduring inhumanities partially described in his *Memoirs from the House of the Dead*. Another four years were spent in military service at a remote Asiatic outpost.

His first marriage was to a hysteric, his second to his secretary, who seems to have understood his manias and rages. The utopian radicalism of his youth gave way to a religious conversion. Dostoyevsky became orthodox, reactionary, Slavophile. Yet none of these labels is fair to him, for his temperament was a contradictory one in which Christ and Satan struggled continually for mastery. At times he seems to talk almost like a good European—but a very Russian one. The latter part of his life was not much happier than the first part had been, though his supremacy as a novelist and interpreter of the Russian temperament was generally acknowledged. His epilepsy continued to threaten him; debts worried him; for a time he was a compulsive gambler; and there can be little doubt that his sexual nature was unbalanced.

This is the man who wrote some of the most extraordinary novels of all time. They anticipated many of the ideas of Nietzsche [97] and Freud [98]; they influenced such non-Russian writers as Mann [107], Camus [127], and Faulkner [118]; and they dramatized the terrorist theory and practice that we associate with Lenin, Stalin, and Hitler. Indeed it may be said that Dostoyevsky had an intuitive sense of what the twentieth century would have to endure; and this sense plays its part in the fascination of his work.

It is hard to pin this strange man down. His central obsession was God. The search for God, or the attempt to prove God's existence, dominates his stories. Thus tormented, Dostoyevsky seems to approach a vision of love and peace only after long journeying through universes of pain and evil. In his novels the worlds of crime, abnormal psychology, and religious mysticism meet and mingle in a manner difficult to define. He is thought of as an apostle of compassion, but of the true saintly qualities he seems to possess few.

The Brothers Karamazov is generally considered his most profound work. However, if you are going to limit yourself to only one novel, there is something to be said for *Crime and Punishment*. For one thing, *The Brothers Karamazov*, though it does not leave you up in the air, is nevertheless an unfinished book. *Crime and Punishment* is a simpler, more unified one, with a strong detective-story plot of great interest. It can be read as a straight thriller. It can be read as a vision. It can be read on planes in between these two. From its murky, gripping, intolerably vivid pages you emerge with the feeling that you have lived and suffered a lifetime. Its action takes nine days.

C.F.

88

LEO NIKOLAYEVICH TOLSTOY
1828–1910

War and Peace

War and Peace, more frequently than any other work of fiction, has been called "the greatest novel ever written." This need not scare us. However its greatness may be defined, it is not connected with obscurity, with difficulty, or even with profundity. Once a few minor hazards are braved, this vast chronicle of Napoleonic times seems to become an open book, as if it had been written in the sunlight. Just as Dostoyevsky [87] is the dramatist of the unconscious and what is called the abnormal, so Tolstoy is the epic narrator of the conscious and the normal. His tone is one of almost loving serenity, and his characters, though their names are odd and their time is remote, are our brothers and sisters.

Most beginning readers experience three difficulties:

1. The novel is enormously long. As with *Don Quixote* [38] (though less cogently) some sort of case may be made for an abridged version.

2. It's hard to follow both the relationships and the movements of the (to us) strangely named, complex cast of characters. All I can say is that if you persist in your reading, the characters will sooner or later sort themselves out.

3. It's hard to separate the story from the digressions. Many critics have thought this a weakness in an otherwise great novel. Tolstoy was not a formalist, as Turgenev [81] was. He sprawls. He tells you what's on his mind. You must take him as you find him. If you read slowly enough (and you should; the book sets its own leisurely tempo) you will probably discover that the digressions are no harder to take than were the essays scattered through *Tom Jones* [55].

When I first wrote about *War and Peace* many years ago, I singled out for special praise three qualities: its inclusiveness, its naturalness, its timelessness. Rereading it fifteen years later, I discovered other qualities, particularly Tolstoy's ability to reveal one to oneself. Now, reading it once more, I am impressed with a virtue that may be simple to the point of banality. Tolstoy once said, "The one thing necessary, in life as in art, is to tell the truth." When your canvas is narrow enough, this may not seem so difficult—Hemingway [119] tells the truth about bull-fighting. But your task is overwhelming when you take human life for your subject, and human life is the real subject of *War and Peace*.

Tolstoy meets his own test. In this gigantic story of the impact of Napoleon's invasion on a whole country, he never fakes, he never evades, he grasps life at the middle, he conveys the essence of a character by seizing upon precisely the true, the revelatory gesture or phrase. That is why, though it deals in part with war and destruction, it seems one of the sanest novels ever written. And its sanity flows from Tolstoy's love for his characters, his love for the "procession of the generations," his love for the spectacle of life itself.

Less demanding than *War and Peace*, and considerably shorter, is Tolstoy's classic love story *Anna Karenina*. I hope you will find time to read both books.

C.F.

89
HENRICK IBSEN
1828–1906

Selected Plays

Of all the dramatists discussed in this Plan, Ibsen, though by no means the greatest or most readable, has perhaps had the widest influence on the modern theater. Single-handed he destroyed the lifeless, mechanical, "well-made play" that dominated Europe when he began his life work. He turned the theater into a forum for the discussion of often disruptive ideas. He introduced a new realism. He made plays out of people rather than situations. And, being partly responsible for Shaw [99], he is the grandfather of modern Western social drama.

The son of a Norwegian merchant who went bankrupt in Henrik's eighth year, Ibsen passed through a difficult boyhood and youth. In his twenties he began to write poems and romantic historical dramas, but was at first no more successful as author than he was as stage manager and theater director. In 1864 he left Norway for Rome, on a traveling scholarship. For the next twenty-seven years, except for two brief visits home, he lived abroad, mainly in Germany and Italy. During this fertile period he wrote most of the plays that astounded, shocked, or delighted Europe. Mental illness clouded the last few years of his long and probably not very happy life.

There are at least three ways of looking at Ibsen.

To H.L. Mencken and many others he is no iconoclast but "a playmaker of astounding skill," a superlative craftsman without a message, whose originality consisted in taking ideas generally accepted by intelligent people and giving them a novel setting: the stage. Mencken quotes with approval Ibsen's statement: "A dramatist's business is not to answer questions, but merely to ask them."

However, to Ibsen's disciple George Bernard Shaw, the asking of questions, if they be the right ones, can itself be a revolutionary act; and the Plato [12] who recorded or created Socrates would agree with him. Shaw sees Ibsen's theater as the means by which the nineteenth-century middle class was enabled to free itself from false ideas of goodness, from what Shaw calls "idealism." To him Ibsen is essentially a teacher, we may even say a teacher of Shavianism. Whether or not Shaw's interpretation is accurate, it does seem fair to say that Ibsen's plays, particularly those dealing with marriage, the position of women, and the worship of convention, had a decisive effect on the ideas of his generation and the succeeding one. My collaborator on this book suggests that I also mention Ibsen's powerful influence in the non-Western world. He points out that translations of *A Doll's House*, for example, had a huge impact on the literary worlds of China and Japan: That one play helped to liberate an entire generation of writers.

There is still a third Ibsen, and that is Ibsen the poet, whom in translation we can only dimly glimpse. To Norwegians his early *Peer Gynt,* written in verse, is, though not at all nationalistic, a kind of epic, an ironic-fantastic résumé of the Norwegian character. It is possible that the so-called social plays, such as *A Doll's House, Ghosts,* and *Hedda Gabler,* will soon be forgotten; and that the more difficult, imaginative, symbolic dramas *(Peer Gynt, The Master Builder, When We Dead Awaken)* will eventually be ranked among the dramatic masterpieces of the last two centuries.

The plays here recommended are arranged in their order of composition. To my mind the finest are *Peer Gynt* and *The Wild Duck,* but there is no absolute agreement on Ibsen's best work. At any rate try *Peer Gynt, A Doll's House, Ghosts, An*

Enemy of the People, The Wild Duck, Hedda Gabler, The Master Builder, and *When We Dead Awaken.*

C.F.

90
EMILY DICKINSON
1830–1886

Collected Poems

What has long fascinated readers of Emily Dickinson is the seeming discrepancy between the uneventfulness of her life and the depth of her insight into the human condition. She once wrote "The Soul selects her own society—/Then—shuts the door—"; and again, "This is my letter to the World/That never wrote to Me—". The door has opened, the letter has been answered, and this solitary has now become part of the canon of the world's major poets.

Emily Dickinson came of good family, was educated at Amherst Academy and Mt. Holyoke Female Seminary until the age of eighteen. She never married and from her late thirties to her death she did not stir from her family's house and her beloved garden. From her early forties she dressed only in white. While her letters reveal certain romantic attachments, her erotic energy seems to have displayed itself only in her poetry.

She wrote some 1775 poems, of which only a tiny handful were published in her lifetime. Thus, in a sense, her work is a series of terse soliloquies, all untitled. Even today her temperament and her way—willful—with the language are so original that we can't fit her in. She is the despair of critics. What can they do with lines such as these?

> And then, in Sovereign Barns to dwell—
> And dream the Days away,
> The Grass so little has to do
> I wish I were a Hay—

When reading Dickinson, it's best not to expect immediate comprehensibility. Sometimes the thought is so dense or so odd as to confound most of us. Sometimes the syntax itself is off-putting. Try at first merely to submit yourself to the pitch and tone of her voice. Read twenty or thirty poems, no more, at one go, and get what you can. However, not all of us will be satisfied with this impressionistic reading experience. For those who wish help in decoding Dickinson's odd metaphors and eccentrically slanted approach to such major themes as love and religion, I would suggest recourse to such works as Cynthia Griffin Wolff's *Emily Dickinson* (Knopf, 1986).

On occasion the poet reflects the sturdy individualism of Thoreau [80] and Emerson [69] and is often characterized as a transcendentalist:

> I wonder how the Rich—may feel—
> An Indiaman—An Earl—
> I deem that I—with but a Crumb—
> Am Sovereign of them all—

One collection of her poems published in 1945 was titled *Bolts of Melody*. The phrase is hers, and illuminates the creative ebullition she felt when writing verse. One of her trademarks, the dash (see preceding quotation), does not prove that she was ignorant of punctuation. It is more probable that the dash expresses the physical excitement accompanying composition, the quick inhalations and exhalations as ideas and words crowd in upon her mind.

For human society Emily Dickinson substituted her garden. Flowers, bees, the oriole and spider, the dandelion, the twig, the leaf, the caterpillar worms—these, to the recluse, are her constant companions, her social circle. Out of these she made the metaphors that expressed her sense of her own life. She capitalized on its seeming restriction. She writes "A Prison gets to be a friend—."

Emily Dickinson wanted an audience, but in the end wrote

only for herself. It took many years to become clear that she wrote also for us.

C.F.

91
LEWIS CARROLL
1832–1898

Alice's Adventures in Wonderland, Through the Looking-Glass

Some may think Lewis Carroll has strayed into this rather formidable list through some error. But he belongs here, for he proved, possibly not quite knowing what he was doing, that the world of nonsense may have strange and complex relations with the world of sense. I do not include him because he is a juvenile classic, for in that case we should also have Grimm and Andersen and Collodi and E.B. White and a dozen others. I include him because he continues to hold as much interest for grownups as for children.

In fact he is more alive today than he was in the Sixties and Seventies of the last century, when the two Alice books were published. He continues to fascinate not only ordinary men and women of all countries and races, but the most sophisticated intellects: critics such as Edmund Wilson, W.H. Auden [126], Virginia Woolf [111]; logicians and scientists such as Alfred North Whitehead, Bertrand Russell, and Arthur Stanley Eddington; and philosophers, semanticists, and psychoanalysts by the score.

His real name was Charles Lutwidge Dodgson (pronounced Dodson). The son of a rector, he had seven sisters, a circumstance that may in part account for his seemingly arrested masculinity. From age nineteen to his death he passed his life at Christ Church, Oxford, as student, mathematics master, and ordained dean. He remained, as far as we know, chaste. His life was proper, pleasant, and donnish, marked by fussy little academic controversies, many hobbies (he was a first-rate pioneer photographer and invented something very much like Scotch Tape), and the one passion of his life, an apparently innocent attraction to little girls.

He was a dull teacher, a mediocre mathematician, but a rather exceptional student of Aristotelian [13] logic—defective syllogisms are among the many slyly hidden features of *Alice*. A queer chap on the whole, kind, testy at times, prissy, shy (he even hid his hands continually within a pair of gray-and-black gloves), with a mind that seems to be quite conventional, but which in his letters and diaries flashes forth from time to time with some startling insight that it is hard not to call Freudian [98] or Einsteinian.

Doubtless, like many Victorians, he was an internally divided man, and some of these divisions and tensions can be traced by the careful and curious reader. In *Alice* four worlds meet, worlds that he knew either consciously or intuitively. They are the worlds of childhood, dream, nonsense, and logic. They partly fuse, drift in and out of each other, undergo mutual metamorphoses. Their strange interaction gives *Alice* its complexity and, more important, its disturbing reality. The adult reader continues to delight in its fanciful humor but feels also that this is more than a child's book, that it touches again and again on half-lit areas of consciousness.

Many years ago I wrote an essay on Lewis Carroll, from which I extract this sentence: "What gives the *Alice* books their varying but permanent appeal is the strange mixture in them of this deep passion for children and the child's world, with an equally deep and less conscious passion for exploring the dream world, even the nightmare world, filled with guilts and fears, which is a major part of the child's life, and therefore a major part of our grownup life."

C.F.

92
MARK TWAIN
1835–1910

Huckleberry Finn

Many of us who read *Huckleberry Finn* in our youth still think of it as a "boys' book"—which of course it is, and a very good one, too. Against this view place Ernest Hemingway's [119] famous statement: "All modern American literature comes from one book by Mark Twain called *Huckleberry Finn*." Somewhere between these two judgments lies the truth. But it lies much closer to the second judgment than to the first.

Mark Twain (real name: Samuel Langhorne Clemens) had a good deal of trouble writing *Huckleberry Finn*. It's doubtful that he knew, when he had finished, that it would turn out to be, along with Thoreau's *Walden* [80], one of the two central and generative books of the American nineteenth century. In a way he wrote it out of his unconscious, through which the great river that had nourished his early imagination still rolled and flooded. Into it he put his youth—but also, perhaps without quite knowing it, the youth of the Republic. He did more. The division in Huck's mind between his natural social genius (for Huck is a genius as well as a boy; indeed this boy is a great man) and his distaste for "sivilization" mirrored a split in our national soul. We, too, as a people have been torn and are still being torn between a desire, based on our frontier heritage, to "light out for the territory," and our apparently stronger desire to convert that territory into one great productive mill. Furthermore, Huck reflects the racial tensions still vibrating in the national conscience; reread the chapter in which Huck debates whether or not he will turn in Jim, who is that criminal thing, an escaped slave, but who also happens to be a friend.

In this book there is no sentimentality. The preindustrial "natural" America it depicts is one of violence, murder, feuds, greed, and danger. The river is supremely wonderful but also, as this ex-pilot author knew, supremely treacherous and even sinister. Nevertheless, no grownup American who loves his country, its present no less than its past, can read *Huckleberry Finn* without a poignant sense that it is a kind of epic celebration of a lost paradise. We all feel, North and South, that with Appomattox a certain innocence, a certain fresh and youthful freedom left us forever. The sophisticated Periclean Greek, reading his Homer [2,3], must have felt somewhat the same way. *Huckleberry Finn* is our *Odyssey*.

Mark Twain, referring to the greatly inferior *Tom Sawyer*, called it "simply a hymn, put into prose form to give it a worldly air." That is also true of *Huckleberry Finn*. It is a hymn to the strange, puzzled, disorderly, but still rather beautiful youth of our nation.

Hemingway implied all this in his statement. But he also meant something more precise. He meant that Mark Twain was the first great American writer to use the vernacular (indeed a dozen vernaculars) creatively. *Huckleberry Finn* deliberately destroyed the conventional English literary sentence. It introduced a new rhythm that actually followed the twists and turns of our ordinary speech, without trying for phonographic accuracy. It showed us what can be done with a de-academicized language.

For all his later worldliness and big-city culture, Mark Twain was one of those "powerful, uneducated persons" saluted by Walt Whitman [85]. This does not make him any the less a great writer. But it makes him a great writer who heads a tradition radically different from that headed by his contemporary Henry James [96]. They reflect two powerful forces in our literature and our thought. The first is native, humorous, and in the best sense, popular. The second is Anglo-European-American, deeply analytic, and in the best sense, aristocratic.

C.F.

93
HENRY ADAMS
1838–1918

The Education of Henry Adams

Henry Adams was born with a complete set of sterling silver in his mouth. A scion of what is probably the first family of the United States, he was the great-grandson of John Adams, the grandson of John Quincy Adams, and the son of Charles Francis Adams, who represented us at the Court of St. James. The fascination of his life lies in the unexpectedness of what he did with his inheritance.

The family tradition of service virtually demanded that he grow up to wield high political power for his country's good. The presidency itself would not have been inconceivable. Henry Adams became a scholar, a major historian, an influential teacher, a philosopher, a marvelous letter writer, a world traveler of genius, and the author of the finest of American autobiographies. He never became a leader. His influence has been profound, but it has been indirect. At one point he remarked, "So far as [I] had a function in life, it was as stable-companion to statesmen." Acquainted with everyone of importance here and in England, he rarely departed from his role of ironic observer, the irony directed inward as well as outward.

From one standpoint (and it was also his own) he was a failure. From another, he was a success, though largely a posthumous one. His failure lay in disappointed ambitions, in his inability to live up to the family tradition. He felt—this is a major motif in the *Education*—that his eighteenth-century upbringing, with its emphasis on humane letters and strict moral accountability, had ill-equipped him for the twentieth century, with its emphasis on energy, science, and industry. His success lay in the fact that this very dissatisfaction with himself (a dissatisfaction out of which he made a virtual career) led him to probe deeply the age for which he was temperamentally unsuited. His books, particularly the *Education*, are pearls produced by irritation.

The Education of Henry Adams, written in a severely ironic third person, is an attempt to explain the author to himself and his time to the author. Adams was greatly influenced by late-nineteenth-century physics. He felt that civilizations, like matter, were subject to inexorable laws of change and degradation. In the thirteenth century (see his beautiful book of medieval studies, *Mont-Saint-Michel and Chartres*) he believed Western civilization to have achieved a state of coherence and unity, symbolized by the figure of the Virgin. Our time, symbolized by the Dynamo, he saw as one moving further and further away from unity toward multiplicity. The rate of disintegration was rapidly increasing; mankind had little to look forward to beyond a series of graver and graver catastrophes. The *Education* is remarkable for wit, elegance, wonderful on-the-scene reporting; but what gives it its sharp edge of emotion is Adams's constant cold prescience of tragedy. It makes the *Education* a work of poetry as well as truth.

The critic Paul Elmer More has decried its "sentimental nihilism," and it is true that Adams's special brand of pessimism sometimes strikes tediously on the ear. Yet, when one looks about at the world today, it is hard to find many writers who foresaw as clearly as Adams did the shape of the future. We have experienced several of the catastrophes he foretold; and it is clear that we are to experience others. Disintegration rather than coherence seems more and more to mark our era. It required a considerable depth of imagination to say in 1862, as Adams did, "Some day science may have the existence of mankind in its power, and the human race may commit suicide by blowing up the world."

Henry Adams was by nature a rather unhappy man, and his beloved wife's suicide in 1885 further predisposed him to pessimism. He was snobbish, intellectually cocky, vulgarly racist, and his self-depreciation is often spurious. Yet from these weaknesses as well as from his strengths he drew the materials that make the *Education* a great book. Being an Adams, he could not write a *Confessions*. His aim is not the revelation of a human heart but the unflinching consideration of a historical character, who happens to be the writer himself. As an intellectual analysis of a labyrinthine mind and of the changing and, as he thought, disintegrating society he knew intimately, the *Education* remains unrivaled.

C.F.

94
THOMAS HARDY
1840–1928

The Mayor of Casterbridge

Thomas Hardy came of Dorset stock and lived the larger part of his life just outside Dorchester. The beautiful, history-freighted, and rather desolate countryside around Dorchester (Hardy calls it Wessex) is in a way the main character in his novels. His formal education—he was the son of a builder—lasted only from his eighth to his sixteenth year. He was then apprenticed to a Dorchester, and later to a London, architect. At twenty-seven he started what turned out to be a quarter-century of increasingly successful novel writing. The indignation aroused by supposedly shocking situations and passages in *Jude the Obscure* (1895) made the sensitive Hardy turn back to his first love, poetry. At his death he had written over a thousand poems, not including his gigantic cosmic panorama of the Napoleonic wars, *The Dynasts*. Many rate his verse above his novels. Certainly he is one of the two dozen or so English poets you may wish to read most closely.

It may be some time before the cycle of taste returns Hardy to favor, just as it has brought back Dante [30], Conrad [100], Stendhal [67], Melville [83], and Henry James [96]. This Plan, however, is not designed to take more than casual account of fashion. It deals mainly with writers of generally acknowledged long-term influence and interest. Among these Hardy will doubtless occupy a secondary rank. But not a minor one.

He died at eighty-eight. Just as his life linked two centuries, so his work acts as a kind of bridge between Victorian and modern fiction. Bravely (for their time) his novels defied many of the sexual, religious, and philosophical taboos to which even so independent a mind as George Eliot's on occasion succumbed [84]. Hardy, influenced by Darwin [73] and by a generally mechanical-determinist nineteenth-century view of the universe, dared to show man as the sport of Nature. His view is sometimes bleak, sometimes merely sorrowful; and it proceeds not only from theory, but from the bias of his own brooding temperament. His humor and his remarkable sensitivity to the magic of landscape and weather prevent his novels from being merely depressing. But if you find modern fiction on the whole uncheerful, that is partly because Hardy pioneered the campaign against the unrealistic optimism of some of his contemporaries.

The Hardy novels most generally admired are *The Return of the Native, Tess of the D'Urbervilles, Jude the Obscure,* and the one suggested here. In *The Mayor of Casterbridge,* I find in balance the most striking constituents of Hardy's art: A complex plot, which despite some concessions to melodrama, such as the secret document, is powerfully constructed; that sense of place and of the past that gives his work such deep-rooted solidity; the sympathetic portrayal of rustic character, often compared to Shakespeare's [39]; the ability to work out with relentless elaboration a succession of tragic fates; and finally his special atmosphere of ruminative compassion.

The opening scenes, in which a man auctions off his wife, are extraordinary in their capacity to catch our interest. That interest is sustained, page after deliberate page, as we watch Michael Henchard, "the self-alienated man," devising his own self-destruction and expiating his guilt.

The English critic Desmond MacCarthy, speaking of Hardy, says that "it is the function of tragic literature to dignify sorrow and disaster." By this criterion the creator of *The Mayor of Casterbridge*, for all his faults of style and taste, is a true master of tragedy.

C.F.

95
WILLIAM JAMES
1842–1910

The Principles of Psychology, Pragmatism, **Four Essays from** *The Meaning of Truth, The Varieties of Religious Experience*

The psychologist-philosopher William James was the slightly elder brother of the novelist Henry [96]. A warm affection linked these two very different beings. Henry's nature was fastidious; it concerned itself with the relations existing among other rarefied temperaments; and though reflective, it was not speculative or able to handle high-order abstractions. William was, like Emerson [69], a natural democrat, hearty, humorous, with a deep interest in problems of science, religion, and morality. Henry was the pure artist, affecting the world by his books alone. William was a vital teacher whose personality still exerts great influence. Henry opted for upper-class and intellectual English society. William delighted in the vigorous, growing America of his time and entered into its public life in a way that would have been difficult for his more detached brother. The British philosopher Alfred North Whitehead called William "an adorable genius." The noun would also apply to Henry; the adjective (though he did have a fussy charm) hardly.

A word about the suggested reading. Very little of James is unrewarding, but these three books will give you a fair idea of both his personality and his ideas. *The Principles of Psychology*, though now partly superseded, remains James's most permanent work. Difficult in part, it succeeds wonderfully in dramatizing the life of the mind. James himself later spoke of its content as "this nasty little subject," but the world has not accepted his judgment. *Pragmatism* should be read not only because the word is so closely connected with James, but also because the idea behind the word is so closely connected with our character as a people. If you have read Mill [72] you may find it interesting to figure out why the book is dedicated to him. James's most purely *interesting* book is *The Varieties of Religious Experience.* One of the cornerstones of the literature of religious psychology, it illustrates concretely what he meant by the pragmatic test.

The pragmatic test sounds simple and to many it is at once convincing. However, it is open to philosophical objections into which it is not our present business to go. Briefly, James argues that an idea's meaning and truth depend on its practical consequences. A problem is real if its solution makes a difference in actual experience, if it performs an operation on our behavior. Thus James stresses not origins but results. In the *Varieties* he asserts that the religious states he is describing are, like all states of mind, neurally conditioned. But he goes on to say that "their significance must be tested not by their origin but by the value of their fruits." Thus religion, whether or not determinably "true," is valuable to the individual and therefore to the race. Its truth is not absolute but functional. Ideas are good only as instruments, and it is by their instrumentalism that we must judge them. To sum up, "an idea is 'true' so long as to believe it is profitable to our lives." James's moral ideals were of the highest and purest; "profitable" does not refer to the marketplace; nor is it fair to vulgarize James's pragmatism by saying that what he meant was "Anything is O.K. if it works."

There is more in James, far more, than the pragmatic idea, though it is central both to him and to our vague national philosophy, if we may be said to have one. One should understand it. But that is not the main reason for reading him. The main reason is the man himself. He is one of the most attractive figures in the history of thought—vital, alert to the whole world of experience, mentally liberating, emotionally refreshing. In addition he is master of a style of great freshness and clarity. One may disagree with the pragmatic test (believers in fixed religious and moral values are bound to do so) and still emerge from reading James feeling more alive and hopeful than before. He is the philosopher of possibility. By his own pragmatic test, he is apt to succeed with the reader. Reading him can make a difference.

C.F.

96
HENRY JAMES
1843–1916

The Ambassadors

During his seventy-two years, nothing much happened to Henry James, brother of the great American philosopher-psychologist William James [95]. He never married. Indeed, so far as we know, he had few passionate relations with men or women. (He had a close, but entirely chaste, friendship with Edith Wharton [102].) The one decisive external event of his long, industrious life was his decision in 1876 to live permanently in England. There, varying his desk labors with trips to his native country and the European continent, plus much dining out, James spent the rest of his days.

It seems a bit passive. Yet on balance James probably lived one of the most active lives of the century. Nothing happened to him except everything—everything he could observe, feel, discriminate, ponder, and finally cast into his elaborately wrought stories. He made everything pay artistic dividends. His books are his real biography.

Conrad [100] called him "the historian of fine consciences," an excellent phrase if we extend the last word so as to include the idea of consciousness. James excels in the careful tracing of subtle relationships among subtle characters. He exhausts all the psychological possibilities of any given situation; and the situations he chooses, at least in his major novels, are dense with meaning. His mastery flows in part from his perfect recognition of his own immense powers. These depend on sensibility and high intelligence, and the ability to find and mold the exactly right form for his ideas and themes. As pure artist he is the most extraordinary figure in the history of the American novel.

James himself thought *The Ambassadors* his finest book. Though written in his late period it does not suffer from the overelaboration of which many readers complain. (One well-known witticism of Philip Guedalla's thus describes James's three phases: James I, James II, and the Old Pretender.) All his powers are here held in beautiful balance and suspension. He handles one of his major themes—the impact of Continental moral realism on the rigid and sometimes naive ethical outlook of Americans—on the level of the highest comedy. That last word should not make you think *The Ambassadors* is not a serious work. For all its grace and wit, it is weighty enough, with its grave and reiterated plea for more life, for more perception, for the claims of the intelligence as an instrument for seizing and interpreting experience. "Live all you can," cries Lambert Strether to Little Bilham, "live, live!" In Strether, who is superbly equipped to react to the new experience that comes to him, alas too late, I think James felt he had created a peculiarly American type.

As with most of James's work, *The Ambassadors* must be read slowly. Every line tells. All is measured for its possible effect. There is no trace in it of what the author called "the baseness of the arbitrary stroke." It may take you ten times as long to read *The Ambassadors* as to read *Tom Jones* [55]—but for some readers there will be ten times as much in it.

One of the most voluminous of great writers, James cannot be known through any single book. He worked brilliantly in the fields of the novel, the long and short story, the memoir, the biography, the critical essay, and the travel sketch, as well as, unsuccessfully, in the theater. In addition to *The Ambassadors*, I should like to nominate for your attention two other works of Jamesian fiction: *The Portrait of A Lady* and *The Turn of the Screw*.

C.F.

97
FRIEDRICH WILHELM NIETZSCHE
1844–1900

Thus Spake Zarathustra, The Genealogy of Morals, Beyond Good and Evil, and other works

The rhapsodic singer of the strong, triumphant, joyful super-man led a life of failure, loneliness, obscurity, and physical pain. Son of a Lutheran pastor in Saxony, he was brought up by pious female relatives. A brilliant student, he specialized in classical philosophy. At twenty-five he was professor of Greek at Basel University. He resigned ten years later, in 1879, because of poor health. One of the major influences in his life at this time was Wagner, whom he at first adored. (Bertrand Russell remarks: "Nietzsche's superman is very like Siegfried, except that he knows Greek.") Gradually, however, as Wagner succumbed to philistinism, anti-Semitism, German racism, and the sick religiosity of *Parsifal*, Nietzsche drew away from the great composer, and at last broke with him. From 1879 to 1888 he wandered about Germany, Switzerland, and Italy, living a lonely life in seedy boardinghouses. Yet during these nine years, working under the most depressing conditions, he produced most of his famous books. In December of 1888 he was found in a Turin street, weeping and embracing a horse. His mind had given way. For the remaining eleven years of his life he was insane, possibly—there is no proof—as a result of general syphilitic paresis.

Nietzsche is still a controversial figure. At times he writes like a genius. At times he writes like a fool, as if he had never been in touch with ordinary realities. (His views on women, for example, are those of a man who simply didn't know any very well.) And so, though he has been dead for almost a century and has been the subject of countless commentaries and interpretations, there is still no generally agreed-upon judgment of this extraordinary man. Those naturally inclined to moderation, decent intellectual manners, rationality, or plain common sense, find him ridiculous or even hateful. Others see in him a prophetic figure, a constructive destroyer of false moral values, an intuitive psychologist who anticipates Freud [98]. And positions in between these extremes have been set up all along the line.

One general misconception is worth mentioning. The Nazis and Fascists in general did exploit, often by falsifying, Nietzsche's celebration of the virtues of war, ruthlessness, blood-thinking, and an elite class—or his presumed celebration, for his admirers translate his words rather differently. But Nietzsche would have despised Hitler and all the little Hitlers. He was not anti-Semitic and he condemned German nationalism. "Every great crime against culture for the last four hundred years lies on their conscience" is his summing up of the Germans. Nietzsche in one of his aspects was a good European, a defender of the culture the Nazis hated. It cannot be denied that his political influence has been deplorable. But this is not the same as saying that he was a proto-Fascist.

Yet, good European that he may have thought himself, Nietzsche in a certain sense stands outside the Western tradition. He is a total revolutionary, more total, if that is possible, than Lawrence [113] or Marx [82]. At times he seems to reserve his admiration for only a few: the pre-Socratics, Socrates himself [12], and a few "artist-tyrants," such as Frederick II of Sicily. He indicts Christianity as a "slave morality." He rejects the traditional virtues of compassion, tolerance, mutual accommodation, in favor of the "will to power," a phrase variously interpreted. He detests the liberal democratic humanitarianism of Mill [72], whom he called, with typical courtesy, "that blockhead." He exalts the heroic, the "Dionysian," and, it would seem, the irrational and intuitive elements in the human mind. He has no interest in the ordinary conception of progress, substituting for it a somewhat misty doctrine of eternal cyclical recurrence, and stressing the positive power of heroic suffering, exultant pessimism, and tragic experience. On the whole, not a comfortable chap.

No one can deny his extraordinary, though uncontrolled, gift for language; his command of invective and irony; the variety of his poetical images; and the torrential, paradoxical inventiveness of his tortured mind. If taken in large, uncritical doses he can be not only antipathetic but dangerous; the God he denied seems to have formed him to attract the lunatic fringe. On the other hand it is true that, like Ibsen [89] and Shaw [99], he helped to point out to his century and ours many of our shams, cowardices, and hypocrisies.

Suggestion: Use the edition called *The Portable Nietzsche*, if available. The translations are intelligent, the notes and other apparatus helpful. You might read the whole of *Zarathustra*, uneven as that strange work is; the selections from *Beyond Good and Evil*; *Toward a Genealogy of Morals* and *Ecce Homo*, and perhaps *The Antichrist*.

C.F.

PART FIVE

98
SIGMUND FREUD
1856–1939

**Selected Works, including *The Interpretation of Dreams,
Three Essays on the Theory of Sexuality,* and *Civilization
and Its Discontents***

Freud died September 23, 1939. In his memory W.H. Auden
[126] wrote a superb poem from which I quote:

> To us he is no more a person
> Now but a whole climate of opinion.

That is the heart of it. To the discomfiture or horror of
many, Freud is one of the major components of our mental
world. There is hardly an area of thought, and there are few of
conduct, untouched by him, his disciples, his ex-disciples, or
his opponents. You will have to determine for yourself whether
this is a good thing, a bad, or a mixture of both.

When we talked about Shakespeare [39] it was suggested
that most of us think we know him when what we really know
is some handed-down opinion of him. That is true of Freud.
Many of us still vaguely believe that his doctrines encourage
sexual license, or that "he sees sex in everything," or that he
did little beyond shifting the confessional from the grating to
the couch. A reading of his major works will clear up these and
dozens of other vulgar errors.

Freud began his training in medicine, specializing in clini-
cal neurology. In 1884 he became interested in some work
done by Breuer, with whom he later worked. Breuer had with
some success treated a female hysteric by encouraging her to
"talk out" her past under hypnosis. The case is classic; it

marked the birth of psychoanalysis, whose actual origin Freud, himself no humble type, always credited to Breuer. By replacing hypnosis with "free association" Freud found the key that unlocked his system. By 1896 he had named it psychoanalysis. The rest of his life was devoted to the widest possible development of the new conception of mental processes. Against misunderstanding, abuse, and moralistic prejudice he worked unceasingly, deepening his insights as he extended his experience. In 1938 his books were burned by the Nazis. As he was already suffering torture from cancer of the mouth, they waived their usual methods of dealing with the weak, the good, the great, and the non-Aryan. In return for a large ransom they permitted Freud to remove to England, where he passed the last months of his phenomenally productive life.

Psychoanalysis claims to be two things: a science (at least to its adherents) and a method. It is a theory of mental life and a specific technique for the cure of neuroses. Both theory and technique are based on a few fundamental concepts. They seem trite to us now, but they were not so a century ago. Among them are: the unconscious; the mechanism of repression; the formative power of infantile sexuality (Freud did not invent the Oedipus complex, he observed it); the dream life as the disguised expression of fears and desires; and, more generally, the frightening power of the irrational in determining human behavior.

Sometimes with insufficient caution, Freud and his followers applied their novel insights to fields seemingly remote from mental disease: religion, morality, war, history, death, humor, mythology, anthropology, philosophy, art, and literature. Particularly in literature Freud has had a pronounced influence, not always for the good.

I must alert the reader of this new edition to the fact that if W.H. Auden were alive today his reverential lines, quoted above, might possibly be qualified. During the last two decades many scholars have submitted the Freudian doctrine to rigorous re-examination, and have questioned the validity and weight of his evidence. Furthermore, we know today far more than Freud did about the brain's electrical behavior, knowledge that makes us question Freud's interpretation of the dream work. There is no doubt that on the intellectual stock exchange Freud has slipped several points since his death.

With respect to your choice of reading, two difficulties present themselves. The first is the vast volume of Freud's work. The second is the change and development of his thought, which means that an early (yet still valuable) book may be in part superseded by a later one. I list herewith eight titles. Experts will quarrel over all of them, and doubtless champion others. The first five books, arranged chronologically, contain much of the general theory. The last three, similarly arranged, are more specialized or exemplify Freud's thinking on a philosophical level.

> *The Interpretation of Dreams*
> *The Psychopathology of Everyday Life*
> *Three Essays on the Theory of Sexuality*
> *A History of the Psycho-Analytical Movement*
> *New Introductory Lectures on Psychoanalysis*
> *Beyond the Pleasure Principle*
> *The Ego and the Id*
> *Civilization and Its Discontents*

I would suggest starting with these three titles: *Three Essays on the Theory of Sexuality*, *The Interpretation of Dreams*, and *Civilization and Its Discontents*.

C.F.

99
GEORGE BERNARD SHAW
1856–1950

Selected Plays and Prefaces

For the better part of a century GBS explained and advertised himself and his intellectual wares with dazzling wit, energy, clarity, and persistence. A man who lived to be ninety-four; who probably began thinking in his cradle if not in the womb; who left behind him, in addition to a vast library of correspondence, thirty-three massive volumes of plays, prefaces, novels, economic treatises, pamphlets, literary criticism, dramatic criticism, musical criticism, and miscellaneous journalism dealing with every major preoccupation of his time and many trivial ones; and who, like all his favorite supermen, lived forward, as it were, toward an unguessable future—such a man reduces to no formula.

Except perhaps one, and it is his own: "The intellect is also a passion." Whether or not one agrees with Shaw at any point in his long mental wayfaring is less important than the solid fact that he made intellectual passion exciting, or at least modish, for hundreds of thousands, perhaps millions, of human beings. He was a ferment, a catalyst, an enzyme. He left neither system nor school. But one cannot come fresh to any half-dozen of his best plays and prefaces without having one's mind shaken, aerated, and often changed.

At the moment, the more rarefied critics tend to pass him by, or to stress his lacks: lack of any other than intellectual passion; lack of the tragic sense we find in the Greeks or in Shakespeare [39]; lack of what we call poetry. My own opinion is that he will be recognized as a master prose writer in the plain or unadorned style; and that, merely as a nonstop influential *personality*, he will rank with Voltaire[53], Tolstoy [88], and Doctor Johnson [59].

It will help us, as we read Shaw, to remember a few simple facts.

First, he was Irish—or, as he put it, "I am a typical Irishman; my family came from Yorkshire." Hence he viewed English life, his immediate world, with a detachment and an irony difficult for an Englishman.

Second, he was a Fabian (antiviolent, gradualistic) Socialist who never recovered from Karl Marx [82]. Hence, in his work economic knowledge, as he says, "played as important a part as the knowledge of anatomy does in the work of Michael Angelo."

Third, he had a deep faith in the capacity of human beings

to rise by effort in the scale of mental evolution. His mouth-piece Don Juan in *Man and Superman* speaks for him: "I tell you that as long as I can conceive something better than myself, I cannot be easy until I am striving to bring it into existence or clearing the way for it."

Fourth, he is probably the greatest *showman* of ideas who ever lived. He is continually using all his resources of wit, paradox, clowning, humor, surprise, invective, and satire, plus a thousand stage tricks, in order to fix firmly in the reader's or playgoer's mind ideas ordinarily found in volumes of sociology, economics, politics, and philosophy that would be inaccessible to the average intelligence. He is always preaching—but from the middle of the center ring of the circus.

You will see below the titles of eleven of Shaw's forty-seven plays. (He wrote ten more than Shakespeare, a man he considered rather inferior to himself as a dramatist—but then he lived almost twice as long.) Always read the prefaces that usually accompany the plays. As prose they are masterly. As argument they are often more comprehensive and persuasive than the plays—see, for example, the astounding Preface to *Androcles and the Lion* on the prospects of Christianity. Arranged in order of publication or production, this list suggests a little of the evolution of Shaw's mind over his most fertile quarter century, from 1894 to 1923: *Arms and the Man; Candida; The Devil's Disciple; Caesar and Cleopatra; Man and Superman; Major Barbara; Androcles and the Lion; Pygmalion; Heartbreak House; Back to Methusela;* and *Saint Joan.*

C.F.

100
JOSEPH CONRAD
1857–1924

Nostromo

The same year, 1895, in which Thomas Hardy [94] gave up novel writing saw the publication of Joseph Conrad's first book,

Almayer's Folly. The traditional English novel—a large, loose, free-flowing narrative, depending largely on external action and easily grasped characters—has begun to die. A new kind of fiction—original in form, full of technical devices, its tensions flowing from the exploration of mental life—is being born. Sterne [58], Austen [66], George Eliot [84], and Hardy had all helped to clear its path. But it is really Conrad who announces its themes and methods. At this point in our reading we will feel a greater richness if we see Conrad as helping to make possible our understanding of Henry James [96], D.H. Lawrence [113], Joyce [110], Mann [107], Proust [105], Faulkner [118], and others, such as André Gide, not included in the Plan.

Strangeness, somberness, nobility: these mark Conrad's career. He repels affection, he compels admiration. Born a Pole, of a family tragically dedicated to the desperate cause of Polish freedom, he was left an orphan at twelve. At seventeen he turned westward "as a man might get into a dream." Without ever forgetting his aristocratic Polish heritage, he committed himself to a new world. Some years of curious, almost cloak-and-dagger adventure followed, during which, for instance, he smuggled arms for the Carlist cause in Spain. Then, adopting the life of a seaman and an Englishman, he spent twenty years in the British Merchant Service, rising to the rank of master. He pursued his vocation on most of the seas of the world and particularly in the fabled East Indies, the setting of many of his stories. At last came the fateful decision which had doubtless been incubating in his mind for years. With a certain reluctance he abandoned the sea and, now a mature man, using a language not his own, and interpreting the world as a Continental writer would, this Polish sailor in the end became (this is my own opinion, though shared by many others) one of the half-dozen greatest novelists to use our magnificent tongue.

For years, stoically suffering neglect and, what is worse, misunderstanding, Conrad toiled at his desk. He tested his craft by a set of standards unfamiliar to the Victorians. He sought the perfect form for each of his stories. He searched human character in depth, fearless of what he might find there. He sought out wonderfully suggestive symbols (such as the silver mine in *Nostromo*) to mirror large areas of emotion. Just as Flaubert [86] did, he consciously forged a style suited to his special view of human nature under special conditions of moral stress. He thought of himself as an artist fiercely dedicated to his calling. He had no friendly relation to his public as Dickens [77] and Thackeray [76] had. His relation was to the vision within himself.

Nostromo is not an easy novel to read, and it is best to take it slowly. It does not tell itself, as *Tom Jones* [55] seems to. It uncoils, retraces its steps, changes its angle of attack. Into it Conrad put his most anxious effort, and if he has a masterpiece this is probably it.

But before we read *Nostromo* it is best to clear our minds of some notions about Conrad still entertained by many.

First, he is not a writer of "sea stories," much less of adventure stories. He is a psychological novelist who happens to be exploiting material he knew intimately.

Second, though he wrote many tales of the East Indies, he is not an "exotic" novelist. Local color is there, of course, laid on with a painter's eye, but again this is subordinate to his interest in the roiled depths of the human heart.

Third, he is not, except superficially, a "romantic." The tests of fidelity, fortitude, and understanding to which he submits his characters are ruthlessly true to the human condition as seen by a most unsentimental eye. Conrad does not flee or evade, nor, despite his sense that life itself is a kind of dream, does he take refuge in dreams. He is far more realistic than a Sinclair Lewis.

Critics always quote one sentence from his famous Preface to *The Nigger of the Narcissus*. I will quote it, too. But we must understand what Conrad means by the word "see." He is not talking like an Impressionist painter. He means the kind of seeing that has the depth, clarity, and often agony of a vision, visible only when the mind and the imagination are at full tension. Once we grasp this, the sentence may stand as a shorthand summary of Conrad's ideal relationship to the ideal reader: "My task which I am trying to achieve is, by the power of the written word, to make you hear, to make you feel—it is, above all, to make you see. That—and no more, and it is everything."

For additional reading in Conrad I would suggest three long short stories: "Heart of Darkness," "The End of the Tether," and "Youth."

C.F.

101
ANTON CHEKHOV
1860–1904

Uncle Vanya, Three Sisters, The Cherry Orchard, **Selected Short Stories**

The experience of reading Chekhov's plays is never quite satisfactory, because the reader's imagination must meet a difficult challenge. The page cries out for the stage. The words demand the actor's voice. The dialogue is not tidy and explicit, as with Shaw [99], but more like ordinary conversation. It is marked by breaks, pauses that make their own statements, involuntary gestures, small digressions, abrupt transitions, incomplete thoughts, careless syntax. Chekhov's apparently inconsequential talk is designed to reflect the contradictions, the confusions, the frustrations hidden deep within his characters.

Chekhov has no program. A doctor by profession, he has some of the physician's requisite detachment. He does not care about changing your mind; he cares only about telling the truth about the human heart. He wants to make you feel what lies behind the daily, the ostensibly trivial. As playwright he has no option, words are his only medium. But these words he thinks of as a mere screen. His business is to reveal holes and gaps in the screen, thus allowing us glimpses of the reality it conceals.

In these respects, as in others, Chekhov contributed something new, as did Ibsen, to the art of the playwright. Since Chekhov, the serious theater has never been quite the same.

The theme of the three major plays I have suggested is human wastage. His characters, the provincial intelligentsia, the petty aristocracy, the small landowners and bureaucrats of prerevolutionary Russia, are in effect functionless. Essentially they have nothing to do except to contemplate their unsatisfactory lives. They are talkers, not doers. And they sense their own weakness. They know, as Yeliena Andryeevna puts it in *Uncle Vanya* that "things have gone wrong in this house," and we cannot but feel that the house is Czarist Russia. In *Three Sisters* Baron Toozenbach says, "The time's come: there's a terrific thundercloud advancing upon us, a mighty storm is coming to freshen us up!" (*Three Sisters* premiered sixteen years prior to the Revolution.) In the same play Olga offers the vague consolation: "Our suffering may mean happiness for the people who come after us."

But we must not think of Chekhov as a leftist, much less a revolutionary. He would not have welcomed 1917. His mind was not political, only contemplative.

That contemplation is pessimistic; perhaps melancholy is a better word. Chekhov's exposure of the provincial middle class is sad rather than indignant. And even that sadness is qualified by humor; he once wrote to a friend that *The Cherry Orchard* (which to most readers seems so downbeat) was "not a drama but a comedy: in places almost a farce."

The mood of many Chekhovian characters is one many of us have felt. It is expressed by Chebutykin in *Three Sisters*: "What difference does it make?"

Yet Chekhov is no nihilist. His own life was marked by generosity, adherence to traditional moral values, and a persuasive compassion. He has no fixed or comprehensive view of life.

What interested him was detection of the almost unseizable reality of human behavior. Few dramatists have done this more successfully. To his friends he would say, "Let the things that happen on the stage be as complex and yet just as simple as they are in life."

The social world of his plays is rather restricted. To perceive the full extent of his understanding of other Russian types, including the peasant, we must go to his short stories. In this field he is one of the few great names. He helped revolutionize the short story as he helped revolutionize modern drama.

C.F.

102
EDITH WHARTON
1862–1937

The Custom of the Country, The Age of Innocence, The House of Mirth

Born into an upper-class but only moderately wealthy New York family, Edith Jones spent her early years as a shy and bookish young woman who was much more comfortable as an observer of high society than a participant in it. Her rigorous intelligence took note of the pretensions of the "Old New York" families guarding their dwindling wealth and clinging to the prestige inherited from their Dutch forebears, and of the social climbing and vulgar display of the new millionaires who were jostling to replace them. In the drawing rooms of Fifth Avenue mansions and in modest side-street brownstones, in elegant hotels and shabby rented rooms, in fashionable summer resorts, she found material that would serve her well during a lifetime as one of the most successful and admired novelists of her era. Soon after her death her reputation went into decline, and she was dismissed as merely a "popular writer"; in recent years her work has enjoyed a well-deserved revival.

Her own life had its novelistic elements. In 1885 she married, with no great enthusiasm, Teddy Wharton, a well-to-do but vapid Bostonian who was conspicuously her intellectual inferior. For a few years she lived a life of idle affluence, building her dream house, The Mount, in Lowell, Massachusetts, and frequenting the haunts of the wealthy in Saratoga, Newport, and New York. At the same time she began, tentatively, the literary career she had dreamed about as a young girl; her collection of short stories, *The Greater Inclination* (1899) won some favorable notice. She began to achieve real celebrity as a writer with a steady output of novels in the early 1900s; by that time her marriage was showing serious strains (Teddy began embezzling money from her trust fund and spending it on more compliant young women) and she was living mostly in Europe, with or without her husband. In 1906–09 she had an affair with Morton Fullerton, the great love of her life, who unfortunately turned out to be a cad. She and Teddy were divorced in 1913, and her relations with men thereafter were confined to warm but asexual friendships with men prominent in the arts—most notably Henry James [96], but also Walter Berry and Bernard Berenson. (The dark tone of her best-known short novel, *Ethan Frome*, published in 1911, very likely reflects her disenchantment with the institution of marriage.) Edith Wharton settled permanently in Europe, living on her ever-increasing royalties and acting as a literary hostess and generous friend to young writers at her sumptuous Paris apartment and her garden home in the south of France.

The strength of character that saw her through her difficult youth and her impossible marriage made Edith Wharton a disciplined and hard-working writer who achieved both popular and critical success. Of her many excellent novels (and I find it hard to choose), I recommend especially *The Custom of the Country* (1913), whose heroine, the ambitious Undine Spragg, finds none of her conquests satisfactory; *The Age of Innocence* (1920), the story of an irresolute young man in the New York of the 1880s, caught between his feelings for his fiancée and his rekindled passion for an earlier lover; and her first best-seller, *The House of Mirth* (1905), whose heroine Lily Bart, in my view, is Wharton's finest character. Like Becky Sharpe [76], Lily finds little she will not do to win a place in society; but whereas Thackeray tried to suppress his own and the reader's potential affection for his spunky adventuress (by making her a bad mother), Wharton clearly has every sympathy for Lily, but nevertheless finds no way to avert the doom that a rigid and censorious society reserves for her.

In these novels, and in all of her work, Edith Wharton viewed the world with a sympathetic but unsparing eye.

J.S.M.

103
WILLIAM BUTLER YEATS
1865–1939

Collected Poems, Collected Plays, *Autobiography*

Exclusive of Shakespeare [39] and Chaucer [32], the Plan suggests for extended reading a small number of English and American poets. Among these, posterity will assign Yeats his proper rank. That he will not be at the bottom of the list we may be sure.

Yeats offers difficulties. He was a complex man who offers inadequate satisfaction when read in anthological snatches. Also, he is more than a poet. Among his tremendous output are poems, plays, memoirs, essays, literary studies, folk and fairy tales, mystical philosophies, letters, speeches, translations from Sophocles [6]. Like Goethe's [62], his long life comprised a series of evolutions. There is a vast space between the aged poet of the *Last Poems and Plays* (1940) and the young Celtic dreamer of *The Wanderings of Oisin* (1889). To bridge this space the reader must absorb a great deal of Yeats and also know something about the Ireland whose soul he tried to find and form.

That is why I suggest his *Autobiography,* a one-volume omnibus. It contains reminiscences of his life through 1902, together with extracts from a diary kept in 1909, some notes about the death in 1909 of the fine Irish dramatist Synge, and an account of his reception in Sweden, which he visited in 1923 to receive the Nobel Prize.

Yeats grew and changed and deepened; his life was not simple, any more than his thought. We may identify a few influences: his early childhood in the beautiful Sligo country; his readings in the romantic English poets; the mythology and folklore of Ireland, together with the Irish literary revival that he led; theosophy, spiritualism, occultism, astrology, and Indian philosophy; the beautiful Irish revolutionary Maud Gonne, whom he loved in vain for twenty years; the psychic powers of his mediumistic wife; and toward the end such cyclical theories of history as are to be found in Vico, Spengler, and Toynbee.

The major movement of his creative life is away from the delicate, suggestive, vague but often beautiful lyricism of the early verse toward the hard, spare, condensed, intellectual, tightly passionate, often obscure poetry of his later years. The change was already apparent in a poem called "September 1913," with its plain statement: "Romantic Ireland's dead and gone." Yeats's development is exactly polar to Wordsworth's [64]: aging, he became greater as man and artist. The growth was fed by deep conflict, not only personal but political and social, for he despised much of our world ("this filthy modern tide") and used it as nourishment for his noble rage.

The bias of his mind is aristocratic (even feudal), mystical, symbolical. Though the symbols are not as wildly private as in Blake [63], who greatly influenced Yeats, they cannot be understood without a considerable knowledge of his work and life. Unless this is frankly admitted, the reader is apt to be at first puzzled, then irritated, finally antagonistic.

Yeats often seems esoteric, remote, impersonal, wrapped up in a world of strange images drawn from antiquity or the

East or his own occult thought system or Irish legend. But the more one lives with him, the more clearly one feels his unflinching closeness to reality. He may be taken in by visions; but he is not taken in by illusions. In his mature work there is a bracing tragic bitterness:

> Whatever flames upon the night
> Man's own resinous heart has fed.
> His wisdom is not for children, optimists, or the comfortable:
> I must lie down where all the ladders start,
> In the foul rag-and-bone shop of the heart.

In the final lines of one of his last poems, "Under Ben Buiben," he compresses his seeming arrogance, his patrician elevation of spirit, his horror of self-pity. He is leaving instructions for his own gravestone:

> No marble, no conventional phrase;
> On limestone quarried near the spot
> By his command these words are cut:
> *Cast a cold eye*
> *On life, on death.*
> *Horseman; pass by!*

C.F.

104
NATSUME SOSEKI
1867–1916

Kokoro

Commodore Matthew Perry's unwelcome arrival in Edo Bay in 1854 ended a period of more than two centuries during which Japan had almost no contact with the outside world. The "opening" of Japan by the West provoked fifteen years of irresolution, and even a civil war between proponents of different responses to the crisis; the issue was settled when advisors to the young Emperor Meiji (reigned 1868–1912) embarked upon a program of modernization and aggressive diplomacy designed to beat the West at its own game. Japan's effort to catch up with the West bore results with astonishing speed, perhaps in part because of the unusual homogeneity and discipline of the Japanese people. One effect of the modernization effort was to create a generation of young people educated in Western studies and equipped to guide their country from a traditional, feudal past into a hopeful new future. Among them was Natsume Soseki.

He was born into a minor samurai family in 1867, a year before the Emperor Meiji took the throne, and was one of the first Japanese students to come up through the newly reformed educational system. After graduating from Tokyo Imperial University he was sent to study in England in 1900. On his return in 1903 he became Lecturer in English Literature at his old university, succeeding his mentor, the noted American Japanophile Lafcadio Hearn. In 1907, however, he gave up his academic post to work as a full-time writer; he was already beginning to feel afflicted by the anxiety and cultural alienation that made him unable to stay in the front lines of Westernization in Japanese education, and that was to make his fiction steadily darker in tone and less hopeful in the years before his early death in 1916.

He achieved national celebrity with his first two novels, *I Am a Cat* (1905) and *Botchan* (1906), both of which are still widely read and admired in Japan; both are satirical novels that puncture the pretenses of Japan's new Westernized urban elite. In my view, however, the first suffers from an excess of cuteness, the second from an excess of sentimentality; neither seems to survive the translation process very well, nor to cross cultural frontiers with any success. Where the tone of these early novels is one of comic irony, that of *Kokoro* (1914) is somber and elegiac.

The word "kokoro" means "heart," with overtones of the soul, the center, the authentic. As a book title it is nearly equivalent to Graham Greene's *The Heart of the Matter*. In Natsume's novel, narrated in the first person, the heart of the matter is precisely what the young protagonist is unable to express. The book deals with his obsessive relationship with "Sensei" (the word means "teacher," but more than that, too— "master" or "mentor"). The narrator is consumed by loneliness and alienation, by feeling poised between the old Japan to which he is sentimentally attached (he admires the suicide of General Nogi upon the death of Emperor Meiji: a vassal fol- lowing his master to the grave) and the new Japan of which he is part but to which he cannot relate. His only salvation seems to lie in explaining himself to Sensei, but as he reveals himself he cannot stand what he sees: "You wished to cut open my heart and see the blood flow. I was then still alive. I did not want to die. . . . Now, I am about to cut open my own heart, and drench your face with my blood. . . ."

Natsume Soseki has been called Japan's first fully modern writer; certainly he is one of a handful of Meiji Period intellec- tuals and writers who helped to create a modern revolution in Japanese art and literature.

J.S.M.

105
MARCEL PROUST
1871–1922

Remembrance of Things Past

This is the longest first-rate novel ever written, at least in a Western language. Its difficulties, like its rewards, are vast. If you respond to it at all (many do not) you may feel quite justi- fied in spending what time you can spare over the next five or ten years in making it a part of your interior world.

Though it shares some features with *Ulysses* [110] and in a minor way with *Tristram Shandy* [58], it is basically unlike any novel we have so far discussed. It has a story, of course, and characters, and a clear setting in time and place—and all are most interesting indeed. But Proust is less concerned with these matters than with dramatizing a metaphysical system. Metaphysics tries to answer the question, What is the fundamental nature of reality? Proust devoted his life to answering the question in the form of a work of art. Of course he answers only part of the question. He tells us what reality means to Proust. But the answer has enormous scope and range.

Proust never had to work for a living. His family was moderately wealthy, and from an early age the brilliant boy had access to the worlds of fashionable and intellectual Paris, as it was before World War I. His attachment to his Jewish mother, a sensitive woman of fine character, was powerful and neurotic. Though Proust loved women as well as men, there is little doubt that his later homosexuality was caused partly by his relationship to his mother. Her death in 1905, together with his own physical weaknesses (particularly asthma), determined the shape of his life. He withdrew to the seclusion of a dark, vapor-filled cork-lined room. There, sleeping by day, working by night, with occasional sorties into the outer world (with which he also kept in touch through a huge correspondence), he slowly, painfully elaborated his masterpiece.

The hero of *Ulysses* is a place, Dublin. The hero of *Remembrance* is Time. To project in art the very "form of Time" was Proust's passion, his answer to the question, What is it to be? He jettisoned completely the methods of the conventional novelist. For him, being is not a chronological succession of events. Being is the complete past, "that past which already extended so far down and which I was bearing so painfully within me."

How shall we grasp this past, this reality? Quantum theory tells us that in a sense reality is unseizable because observation itself changes the thing observed. Proust understood this. He therefore gave us the past as well as he could, by a series of approximations, by presenting it to us in a thousand aspects, by showing it for what it really is—not a smooth flow of discrete events, but an ever-changing continuum. Parts of our past are continually erupting in us. These parts are felt differently at different times, by different people, under different circumstances. Proust evades none of these difficulties; he triumphs over them.

The past is evocable, we say, by memory. But this memory is not under our control. The taste of a small cake dipped in tea, the outline of some towers against the sky—such small events reawaken in Proust a stream of memories and half-forgotten experiences, which color his whole life. We cannot understand ourselves at any given moment, nor are we merely the static sum of all the moments we have lived—because we are continually reliving them, and so the sum is always changing. Only through a complete evocation of the past can the content of any moment be even approximated. Because this is so, reality, as we say, eludes us, and life seems sad, evanescent, and puzzling. Only art, Proust's religion, by imposing on life's mutations an orderly form, can give us consolation.

Proust's method, even the structure of his interminable sentences, flows from this conception of time, from this enthronement of subjectivism. In his book, time turns and twists upon itself like a snake, past and present merge, motifs and themes are recalled and redeveloped and answer each other in echo and counterpoint. Every critic has pointed out that the book is less like a narrative than like a symphony.

But had Proust done nothing more than incorporate a metaphysic he would not be as interesting as he is. In addition to his peculiar, neurotic sensibility and his phenomenal memory, he possessed most of the gifts of any first-rate novelist. His book, for example, is a social panorama of unprecedented depth (though not of range): compare his Vanity Fair with Thackeray's [76]. He describes the agonies and death of a whole aristocratic and upper-middle-class society. He analyzes, sometimes with intolerable exhaustiveness, the baffling and to him frustrating nature of love, and particularly of homosexual love. He creates at least a half-dozen characters comparable to the most living in the literature of the novel. And he invents a prose, often opaque, but always, in its slow sinuosities and plangent rhythms, proper to his difficult theme. His realism is unlike that of any novelist we have so far met. It is the realism of the symbolist, not the naturalist. When he wishes, he can describe to perfection. But he omits all details that do not reinforce his conviction that our only reality is the aspect of things remembered. This partial reality is not all we need to know, but it is all we do know; and that limitation is the cause of the tragedy of life.

For some this is the greatest novel in the world. For others it is unreadable. For still others it is, as one good critic wrote, "mammoth but minor." You must pass your own judgment. I will, however, in conclusion quote the considered estimate of the finest American critic of his time, Edmund Wilson: "We must recognize in Proust, it seems to me, one of the great minds and imaginations of our day, absolutely comparable in our own time, by reason both of his powers and his influence, to the Nietzsches [97], the Tolstoys [88], the Wagners and the Ibsens [89] of a previous generation. He has recreated the world of the novel from the point of view of relativity: he has supplied for the first time in literature an equivalent on the full scale for the new theory of modern physics."

C.F.

106
ROBERT FROST
1874–1963

Collected Poems

Though not *very* near, Frost is probably the nearest thing we have to a national poet. He is constantly anthologized. Schoolchildren are regularly exposed to his simpler work. The television screen, the lecture platform, and the college class-room made his remarkable and sometimes disquieting person-ality familiar to many Americans who do not think of them-selves as poetry lovers. A citizen of a prize-respecting country, he won the Pulitzer Prize four times. Finally, together with other talents, he possessed that of longevity. All these factors combined to make him a kind of unofficial poet laureate. Insofar as this has helped to raise the status of poetry in a poetry-resistant age, it is a fine thing. Insofar as it has created a fuzzy or sentimentalized or incomplete image of a great writer, it is less so.

"Literature begins with geography," says Frost. The litera-ture he created did indeed begin with the hilly, lonely, past-conserving, Yankee land north of Boston. Yet Frost is no regional poet. He may begin with geography, but he advances into unmappable country. Nor is Frost, though deeply American, merely a representative voice; he is his own man. Nor is he a "poet of the people," as Sandburg may be. He writes often about farmers, hill folk, lonely small souls. But the slope of his temperament is as aristocratic as Yeats's [103], though more sociable, flexible, and humorous. As is often the case with him, he is half serious, half kidding in such a casual remark as "I have given up my democratic prejudices and have willingly set the lower classes free to be completely taken care of by the upper classes." Finally, though he uses simple words and weaves into his verse the actual tones of common speech (so that it "says" itself), his technique and imagination are both extraordinarily complex. In other words, Frost is no Yankee sage, rhyming cracker-barrel philosophy, but a sophisticated mind who scorns the usual lingo of sophistication. His under-statement conceals a rich growth of statement.

Frost is an uncornerable man. He will say "I never take my own side in a quarrel." He will say "I'm never serious except when I'm fooling." About his own art he has ideas no one else ever seems to have thought of: "Like a piece of ice on a hot stove the poem must ride on its own melting." He absorbed

Thoreau [80] and Emerson [69] and reflected some of their independence, even their crankiness; but, that said, we have said little. Frost outwits classification, as he outwitted his own time, refusing to bow to it, refusing to be intimidated by it, using it always for his own secret, sly purposes: "I would have written of me on my stone: I had a lover's quarrel with the world."

The poems most of us know—"Mending Wall," "After Apple Picking," "The Road Not Taken," "Stopping by Woods on a Snowy Evening"—remain beautiful. But to find and wind your way into this cranky, ironic, humorous, elusive mind it is necessary to read the less familiar Frost of the later years. Aging, he grew more difficult, more philosophical, far more daring, satirical, funny, scathing. Absorb him slowly, over a long period.

C.F.

107
THOMAS MANN
1875–1955

The Magic Mountain

Some books (they can be first-rate ones, like Jane Austen's [66]) isolate parts of human experience. Others sum up these parts. Thus the masterpieces of Dante [30] and Homer [2,3], though they do other things as well, sum up their cultures. So does *The Magic Mountain*. The reader will get more out of it by seeing it as a synthetic, inclusive work. Mae West once remarked, in a somewhat different connection, "I like a man who takes his time." In his Foreword to *The Magic Mountain* Mann puts it thus: "Only the exhaustive is truly interesting." His great novel is exhaustive, and it is truly interesting.

It is a story about a rather simpleminded young German who comes to visit a sick friend at a Swiss tuberculosis sanitarium; finds that he is himself infected; stays on for seven years;

listens, talks, thinks, suffers, loves; and is at last swept up into the holocaust of the First World War. As you read this story you will feel, slowly and almost imperceptibly, that it is more than the usual narrative of the education of a young man. In dialogue, in symbol, in fantasy and dream, in argument, in soliloquy, in philosophical discourse, Mann is trying to sum up the mental life of the West.

All of our authors are engaged in a Great Conversation, as it has been well called. A minor proof of this is the number of these authors who have helped to form Thomas Mann and whose ideas are orchestrated in *The Magic Mountain*. I could name dozens. Here are a few acknowledged by Mann himself: Goethe [62], Nietzsche [97], Turgenev [81], Tolstoy [88], Conrad [100], Whitman [85], Ibsen [89], and Freud [98]. In this sense, too, *The Magic Mountain* is summatory.

Look at it another way. As you read, try to see the Berghof sanitarium as Europe, the Europe (which means America, too) that in 1914 died violently. Think of its characters as being not only themselves but incarnations of powerful modes of thought and feeling: Settembrini is liberal humanism; Naphta is absolutist terror (Lenin, Stalin, Hitler, Mussolini, Khomeini, Saddam Hussein, and all the others still to come); Peeperkorn we have perhaps already met, for his message is not unlike D.H. Lawrence's [113]. And the patients are drawn from so many countries and social levels—what are they but the sickness of the West, which Mann understood clearly in 1924 and which in the last years of our century may reach its feverish crisis?

In this gigantic work Mann touches on a dozen themes and issues that have since come to pervade the thought of our day: psychoanalysis and spiritualism; the links connecting art, disease, and death; the relative nature of time, to which Einstein has accustomed us; the nature of Western man, and particularly of middle-class man; the relations between the artist and society; the proper education of a human being. Mann's special genius lies in his ability to combine high-level reflection with the creation of character and atmosphere.

The Magic Mountain takes place in two worlds. One is a world of ideas. The other is a world of subtle human relationships, which we can sense all the more clearly because they are cut off from the confusing contingencies of the "flatland," the clock-bound "healthy" world you and I inhabit.

Once we have read Conrad, Lawrence, Joyce [110], Mann, Proust [105], and Henry James [96], we are borne on the full tide of the modern novel. We can begin to see its character. It is marked by enormous self-consciousness, profound delvings into the human spirit, technical innovations of bewildering variety. Its main difference from the simpler fictions of the English authors of the eighteenth and early nineteenth centuries lies in its receptive openness to the whole creative life of humanity. It intellectualizes without dehumanizing. Its entire drift is perhaps most clearly exemplified in Thomas Mann's masterpiece, one of the most magnificent works of art produced in our unhappy century.

Among Mann's shorter works you might want to read the masterly *Death in Venice* and *Mario and the Magician*.

C.F.

108
E.M. FORSTER
1879–1970

A Passage to India

Compared with a Faulkner [118] or a Hemingway [119], E.M. Forster has made little noise in the world. He wrote only five important novels, none of them radiating a portentous air. Of these, four are pre-First World War. The fifth, A *Passage to India*, was published in 1924. Only this title has attracted many readers (although, together with A *Room with a View* and *Howards End*, it has become familiar through brilliant film versions). Why, then, is Forster included in our short, highly debatable list of twentieth-century novelists?

One reason is that the most perceptive critics consider him among the finest. Finest, not greatest. The latter adjective somehow seems inappropriate to Forster; he would have rejected it himself. The second reason is that, though his output is small and the publication dates seem remote, it is rich in import and as modern as you wish.

Forster's quiet power of survival springs from his special gift for treating crucial problems in human relations in a style showing not even a chemical trace of journalism, a style marked by grace, delicacy, and a pervasive sense of comedy. Comedy, rather than satire. Except for a generally liberal viewpoint (which he was quite capable of mocking) he was an uncommitted writer. His values are those of civilization—not Anglo-Saxon civilization or even European civilization, but a kind of timeless civilization of the heart unlinked to any special group or creed.

In *A Passage to India* there are no heroes or villains. The Hindus, the Moslems, the English—they are all at times "right," at times "wrong." Each character, even those the author dislikes, has a certain dignity; each character, even those the author admires, has a certain absurdity. But one quality they all share: they are incapable of perfect communication. This strange and wonderful book (see whether the worn adjective wonderful does not properly apply to the scene in the Marabar Caves) is not about the claims of Indian nationalism; nor about the obtuseness of English imperialism; nor about the appeal of Hindu mysticism. All three themes are involved. But if their involvement were the book, *A Passage to India* would now, since the liberation and partition of that subcontinent, be unreadable. This novel is about separateness, about the reverse of Donne's sentence [40], for every man is also an island unto himself. It is about the barriers we or Fate or God throw up and that isolate us one from another. It is about that permanent tragic condition in human intercourse arising from poor connections.

If you have read *A Passage to India*, reread it. If you have reread it, try Forster's other major novel, *Howards End*. Many consider it his masterpiece.

C.F.

109
LU HSÜN
1881–1936

Collected Short Stories

The twentieth century has on the whole been a terrible time for Chinese writers. For most of the century repressive governments, civil and international wars, poverty and social dislocation, and outright political repression have choked off the careers of many writers, killed some, and turned many others into party-spokesmen hacks. Chinese literature has only begun within the past few years to recover from these onslaughts.

Lu Hsün [Lu Xun] had the good fortune to spend the prime of his life in the 1920s, when a modernist movement briefly flourished in China before it was killed in adolescence. He was a leading light of what is known as the May Fourth Movement, named for a student-led demonstration on May 4, 1919 protesting pro-Japanese provisions in the Treaty of Versailles. This protest movement came to symbolize a decade or so of relative intellectual and artistic freedom, during which young writers and thinkers questioned traditional Chinese culture and society and found them wanting, and began to look for substitutes to take their place. (The pro-democracy students who protested and died in Tiananmen Square in 1989 consciously modeled themselves on the students of the May Fourth generation.)

Lu Hsün's real name was Chou Shu-jen [Zhou Shuren]. He was born into a prosperous and socially progressive family and, along with his brothers, studied Western science and medicine. (His brother Chou Tso-jen [Zhou Zuoren] became a psychologist, and translated the works of Havelock Ellis into

Chinese; Chou Chien-jen [Zhou Jianren] was a biologist and eugenicist, the first translator of Darwin into Chinese.) Lu Hsün abandoned his medical studies to play a full-time role in the May Fourth Movement as a pioneering writer of modernist, socially critical fiction. His reputation was assured with the publication in 1918 of "Diary of a Madman" (the title deliberately taken from Gogol [74]), which depicted Chinese society through the madman's eyes as cannibalistic. His story collection *Call to Arms*, published in 1923, included his most famous story, "The True Story of Ah Q," in which a hopelessly befuddled Chinese everyman bumbles his way through life until he is eventually dragged off to the execution ground for reasons he cannot understand; this is plainly an allegory for a traditional Chinese culture that, in Lu Hsün's eyes, has left China utterly unprepared to deal with the impact of Western culture and technology.

Beginning in the mid–1920s Lu Hsün closely associated himself with the nascent Chinese Communist Party, but infuriated the party's leadership by refusing to join the party formally. A resolute independent at a time when it was extremely difficult for people to avoid choosing sides in China's growing civil conflict, Lu Hsün maintained his status as an independent but leftist artist. Perhaps it is fortunate in some respects that he died before the Japanese invasion of China and then the Communist-Nationalist civil war would have made his independence insupportable. Since his death he has proven his independence by making all political factions in China slightly nervous about his legacy. But from our point of view his legacy is plain: No matter who claims or repudiates him politically, he is China's greatest twentieth-century writer.

There are many translated editions of Lu Hsün's selected or collected stories; read "Diary of a Madman," "The True Story of Ah Q," and a good sampling of others. You will find him a deft and entertaining storyteller as well as a penetrating social critic.

J.S.M.

110

JAMES JOYCE
1882–1941

Ulysses

With *Ulysses* we at last meet a novel that seems impenetrable. It is best to admit that this mountain cannot be scaled with a single leap. Still, it is scaleable; and from the top you are granted a view of incomparable richness.

Here are five simple statements. They will not help you to enjoy or understand *Ulysses*. I list them merely to remove from your mind any notion that this book is a huge joke, or a huge obscenity, or the work of a demented genius, or the altar of a cult. Here is what a large majority of intelligent critics and readers have come to believe about *Ulysses* since its publication in 1922.

1. It is probably the most completely *organized,* thought-out work of literature since *The Divine Comedy* [30].

2. It is the most *influential* novel (call it that for lack of a better term) published in our century. The influence is indirect—through other writers.

3. It is one of the most *original* works of imagination in the language. It broke not one trail, but hundreds.

4. There is some disagreement here, but the prevailing view is that it is not "decadent" or "immoral" or "pessimistic." Like the work of most of the supreme artists listed in the Plan, it proposes a vision of life as seen by a powerful mind that has risen above the partial, the sentimental, and the self-defensive.

5. Unlike its original, the *Odyssey* [3], it is not an open book. It yields its secrets only to those willing to work, just as Beethoven's last quartets reveal new riches the longer they are studied.

These statements made, I have three suggestions for the reader:

1. Read Joyce's A *Portrait of the Artist as a Young Man.* This is fairly straightforward, as compared with its greater sequel. It will introduce you to Stephen Dedalus, who is Joyce; and to Joyce's Dublin, the scene of both novels.
2. In this one case, read a good commentary first. The best short one, I think, is by Edmund Wilson, the best long ones by Stuart Gilbert and Anthony Burgess.
3. Even then *Ulysses* will be tough going. Don't try to under-stand every reference, broken phrase, shade of meaning, allu-sion to something still to come or buried in pages you've already read. Get what you can. Then put the book aside and try it a year later.

As you read it, try to keep in mind some of Joyce's pur-poses:

1. To trace, as completely as possible, the thoughts and doings of a number of Dubliners during the day and night of June 16, 1904.
2. To trace, virtually completely, the thoughts and doings of two of them: Stephen Dedalus, the now classic type of the mod-ern intellectual, and his spiritual father, the more or less aver-age man, Leopold Bloom.
3. To give his book a form paralleling (not always obviously) the events and characters of the *Odyssey* of Homer. Thus Stephen is Telemachus, Bloom Odysseus (Ulysses), Molly an unfaithful Penelope, Bella Cohen Circe.
4. To invent or develop whatever new techniques were needed for his monumental task. These included, among dozens, inte-rior monologue, stream of consciousness, parody, dream and nightmare sequences, puns, word coinages, unconventional punctuation or none at all, and so forth. Ordinary novelists try to satisfy us with a selection from or summary of their charac-

ters' thoughts. Joyce gives you the thoughts themselves, in all their streamy, dreamy, formless flow.

Even the attempt to read *Ulysses* can be a great adventure. Good fortune to you.

At this writing probably the best edition to use is the 1986 Vintage Books (Random House) paperback, described as "The corrected text edited by Hans Walter Gabler with Wolfhard Steppe and Claus Melchior." Perhaps even better is the edition by John Kidd (Norton, 1994).

C.F.

I I I
VIRGINIA WOOLF
1882–1941

Mrs. Dalloway, To the Lighthouse, Orlando, The Waves

Three names among the brilliant but overpublicized Bloomsbury group have not only survived but grown more impressive with the passage of time: those of the economist John Maynard Keynes and the novelists E.M. Forster and Virginia Woolf. Long before her death in 1941 Woolf had already begun to influence decisively the course of the English novel. That influence has continued to expand. We can legitimately claim that, along with Conrad [100], Henry James [96], Proust [105], and Joyce [110] (whom she did not admire), she is truly seminal.

To put it in formula terms, she demonstrated that the accepted realistic English novelists of the first quarter of the century—Arnold Bennett, John Galsworthy, H.G. Wells—suffered from an inadequate view of the resources of their art. They dealt in surfaces, as she argued in her trail-breaking essay "Mr. Bennett and Mrs. Brown." She proposed to get underneath these surfaces by using devices that have become familiar—stream of consciousness, interior monologue, the abandonment of linear narrative, and a sensitive adaptation of some of the techniques of poetry. At times she failed in her endeavor; more often she succeeded.

Of the four novels here recommended, *Mrs. Dalloway* is perhaps the most accessible. Through the central figure, a wealthy political hostess, Woolf gives us a picture of the London upper class, of a whole society at its highest peak of self-confidence. The great themes of love and death dominate. But there are interesting minor ones such as snobbery (Woolf herself was partly a snob), rebellion against privilege, and, more faintly, lesbian attachment. Her own intervals of madness, which were to culminate in suicide, gave her extraordinary insight into the mind of the shell-shocked veteran Septimus Smith, a character as firmly realized as Mrs. Dalloway herself.

In *To the Lighthouse,* as in all the novels beginning with *Mrs. Dalloway,* we slip in and out of people's minds, sometimes with no warning. The personages, drawn from Woolf's own family memories, are consciousnesses rather than characters. Not chronological time but moments of epiphany determine the novel's form and structure. She writes, ". . . any turn in the wheel of sensation has the power to crystallize and transfix the moment."

The original of Orlando, in the book so titled, was Virginia Woolf's great friend, the aristocratic Vita Sackville-West, wife of the writer-diplomat Sir Harold Nicolson. This elaborate fantasy glancingly recapitulates parts of English history from Elizabethan times to 1928. It seems to anticipate the Latin American school of magic realism [132]. An element of play enters; perhaps *Orlando* bears the same relation to Woolf's total production that Graham Greene's Entertainments bear to his.

The Waves is her most difficult novel. Six members of the privileged class, three of each sex, are carried rapidly from childhood through youth, university, and middle age. There is no movement in the usual sense, merely six souls soliloquizing in turn. As one of them, Bernard, reflects: "There is nothing one can fish up in a spoon; nothing one can call an event." Not everything the characters say or think or feel is graspable by even the most sensitive reader. The effect is of beauty without clarity. Not her most successful book, *The Waves* is nevertheless probably the most original development-novel of the first half of the century.

C.F.

112
FRANZ KAFKA
1883–1924

The Trial, *The Castle*, Selected Short Stories

If we think only of the West, there are perhaps five creative writers of the century who have most influenced other twentieth-century writers. Franz Kafka's name would probably be among them. He would be classed with Joyce [110], Proust [105], Yeats [103], and T.S. Eliot [116]. About two decades after Kafka's death the poet W.H. Auden [126] wrote: "Had one to name the author who comes nearest to bearing the same kind of relation to our age as Dante [30], Shakespeare [39] and Goethe [62] have to theirs, Kafka is the first one would think of." Even less restrained praise was accorded him by the great French poet and dramatist Paul Claudel: "Besides Racine, who is for me the greatest writer, there is one other— Franz Kafka."

These judgments were expressed at perhaps the peak of the Kafka boom. I say boom because his reputation is in part cult-inspired. But it remains true that the dark anomie and spiritual hunger of our unhappy epoch are both classically reflected in the dreams and nightmares of Kafka's fictions.

None of this was apparent during his brief lifetime. His enormous reputation is almost entirely posthumous. It is based, furthermore, on very little actual production: three not-quite-finished novels, a dozen short stories, and a scattering of brief parables, plus some correspondence. It may in part be explained, as in the cases of Stendhal [67] and Tocqueville [71], by Kafka's powers of prophecy. Though he died as long ago as 1924, his symbolic visions seem to us to foretell our own period, marked by the German near-imposition of a state of total terror; by the bureaucratic maze that is the essential structure of all modern governments; by a sense that, as spiritual beings, we have lost our way and must rediscover it; by the invasion of our very souls by the machine; by a pervading feeling, hard to pin down, of universal guilt; by dehumanization. Borges [121] speaks of "the Kafka of somber myths and atrocious institutions."

Kafka's external life, though not notably happy, was sheltered, reasonably rich in interesting friendships, and untouched by war. (His three sisters, however, were murdered by the Nazis; he would not have been surprised.) His personality was intensely neurotic. This neurosis he put to creative use in his disturbing fictions. He suffered all his life from an obsessive sense of domination by his materialistic father, a Jew who acted more like a Prussian. This obsession reflected itself in his two major works, *The Trial* and *The Castle,* though their symbolism is so intricate and multileveled that biographical interpretation becomes hazardous. Yet it is clear that these novels turn on feelings of guilt and inferiority. *The Trial* tells the story of a man who feels guilty but is never able to discover just what he is accused of. *The Castle* is about a similar figure enmeshed in a bureaucratic system with which he can never make contact but which nevertheless represents some kind of redeeming authority.

Kafka is not difficult to read, because he employs a style of the utmost calm, lucidity, and simplicity. The surface narrative, however, is deceptive. He is trying to suggest, using familiar images and seemingly commonplace episodes, the disturbed condition of modern man. We may put it this way: There is, for Kafka, a Goal. But is there a Way? Kafka, though he belonged to no sect and was devoid of any trace of mysticism, was a deeply religious man. He thought of his writing, not as a profession, but as a form of prayer to a God who continually eluded him. His heroes suffer from lostness, alienation, an inability to identify themselves. It is a feeling many of us have had. But at the same time they are seeking some redemptive grace (the Castle perhaps symbolizes this), which they vaguely sense. They have no place in the universal order; yet surely there must be one. In this sense Kafka may be said to be a metaphysical novelist, in some respects akin to the less agonized Borges.

In some of his shorter works—especially *The Metamorphosis* and *In the Penal Colony*—Kafka seems to foresee the dehumanization, the terror, and the bureaucratic tyranny of our epoch. They are chilling stories, recounted in quiet prose, parables of guilt and punishment, that strike to the very heart of our age of anxiety.

Though he died over seventy years ago, Kafka is contemporary. A neurotic genius, he was perfectly equipped to create a visionary world that reminds us of our real one.

C.F.

113
D.H. LAWRENCE
1885–1930

Sons and Lovers, Women in Love

It is hard to realize that when Lawrence died of tuberculosis he was only forty-five. From 1911, when his first novel appeared, to his death in 1930, no year passed without the appearance of at least one book. In 1930 there were six, and his posthumous works (excluding the extraordinary *Letters*) total another dozen or so. While producing so prodigiously, Lawrence was traveling widely, meeting and influencing large numbers of people, working at various hobbies, and engaging in the unhappy controversies caused by his uncompromising ideas. This frail, thin, bearded man—novelist, poet, playwright, essayist, critic, painter, and prophet—had a central fire of energy burning inside him. He stands out as one of the most alive human beings of his time.

Lawrence was born of a Nottinghamshire coal miner and a woman greatly superior to her husband in education and sensitivity. His early life, dominated by his mother's excessive love and his excessive dependence on it, is portrayed quite frankly in the first part of *Sons and Lovers*. Lawrence excelled at school and for a few years was a schoolmaster. In 1912 he eloped with Frieda von Richthofen Weekley, a member of a patrician German family, and in 1914 married her. The latter part of his life was one of almost continuous wandering. In exotic primitives and undeveloped countries he sought the equivalent in fact of the life-feeling that blazes in his fiction.

This life-feeling attracts some readers, alienates or shocks others. You will not be able to tolerate Lawrence at all unless you understand that he was neither poseur nor hysteric, but a prophet with a message fervently believed in, a message with which he sought to change the day-to-day behavior of the human race. The message is implicit even in so early a book as *Sons and Lovers,* which is certainly the one with which to start one's reading of Lawrence. It is to be found more particularly in *The Rainbow, Women in Love* (perhaps his masterpiece), and *Lady Chatterley's Lover,* one of his poorest novels.

We must understand that Lawrence was an absolute revolutionary. His rejections were complete. He made war against the entire industrial culture of his and our time. He felt that it had devitalized us, dried up the spontaneous springs of our emotions, fragmented us, and alienated us from that life of the soil, flowers, weather, animals, to which Lawrence was preternaturally sensitive. Worst of all, he thought, it had withered our sexual lives. For Lawrence sex was not merely something to enjoy. It was the key to the only knowledge he prized— direct, immediate, nonintellectual perception of reality. As early as 1912 he was writing, "What the blood feels, and believes, and says, is always true." (To some readers this will seem pernicious nonsense.)

He hated science, conventional Christianity, the worship of reason, progress, the interfering state, planned "respectable" living, and the idolization of money and the machine. It is easy to understand therefore why he was forced to live, though bravely and even joyfully, a life of poverty, struggle, and defiance. Aldous Huxley [117], who knew him well, described him as "a being, somehow, of another order." It does at times seem that he drew his energy from some primal source most of us cannot tap. In this respect as in others he reminds us of the prophet-poet Blake [63].

His books are not constructed, as Conrad's are [100]. They flow, eddy, flash, erupt, or sing in accordance with the electric changes in the author's own personality as he composed. Unless you are willing temporarily to accept this personality, his books may seem intolerable.

But Lawrence wants you to do more. His view of the novel was deeply moral. The novel, he passionately believed, "can help you not to be a dead man in life." He wants nothing less than to change you, to reawaken in you an intensity, a joy in life that he felt humanity was losing or had lost.

It is hard to say whether a century from now Lawrence will be thought of as a major prophet (as well as a remarkable artist) or merely as an oddity of genius.

The careful reader of the above paragraphs will suspect that I do not really like Lawrence as a human being and that I am doing my best to disguise my feelings. This new edition gives me an opportunity to be more honest. There was a fascist streak in Lawrence and we cannot really tell how wide it was. He once wrote: "The great mass of the population should never be taught to read and write. Never." As I have elsewhere noted, this is "one of the most remarkable statements ever made by a man who lived largely on his royalties." It is also worth remembering that, as the son of a poor miner, Lawrence was himself born into "the great mass." Had it not been for his country's enlightened universal education, he might never have become D.H. Lawrence. Never.

It has taken us some time to acknowledge that Wagner was both a genius and a swine. Of the genius Lawrence we may say, at the very least, that his character included some unpleasing traits.

C.F.

114
TANIZAKI JUNICHIRO
1886–1965

The Makioka Sisters

Tanizaki was born only two decades after Natsume Soseki [104], but he clearly belongs to another generation, walking confidently on the modernist path blazed so arduously by Natsume and other Meiji Period intellectuals. He was born into a prosperous Tokyo merchant family at a time when Japan's commercial prospects were booming, and grew up feeling quite comfortable with the modern, highly Westernized urban environment of Tokyo at the turn of the century.

Tanizaki attended Tokyo Imperial University but was expelled for nonpayment of fees before graduating—an act of rebellion, one supposes, since he was not short of funds. He began to publish short stories while he was in his early twenties; "The Tattooist" (1910) first brought him to the attention of Japan's literary world. He became infatuated with Western literature and material culture, and this is reflected in his early stories and film scripts.

In 1923, however, Tanizaki's life underwent a radical change, which in turn affected his point of view. He was living in the fashionable foreign enclave of Yokoyama at the time of the great Kanto earthquake of 1923; when his house, along with thousands of others, was leveled by the quake, he abandoned his wife and child and moved forthwith to Osaka, a much more conservative commercial city in western Japan. There he became an ardent Osaka patriot (as if a New Yorker were to move to Chicago and become a confirmed booster of the Second City), and was increasingly intrigued by the cultural tensions in the lives of modern Japanese of his day, people caught (like Tanizaki himself) between the fads, fashions and material allure of the West and a nostalgia for traditional Japanese culture. His first truly major novel, *Some Prefer Nettles* (1928), is a tale of a marriage that is unable to survive the tensions between the traditional and the modern.

I suggest that you begin your reading of Tanizaki with his finest and most famous novel, *The Makioka Sisters* (written 1942–44, published 1946–48). It cannot be described as autobiographical, though some of the main characters are based on his third wife and members of her family, and the setting of the novel, in Osaka in the mid–1930s, in some respects mirrors the actualities of Tanizaki's own situation there. It is a work of the imagination, and in it Tanizaki succeeds in creating an exceptionally vivid portrait of a wealthy family's struggles to reconcile their privileged and leisurely way of life with the harsher realities of modern times.

In the novel there are four Makioka sisters, and they have a delicate problem. The third sister, Yukiko, is unmarried, and remains so almost throughout the book despite the determined efforts of the second sister, Sachiko, to find her a suitable husband. Meanwhile the fourth sister, the liberated and rather "loose" Taeko, would be only too glad to get married, to whomever is her unsuitable beau of the moment, but is prevented from doing so by the polite social convention that the sisters must marry in order of age. This sets the stage for a prolonged and subtle comedy of manners that shows Tanizaki's literary talents at their fertile best.

Relatively subdued in *The Makioka Sisters*, in comparison to some of his other works such as *Naomi* (1924) or *A Cat, a Man, and Two Women* (1936), is the undercurrent of obsessive and somewhat fetishistic sexuality that many readers identify as the hallmark of Tanizaki's writing. A critic once quipped that all of Tanizaki's novels are about a man's search for a perfect woman to be abused by. This element of suppressed weirdness lurking beneath the surface of things leads some people to regard Tanizaki as an acquired taste, and others (I, among this group) to find him oddly wonderful. I invite you to see for yourself.

J.S.M.

115
EUGENE O'NEILL
1888–1953

Mourning Becomes Electra, The Iceman Cometh, Long Day's Journey into Night

Despite his unquestioned position as the greatest of American dramatists, the original edition of this book omitted Eugene O'Neill. At that time (1960) I did not feel that he ranked with such figures as Shaw [99] and Ibsen [89]. I still hold to this opinion. During the years since his death, however, it has become clear that his appeal did not die with him. His plays continue to be revived both here and abroad. He has become a classic figure, exerting an influence far transcending his historical importance as the first truly serious dramatist ever to write for the American stage.

It is interesting that O'Neill maintains and even strengthens his position despite the fact that his plays, when read, lack certain literary qualities. He is almost entirely humorless. When he essays the lyric flight, trying for elegance or beauty of language, he sounds mawkish, even naive. Worst of all, for a playwright specializing in characters who use the vernacular, he has a tin ear for dialogue. There is something not grossly but subtly wrong, for example, with the presumably low-life phrasing of the speakers in one of his finest plays, *The Iceman Cometh*.

Yet on the stage these defects, and other literary weaknesses, are hardly noticed, so powerful is his emotional thrust, so insistent the reiteration of his bleak theses. And even on the page his power forces its way through, at least in his best work.

Much of O'Neill is, or was in its day, experimental in technique: the use of masks; the fresh employment of that old standby, the soliloquy; enormously long and multidivisional dramas; the abandonment of realism in favor of an expressionism influenced by the Swedish dramatist Strindberg; the rehandling in modern terms of plots from the classical Greek drama that we have discussed under Aeschylus [5], Sophocles [6], and Euripides [7].

The most successful example of the latter is the trilogy *Mourning Becomes Electra*. The Clytemnestra-Agamemnon-Electra-Orestes story is ingeniously transferred to a New England post-Civil War setting. O'Neill, decisively influenced by the Greeks, is trying here to write pure tragedy, a dramatic mode rather foreign to the American stage tradition. Its force, however, derives less from the fatalities implicit in the plot than from a sense the reader gets that O'Neill's own conflicts are here transmuted.

This is even truer of the other two recommended plays. To my mind they are his masterpieces, both derived from intense personal experience, both dealing not with the periphery of life, but with the most agonizing questions man can ask of the cosmos.

The Iceman Cometh is about failure, not only the failure of the whisky-sodden derelicts in Harry's Bar, but the failure of perhaps all of us. It is relentless both in its stripping away of the illusions by which we live and its bitter demonstration that without them we could not live at all.

Long Day's Journey into Night is probably the most striking example in dramatic literature of a nakedly autobiographical play. Its characters are O'Neill's family, its tragedy theirs, its hopelessness his own.

O'Neill once remarked, "I am interested only in the relation between man and God." One must not take this literally, for O'Neill did not, as did his master Aeschylus, have a truly metaphysical mind. But the statement points to the underlying and intense preoccupation of O'Neill's intelligence with the deepest and most permanent concerns of humankind. It is this anguished seriousness that sets him apart from every other American dramatist.

C.F.

116
T.S. ELIOT
1888–1965

Collected Poems, Collected Plays

In our short list of leading twentieth-century writers the inclusion of T.S. Eliot is inescapable. Not because in 1948 he won the Nobel Prize—on balance the prize has just as often gone to mediocrities as it has to those of high talent. Nor because he was the (involuntary) leader of a highly vocal and influential school of poets and critics. Nor because he occupied a position in England held in previous eras by such literary popes as Dryden, Addison, and Samuel Johnson [59]. Nor because he was in his time one of the most controversial figures in contemporary English letters. Nor because the klieg lights of publicity were switched on him when he declared himself "Anglo-Catholic in religion, royalist in politics, and classicist in literature"—a description fitting hundreds of thousands of virtuous and intelligent Britishers. (The fuss made over it sprang from the liberal temperament's besetting weakness, parochialism.)

Except in his lucid essays (some of which I recommend you try), Eliot is a difficult writer, though as the years pass he seems less so, for he educated us to understand him. His achievement may be stated simply. He altered, deepened, and refined the character of English and American poetry in our time. He supplied modern criticism with a set of elevated and rigorous standards useful as a counterweight to the prevailing sleazy impressionism. In so doing he retrieved for us or set in a new light a whole series of writers: the minor Elizabethans, the seventeenth-century divines, Dante [30], Dryden, Donne [40].

Read his poetry in chronological order. Eliot—and this is not true of all the Plan's writers—was by nature a developer. His growth was both technical and spiritual. Technically he passed from verse filled with allusions and quotations, verse often rather tricky and fantastically clever, to verse of great purity, sonority of rhythm, and symphonic form. Spiritually he moved from the dandyish irony of the Prufrock poems of 1917 through the detached, terrible despair of *The Waste Land* (1922) to the brooding metaphysical religiousness of *Four Quartets* (1943).

During the whole of this evolution he held fast to his original aim: "to digest and express new objects, new groups of objects, new feelings, new aspects." Many of these objects and feelings are unpleasant, corresponding to our modern wasteland as the traditionalist eyes of Eliot saw it. But his purpose was neither to enjoy the luxury of misery nor to shock us with the disagreeable. "The essential advantage for a poet is not to have a beautiful world with which to deal; it is to be able to see beneath both beauty and ugliness; to see the boredom, and the horror, and the glory." All three—the boredom, the horror, the glory—are woven into his verse.

Though it has forebears, Eliot's poetry is nonetheless truly revolutionary, like the fiction of Proust [105] or Joyce [110] or the plays of Beckett [125]. It is exact and condensed on the one hand and rich in magical suggestion on the other. Every word or allusive echo carries its proper weight, and all is borne upon a rhythmic current whose effect becomes evident when you read the lines aloud or listen to Eliot's own recording of them. At first the language seems private, impossible to penetrate. But as one gains familiarity, it begins to emerge as a marvelously precise and evocative rendering of states of mind peculiar to sensitive Western men and women at this particular stage of our evolution or devolution. And it shares at least one quality with the greatest verse, Shakespeare's [39] or Dante's: It is rich in lines so finally expressive that they remain in our heads forever and become part of our emotional world.

C.F.

117
ALDOUS HUXLEY
1894–1963

Brave New World

T.S. Eliot [116] and Huxley had much in common. Both were formidably intelligent, as well as formidably learned. Both summed up in their personalities a large part of the Western tradition. Both moved from a position of destructive critical irony to one of faith—Eliot to Anglo-Catholicism, Huxley toward a mysticism drawn from the East but also from such Western visionaries as Blake [63], Eckhart, Tauler, and others. Eliot's may have been the profounder intellect, as he was certainly the greater artist. But Huxley's intellect was more adventurous, more playful, and more closely involved with insistent concrete problems of our time, particularly those pointing the way to race suicide, such as total war and murderous overpopulation.

The variety, the flexibility, the erudition, the sheer brilliance of Huxley's restless mind may be enjoyed through a reading of his essays. He leaves few of humanity's major concerns untouched. His skepticism, never cheap or easy, has a cleansing power still to be properly estimated. I know no other single English or American writer of his time who reflected with such clarity certain shifts and modulations in the Western intellect, including a shift toward the thought of the East.

Huxley was famous before he was thirty, a circumstance

perhaps not entirely fortunate for him. But the book that gave him a worldwide audience was *Brave New World*, published in 1932, reissued in 1946 with an important new Preface by the author. Probably this terrible fable will lose its point and force as unconsciously we take on in reality the condition he describes in fantasy. For our period, however, it is what might be called a temporary classic. No one who really wishes to learn what is happening, not to our environment but to our souls, should remain unacquainted with this nightmare of a book.

The utopian literature of the twentieth century, unlike that of the Renaissance, is negative, dystopian. In it we hear not shouts of encouragement but cries of warning. As Berdiaeff, quoted by Huxley, puts it, our concern now is not how to attain but how to avoid Utopia. For the Utopia we are so busy preparing is, according to Huxley, Orwell [123], and dozens of other thoughtful writers, a hell of dehumanization.

Huxley's *Brave New World* projected six hundred years into the future, is populated by animals (still known as human beings) and their managers. The managed animals have been taught to love their servitude; they are happy, or, as we proudly say, adjusted. The Constitution of the state has but three articles: Community, Identity, Stability. Religion as we know it, art, theoretical science, the family, emotions, individual strivings and differences—all have vanished.

Not a good novel, *Brave New World* should be read as a prophetic fable, differing from other prophecies in that it is the product not of intuition but of cold intelligence. Its ideas (and all its characters are ideas), first advanced more than sixty years ago, have proved prescient. All the gambits of then-current cocktail party conversation are prefigured in *Brave New World*—the conformist, the nonconformist, the relapse to primitivism, the new chartered sexuality, the organization man, the lonely crowd—they are here extended into a future that seems less remote today than it did in 1932.

I do not suggest that *Brave New World* be taken literally. It is not a textbook of the future but a purposely exaggerated satirical vision, in the tradition of *Gulliver* [52]. Doubtless Huxley will rank below Swift. But not too far below. And what he has to say is perhaps more immediate, if less crushing, than Swift's total misanthropy.

C.F.

118

WILLIAM FAULKNER

1897–1962

The Sound and the Fury, As I Lay Dying

William Faulkner has been hailed (except by a few uninfluential dissenters) as the greatest American novelist of his generation. Some critics rank him among the greatest of all time. In 1949 the award of the Nobel Prize marked the official peak of an extraordinary career.

Most of his novels and short stories are laid in Yoknapatawpha County, Mississippi. This invented region has now become hallowed literary ground, like Hardy's Wessex [94]. The novels' time span covers almost a century and a half, beginning in 1820. They form a connected series, something like Zola's Rougon-Macquart family chronicle or Balzac's more loosely linked "Human Comedy" [68]. Through accounts of the fortunes of a number of related families, Faulkner exposes, in a style of great complication and variety, the tragedy, and some of the comedy, of his violent, haunted, guilt-ridden Deep South. Mainly represented are three worlds: that of the black; that of the degenerate aristocracy, typified by the Compsons in *The Sound and the Fury;* and that of the even more degenerate emergent commercial class, whose emblem is the horrifying Lem Snopes.

The two novels recommended above are considered by most critics among Faulkner's finest; they are certainly among his most violent in theme and trail-blazing in technique. His champions also single out for high praise *Light in August* and *Absalom, Absalom!* as well as the Snopes trilogy (*The Hamlet, The Town, The Mansion*). My own favorite is *The Reivers.*

Faulkner is a serious, difficult, and daring writer. He is also, to some, a shocking writer. And finally, to a few, he is a writer only intermittently readable. The latter do not have the key to his mind, which may well be their loss. To this class I belong. If you need guidance through Faulkner's special inferno, I suggest Malcolm Cowley's Introduction to his *Portable Faulkner,* a brilliant exercise in sympathetic clarification.

C.F.

119
ERNEST HEMINGWAY
1899–1961

Short Stories

In perspective it is Hemingway's short stories, rather than his more ambitious fiction, that stand out. In them the defects of his attitudes have neither time nor space in which to expose themselves. The bellicosity, the conscious virility, the exaltation of violence and toughness, the bravado, the conception of women as romantic receptacles—these are all muted in his marvelous tales. By the same token the famous style, perfectly suited to the illumination of intense moments or isolated situations, gains a power in the short story it does not always possess in the longer works. It seems fair to say that, by virtue of his reverence for truth, the originality of his prose, the bone-bare exactness of his dialogue, and the charge of his emotion, Hemingway ranks among the first half-dozen of the world's masters of the short story.

Though he seems to grapple with ultimates, such as death, passion, and the defeat or persistence of human hopes, Hemingway's total world is actually not a large one. In even the lesser novelists we have already met more and wider gateways to human nature. To match him with the greatest is probably pointless. Beside Stendhal [67] he seems young; beside Henry James [96], primitive; beside Tolstoy [88], simply minor. Yet his achievement is solid. Building on a foundation laid down by Mark Twain [92], he quite literally remodeled the English sentence. He forced it to reveal, without wasted motion, the exact truth of a moment, an insight, an experience. This contribution to literature is not merely technical. It is moral. Hemingway taught language honesty.

His greater tales (with which we must class the novella *The Old Man and the Sea*) are now as much a part of our American heritage as "Rip Van Winkle" or "The Fall of the House of Usher." "The Snows of Kilimanjaro," "The Undefeated," "My Old Man," "The Killers," "Fifty Grand," and dozens of others compel us, no matter how often we reread them, to relive the experience the creator once felt so deeply. Whether or not we accept Hemingway's view of life, we cannot reject these tales of the veld, the bull ring, the barroom, the ski slope, the racetrack, the prize ring, the Michigan woods. For they pass beyond the novel settings and beyond the once-novel style. Emotion and the control of emotion are here held in exquisite poise. An artist who is also an honest man succeeds in telling the truth.

Note: The 1987 *Complete Short Stories of Ernest Hemingway*, the so-called Finca Vigía edition, is the only exhaustive collection.

C.F.

120
KAWABATA YASUNARI
1899–1972

Beauty and Sadness

Kawabata was orphaned early and grew up under difficult circumstances, a fact that some critics have seen as the source of the atmosphere of deep melancholy that pervades his writing.

In my view, however, Kawabata's stance is less likely to have to do with the hardships of his childhood than with the tension he seemed to feel throughout his life between beauty and sadness, or more precisely between sexuality and a sense of loss. Although his work, like that of other Japanese writers of his generation, shows strong European influence (particularly, in Kawabata's case, from the French Symbolists), he is in many ways a traditionalist, closer in *mentalité* to Murasaki [28] than to Tanizaki [114].

When Kawabata was awarded the Nobel Prize for Literature in 1968, the novel most often mentioned as his great work was *Snow Country* (1948), a tale of sexual obsession set in the snowy mountain fastness of northwestern Japan. I commend that book to your attention, but to my own taste *Beauty and Sadness* (1961) is a more subtle, and a more moving, work. It tells of the reunion of an elderly man and a woman artist whom he loved long ago, of the jealous rage the artist's young protégée conceives on her behalf for having been jilted in that affair, and of the terrible revenge she wreaks on the old man's family. Love, regret, obsession, eroticism, and evil blend in Kawabata's slight, almost ephemeral prose, where more is implied than is ever made explicit, and where throat-catching beauty goes hand in hand with the *frisson* of danger. Kawabata is said to have been greatly influenced by Bashō [50] and other *renga* (linked verse) poets of the seventeenth century, and something of this can be seen in the leaps of imagination and the mental filling-in of plot development that he requires of his readers. His prose is a sort of gossamer that seems to shimmer in one's consciousness, engaging the imagination but never revealing itself fully.

If you find yourself becoming a fan of Kawabata's work, I would suggest reading also one of his less-well-known novels, *The Master of Go*, about an old champion and a young challenger in Japan's chesslike national game of strategy. It is particularly interesting to read this novel alongside Nabokov's great tale of chess obsession, *The Defense* [122].

In 1972 Kawabata became despondent over the grotesque public suicide of his friend and protégé Mishima Yukio [131] and, far more quietly and decorously, committed suicide himself. Given the obsessive qualities of Kawabata's work, it is somehow difficult to imagine his life ending otherwise.

J.S.M.

121
JORGE LUIS BORGES
1899–1986

Labyrinths, Dreamtigers

Since this book's first appearance, Latin American writers have been looming larger on our literary horizon (see also Gabriel Garcia Marquez [132]).

Borges, scion of an intellectual middle-class family, was born in Buenos Aires, where most of his life was lived. His ancestry was Spanish and English, with a small infusion of Portuguese-Jewish blood. Like Nabokov [122], he learned English prior to his native tongue. He was strongly influenced by English writers from Caedmon to Chesterton and H.G. Wells.

Following his partially European education Borges began his career as a poet. His father's death and a near-fatal illness made 1938 a year of crisis for him. From this year dates the finest of his "fictions," a form peculiarly his own in which his genius is most clearly reflected. Slow in growth, his reputation became international with the publication in 1944 of his collection *Ficciones*. It was more formally recognized in 1961 when Borges shared with Samuel Beckett [125] the coveted international Formentor Prize.

Although hardly a political man, Borges opposed the Perón dictatorship and as a result was demoted from his post of librarian to that of poultry and rabbits inspector. After Perón's fall in 1955 he was named director of the National Library of

Argentina. By that time his always defective eyesight had worsened; from the age of fifty-six he was totally blind, this man who described himself as one "who imagined Paradise in the shape of a library."

Borges's vast and esoteric learning, which pervades his stories, makes his range of allusion somewhat forbidding to many readers and on occasion imparts to his work a bookish flavor. But these seeming hindrances are little more than a façade of irony. Behind it works a mind of almost dismaying subtlety in which a metaphysician, a logician, and a visionary (but not a mystic) occupy continually shifting positions. His constant theme, whether he offers us science fiction, detective stories, tales of violence, or logical nightmares, is the "hallucinatory nature of the world." For him the universe is not something made. Rather it is dreamt. Or perhaps it is a great Book, whose tone is that of "irreality, one of art's requisites."

Certain metaphors recur: images of infinite regression, of cyclic reappearance, the maze, the mirror, the double, tigers, libraries, time itself. "I have some understanding of labyrinths," says his narrator in "The Garden of Forking Paths." For Borges "ambiguity is richness." Thus his endless series of possible worlds differs essentially from the alternate world of a Tolkien, which is unambiguous, solid, roughly congruent point by point with our familiar one. Borges plays with ideas like a magician with his props, but the magic is more than legerdemain. His Library of Babel is also a universe and an emblem of infinity; his science fiction tales are not arbitrary fantasies but serious attempts to refute ordinary notions of time; and his many stories of betrayal and frustration penetrate the dream life that floats, dense, shifting, troubling, below the consciousness threshold of all of us.

As you read Borges you may feel his affinities with other writers discussed in his book: with Cervantes [38], about whose masterpiece he has written the most coolly outrageous story one can well imagine; with Lewis Carroll [91], Kafka [112], surely Garcia Marquez [132], and perhaps Nabokov [122]. But the Borges voice is unique. He has influenced many, but his magic is his own.

I have suggested you try two of his books. *Labyrinths* contains his finest fictions, essays, and parables, as well as a useful bibliography for those who wish to know him better. *Dreamtigers* contains more parables and a fair selection of his verse, conscientiously translated.

C.F.

122
VLADIMIR NABOKOV
1899–1977

Lolita; Pale Fire; Speak, Memory

One (but only one) way of viewing modern novelists is to divide them into two classes: the engaged and the unengaged. The engaged have a statement to make, often something about the state of our society. They are not necessarily propagandists or message bearers, but they have something on their minds, some special view of the world they are anxious to pass on to us. We may recognize engaged writers in such figures as Swift [52], Huxley [117], Solzhenitsyn [129], and Camus [127], different as they are in other respects. The unengaged are less interested in getting something off their own minds than in revealing the configurations, the patterns of other minds. They do not care greatly about altering our view of life. They do care greatly about displaying symbolic structures we may admire or vibrate to. Both the engaged and the unengaged may produce first-rate works of art, but the engaged writer tends to operate on our intelligence, the unengaged on our esthetic sensibility. Borges [121] is such an unengaged writer; and so, preeminently, is Nabokov.

Nabokov's Slavic background, his aristocratic stance, his checkered career, his mastery of two national cultures, and his keen interest in formal literary problems—all connect him with another towering innovator in modern fiction, Joseph Conrad [100]. Born in what was then (and is now again) St. Petersburg, Nabokov was the scion of an aristocratic family that lost its fortune in the Revolution. Educated at Trinity College, Cambridge, he spent formative years (1922–40) in Germany and France as a struggling and largely unrecognized writer. From 1948 to 1958 he taught Russian and European literature at Cornell, continuing also his extensive researches in entomology. He became a recognized authority on butterflies, as well as a remarkable chess player, and these themes from time to time reflect themselves in his novels.

The worldwide success of *Lolita* (1955) gave him financial independence, though he never at any time wrote seriously for any reason except to please himself. He spent his last years living quietly in a Swiss hotel, dying in 1977.

Complete familiarity with the Nabokovian universe is a major adventure of the mind and imagination. To accomplish this it would be necessary to read all of his novels, plays, stories, and criticism—including a brilliant, cantankerous study of Gogol [74] and such marvelous fiction as the sad-hilarious *Pnin*, the metaphysical-sexual time-fantasy *Ada*, and the tragic *The Defense*, the best piece of fiction ever written about the passion for chess. But the three books here suggested will supply a first acquaintance with the greatest stylist of our period, who wrote equally well in English and Russian, and whose elegant, allusive, and witty prose sets him apart.

Lolita, which deals with Humbert Humbert's passion for nymphets, is of course a recognized classic. Completely original, it is an examination of love that is funny, shocking to some, sad, and sophisticated in a manner quite remote from our American notion of sophistication. *Pale Fire* is partly a one-thousand-line poem in heroic couplets, partly a commentary on them by a mad exiled king—or perhaps a king only in his fantasy. It is a literary joke of enormous intricacy and at the same time, in the opinion of good critics, an addition to world literature. *Speak, Memory* is autobiographical, a unique recollection of Nabokov's childhood and youth, set mainly in pre-revolutionary Russia.

The mad Kinbote, in *Pale Fire*, describes himself in terms that might apply to his creator: "I can do what only a true artist can do—pounce upon the forgotten butterfly of revelation, wean myself abruptly from the habit of things. . . ."

The critic Gilbert Highet, reviewing the remarkable thriller *King, Queen, Knave*, summed up Nabokov as "the most original, the most tantalizing, the most unpredictable author alive." Since then, Nabokov has passed on. But his genius is so unbound by mere chronology that the judgment will stand.

C.F.

123

GEORGE ORWELL

1903–1950

Animal Farm, Nineteen Eighty-Four, Burmese Days

Eric Blair (George Orwell is a pen name) attended Eton, passed up university, and in 1922 shipped out to Burma where for a few years he served in the Burma Imperial Police. The values of the British Establishment did not take; indeed he spent the rest of his life repudiating them. Returning to England, he immersed himself in the culture of the poor, calling himself an anarchist, later a socialist. Unlike many British intellectuals of his time, Orwell was never seduced by Communism. The Spanish Civil War, in which he was wounded while fighting on the Republican side, intensified his distrust of all totalitarian doctrines. Back in England he engaged in journalism and book writing, gradually working out for himself a libertarian-socialist political stance quite at variance with doctrinaire Labour Party socialism.

Animal Farm made Orwell famous. Like parts of *Gulliver's Travels* [52] it is a sophisticated adaptation of a simple and ancient literary form, the animal fable. Just as *Candide* [53] ranks as the classic satire on Leibnizian optimism, so *Animal Farm* has become the classic satire on Soviet Communism, and its pertinence is unchanged by the breakup of the Soviet Empire. Its lively movement, directness, and wit recall some of Voltaire's outstanding qualities.

The two pigs Napoleon and Snowball may make us think of Stalin and Trotsky, but Orwell is not really playing *roman á clef* games. He is questioning the whole notion of the ordered state, perhaps questioning the value of any revolution that sets the ordered state as its goal. Funny as *Animal Farm* often is, it is also full of dismaying insights into the venality and hypocrisy of all power-obsessed natures. One of these insights has entered the language: All animals are equal, but some animals are more equal than others.

In an article headed "Why I Write" Orwell made his purpose clear: "*Animal Farm* was the first book in which I tried, with full consciousness of what I was doing, to fuse political purpose and artistic purpose into one whole."

Nineteen Eighty-Four is not only his finest work but one of the most influential books of our time. You might want to compare it with *Brave New World* [117] to feel how much blacker the world became during the seventeen years, 1932 to 1949, separating these two exercises in dystopian thought.

To avoid despair we must interpret *Nineteen Eighty-Four* as warning rather than prophecy. We are still some distance away from the picture of the future imagined by O'Brien, the book's most important character: "Imagine a boot stamping on a human face—forever." But Stalin's ruthlessness and the Nazi mechanized techniques of mass torture and murder, not to mention the Cambodian, Iranian, and other horrors, have to some degree changed *Nineteen Eighty-Four* from a cautionary tale to a bleak commentary on our era. Newspeak, the art of the Big Lie, may have been developed by the Russians and the Germans, but it has been adopted by many quick-study leaders of the Free World. To Huxley's vision of a dehumanized future Orwell adds new dimensions of terror and torture; and of course terror and torture are now prominent features of our world's political landscape.

As a novel *Nineteen Eighty-Four* hardly ranks with the greats. Yet some of its scenes—for example, the keystone Smith–O'Brien dialogue—are almost as telling as similar ones in Dostoyevsky [87]. The episode in which Winston Smith actually does begin to believe that 2 + 2 = 5 is a remarkable translation into imaginative terms of the terrifying power of propaganda backed by force.

Burmese Days is considered by many to be the most devastating fictional account we have of the evils of colonialism.

In addition to the three recommended books, you will find some of Orwell's essays worth reading. One realizes, viewing his work as a whole, that the style is truly the man. It is plain, honest, without a hint of striving for effect. Now that we can survey his whole career, Orwell himself seems an admirable example of the nonconformist temperament at its best, integrated and unfoolable.

More than that of any other writer of his generation, his reputation has steadily risen since his death. It is often said that the engaged writer must pay for his engagement by becoming outmoded. In Orwell's case this does not appear to be true.

C.F.

124
R.K. NARAYAN
1906–

The English Teacher, The Vendor of Sweets

It is easy to overlook the fact that India is one of the world's largest and most important English-speaking countries; after all, it is famous for its numerous mutually unintelligible languages, and English is not native to the subcontinent. But a consequence of three centuries of British commercial domination and colonial rule was to create an English-speaking Indian elite, educated in English-style schools and conditioned to think of England as, in some sense, their true mother country. Cultural and political loyalties have changed in postindependence India, of course, but English lives on—in part because it provides a prestigious and culturally neutral way of bridging the country's inherent linguistic chasms as a second language for everyone. (Most Tamil-speakers, for example, would rather converse with a Hindi-speaker in English than in Hindi.)

A further consequence is that the family tree of English literature has grown a branch of works written in India in the English language. Indian English is as distinctive a dialect as American, or Australian, or West Indian; and Indian English literature has tended to take advantage of the distinctiveness of its linguistic voice to explore questions of identity and interculturality. Of the older generation of Indian English novelists, the grandest old man is R.K. Narayan, a patriarch who has paved the way for a vocal and highly talented younger generation of writers like Vikram Seth and Bharati Mukerjee.

Rasipuram Krishnaswami Narayan was born in Madras, the lively and cosmopolitan capital of the Indian state of Tamil Nadu, and received a thoroughly bicultural education in Tamil and English literature. He worked briefly as a teacher but always saw himself as destined to be a writer. In his first novel, *Swami and Friends*, published in 1935, he created the fictional milieu that was to sustain his literary career for the next sixty years.

Swami and Friends, like virtually all of Narayan's novels and stories, is set in the imaginary small south Indian city of Malgudi, which has taken on, in the minds of Narayan's readers, a reality of its own. Narayan is as identified with Malgudi as Faulkner [118] is with his fictional Yoknapatawpha County; but Narayan's imaginary landscape is altogether a more genial and pleasant place than Faulkner's—a closer parallel might be with Lake Wobegone in Garrison Keillor's *Prairie Home Companion* radio programs, though with much greater subtlety and depth.

Narayan's method, in his numerous Malgudi novels and stories, is to look with a gently ironic eye at one or another of his fictional town's citizens, someone who finds himself in a position of difficulty and who needs to muddle through with a little help from his friends. We see grand schemes yielding less than grand results through ineptitude and sloth; personal preferences thwarted by the overwhelming weight of family pressures; pride and pomposity punctured by demotic wit and passive resistance to anything that smacks of grandiosity. Nothing in Malgudi turns out quite as well as people would want it to, but nothing ever turns out too badly either.

Narayan's work has been criticized as being too slight, or for lacking gravity and seriousness. Certainly one cannot find in it many of the hallmarks of modernist fiction; one looks in vain in his books for alienation, or anomie, or dysfunctional sexuality, or doomed antiheroes. Narayan's fiction is gentle, good-natured, subtle, ironic, simple, and graceful; he is not uncritical of his subjects, but his criticism is delivered with a smile, not with a bludgeon. He is perhaps not profound; he is merely delightful.

Of Narayan's many novels, my personal favorites are *The English Teacher* and *The Vendor of Sweets*; you might want to start with those, and I suspect you will go on to read many others. Followers of this Plan will also be interested in Narayan's very good prose abridged versions of the *Ramayana* [15] and the *Mahabharata* [16].

J.S.M.

125
SAMUEL BECKETT
1906–1989

Waiting for Godot, Endgame, Krapp's Last Tape

In *Waiting for Godot* Estragon remarks to his pal Vladimir, "We always find something, eh Didi, to give us the impression we exist?" Perhaps Beckett's entire lifework is the "something" designed to give his audience and himself the impression that they exist. However absurd or painful life may be, art somehow ratifies or vindicates it. Of his own motivation he has said, "With nothing to express, no desire to express, but with the artist's need to express."

What kind of art is Beckett's? It completely ignores the traditional conventions of the stage, among them clarity. Beckett's most famous play is *Waiting for Godot.* Asked who Godot was, Beckett replied, "If I knew, I would have said so in the play." As for form, he once wrote to his younger disciple Harold Pinter, "If you insist on finding form [for my plays] I'll describe it for you. I was in hospital once. There was a man in another ward, dying of throat cancer. In the silences I could hear his screams continually. That's the only kind of form my work has." Ever since the Greeks, physical or mental action, adding up to some kind of statement or resolution of conflict, has been a staple of drama. But early in *Godot* we have:

ESTRAGON *(giving up again):* Nothing to be done.

and the curtain lines are:

VLADIMIR: Well, shall we go?
ESTRAGON: Yes, let's go.
They do not move.

Shakespeare [39] has accustomed us to a mixture of humor and tragedy in the same play, but the dominant tone is always clear. Beckett, however, in accord with absurdist doctrine, deliberately carries this confusion of genres to almost frightening extremes. Once, directing the Berlin production of *Endgame,* he remarked that the most important line in the play was:

NELL: Nothing is funnier than unhappiness, I grant you that.

Beckett has removed himself completely from Aristotle's mimetic theory of drama [13]. He throws out all the play's traditional furnishings, somewhat as Virginia Woolf [111] has done for the novel and minimalist painters for art. One playlet *(Come and Go)* contains only 121 words. Another, *Breath*, lasts thirty seconds.

Beckett's triumphs as a dramatist may make us forget that he is also a novelist of extraordinary originality. Among his fictions are *Watt* and the trilogy composed of *Molloy*, *Malone Dies*, and *The Unnameable*.

Interpretations of Beckett have been as endless as they are ingenious, but each reader or viewer must make up his or her own mind. Perhaps mind is the wrong word, because the meaning is the play itself, to be felt rather than understood, as with music. Beckett is trying to make us share his agonized inability to answer the two darkest questions: Who are we? Why are we? All his work is an elaboration, sometimes bleak, sometimes comic, of Hamm's statement (in *Endgame*): "You're on earth, there's no cure for that!"

So far more than twenty-five volumes of Beckett have been published, certainly the most comprehensive treatment in all literature of the theme of negation. Yet he is no cynic—indeed he is deeply moved by human misery, and his own life (he performed nobly during the French Resistance) evinces great purity of character. His *nada*, unlike Hemingway's [119], is not a response to the dislocation of our time but is deeply metaphysical, a vision of life as eternally the same and eternally incomprehensible. It is interesting that a dramatist so obscure, so nightmarish, so uncompromising, and so oblivious to what we normally expect from drama should have met with worldwide acclaim. However strange his way of saying it, he must be saying something to us.

The last words of *The Unnameable* are "I can't go on, I'll go on." Of that, make what you will.

C.F.

126
W.H. AUDEN
1907–1973

Collected Poems

It is a minor paradox that in our hypertechnological era poetry should be alive and well. Poets proliferate; more to the point, many are producing work of high quality. Nor can their influence be gauged by sales figures alone. Their work seems, rather, to be absorbed somehow into the mental climate of intelligent men and women who are not necessarily assiduous poetry readers.

In our country Yeats [103] and Eliot [116] would probably figure as the two most pervasively influential English-language poets. To them I would add a third: W.H. Auden. For me and many others his is the most eloquent and representative poetic voice of what he dubbed the "Age of Anxiety." The tonality of that age was announced by Eliot's *The Waste Land* and by Yeats's "Things fall apart; the centre cannot hold." This preoccupation with our dysfunctional society Auden developed in his long and short poems, in his plays (several written in collaboration with Christopher Isherwood), and in his somewhat undervalued critical essays.

There are ways in which Auden reminds one of Goethe [62]. Like Goethe he was no garret-poet, but led a very active life, traveling extensively, constantly in touch with the extraliterary world, constantly metamorphosing in the Goethean style. A quester like Goethe, he passed from youthful rebellion against the tradition in which he had been reared to an uneasy leftism to a rediscovered Anglo-Catholicism. One wonders whether, had he lived another fifty years, he would have remained an Anglo-Catholic. Like Goethe he was a man in motion, the carrier of possibility.

Born a British subject, Auden became an American citizen in 1946, and so his work achieved a certain amplitude by drawing from two major historical traditions. The name Audun (so spelled) appears in Icelandic sagas, and Auden was much influenced, particularly in the actual techniques of his verse, by the great body of poetry of the far North.

Auden's father was a distinguished physician, and the son was brought up in an atmosphere of scientific inquiry and discussion. At one time in his undergraduate years he planned to become a biologist, and his work is filled with metaphors and allusions drawn from the earth sciences and the revolution in physics, as well as from applied sciences such as metallurgy, mining, and railroad-building. Here, too, he reflects the drift of our time, as does his involvement with Freudian [98] and Jungian thought, metaphysics, ethics and politics. He was master of a treasury of language, often extending to a difficult-to-follow private symbolism. But even his more incomprehensible phrases have magic.

Auden was homosexual, but this does not seem to have affected his openness to the erotic drives that sway all men and women. A large fraction of his poetry deals with love—usually frustrated, incomplete, longed-for, distrusted love. But the poetry is simply good love poetry.

Perhaps the wittiest English poet since Donne [40], Auden erases the line between light and serious verse. Like Eliot and the later Yeats, he throws away the romantic lexicon of the great nineteenth-century English poets. Into his intricate metaphysical verse he cunningly introduces the vernacular and creates the unique Auden poetic sentence. Thus his work is full of linguistic surprises, often turning on near-rhymes or odd alliterations. A technical experimenter, he invented new forms, along with ringing the changes on all the older forms, including those to be found in Anglo-Saxon and Icelandic poetry. He often felt that his critics had not sufficiently appreciated his capacities as a metrist.

Auden is not an "easy" poet, and his density tends to increase in his later poems. He cannot be read straight through. Try the shorter poems first, including such classics as

"In Memory of W.B. Yeats," and "In Memory of Sigmund Freud." Then make your way as best you can. Five years from now, come back to him—and you may find that somehow he has become part of you. Great poets have a way of creating and educating their own audiences.

No brief quotation can even suggest the range of Auden's emotional world, but here are three Auden quatrains, written in wartime, which reveal something of his sense of the poet's role in "the nightmare of the dark":

Follow, poet, follow right
To the bottom of the night,
With your unconstraining voice
Still persuade us to rejoice;

With the farming of a verse
Make a vineyard of the curse,
Sing of human unsuccess
In a rapture of distress;

In the deserts of the heart
Let the healing fountain start,
In the prison of his days
Teach the free man how to praise.

C.F.

127
ALBERT CAMUS
1913–1960

The Plague, The Stranger

Like many of his generation, Camus was much preoccupied by man's incomprehensible situation within a seemingly absurd universe. Appropriately enough, he was killed at the age of forty-six in an automobile accident. For the world of the mind, though perhaps not for the absurdist, this was a major tragedy. With unmatched eloquence and moral seriousness Camus spoke for his disillusioned postwar contemporaries. Because his underlying theme was the permanent human condition, he speaks to us today.

Camus was born in Algeria of impoverished parents, and the countryside and cityscapes of that sun-dried land are reflected with joyful intensity in many of his narratives. From the start he was a brilliant student, specializing in philosophy. Surviving a brief infection of Marxism, he retained for the rest of his life a sense of community with the poor and oppressed. As a journalist he was among the first to document the injustices from which the Algerians suffered and which were to spark the independence movement. During the German occupation of France and for part of the post-Liberation period he edited the Resistance paper *Combat*. During the Forties and Fifties he achieved his major work. In 1957 it was recognized by the award of the Nobel Prize. He was only forty-four. Three years later he was dead.

Camus is distinguished as journalist, polemicist, memoirist, and philosopher. He also contributed, as playwright and worker in the theater, to the tropical growth in the Forties of the theater of the absurd. But his most enduring work lies in his handful of novels and especially in his major effort, *The Plague*. He once wrote: "We only think in images. If you want to be a philosopher, write novels." For him this was true; his novels (as also his plays) dramatize involved moral and metaphysical problems.

While it is useful to have some acquaintance with his specifically politico-philosophical works, such as *The Myth of Sisyphus* and *The Rebel*, one can, I think, effect entrance into Camus's beautiful mind through a reading of his short novel *The Stranger* and his full-length effort *The Plague*. *The Stranger*, concerned with an act of seemingly gratuitous murder, is one of many studies of the rootless nonconformist sensibility so symptomatic of our time. The gesture of violence that delivers the hero up to society's power to punish also measures the gap separating him from the values that society takes for granted, but which are open to troubling questions. In an absurd universe, how may evil and good be distinguished or perhaps even identified?

His masterpiece, *The Plague,* may be interpreted (but there is no single interpretation) as Camus's resolution of the problem. In his Preface to *The Myth of Sisyphus* he writes: "Even within the limits of nihilism it is possible to find the means to proceed beyond nihilism." Just because the universe seems absurd man must rebel against that very absurdity, guiding his actions by the twin lights of truth and justice. It is precisely in a world of apparently meaningless disaster that some develop, almost unconsciously, the power to recognize and act by truth, justice, and compassion.

This sounds very moralistic and old-fashioned, does it not? But *The Plague,* you will find, is neither one nor the other. Sometime in the Forties, Camus imagines, bubonic plague strikes the Algerian city of Oran. Quietly, coolly, Camus records in detail the differing ways in which men, women, and children react to agony, isolation, and death. Our eyes are never allowed to wander from a definite city, identifiable people, specific fates, and the particular character of the pestilence. And yet, as we read, we become deeply aware that this study of the effects of plague is also a study of the isolated condition of man in an uncaring universe and his attempts to transcend that condition. Camus prefaces his novel with a quotation from Defoe [51]: "It is as reasonable to represent one kind of imprisonment by another, as it is to represent anything that really exists by that which exists not." At no time does Camus offer us a parable or allegory. The narrative is rigorously realistic. Yet reading it, we feel that, as Dorothy Canfield wrote in her review of *The Plague,* it "casts a light on all catastrophes which shut men and women up in misery together." Life itself is such a catastrophe, Camus seems to be saying. But the catastrophe is not total; such men as Dr. Rieux and Tarrou, such women as Dr. Rieux's mother, can compel, by the force of their moral character, community to emerge from isolation and a qualified freedom from human bondage.

C.F.

128
SAUL BELLOW
1915–

The Adventures of Augie March, Herzog, Humboldt's Gift

Saul Bellow may be the most intelligent imaginative writer now at work in our country. He also seems to me to exemplify beautifully the Western cultural tradition as a whole. The moral dilemmas at the heart of his fiction are not constructs; they evolve from the very nature of his characters. He is penetrating rather than merely observant, wise rather than merely shrewd. A noble word currently derided in some quarters applies to him. He is a humanist.

Bellow was born in Lachine, Quebec, of Canadian-Jewish parents but has lived most of his life in Chicago, generally the setting of his fiction. He received an excellent college and university education, has taught at Princeton, Bard, and the University of Minnesota, and is, I believe, still connected with the University of Chicago. He is not ashamed of being an intellectual or of presenting in his work evolved rather than semi-barbarian minds.

Many of his characters are Jewish, but he hardly belongs to any ethnic school. While his creations are pure urban-American, his general temper often suggests the mainstream of European fiction. Perhaps his harmonious fusion of these traditions influenced the Nobel Committee when they conferred on him the Prize in literature for 1976.

Though any of his books will reward you, I have recommended three. *The Adventures of Augie March* (1953) is a modern picaresque with scenes laid in Chicago, Mexico, and Paris. The form is well suited to Bellow's sense of the free flow of big-city life. In it he exhibits masterfully a style peculiarly his own. The street vernacular of the period merges with more classical and elegant uses of the language. Two of his outstanding qualities—energy and a sense of comedy—here assert themselves as, under great control, they will in all of his work to follow.

Most of his major characters have trouble with women, as is the case with Charlie Citrine, the writer whose memories generate the structure of *Humboldt's Gift* (1975). The title derives from Citrine's friend Von Humboldt Fleischer whose sad life is said to be based on that of Delmore Schwartz, a remarkable poet and critic who died in sordid circumstances in 1966.

Many readers and critics feel that Bellow's finest work is *Herzog* (1964), perfect in its fugal form, impressive in its insight into our troubled time, and enormously skillful in the portrayal of a suffering human being whose irony is continually exercised on himself and the American scene against which he is limned. Moses Herzog is a forty-seven-year-old intellectual, a womanizer without being a libertine. He spends about a week in a crazy zigzag flight, searching for self-understanding, stability, comprehension of his country and his period. Part of the time is occupied in writing letters (unmailed) to those who have figured in his life, as well as to Adlai Stevenson, Eisenhower, and the eminent dead. He recollects his miserable childhood ("a great schooling in grief"); tries to connect his surplus store of book learning with the baffling requirements of real life; meditates on history; passes from "the dream of existence" to "the dream of intellect." He achieves almost archetypal dimensions, doing for the American intellectual what Babbitt did for the American businessman. Like many of Bellow's characters, he is an emotionally displaced person, but even those readers who consider themselves well adjusted will recognize in the comic-pathetic-heroic Herzog not a stranger but a part of their very selves.

"The soul requires intensity," thinks Herzog. We smile, but we cannot laugh off the sentence. It suggests what is perhaps Bellow's major distinction: the high charge of feeling and thought that vibrates in all his work but most notably in this novel. At the center of his preoccupations lies a concern, often tinged with irony, with the impingement of the long humanist tradition on a "posthistorical" culture.

C.F.

129
ALEKSANDER ISAYEVICH
SOLZHENITSYN
1918–

The First Circle, Cancer Ward

If we exclude Nabokov [122], who was at least fractionally an American novelist, Solzhenitsyn emerges as the greatest modern Russian writer. This is not in itself high praise: Soviet authors, though doubtless excellent employees, have not been greatly esteemed by the rest of the world. But Solzhenitsyn is major, even when compared with the towering Russians we have already met: Gogol [74], Turgenev [81], Dostoyevsky [87], Tolstoy [88], Chekhov [101]. He ranks not too far below them, both as an artist and as a human being passionately concerned with the welfare of Russia and with the idea of freedom—though doubtless he attaches to this shapeless concept meanings not entirely identical with our own.

Descended from an intellectual Cossack family, Solzhenitsyn was educated as a mathematician, fought bravely in World War II, was arrested in 1945 for a letter criticizing Stalin ("the man with the mustache"), was imprisoned for eight years, placed in a detention camp for another three years, began to write after his "rehabilitation," and electrified thinking Russia when in 1962 Khrushchev permitted him to publish *One Day in the Life of Ivan Denisovich*, a labor-camp novel that dared to tell the truth.

In 1963 he ran into trouble with the bureaucracy. In 1970 he won the Nobel Prize, but was not allowed to go to Stockholm to receive it. In 1973 he publicly indicted the Soviet system, was denounced, and left for the West. At this writing he has returned to Russia.

He has made himself the voice, heard worldwide, of the Russian conscience, as Dickens [77] and Zola were for their countries. His notion of democracy, though it breaks absolutely with Soviet totalitarianism, is infused with an old-Russian mysticism and theocracy that would perhaps bewilder Jefferson [60], Lincoln, and the ordinary American citizen. But of his courage and high moral character there can be no question. Whatever his final place in the hierarchy of literature, he is a great man.

I suggest that you try his two finest novels, *The First Circle* and *Cancer Ward*.

The First Circle narrates four days in the life of a mathematician (clearly a self-portrait) who is enclosed in a scientific institution outside Moscow, along with others who have committed "crimes against the state." What is described is a whole world, certainly the whole world of Soviet Russia, for the institution is a microcosm of Russian life and characters.

Equally powerful is *Cancer Ward*. Solzhenitsyn himself was treated for cancer, so far successfully, in the mid–Fifties. In this beautiful and by no means morbid study he achieves for Russian literature—though on a lower level—something like what Mann with his *Magic Mountain* [107] did for German literature. *Cancer Ward*, like all his work, is really about a prison, all Russia being so conceived. "A man sprouts a tumor and dies—how then can a country live that has sprouted camp and exile?" For all its external atmosphere of the clinic, *Cancer Ward* is basically a celebration of human life, as is Camus's *The Plague* [127].

Solzhenitsyn requires close attention. He lacks elegance, mastery of form, and his humor may seem to us flavorless. But he has enormous drive, compassion, and the capacity to create hundreds of characters. The poet Yevtushenko has dared to call him "our only living Russian classic." That would appear to be the case.

C.F.

130
THOMAS KUHN
1922–1996

The Structure of Scientific Revolutions

"Paradigm" was an unusual, even an abstruse, word in the English lexicon back in the days before anyone had ever heard of Thomas Kuhn; he put the word into our vocabulary. If you have ever described something as representing a "paradigm shift," you were quoting *The Structure of Scientific Revolutions*, whether you knew it or not. And although by the end of his life Kuhn professed himself to be heartily sick of hearing the word, his deployment of the concept of a paradigm in the history of science revolutionized the way we think about science in our own time.

Kuhn was trained as a physicist, but found his true vocation as a historian and philosopher of science, fields that he taught at Princeton, and later at M.I.T., for most of his career. The first edition of *The Structure of Scientific Revolutions* appeared in 1962, and a revised edition in 1970; it went on to become, as very few serious scientific books have done, a genuine bestseller. In a modest and low-key style, Kuhn argued in that book that our view of what science is and how it works was based on deeply flawed assumptions.

The pre-Kuhn picture of scientists at work was highly idealized: Scientists were men of pure and lofty minds, believing nothing that could not be proved by the scientific method, devising experiments designed to conjure up new knowledge by a rigorous process of hypothesis formation, experimentation, and proof. Kuhn's genius lay in an ability to look at the historical record and see how things really worked; what he told us is that science doesn't work as we were taught to believe.

Instead, Kuhn said (and like many good ideas it seemed obvious after he said it), scientists are men (usually men, at least in the past) of their times, sharing a world view with the majority of their fellow citizens, and differing from them primarily in having access to a more refined and technical understanding of that world view's implications, and by knowing more about how to expand the state of their knowledge. But their work is not done on a blank slate, but on the basis of a paradigm: a set of assumptions about how the world works. Gradually, as knowledge accumulates through the work of scientists, philosophers, and others, anomalies arise to disturb the seemingly smooth explanatory power of the paradigm, and questions arise as to its validity. When a sufficient number of anomalies accumulate, the paradigm loses its claim on peoples' minds, and a new one forms to take its place. This model explains, for example, how the Aristotelian-Ptolemaic model of the universe endured for almost a century after Copernicus published his first hypothetical challenge to it; only with the work of Galileo [42] and Newton did the old paradigm collapse in the face of insupportable contradictions that they pointed out.

Kuhn showed that science is neither value-free nor immune to the cultural context in which scientific investigation takes place. His work has been used in recent years by some radical critics of science to argue that science is incapable of discovering truth in any objective sense, and that all scientific results are merely expressions of cultural assumptions. Kuhn never said that, however, and he rejected the assertions of those who tried to use his theoretical work in that way. He was convinced, as any physicist would be, that science can and does discover truth; but he argued that within a given paradigm some truths cannot be discovered (which is why there will always be paradigm shifts). The question of the reliability of science has been central to the so-called culture wars of our time.

The Structure of Scientific Revolutions is a serious book, but there is nothing in it to deter a general reader who brings to it a willingness to think seriously. It is an eye-opening study of how we, as a civilization, have come to know what we know about the universe, and of the factors that will condition the expansion of our knowledge in the future.

J.S.M.

131
MISHIMA YUKIO
1925–1970

Confessions of a Mask, The Temple of the Golden Pavilion

Although both Tanizaki [114] and Kawabata [120] published extensively after World War II, in effect Mishima was Japan's first true postwar writer. Excused from military service during the war on medical grounds (a source of shame that plagued him throughout his life), he burst upon the postwar literary scene in 1949 with the publication of *Confessions of a Mask*.

Confessions is a highly autobiographical work about a young man growing up as a homosexual, and the "mask" he needs to don to protect himself from social scorn. Mishima's own mask was that of hypermasculinity; he became a bodybuilder obsessed with sculpting himself into a form of perfect beauty, a latter-day samurai obsessed with a largely made-up version of the warrior's cult of the sword, and an actor whose roles were virtual parodies of noble manhood. At the same time he was a sadomasochist fascinated by suicide and self-sacrifice; it seems likely that his bodybuilding was related to a desire to create himself as a perfect sacrificial victim, and to prepare his body to be a beautiful corpse. He liked to pose for homoerotic-masochistic photographs in such roles as a dead shipwrecked sailor washed up on the rocks, as St. Sebastian riddled with arrows, and as a samurai committing *seppuku* (ritual suicide).

But for what cause was he to sacrifice himself? Here again one finds contradictions. Mishima was in some respects a playboy and a materialist; he lived in a luxurious Western-style house, dressed in Western clothing, and had cosmopolitan interests. At the same time he became increasingly devoted to a cult (of his own devising) dedicated to restoring Japan's samurai spirit, expressed as reverence for the emperor. He recruited a private army, the Shield Society, of handsome young men, and drilled his troops both in his ideology and in traditional martial arts. On November 25, 1970, he led some of his followers onto a base of Japan's National Self-Defense Force and addressed the soldiers, calling upon them to join him in an uprising to restore the emperor to power. His speech was met with derision, whereupon he drew a sword, slit open his abdomen in ritual fashion, and was decapitated by his chief lieutenant: the ultimate acting-out of fantasies that had driven his intensely troubled but also brilliantly creative life.

Mishima was regarded as a literary genius even by the great majority of Japanese who thought that his political beliefs were loony. His personal obsessions inform his writing to such an extent that his work really does not resemble anyone else's very closely, except insofar as a confessional attitude is one common aspect of modernism. His work was highly regarded by Kawabata, who befriended his much younger fellow writer and championed his career. The work of contemporary Japanese writers like Oe Kenzaburo and Murakami Haruki has clearly been influenced by Mishima's style.

I recommend that you read *Confessions of a Mask*, and also *The Temple of the Golden Pavilion*, a novel based on real events, in which a young monk, deranged by the American occupation of Japan, burns down a famous old temple to prevent it from falling into foreign hands. If you find yourself drawn into Mishima's weirdly brilliant mind, you might also want to try *The Sailor Who Fell from Grace with the Sea* and his four-volume masterpiece and final testament, *The Sea of Fertility*.

J.S.M.

132
GABRIEL GARCIA MARQUEZ
1928–

One Hundred Years of Solitude

Garcia Marquez and Borges [121] are usually considered the two world-famous Latin American writers of our time. The term *magic realism* is often applied to their work and to that of others of the same school, such as the Cuban Alejo Carpentier, the Mexican Carlos Fuentes, the Argentinian Julio Cortizar, and the Peruvian Mario Vargas Llosa. The rather tired critical cliché does suggest their slant on the world, which diverges sharply from the mainstream tradition of English and American fiction.

"Magic realism" was first used back in 1925 to describe a group of German painters who used precise literal techniques to image fantastic events flowering in the unconscious. These artists addressed the nonlogical element deeply buried in all of us; and so do the contemporary novelists of magic realism.

Garcia Marquez speaks somewhere of "the mistaken and absurd world of rational creatures." The phrase would seem perfectly acceptable to many South American and Central American writers. They have all been affected, to the point of obsession, by the disorderly, often nightmarish history of their native lands. Thus, though their magic realism was also influenced by French symbolism and surrealism (and in Garcia Marquez's case by Faulkner [118]), it developed as a special technology of the imagination, designed to cope with the abnormal experience of a whole people.

One Hundred Years of Solitude traces the rise, decline, and fall of Macondo, presumably the author's hometown of Aracataca, Colombia. The era is marked by civil strife, frightful violence, political corruption, and the abuse of power. Five—perhaps seven—generations of the Buendia family compose the materials with which the narrative is constructed. Over the years, first names (Aureliano, José Arcadio) recur, identities blur, family traits reassert themselves, making us feel that Macondo's life is cyclical, without forward movement, devoid of a goal. While the outside world of industry and progress at times touches them, essentially the Buendias remain immured in their sad and sometimes mad solitude.

Winner of the 1982 Nobel Prize in literature, Garcia Marquez has spent much of his life as a working journalist. Thus he has a keen nose for fact; much of *One Hundred Years* is realistic enough. But the story is also full of ghosts, visions, monsters, prescient dreams, happenings contrary to nature (such as mass insomnia), a man two hundred years old, another returned from the dead, others who levitate.

The book is a kind of allegory of Latin American history, as much hallucination as family chronicle. Macondo is "the city of mirrors (or mirages)." Past and present fuse. One historian of the Buendia family, the author tells us, "had not put events in the order of conventional time, but had concentrated a century of daily episodes in such a way that they co-existed in one instant." José Arcadio Buendia, we learn, "was the only one who had enough lucidity to sense the truth of the fact that time also stumbled and had accidents and could therefore splinter and leave an eternalized fragment in a room."

In its energy, its humor (for it has a kind of grim humor), its conscious exaggeration, its distortions of language, and its drive to transform human experience into myth, *One Hundred Years* recalls *Gargantua and Pantagruel* [35] as much as any title suggested in this volume.

One is tempted to say that *One Hundred Years* has a certain claim to be called the Great Latin American Novel. At any rate, for all its concentration on the sufferings, madnesses, delusions, incestuous loves, and outsize passions of a single family, it seems to evoke the tragic real life and dream life of a whole continent.

C.F.

133
CHINUA ACHEBE
1930–

Things Fall Apart

Just as the inclusion of Garcia Marquez [132] in earlier editions of the Lifetime Reading Plan acknowledged the growing importance of Latin American writers in modern world literature, so also it is fitting that the final work in the New Lifetime Reading Plan be the masterpiece of Chinua Achebe, in recognition not only that *Things Fall Apart* has already entered the worldwide modern canon, but that henceforth African literature will claim its due as part of the literary heritage of readers everywhere. Achebe in this sense also stands here as a surrogate for Senghor, Soyinka (for both of whom see Going Further, below), Diop, and many other African writers whose works transcend merely regional significance.

Chinua Achebe was born and educated in Nigeria, a member of that country's Ibo ethnic group. After graduation from University College, Ibadan, he pursued a career in the public radio corporation, but resigned abruptly in 1966 during the turmoil surrounding the attempted secession from Nigeria of the Ibo ethnic province of Biafra. Thereafter he has spent much of his time abroad, primarily in the United States, where he now lives and pursues a career as a college professor.

Although Achebe has been a prolific writer of novels, short stories, plays, and other works, his international reputation rests overwhelmingly on his first novel, *Things Fall Apart*, published in 1958. Achebe himself was raised in a Nigerian village in the midst of a difficult transition from traditional society to life under British missionary and colonial government influence. His novel, drawn from his childhood experiences, tells the story of a traditional village "big man" whose life is destroyed by changes he can neither understand nor halt.

Okonkwo is a man of wealth and power in the village of

Umuofia. His gardens yield heavy crops of yams, his compound is large and comfortable, his wives desirable and his children satisfactory; most importantly he enjoys the respect of his fellow villagers, and his words are listened to as those of a man to be reckoned with. He is not immune to difficulties and troubles; when, for example, he accidentally kills a fellow clansman, he must endure the obligatory seven years' exile in his mother's native village. But he understands troubles in a traditional context, and knows how to cope with them. What is completely beyond his grasp is the appeal of the newly built missionary church, which seduces even some of his clansmen with its bizarre new doctrines, and the authority of the British District Commissioner and his hated retinue of constables recruited from outside the village. What is tragic about Okonkwo's downfall in the face of these new circumstances is that, in terms of the traditional world that he understands, he makes all of the right moves, says the right things, asserts his power in strategically effective ways; the only problem is that things have changed, things have in fact fallen apart, and every move he makes to assert his authority makes his downfall more certain.

Achebe, in other words, has created a figure who would be recognized by Sophocles [6] or by Shakespeare [39], an African Oedipus or Lear brought down not only by fate but by his own stubborn pursuit of inappropriate goals and his blindness to circumstances. This, I think, is what accounts for the extraordinary appeal of *Things Fall Apart*, and why it has become established as a modern classic in dozens of translated versions around the world.

J.S.M.

GOING FURTHER

Below we list, with brief comments, one hundred twentieth-century authors—primarily novelists, but also poets, playwrights, and writers of nonfiction—whose works we think will be of interest to readers of *The New Lifetime Reading Plan*. Like any such list, this one is subjective, idiosyncratic, and open to challenge. We expect that both critics and lay readers will quarrel with our selections. (Where is C. S. Lewis? Where is Lawrence Durrell? The list could be expanded indefinitely.) So be it: Readers should feel free to augment our suggestions as they wish.

The authors discussed below fall into at least three subgroups. First are acknowledged modern masters: Musil, Rilke, Greene, and others. Second are writers whom we believe are of the first rank but who so far have not had the widespread recognition they deserve; among these would be Pym, Lodge, and Davies. Third, and perhaps most controversially, are writers of the post-war period whose books—for many of them, only one key book—helped to define the literary and intellectual terrain of our time; among them are Kerouac, Salinger, and Irving. There is no way to know how many of these authors will still be read in fifty or one hundred years; "some, but not all," is the best one can do. Meanwhile we regard them as "temporary classics," a deliberate oxymoron intended to emphasize that these books have been important in our own time, if not forever.

The authors are listed below in alphabetical order; we have no recommendations for the order in which they should be read. For most we mention only a book or two; some of these writers, though, have been very prolific, and readers who enjoy their work will want to explore it further.

J.S.M.

1   **RICHARD ADAMS** (1920–) served with the British armed forces in
World War II, took a degree at Oxford, and became a civil servant,
writing children's books on the side. He won widespread notice with
Watership Down (1972), written as a children's book but widely
read by adults as well. It is a gripping and beautifully written allegorical tale of rabbits driven from their native warren and forced to
find a new home elsewhere; it deserves its enduring popularity. Try
also his *The Girl in a Swing* (1980), a beautiful and shocking love
story written for a decidedly adult audience.

2   **KINGSLEY AMIS** (1922–1995) is regarded as one of the foremost of
the "Angry Young Men," iconoclastic British writers of the post-
WWII period (he denied the affiliation). He cultivated a supercil-
ious and curmudgeonly persona that resonates strongly in the general tenor of his books. *Lucky Jim*, his best-known novel, portrays
the unruly life of a loutish but engaging provincial professor; it is a
savagely funny book.

3   **SHERWOOD ANDERSON** (1876–1941) was a prolific and influential
writer of novels and short stories, but he is deservedly best known
for his first novel, *Winesburg, Ohio* (1919). It is a loosely linked
series of stories and sketches about the emotionally shrunken lives
of the citizens of a small Ohio town, seen through the eyes of a brilliantly realized narrator persona, a callow local newspaperman.

4   **MARGARET ATWOOD** (1939–) shares with Robertson Davies the
reputation of being modern Canada's foremost writer. An articulate
and persuasive feminist, she is a prolific and versatile writer, the
author of poetry, short stories, and essays as well as novels. Start by
reading *The Handmaid's Tale*, her best-known work; you will find
yourself wanting to devour the rest of her books as well.

5   **LOUIS AUCHINCLOSS** (1917–), like Edith Wharton a descendant of
the old New York WASP aristocracy, portrays the manners, customs,
and moral conflicts of his tribe with a deft pen and an insider's eye.
He is a lawyer, and the leading characters of many of his novels
inhabit the upper reaches of the legal and corporate worlds. Most
people regard *The Rector of Justin* (1964) as his finest novel; try also
his wonderfully focused short stories (*Collected Stories*, 1994).

6   **JAMES BALDWIN** (1924–1987) was torn between the legacy of a
Harlem childhood of poverty, racial oppression, and religious inspiration, and the reality of an adult life as a gay Black intellectual living in Greenwich Village and France. His novel *Giovanni's Room*
(1956) addresses the issues of exile and conflicted homosexuality; in
The Fire Next Time (1963) Baldwin produced a powerful meditation
on Black identity, the Civil Rights Movement, and the temptation of
Black separatism. Both the agony of his conflicted personality and
the power of his commitment to racial justice continue to resonate
in his work.

7   **JOHN BARTH** (1930–) was born and raised in the Tidewater country of Maryland, and his native region is in effect the principal character of all of his work. His very distinctive writing style is often quirkily humorous, erotically charged, and sardonic in tone. His best known work, *The Sot-weed Factor* (1960), is a burlesque "history" of the Chesapeake Bay region in colonial times; his beautifully realized short stories (*Tidewater Tales*, 1987, for example) tend to be more sober in tone.

8   **SIMONE DE BEAUVOIR** (1908–1986) met Jean-Paul Sartre in 1929, and the two soon became lifelong companions. Perhaps influenced in part by her own struggle for independence and autonomy in the face of Sartre's powerful and autocratic personality, de Beauvoir became an articulate and influential feminist thinker. *The Second Sex* is by far the most famous of her many books; in it she calls for an end to the patriarchal systems—and the feminine accommodations to them—that have kept women in a secondary and subservient position since time immemorial.

9   **PAUL BOWLES** (1910–) has expressed a wish to be remembered primarily as a composer, and his music is highly esteemed; still for the moment most people probably think of him first as a writer. Born in America, he spent much of his young adulthood in Europe and has lived mostly in Morocco for the past fifty years. He writes marvelously crafted travel essays and short stories; by far his best-known literary work is *The Sheltering Sky* (1948), a horrifying tale of an American couple traveling in Morocco who become caught in a web of fear and sexual obsession.

10   **FERNAND BRAUDEL** (1902–1985) was a leading member of the French *Annales* school of historians, the followers of which attempted to get beyond the mere events ("ephemera") of history to achieve an understanding of the "deep structure" of the past. Braudel's *The Mediterranean and the Mediterranean World in the Age of Philip II* (1945) perfectly exemplifies the *Annales* approach at its best, with the structure of history delineated through "thick description" of the past and through attention to such factors as geography, ecology, economics, and social and religious movements. The aims of these historians might sound ponderous, but in Braudel's hands the results are not; this is both an intellectually challenging and highly readable book.

11   **BERTHOLD BRECHT** (1898–1956) was a poet and playwright whose early work showed the influence of the German Expressionist movement of the 1920s. He became a Marxist and developed a theory of "epic theater," in which plays would be objectified by abandoning the illusion of realism (by such techniques as having the players directly address the audience). Of his many plays, try reading *Mother Courage*, *The Good Woman of Szechuan*, and *The Caucasian Chalk*

Circle; attend performances of, or listen to recordings of, his collaborations with composer Kurt Weill, *The Threepenny Opera* and *The Rise and Fall of the City of Mahagonny*.

12 **JOSEPH BRODSKY** (1940–1996), perhaps the greatest poet of postwar Russia, was scorned and persecuted in his native country. From his school years he never wanted to be anything but a poet; his refusal to contribute to socialist society in a more practical way led to his being considered a "social parasite," and to his being exiled from the Soviet Union in 1972. His poems have an apparently innate lyrical quality, and deal with transcendent issues of life and death with a graceful and undogmatic hand. Brodsky wrote little poetry in his mature years, concentrating instead on essays and criticism; he was awarded the Nobel Prize for literature in 1987. *So Forth* (1995) is a good collection of his poems.

13 **PEARL BUCK** (1892–1973) was born in America but spent much of her youth in China, where her parents were missionaries. Her novel *The Good Earth* (1931) made her famous; it distills her deep affection and respect for the Chinese people, and was influential in winning American popular support for China in the face of imperialist domination and Japanese aggression. Though its language now seems rather stilted and its values reflect missionary hopes more than Chinese realities, it remains worth reading both for its well-wrought plot and as an important document of its time.

14 **MIKHAIL BULGAKOV** (1891–1940) wrote many books but is truly famous for one, *The Master and Margarita* (1930s). The book was correctly perceived by the Russian authorities as a satire on life under Stalin and therefore banned. (It was finally published in heavily censored form in 1966, and in an unexpurgated edition in 1973.) It depicts the bizarre and often very funny relations between the Master (a writer), his mistress Margarita, and the Devil; the plot is intercut with scenes from the Master's novel set in Jerusalem in the time of Christ. It is an odd but brilliant and compelling book.

15 **ANTHONY BURGESS** (1917–1993) was a prolific and talented writer, but his reputation rests almost entirely on one novel, *A Clockwork Orange* (1962), and that in large part because of the impact of the powerful 1972 film version starring Malcolm McDowell. The mordant and darkly humorous dystopic world of Burgess's novel now looks, in retrospect, like a harbinger of the rebellious spirit of the Sixties; but the book retains its power both to shock and to please the reader.

16 **ITALO CALVINO** (1923–1985) is generally regarded as Italy's greatest modern writer of short stories and novels. His work is richly imaginative, and blurs the line between reality and fantasy; he was deeply interested in folk tales, which in turn profoundly influenced his own work. Representative of the best of his mature fiction is *If*

on a Winter's Night a Traveller (1979); it is confusing, nonlinear, nonsequential, often parodistic; a tale of a novel within the novel, interspersed with still other seemingly unrelated stories. It is not easy reading, but it is rewarding to read.

17 **TRUMAN CAPOTE** (1924–1984), novelist, short-story writer, social butterfly, a New Yorker who remained firmly rooted in his native South, was above all a writer, and more seriously dedicated to his craft than he sometimes let on. He found fame early with *Other Voices, Other Rooms* (1948), his semiautobiographical novel of a teenager in search of his identity, and enhanced his reputation with the novella *Breakfast at Tiffany's* (1958). His best book is *In Cold Blood* (1966) a "nonfiction novel" (a genre he claimed to have invented) about a brutal murder and the trial and execution of its perpetrators.

18 **RACHEL CARSON** (1907–1964). DDT seemed like a miracle when it was developed during World War II, and in some ways it was; certainly it saved the lives of thousands of American soldiers who would otherwise have died of malaria and other mosquito-borne diseases. But after the war DDT and other long-lasting pesticides began to be used in agriculture without restraint; and then the birds started to die. Rachel Carson—whose 1951 bestseller *The Sea Around Us* combined good scientific observation with a talent for poetic description—was the one who put the picture together; her book *Silent Spring* (1962) galvanized the nascent environmental movement and ultimately sparked an environmental revolution. The book itself is still a wonderful read, both as an indictment of human stupidity and greed, and as a principled call to action.

19 **WILLA CATHER** (1873–1947) lived most of her adult life in or near New York City, but used memories of her early years on the plains of Nebraska as the source of her literary inspiration. Her first popular success came with *My Antonia* (1918), which draws on her plains childhood in semiautobiographical fashion. In her later novels she explored the experiences of other early settlers in the Americas; two of the best of these are *Death Comes for the Archbishop* (1927) set in Spanish colonial New Mexico, and *Shadows on the Rock* (1931), set in French colonial Quebec.

20 **JOHN CHEEVER** (1912–1982) was as brilliant a master of the short-story genre as can be found in all of American literature. His most characteristic stories are set in the well-to-do suburbs and exurbs of the Northeast, and scrutinize, with a gimlet eye softened by irony and wry humor, the foibles of people who, away from the office, spend too much time at the country club, drink too much, and are too attracted to their neighbors' spouses. His crystalline prose exemplifies the old "*New Yorker* style" at its best. Feast on his *Collected Stories* (1978).

21 **ROBERTSON DAVIES** (1913–1995), even more than Margaret Atwood, seemed to personify twentieth-century Canadian fiction. Davies was a master storyteller, with such a sure grasp of humor, such control of language, and such a genius for plot that he was able to make ideas the real subjects of his novels without impeding their narrative drive at all. My favorites of his many novels are those of the Cornish Trilogy: *The Rebel Angels* (1981), *What's Bred in the Bone* (1985), and *The Lyre of Orpheus* (1988).

22 **E.L. DOCTOROW** (1931–) is a fluent and exceptionally clever storyteller whose novels characteristically are set in the American past and blend real events with fictional ones, made-up characters with historical figures. His best-known novel, *Ragtime* (1975), is a compelling story of crime, race, and aspirations at the start of the twentieth century.

23 **THEODORE DREISER** (1871–1945) was the leading American practitioner of the school of writing called "naturalism," which attempted to substitute an unflinching realism for the artificial proprieties of the Victorian novel. Dreiser's first novel, *Sister Carrie* (1900), tells the story of a young woman who successfully makes her way in the world as a "kept woman." It would have been considered scandalous had it been noticed at all; instead it was ignored by critics and the public alike. Only very much later was it recognized for the masterwork it is. Read also *An American Tragedy* (1925), Dreiser's most celebrated novel, a harrowing fictional account of a murder and its consequences.

24 **ALBERT EINSTEIN** (1879–1955). I would have liked to include Einstein's *The Meaning of Relativity* in *The New Lifetime Reading Plan* itself, but reluctantly concede that it would prove too heavily mathematical for most general readers. Still, it is worth trying for what you can get out of it—read past the equations, and don't let yourself be deterred by them. In his first American lectures (1921), Einstein presented a systematic explanation of his theory of relativity, one of the great intellectual achievements of our time. This book, based on those lectures but revised and expanded by Einstein himself several times over the years, repays multiple readings; more of the meaning will emerge each time.

25 **RALPH ELLISON** (1914–1994) published only one novel in his life, but *The Invisible Man* (1952) had a literary and social impact sufficient to guarantee him a lasting place in twentieth-century American letters. Ellison's nameless young Black protagonist is literally, to the world, invisible as a person; he is merely a black face. He uses his invisibility as a mask, observing the world that ignores him; but ultimately he must retreat entirely into a world of his own to preserve his sense of wholeness. Part allegory, part realism, this novel of the Black experience continues to resonate strongly today.

26 **F. Scott Fitzgerald** (1886–1940) came from the Midwest and attended college at Princeton, the formative experience of his life. There he found social success and a clear literary vocation that led in the 1920s to three of his most successful and enduring works: *This Side of Paradise* (1920), *Tender Is the Night* (1924), and *The Great Gatsby* (1925)—the latter perhaps the quintessential American short novel. His flame burned brightly, but not for long; by the 1930s his life had begun to be ruined by alcoholism, fecklessness, and a (realistic) sense that he would never again equal his early work.

27 **Ford Madox Ford** (1873–1939). Ford's greatest contribution to modern literature probably came from his tireless (and often unrequited) championing of other modern writers. As editor of the short-lived *Transatlantic Review* in the mid–twenties, for example, he published work by Hemingway, Joyce, Pound, Gertrude Stein, and others of their rank. His own work has gone through a long period of disesteem but may be poised for a critical re-evaluation. See for yourself. His best-known novel, and the best place to start reading his work, is *The Good Soldier* (1915).

28 **William Gaddis** (1922–) is a controversial figure in American literature, much admired by many other writers and perhaps the most influential little-known writer of our time. His works are long and knotty, filled with protracted sentences and a sometimes Joycean opacity of language (opacity, that is, that can become transparent upon repeated reading and reflection). He publishes infrequently; try his first two novels, *The Recognitions* (1955) and *J.R.* (1975), both of which dissect the evils and banalities of modern America.

29 **Federico García Lorca** (1898–1936) was the foremost Spanish poet of the early twentieth century; his verse, obsessed with violence and death, has lost none of the emotional power and technical brilliance that brought the poet fame during his own lifetime. An artist of formidable power and creative range, García Lorca was a dramatist as well as a poet, and was intensely interested in Spanish music—many of his poems are in the form of songs. He himself came to a tragically violent end when he was murdered by Nationalist troops during the Spanish Civil War. Of his *Collected Poems* (1991), be sure to read some of his "Gypsy Ballads," and his masterpiece, the "Lament for Ignacio Sánchez Mejías," mourning the death of a bullfighter.

30 **William Golding** (1911–1993) wrote many novels in the course of his career, most of them extended parables—often set in the past or in exotic situations—on the human condition. He is remembered above all for his first novel, *Lord of the Flies* (1954), a tale of a group of schoolboys marooned on a small tropical island who establish, on their own, a bizarre and savage society. We recommend

also *The Spire* (1964), a gripping psychological study of a medieval clergyman's obsessive determination to build a new spire on his cathedral.

31 **ROBERT GRAVES** (1895–1985) saw himself primarily as a poet and a classicist, though most readers probably remember him most vividly as the author of novels set in classical antiquity. Of those, *I Claudius* (1934) is most famous, perhaps more from the extremely successful BBC television adaptation than from the book itself. But the book deserves to be read, whether you've seen the TV series or not; it is a wholly convincing first-person narrative that makes imperial Rome come alive again in one's imagination. To encounter Graves in a very different mood, read his grim and bitter memoir of World War I, *Good-Bye to All That* (1929).

32 **GRAHAM GREENE** (1904–1991) was an extremely prolific writer and a gifted storyteller. It would be easy to see him simply as the author of genre novels (Greene called them "entertainments"); many of his works, such as *Stamboul Train* (1932), *The Ministry of Fear* (1943), and *The Quiet American* (1955), can be read with pleasure purely as thrillers. But like John LeCarré, whose work he greatly influenced, Greene invested his books with moral dilemmas that give them a seriousness lacking in most genre books. Greene was a convert to Catholicism, and his religious convictions—and doubts—emerge in his most serious fiction, such as *The Heart of the Matter* (1948).

33 **JAROSLAV HASÊK** (1883–1923) served as a soldier in the Austro-Hungarian Army during World War I, was taken prisoner by the Russians, and outlived the end of the war by only four years. That was long enough for him to write four volumes (of a planned six) of *The Good Soldier Schweik* (1920–23), a landmark of modern Czech literature and one of the funniest antiwar novels in any language. Hasêk's naive and hapless hero Schweik bumbles his way through the war, to the rage and despair of his pompous, mentally fossilized officers, but always manages to escape from his predicaments unscathed.

34 **JOSEPH HELLER** (1923–) served as a bombardier in American air force raids over Germany during World War II, an experience that inspired his 1961 novel, *Catch–22*, which was both a popular success and an icon of the Sixties' antiwar movement. Like Hasêk, Heller portrays canny enlisted men and demented officers, but Heller's wartime world is a dark, grim place, where Yossarian, the novel's hero, must plot ceaselessly to stay alive. Heller gave us not only a fine novel but an enduring slang phrase. (Catch–22: If you keep flying combat missions you're insane, but if you're sane enough to request to be relieved of combat duty on grounds of insanity you're not insane enough to be relieved; thus, any bad situation for which there is no solution that is not logically self-contradictory.)

35 **JOHN HERSEY** (1914–1993) was born in China of missionary parents; the milieu of his youth informed his semiautobiographical novel *The Call* (1985). His two best-known works are both fictionalized treatments of actual events during the Second World War: *A Bell for Adano* (1944), set in Sicily, and, especially, *Hiroshima* (1946, first published as the sole editorial content of an entire issue of *The New Yorker*), a narrative of the atomic bombing of Hiroshima based on the testimony of survivors. It has, in my view, never been surpassed as an account of that historically transformative event.

36 **LANGSTON HUGHES** (1902–1967) is the great poet of the Black experience in America, as influential a voice in this country as Leopold Sédar Senghor's has been in Africa. Self-taught as a poet, Hughes first came to public notice with his long free-verse poem *The Negro Speaks of Rivers* (1921). He traveled widely in Europe and Africa, and lived in several American cities, but came to be identified particularly with Harlem, the subject of his most famous short poem ("Harlem," in *Montage of a Dream Deferred*, 1951). He was considered a fiery political radical during his lifetime, but his work—angry yet never undisciplined—was characterized by a kind of classicism. Read widely in his *Collected Poems* (1995).

37 **JOHN IRVING** (1942–) has written a number of novels, but his reputation for the moment mostly rests on *The World According to Garp* (1978). Hailed as a breakthrough novel when it was published, *Garp* has become a sort of "cult classic" book since then, particularly among college-age readers. It presents a wry and gallows-humor funny look at the state of the world through the eyes of a novelist, T.S. Garp; it has the vivid writing and strong, idiosyncratic characters that exemplify Irving's work at its best.

38 **CHRISTOPHER ISHERWOOD** (1904–1986) lived in Berlin during the decadent waning years of the Weimar Republic. His reputation rests primarily on the story "Good-Bye to Berlin" and other fictional treatments of his experiences that he published in the late 1930s, later collected in *The Berlin Stories* (1954). After World War II he lived in California, writing mainly film scripts and pursuing an interest in Indian philosophy. He produced, late in life, another celebrated book, the memoir *Chistopher and His Kind* (1977), a candid and graceful account of his homosexual life in the era before gay liberation.

39 **JAMES JONES** (1921–1977) was on the whole a very minor modern novelist, except that he produced one spectacular book: *From Here to Eternity* (1951). Set in Pearl Harbor before and immediately after the Japanese attack that brought the United States into World War II, the book chronicles the life of a gifted and charismatic serviceman in an army that (like all armies) preferred that its soldiers be conventional, obedient, and interchangeable. Published when the

patriotic fervor of the war had mostly disappeared, the book was perfectly in tune with its time; it has worn well, and it still has a powerful impact today.

40 **NIKOS KAZANTZAKIS** (1885–1957) was a prolific and gifted writer whose work is virtually synonymous with modern Greek prose literature. He is known in the West primarily for *Zorba the Greek* (1946; even better known from the 1964 film starring Anthony Quinn), told in the first-person by an effete urbanite who comes to Crete to run a mine and is fascinated by the exuberantly unfettered but also somehow barbaric character of one of his workers, the eponymous Zorba. The book reaches a tragic climax when the narrator intrudes his emotions into the life of the Cretan community, unaware that he is violating a harsh and unforgiving social code.

41 **JACK KEROUAC** (1922–1969) was the leading spokesman for the Beat Movement of the 1950s. The Beatniks, so-called, were a loosely organized (at best) group of writers, musicians, and artists who saw themselves as being in rebellion against America's postwar materialism, and especially against the suburban conformity of the 1950s. Autobiographical, like all of Kerouac's works, *On the Road* (1957) is a breathless, formless, episodic account of the narrator's car travels across the United States, and his sometimes bizarre encounters with artistic and eccentric folk en route. The book's fascination with alcohol, speed, marijuana, and nonmarital sex of various sorts all seems a bit quaint today; one marvels at how little it took to shock both the middle class and the literary establishment a couple of generations ago.

42 **LAU SHAW [LAO SHE]** (1899–1966), like Lu Hsün a writer of China's May Fourth generation, made his early reputation as a writer of humorous action novels. His one masterpiece is a more serious book, the Chinese title of which could be translated as *Hsiang [Xiang] the Camel* (1936), telling the grim life story of a young rickshaw puller in Beijing. Try to find Jean James's accurate translation, *Rickshaw* (1979); the unauthorized translation by Evan King, titled *Rickshaw Boy*, became a bestseller in the United States in 1945 but is a bowdlerized travesty with a tacked-on happy ending. The novel that Lau Shaw actually wrote is a far tougher and more gripping book than that.

43 **PHILIP LARKIN** (1922–1985) was one of postwar Britain's best poets, and the one whose reputation seems to me most likely to continue to grow after his death. Larkin himself lived a crabbed, often rather unhappy life as a provincial university librarian, a situation that seemed to fit the unsparing scorn that he poured into his verse for a wide range of targets: upper-class boorishness, middle-class complacency, working-class sloth, among others. His great talent was to channel this misanthropic jaundice into superbly inventive

language and beautifully disciplined verse; unlike some poets, his work can be enjoyed even in very large helpings. Try his *Collected Poems* (1993).

44 **JOHN LeCARRÉ** (1931–). It would be easy to dismiss LeCarré (real name: David J.M. Cornwall) as simply a "genre writer," but few writers get to re-invent their genre. In *The Spy Who Came In from the Cold* (1963) and its sequels (and sowing in the fertile ground plowed by Graham Greene), he transformed the spy novel from a simple entertainment of white hats vs. black hats to a dark and morally ambiguous tale of the pretty bad holding out against the truly awful; he became something like a poet of the Cold War.

45 **CLAUDE LÉVI-STRAUSS** (1908–) is the founder of the system of cultural analysis called *structuralism*. Lévi-Strauss originally applied the method to the analysis of mythology in the service of anthropology; he sought to learn how people in different cultures use myths to mediate not only their systems of religious and social beliefs but their practical responses to actual situations. His methods were then adapted by literary scholars and other academic researchers in the humanities. Lévi-Strauss wrote both for specialists and for general audiences; his more popular books are highly readable and even entertaining, as well as erudite. He presented some of his early fieldwork in South America in *Tristes Tropiques* (1955), and developed his methodology more systematically in *Structural Anthropology* (1958) and *The Raw and the Cooked: Introduction to a Science of Mythology* (1964).

46 **SINCLAIR LEWIS** (1885–1951). Not many people get to add a word to our language, but Lewis did just that with "Babbittry," shorthand for mindless middle-class conformity and timidity. The word comes, of course, from his 1922 novel *Babbitt*, one of a string of bestsellers in the 1920s that at least for that decade made him perhaps America's most popular and successful author. His work bears the strong stamp of both his literary style and his personality; the novels and short stories have memorable characters, compelling plots, and a strong element of social criticism. In addition to *Babbitt*, try *Arrowsmith* (1925), *Elmer Gantry* (1927), and *Dodsworth* (1929).

47 **DAVID LODGE** (1935), an English novelist and critic, is much loved by a smallish circle of readers in America; he deserves to be far better known. His work is distinguished equally by penetrating psychological insight and superb literary craftsmanship. His novels *Changing Places* (1975) and *Small World* (1984) rank with, and perhaps surpass, Kingsley Amis's *Lucky Jim* as the funniest satires of academic life in modern times.

48 **NORMAN MAILER** (1923–) has spent much of his unruly life trying to live up to the machismo of his prose. He is sometimes dismissed as a braggart, and is much excoriated by feminist critics for his

aggressive masculinity both in real life and on the printed page. Nevertheless, his finest books—both of fiction and of nonfiction, such as *The Naked and the Dead* (1948), *The Armies of the Night* (1968), and *The Executioner's Song* (1979)—are beautifully crafted works noteworthy for their almost tenderly sympathetic (though not sentimental) point of view. Like Hemingway, he is a master of conveying the plight of men operating under extreme circumstances.

49 **ANDRÉ MALRAUX** (1901–1976) during his lifetime enjoyed a larger-than-life reputation as a writer, archaeologist, art historian, Republican volunteer in the Spanish Civil War, and Resistance fighter; he was for ten years Minister of Culture under Charles DeGaulle. Posthumous revelations suggest that his reputation was based in part on self-promoting exaggerations; but his written work endures. *Man's Fate* (1933), his finest novel, is a grim and dark-hued exploration of conflict between Chinese Communists and Nationalists in Shanghai in the late 1920s; more than half a century later it still brings chills to one's spine.

50 **MARY McCARTHY** (1912–1989) was a novelist, memoirist, and critic whose work employed irony, satire and humor to comment on the position of women in American society, and whose biting, sometimes scathingly unkind (and often untrue) portraits of lightly fictionalized real people made her feared by her friends and enemies alike. Her best-known novel, *The Group* (1963), follows eight women of the Vassar class of 1933 for several years after their graduation, while they gradually shed their collegiate hopes, idealism, and naiveté.

51 **CARSON McCULLERS** (1917–1967) was one of a number of twentieth-century American writers whose work is an argument for the reality of a distinctive Southern sensibility. Her books tend to be peopled with lonely, misunderstood people trapped in a society haunted by the past and ill-adapted to the present; the surprising thing is that she was able to pursue such themes while being neither maudlin nor melodramatic. Her best-known book is *The Heart is a Lonely Hunter* (1940), about the intertwined lives of five people in a small town in Georgia.

52 **MARGARET MEAD** (1901–1978) achieved instant celebrity as a young anthropologist when she returned from her first field research expedition and published *Coming of Age in Samoa* (1928), in which she suggested that Samoan young women, unlike American adolescents, enjoyed guilt-free casual sex and grew up to be well-adjusted adults as a result. Mead later pursued fieldwork in New Guinea, Bali, and elsewhere, and became a sort of grand old wise-woman of American anthropology. Although her early methodology has been criticized and her conclusions called into question, her books remain worth reading as emblems of a twentieth-century rev-

olution in attitudes toward non-Western peoples, and toward adolescence, gender, and sex in our own society.

53 **ARTHUR MILLER** (1915–) has lived long enough to have seen his reputation as a playwright evolve from angry young radical to revered elder statesmen. His great talent has been to combine in his plays an intense dramatic focus on the travails of individual characters with an overarching social conscience expressed in the trajectory of the play as a whole. Read both of Miller's most famous plays: *Death of a Salesman* (1949), in which Miller's finest character, the salesman Willie Loman, uses a tenuous hold on personal pride and self-esteem to forestall realization of the deep inconsequentiality of his life, and *The Crucible* (1953), a dramatization of the witch trials of seventeenth-century Salem, but inevitably also an allegory for the political witch hunts of our own mid-century.

54 **TONI MORRISON** (1931–), the 1993 winner of the Nobel Prize for Literature, is the most famous of a group of Black women writers whose work has enriched the literature of late twentieth-century America. Her novels are noteworthy for the poetic lyricism of their language, their sensitive but by no means uncritical analysis of the dynamics of Black culture, particularly with regard to the position of women, and for her ability to draw on the rich wellsprings of Black folklore and oral literature to illuminate contemporary themes. I recommend particularly *Song of Solomon* (1977) and *Jazz* (1992).

55 **IRIS MURDOCH** (1919–) combined a career as a lecturer in philosophy at Oxford University with a second career as a prolific and popular novelist. Her novels, of which I recommend that you read at least *A Severed Head* (1961) and *Sandcastle* (1978), are distinguished, not surprisingly, by a highly literate style and a general air of erudition; at the same time they are strongly plotted and highly entertaining to read.

56 **ROBERT MUSIL** (1880–1942) was educated in Berlin and served in the Austrian army during World War I. He supported himself as a journalist while pouring his entire literary energy into his masterpiece, *The Man Without Qualities* (unfinished in three volumes, 1933–43; see the new translation by Sophie Wilkins and Burton Pike, 1995). A wide-ranging, psychologically astute panorama of life in the *fin-de-siècle* Austro-Hungarian Empire, even in its unfinished state it is regarded as one of the landmarks of modern European literature.

57 **FLANNERY O'CONNOR** (1925–1964), like Carson McCullers a writer whose work reflects a distinctive Southern sensibility, was a modern master of the short-story form. Her stories typically are set in the rural South, and most often deal with characters deeply involved with, or trying to escape from the grasp of, the powerful and sometimes corrosive evangelical religious life of that milieu. She

was a prolific, though tragically short-lived, writer; you will want to read widely in her posthumously collected *Complete Stories* (1971).

58 **JOHN O'HARA** (1905–1970) was esteemed during his lifetime as the equal of Hemingway and Fitzgerald, but his reputation virtually collapsed after his death. His novels and short stories, regarded in recent years as mere potboilers and period pieces, are ripe for rediscovery. Try *Appointment at Samarra* (1934), the story of the decline and fall of a small-town leading citizen, and *Butterfield 8* (1935), a sensitive and subtle portrait of a woman who uses sex to get what she wants (it was considered very scandalous when it was first published). And don't overlook O'Hara's excellent *Collected Stories* (1985).

59 **JOSÉ ORTEGA Y GASSET** (1883–1955) was a philosopher and humanist whose social criticism was highly admired in his native Spain and beyond. His most influential work, *The Revolt of the Masses* (1929), is now no longer very widely read, but deserves not to be forgotten altogether. In it, Ortega denounced the post-WWI society that had emerged in Europe in the 1920s for its shallowness and vacuity; the economic collapse of that society in the Great Depression and the emergence of fascism made Ortega's critique look, in retrospect, powerfully prophetic.

60 **BORIS PASTERNAK** (1890–1960). In the context of modern Russian literature Pasternak's greatest contribution was in the field of poetry, where his avant-garde and sometimes abstruse verse was unpopular with Soviet authorities but had a great influence on younger poets. His popular fame, however, rests on his novel *Doctor Zhivago* (1957–58); written with the scope of a Dostoyevsky or a Tolstoy, the novel's elegiac account of lives disrupted by the Russian Revolution was banned in the USSR and circulated only clandestinely. When Pasternak was awarded the Nobel Prize for Literature in 1958, he was denounced as a traitor and a cultural saboteur; only with the end of the Soviet system was he given, posthumously, the public honors that his work had earned.

61 **GEORGES PEREC** (1936–1982) was one of the most innovative and inventive prose writers of recent times. In the late 1960s he became one of the leading lights of the Workshop for Potential Literature, a French writers' group dedicated to developing experimental new literary forms. Perec is known in the English-speaking world primarily for his 1978 novel, *Life, A User's Manual*, which uses a montage technique to describe a large apartment building in Paris and tell the life stories of all of its inhabitants; it is a fascinating window into the contemporary French literary sensibility.

62 **HAROLD PINTER** (1930–) has employed his spare, uncompromising dramatic vision and his talent for writing vivid, taut dialogue to transform the character of postwar British theater. Discarding the

old ideal of the "well-made play," clear in its dramatic focus, self-contained, and unambiguous, Pinter created a theater where ambiguity, menace, humor, and open-endedness combine to leave audiences with a feeling of unease as well as gratification. Despite the dark and sometimes difficult nature of his work, Pinter has become a significant figure in commercial theater on both sides of the Atlantic. Of his many plays I would recommend particularly *The Caretaker* (1960), in which a stranger insinuates himself into, and disrupts, the secure and stable relationship of a pair of bachelor brothers.

63 **ROBERT PIRSIG** (1928–) captured perfectly the mood of the Sixties' counterculture movement with his book-length essay *Zen and the Art of Motorcycle Maintenance* (1974). Drawing upon and updating the themes of the road trip and Zen consciousness that had been explored by Jack Kerouac in the 1950s, Pirsig used the image of a cultivated harmony of man and machine to illustrate the importance of "quality" as a transcendent goal of the human experience. Whether the book will seem like more than a period-piece curio fifty years from now is unclear; this may be the paradigm of a "temporary classic." For the moment it's well worth reading.

64 **EZRA POUND** (1885–1972) is notable both as one of the greatest poets of the twentieth century and as an editor who had a profound influence on Eliot and Joyce. Pound was deeply learned in classical and East Asian poetry and was a fine and creative translator; his own verse showed both classical grounding and stunning innovation. His best and most influential collection of poetry is *Personae* (1926). Pound was justly criticized for the odious opinions he expressed late in life; his verse outlives his personality.

65 **ANTHONY POWELL** (1905–), despite a long and successful career as a writer, would not rise above the crowd of very good modern British novelists were it not for his remarkable twelve-volume series of autobiographical novels, *A Dance to the Music of Time*, beginning with *A Question of Upbringing* (1951). In a voice noted for its ironical detachment and its unusually frank honesty (but with no unseemly confessional breast-beating), Powell dissects his own life, especially his intellectual and emotional life, in the context of British society at mid-century.

66 **PRAMOEDYA ANANTA TOER** (1925–), Indonesia's most important writer, has spent much of his life in prison or under house arrest for his leftist political views and his outspoken criticism of the government. His best-known novel, *This Earth of Mankind* (1980), is the impassioned, romantic story of a cruelly oppressed young Javanese journalist in the waning years of Dutch colonial control of the East Indies. The novel was written while Pramoedya was confined to the prison island of Buru; the story of the journalist Minke is continued

in the other three novels of the so-called Buru Quartet: *Child of All Nations* (1980), *Footsteps* (1985), and *House of Glass* (1988).

67 **V.S. PRITCHETT** (1900–1997) was a journalist, essayist, and literary critic, but above all a short-story writer of unusual distinction. His stories, which bring a finely ironical eye to bear on the pretensions and tribal customs of the English middle-class, are directly comparable in a British context to the American short stories of John Cheever; his tone and subject matter are also reminiscent of the novels of Barbara Pym. Try his *Complete Collected Stories* (1992).

68 **BARBARA PYM** (1913–1980) is one of many English novelists who deserve to be more widely known in America. Her novels have a slightly old-fashioned quality, in the best sense; if you like Jane Austen and Anthony Trollope, you will like Barbara Pym. She celebrated but also gently satirized the mannered and compulsively reserved lives of members of the upper-middle class in its long decline from Victorian gentility. You will probably find yourself wanting to read all of her novels; start with *Excellent Women* (1952) and *An Unsuitable Attachment* (1982).

69 **THOMAS PYNCHON** (1937–) has deliberately made himself completely invisible in American life except through his books; no photograph of him as an adult is known to exist, and he communicates even with his publisher only with elaborate precautions designed to protect his whereabouts and identity. Under the circumstances it is perhaps not surprising that his greatest novel, *Gravity's Rainbow* (1973), is in part an exploration of paranoid fantasies. Impossible to describe adequately but fascinating to read, the book, roughly speaking, is a nightmarish study of espionage and rocketry in the waning days of World War II; it is noteworthy especially for its dazzling language, verbal and mathematical puns, narrative complexity, and bizarre humor.

70 **ERICH MARIA REMARQUE** (1898–1970) ranks with, or even ahead of, Ford Madox Ford as the great novelist of World War I. Despite the fact that (from the point of view of the English-speaking world) he served on the "wrong" side during the war, his novel *Im Westen nichts Neues* (*All Quiet on the Western Front* [1929]) won immediate recognition as an expression of the terror, danger and tedium experienced by men in the front lines of that war, no matter which way they were facing.

71 **RAINER MARIA RILKE** (1875–1926) spent much of his adult life in France and Italy, but continued to write in his native German. He began his career as a poet in *fin-de-siècle* Munich and in Paris in the first decade of the twentieth century, finally moving to Italy where he wrote the first several of his *Duino Elegies*. Thereafter he was beset by a paralyzing depression brought on by the grimness of modern life and especially by the catastrophe of World War I. He

wrote nothing for a decade, then completed the *Elegies* in a burst of inspiration that also included writing the fifty-five *Sonnets to Orpheus* (1922); both works assure him a place as one of the twentieth-century's greatest poets.

72 **OLE EDVART RØLVAAG** (1896–1931). It is unfortunate, and unfair, that for many years Rølvaag's great novel *Giants in the Earth* (1927) was a favorite work of assigned reading in high school English classes. Generations of students learned to loathe it while reading it a few pages per night and sitting through stultifying explications of its themes and characters. If you have hateful memories of the book, try anyway to read it again with fresh eyes; if you've not yet encountered it, a treat awaits you. There has never been a better book about the joys and sorrows of the early farming settlers on the northern Great Plains; pioneering, Rølvaag shows us, might have been gratifying, but it was no picnic.

73 **PHILIP ROTH** (1933–) first came to critical notice with the publication of his short-story collection *Goodbye, Columbus* (1959), the title story of which fascinated many readers (and appalled many Jewish readers) by exposing the shallowness and money-grubbing boorishness of a suburban Jewish family. Roth achieved real celebrity with *Portnoy's Complaint* (1969), a first-person confessional account (on a psychiatrist's couch) of the narrator's adolescence, his compulsive masturbation, and his suffocatingly protective mother. Although some readers, myself among them, feel that through a succession of scatological novelistic explorations of the guilts and obsessions of modern Jewish-American life Roth's work has grown rather monotonous, the brilliance and insouciance of his early work retains its luster.

74 **ANATOLI RYBAKOV** (1911–) spent time in Stalinist prison camps during his twenties; after military service in World War II he achieved success as a writer of novels for young people. His great work, *Children of the Arbat*, was written in secrecy in the 1960s and not published until 1987, when the *glasnost* policies of Gorbachev made it safe to criticize the excesses of Stalin's rule. The novel tells the story of several idealistic young people from Moscow's Arbat district whose fates take strikingly different turns during the terror of the 1930s. The Arbat Trilogy continues with *Fear* and *Dust and Ashes*.

75 **J.D. SALINGER** (1919–), early in his career as a writer, turned his attention to the idealism, social ineptitude, and general angst of adolescence, and produced a modern classic, *Catcher in the Rye* (1951). Its protagonist, Holden Caulfield, has often been compared with Huckleberry Finn as the prototypical American boy (though Twain's novel is by far the greater book). After publishing a handful of other novellas and short stories (*Franny and Zooey*; *Raise High the Roof*

Beam, Carpenter), Salinger ceased writing, or at least publishing; he lives a quiet, reclusive life in New Hampshire.

76 **JEAN-PAUL SARTRE** (1905–1980), like André Malraux, energetically cultivated his own reputation, which has gone into something of a decline since his death and the gradual emergence of a recollected picture of him as being a not very pleasant person. But by almost any standard Sartre must be judged an important writer, as a novelist, a philosopher, and a playwright. He was a proponent and theoretician of existentialism, arguing in *Being and Nothingness* (1943) that pure consciousness is the source of human freedom. Being an apostle of existential freedom, however, did not spare him from a pessimistic outlook of "existential dread," explored in plays such as, most famously, *No Exit* (1945).

77 **SIMON SCHAMA** (1945–), born in England of Polish Jewish descent, has spent most of his adult life in America, teaching at Harvard and Columbia. A prolific and wide-ranging historian, his most notable book to date is *Citizens* (1989), a marvelously comprehensive and readable social history of the French Revolution. Schama suggests that the Revolution was the great watershed in modern history because it caused the transformation of European peoples from "subjects" to "citizens."

78 **LEOPOLD SÉDAR SENGHOR** (1906–) became independent Senegal's first president in 1960, and retired from office in 1980. Born in Senegal, he was educated in France and served in the French army during World War II, spending two years as a German prisoner of war. In the 1930s, he and other pioneering Black African and Caribbean writers propounded the theory of *Négritude*, an aesthetic based on the concept of the uniqueness of the Black experience. Many of Senghor's poems are written as songs, set to be accompanied by specified African musical instruments. His poems (written originally in French) have been widely translated; I like the *Selected Poems* translated by Melvin Dixon.

79 **UPTON SINCLAIR** (1878–1968) is the unchallenged personification of the American muckraking novelist. His novel *The Jungle* (1906) was turned down by a succession of commercial publishing houses; Sinclair finally published it privately and saw it become a bestseller; it made his reputation. The book's exposure of the brutal working conditions and disgustingly unsanitary environment of Chicago's meat-packing industry led directly to the establishment of the federal Food and Drug Administration, but not to the labor reforms Sinclair had hoped to inspire; he commented, "I aimed at the public's heart and hit its stomach." He wrote a number of other novelistic exposés, and, rather quixotically, ran as a Socialist for governor of California in 1934 (losing badly). Today the prose of his novels seems rather overheated, but his critical stance still carries weight.

80 **ISAAC BASHEVIS SINGER** (1904–1991) grew up in an orthodox Jewish family and community in Poland, the scion of a long line of Hassidic rabbis, and spent much of his life preserving in Yiddish prose the memory of a community and way of life that was wiped out by the Holocaust. He was established as a writer even before emigrating to America in 1935, and thereafter assumed a role as a leading member of New York's Jewish literary intelligentsia. He continued to write in Yiddish (and took an active role in translating his work into English), finding that language a perfect vehicle for his wry, ironical attitude toward his own characters, and for conveying the air of Jewish folklore and occultism that pervades much of his work. He was a prolific writer; I suggest you start with *Gimpel the Fool & Other Stories* (1957) and *The Magician of Lublin* (1960).

81 **WOLE SOYINKA** (1934–) is one of the leading figures of modern African literature. Born in Nigeria and educated in England, for years he successfully negotiated the hazards of being an intellectual in modern Nigeria, where he held various editorial and academic posts before going into exile in 1994. A writer of extraordinary versatility, he has published poetry, criticism, essays, novels, and plays; he was awarded the Nobel Prize for Literature in 1986. His best novel is *The Interpreters* (1965), about a group of young intellectuals in newly independent Nigeria. Of his plays, I particularly recommend *Death and the King's Horsemen*.

82 **WALLACE STEGNER** (1909–1993) is deservedly regarded as the author of some of our finest literary accounts of the American West. His sense of the West as the eternally beckoning land of promise was captured in his novel *The Big Rock Candy Mountain* (1943), about a family's fitful search for a place to settle down. Of his later novels, my favorite is *Angle of Repose* (1971). Stegner was a very prolific writer, well worth exploring in depth.

83 **JOHN STEINBECK** (1902–1968) more than any other American writer captured the spirit of the Great Depression. His novels, like those of Sinclair Lewis and Upton Sinclair (though better), are marked by a strong social conscience; but instead of outrage, Steinbeck's dominant tone is one of sadness that proletarian nobility and toughness are not always sufficient to overcome obstacles. Many of his novels are as powerful and moving to read now as they were when they were first published; I recommend starting with *Of Mice and Men* (1937) and *The Grapes of Wrath* (1939).

84 **WALLACE STEVENS** (1879–1955) is now recognized as one of the greatest American poets—not only of the twentieth century but of our entire national literature, but he worked in obscurity for most of his lifetime. Stevens published *Harmonium*, his first collection of verse, in 1923; it showed in full flower the verbal inventiveness that would be the hallmark of all of his verse, but it was largely ignored

by the literary community. Recognition came only when he was approaching old age, and his reputation has grown posthumously. Read widely in his *Collected Poems* (1954).

85 **LYTTON STRACHEY** (1880–1932) was a leader of the Bloomsbury set of English writers and critics that included Virginia Woolf, Arthur Waley, E. M. Forster, John Maynard Keynes, and other noted writers and intellectuals. Brilliant, irreverent, and gay, Strachey is remembered for his revisionist biographies. His *Eminent Victorians* (1918), which gives brief accounts of the lives of Cardinal Manning, Florence Nightingale, Thomas Arnold, and General Charles Gordon, and *Queen Victoria* (1921), an unsentimental biography of the late queen, are in large part responsible for the opinions most people still have of the manners, morals, and values of the Victorian era.

86 **JAMES THURBER** (1894–1961) was a writer, essayist and cartoonist closely identified with *The New Yorker* under the editorship of Harold Ross. Both his stories and his drawings are characterized by whimsy, wit, and understated humor. Some of his best work is to be found in *Is Sex Necessary?* (1929, written with E.B. White), and his collected stories, *My Life and Hard Times* (1933). Thurber's sight failed when he was in his forties; he was totally blind in later life, but continued to write prolifically.

87 **J.R.R. TOLKIEN** (1892–1973) was a professor of Anglo-Saxon and Old English at Oxford, and a distinguished scholar of early British poetry such as *Beowulf* and *Sir Gawain and the Green Knight*. Medieval themes permeate his fiction, beginning with *The Hobbit* (1937), a fantasy for children about an Englandlike country menaced by sorcery and evil. Tolkien's vision matured with the writing of *The Lord of the Rings* (1954–56), a trilogy building on themes from *The Hobbit* but with an added allegorical urgency that seemed to reflect England's narrow escape from fascist conquest in World War II.

88 **WILLIAM TREVOR** (1928–) is both a novelist and a short-story writer; he is a fine writer in either genre, but his true métier, I think, is the story. He lives and works in Ireland, and all of his work is set there; typically his stories view with irony tempered by compassion the foibles of people who for one reason or another cannot fit comfortably into the cozy but rigid expectations of Irish family and village life. He continues to write prolifically; for the moment, see his *Collected Stories* (1992).

89 **JOHN UPDIKE** (1932–) is one of America's most visible men of letters because of his phenomenal productivity as a novelist, poet, essayist, and critic. His work is too diverse to pin down easily, but his most characteristic novels deal with suburban ambitions and somewhat kinky sex in villages or towns somewhere in the

Northeast. Updike is best known for his quartet following the life of Harry "Rabbit" Angstrom, his best fictional character: *Rabbit, Run* (1960), *Rabbit Redux* (1971), *Rabbit Is Rich* (1981), and *Rabbit at Rest* (1990).

90 **GORE VIDAL** (1925–), patrician, cosmopolitan, gay, intellectually combative, has made a career of trying to outrage critical opinion, sometimes succeeding. His first great success was *Myra Breckenridge* (1968), a comic novel with a transsexual lead character; it poked fun at American hypocrisies, and was considered shocking at the time, but now is simply fun to read. For much of his career Vidal has devoted himself to fictional explorations of American history; a good example is *Burr* (1974).

91 **DEREK WALCOTT** (1930–) shares with the francophone poet Aimé Césaire the status of being the greatest literary figure of the Caribbean region. Walcott is known in this country primarily as a poet; when he won the Nobel Prize in 1992, special mention was made of his novel-length poem *Omeros* (1990), in which he adroitly weaves themes from Homer into a Caribbean setting. But he is also a prolific playwright; in addition to *Omeros* and his *Collected Poems* (1986), try reading his play, *Ti-Jean and His Brothers* (1958).

92 **JAMES D. WATSON** (1928–) electrified the field of biology with the announcement in 1955 that he and Francis Crick had discovered the double-helix molecular structure of DNA. Their discovery made possible unprecedented advances in molecular genetics, leading to the applied science of genetic engineering. Watson tells the story of how he and Crick worked out DNA's distinctive structure in *The Double Helix*, a fascinating and highly readable, even entertaining (if somewhat immodest and self-serving) insider's account of modern science in action.

93 **EVELYN WAUGH** (1903–1966) served in the British army in World War I and then worked briefly as a teacher before devoting himself to full-time writing. Waugh was known for his finely observed and often extremely funny travel memoirs; he later reworked themes from his travels into his humorous novels of the 1930s, such as *Scoop* (1938). Waugh in this period is noteworthy for his satirical wit, his scathing humor, and his total lack of what today would be called "political correctness." A convert to Catholicism, Waugh turned to more serious themes of faith and introspection in *Brideshead Revisited* (1945), now probably his most famous novel. American readers will also enjoy *The Loved One* (1948), a very funny spoof of the funeral industry.

94 **EUDORA WELTY** (1909–) has devoted her life to capturing, in stories and in photographs, the texture of life in the small towns of her native Mississippi Delta. Her work tends to focus on the complexities of intertwined lives, viewed with compassion and the promise of

redemption. She is a gentle writer, but not a sentimental one. Try her *Collected Stories* (1980).

95 **REBECCA WEST** (1892–1983) wrote a number of novels but is remembered primarily as one of the most astute and energetic journalists of our time, a tireless chronicler of history in the making. Her most ambitious and impressive work is *Black Lamb and Grey Falcon* (1942), a massive, two-volume study of the history, politics and culture of the Balkan region; it comes brilliantly to life again for a reader in our own time for its enduring insights into the problems of Bosnia and other countries that once belonged to the much-battered land of Yugoslavia.

96 **PATRICK WHITE** (1912–1990) was the greatest novelist of modern Australia. His work captures well the vast size of that country, and its potential as a backdrop for the clash of powerful emotions and interests; his novels tend to be expansive in scope and to carry heavy thematic freight. Of his many books, I recommend *Voss* (1957) and *Riders in the Chariot* (1961).

97 **THORNTON WILDER** (1897–1975) is probably most widely known for his play *Our Town* (1938), a portrait of small-town New England life that was considered innovative in its time but which has been thoroughly ruined for most people by too many dreadful high school drama productions. Readers coming to Wilder for the first time would be better off with his landmark novel *The Bridge of San Luis Rey* (1927), set in eighteenth-century Peru, in which a priest tries to find the hand of God in the deaths of five people in the collapse of a bridge.

98 **TENNESSEE WILLIAMS** (1911–1983) may or may not be judged by history to have been the greatest American playwright of the twentieth century (a status of which he himself had no doubt), but he surely will be ranked as one of the greatest. Southern and gay, he focused in most of his plays on the hothouse atmosphere of Southern family life, but his best work transcends any taint of mere regionalism. Read, and if possible see stage productions of, at least *The Glass Menagerie* (1945) and *A Streetcar Named Desire* (1947).

99 **WILLIAM CARLOS WILLIAMS** (1883–1963) spent his working life as a doctor in suburban New Jersey while simultaneously writing the spare, lyrical, beautifully controlled verse that brought him recognition as one of the finest poets of our time. His poems focus exquisitely on ordinary things and experiences observed with such clarity of vision and such invention of imagery as to be transformed in the reader's mind's eye. See his *Collected Poems* (two volumes, 1991).

100 **RICHARD WRIGHT** (1908–1960) grew up in poverty in the rural South; as a young man he moved to Chicago, then to New York, and became part of various leftist literary groups. He briefly joined the Communist Party, but then broke with it and moved to Paris after

the end of World War II, and lived there as an expatriate for the rest of his life. He is remembered less for his later essays and polemical pieces than for two early novels, *Native Son* (1940), which introduced one of the most vivid characters in American fiction, Bigger Thomas, a Black man imprisoned for murder; and the autobiographical *Black Boy* (1945).

J.S.M

BIBLIOGRAPHY

In addition to the titles suggested in the Plan, this Bibliography selectively lists other important works, if any, by the author, and gives some suggestions for further reading about the authors and their works. Many of the titles have been published in moderate-priced paperback editions, though some are available only in hardcover.

Publishing is a very volatile industry. Some long-established paperback series are no longer active; others may have been discontinued by the time this book reaches you. Publishing firms not infrequently change names or disappear. At least some of these books will be out of print at any given time. For these reasons, in this Bibliography (unlike those in earlier editions of the Plan) we do not try systematically to list in-print paperback editions of the recommended books. In the frequent cases where an author's works are widely available in standard editions, we simply say that. In other cases we list editions because they contain superior texts, or especially good introductions and critical apparatus, or are particularly good translations of works written in languages other than English.

In any case, innovations of the information age have made it easier for you to find these books on your own. Most libraries and bookstores will have copies of the current *Books in Print* and *Paperback Books in Print*, both published (each in several volumes) annually by R.R. Bowker Co.; you can consult these to locate good and reasonably priced editions of the books listed in the Plan. Most bookstores and libraries also have on-line access to one or another database (including computerized versions of *Books in Print* and *Paperback Books in Print*), which they will happily use to assist you in finding books. If a book or an edition that you are looking for is out of print, try to find a copy in your local library, or ask the library to obtain one on interlibrary loan. (Computer databases and the Internet have widened and simplified the process of interlibrary loans; even very small libraries are now often part of a lending network.) We also encourage you to look for copies of these books at secondhand bookstores, where you will have both the pleasure of browsing through shelves of interesting books and the satisfaction of buying copies of excellent books at reasonable prices.

The lists of books suggested for additional reading in most cases are both brief and basic. To save space, we list these books only by author and title. Again, new information technology makes it easier for you to go further on your own: Many school and public libraries, and all large research-oriented libraries, have entered their holdings into database programs, and often have access via the Internet to other libraries' catalogues as well. It is a simple matter (and the librarians will be happy to help you) to search these databases by subject—for example, "Gilgamesh"—and compile a bibliography far larger and more complete than anything we could hope to provide here. Remember also that the *Encyclopaedia Britannica* remains an excellent and convenient source of sound biographical and background information on virtually all of the authors listed in *The New Lifetime Reading Plan.*

Here, then, are our suggestions, to be considered as nothing more than a way to help you get started.

1. *The Epic of Gilgamesh*—Translations by R. Campbell Thompson (Clarendon); N.K. Sandars (Penguin); E.A. Speiser (Princeton U. Press); John Gardner and John Maier (Vintage); Maureen Kovacs (Stanford U. Press); Danny P. Jackson (Bolchazy-Carducci); David Ferry (Farrar, Straus and Giroux).

   Further reading: C. W. Ceram, *Gods, Graves and Scholars: The Story of Archaeology*; A. Leo Oppenheim, *Ancient Mesopotamia: Portrait of a Dead Civilization*; Jeffrey Tigay, *The Evolution of the Gilgamesh Epic*; Stephanie Dalley, *Myths from Mesopotamia: Creation, the Flood, Gilgamesh, and Others.*

2. **HOMER,** The *Iliad*—The translations of Richmond Lattimore (Phoenix) and Robert Fitzgerald (Anchor) are excellent, as is the newer translation by Robert Fagels (Viking). Those by W.H. Rouse (Mentor) and E.V. Rieu (Penguin) are quite serviceable, the latter especially in the updated version published in 1991 by Penguin.

   Further reading: Jasper Griffin, *Homer*; Michael Silk, *Homer: The Iliad*; Mark Edwards, *Homer Poet of the Iliad.*

   A comprehensive reference volume covering both Greece and Rome is Paul Harvey, ed., *Oxford Companion to Classical Literature.* For mythology: Zimmerman, *Dictionary of Classical Mythology*; Edith Hamilton, *Mythology*; H.J. Rose, *Gods and Heroes of the Greeks.* A masterly general study of Greek culture: Werner Jaeger, *Paideia.*

3. Homer, The *Odyssey*—Versions by Richmond Lattimore (Harper Torchbooks); Robert Fitzgerald (Anchor); W.H. Rouse (Mentor), Robert Fagels (Viking). Avoid abridgements.

Further reading: M.I. Finley, *The World of Ulysses;* G.S. Kirk, *Homer and the Epic.*

4. CONFUCIUS—The standard translation is by Arthur Waley, *The Analects of Confucius* (Random House); equally good is that of D.C. Lau (Penguin). The translation by James Legge, in *The Chinese Classics* (5 vols., 1861–72, several reprint editions) is old but still much admired by scholars. *The Original Analects*, tr. E. Bruce Brooks (Columbia U. Press), gives a radically new interpretation.

Further reading: For Chinese philosophy in general, see Fung Yu-lan, *A History of Chinese Philosophy*, tr. Derk Bodde (2 vols.), and Benjamin I. Schwartz, *The World of Thought in Ancient China.* For a biography of Confucius, see H.G. Creel's *Confucius: The Man and the Myth* (also titled *Confucius and the Chinese Way*). See also: Herbert Fingarette, *Confucius: The Secular as Sacred*; David T. Hall and Roger Ames, *Thinking Through Confucius.*

5. AESCHYLUS—*The Complete Greek Tragedies,* ed. David Grene and Richmond Lattimore (4 vols., U. of Chicago Press), contains good modern versions of all the works of Aeschylus, Sophocles, and Euripides. For Aeschylus only, see *Aeschylus One. Agamemnon, The Libation Bearers, The Eumenides,* tr. and introd. by Richmond Lattimore (U. of Chicago Press); *Aeschylus Two. Four Tragedies: Prometheus Bound, Seven against Thebes, The Persians, The Suppliant Maidens,* tr. David Grene and Seth G. Benardete (U. of Chicago Press); *The Oresteia,* tr. Robert Lowell (Farrar, Straus).

Further reading: H.D.F. Kitto, *Greek Tragedy*; Bernhard Zimmerman, *Greek Tragedy: An Introduction*; Christian Meier, *The Political Art of Greek Tragedy.* Surveys of Greek literature: Moses Hadas, A *History of Greek Literature* (Columbia U. Press); Albin Lesky, *History of Greek Literature* (Crowell); Gilbert Murray, *The Literature of Ancient Greece* (Phoenix).

6. SOPHOCLES—Highly recommended: *Oedipus Trilogy,* tr. Stephen Spender (Random); *The Oedipus Cycle of Sophocles,* tr. Dudley Fitts and Robert Fitzgerald (Harcourt). Other good editions: *Complete Plays,* ed. Moses Hadas (Bantam); *Sophocles One* (incl. *Oedipus the King, Oedipus at Colonus, Antigone*) and *Sophocles Two* (incl. *Ajax, The Women of Trachis, Electra, Philoctetes*) (U. of Chicago Press).

Further reading: C.M. Bowra, *Sophoclean Tragedy*; Lowell Edmunds, *Oedipus: The Ancient Legend and its Later Analogues.*

7. EURIPIDES—Bantam publishes *Ten Plays of Euripides,* tr. Moses Hadas and John H. McLean. University of Chicago Press publishes

all the plays in five volumes in excellent translations. An interesting version of *The Trojan Women* is the adaptation by Jean-Paul Sartre (Random). Also interesting are the translations of Robert Meagher: *Bakkhai* and *Hakabe* (both Bolchazy-Carducci) and *Helen* (U. of Massachusetts Press). The translations by the great scholar Gilbert Murray (which often can be found in libraries and bookstores) are frequently beautiful in a turn-of-the-century manner, but the more modern versions are probably more faithful to the original.

Further reading: Gilbert Murray, *Euripides and His Age*; G.M.A. Grube, *The Drama of Euripides*; Ann N. Michelini, *Euripides and the Tragic Tradition*.

8. **HERODOTUS**—*The Histories* is sometimes titled *The Persian Wars*. George Rawlinson's classic but rather Victorian translation is findable in *The Greek Historians* (2 vols., Random), ed. F.R.B. Godolphin; and also, introduced by Godolphin, in Modern Library. More modern and readable translations: Aubrey de Selincourt (Penguin); and especially David Grene (U. of Chicago Press)

Further reading: J.B. Bury's *The Ancient Greek Historians* covers other Greek historians as well as Herodotus and Thucydides and is a classic in its field. See also John L. Myres, *Herodotus: Father of History*.

9. **THUCYDIDES**—*The Peloponnesian War,* tr. Benjamin Jowett in *The Greek Historians;* ed. F.R.B. Godolphin (2 vols., Random); ed. Richard Livingstone (Oxford U. Press); tr. Rex Warner (Penguin); *Complete Writings,* tr. Richard Crawley, introd. by J. Finley, Jr. (Modern Library). Especially good is *The Landmark Thucydides: A Comprehensive Guide to the Peloponnesian War,* edited by Robert B. Strassler (Free Press); this augments the Crawley translation with extensive maps, commentary, and other aids.

Further reading: The definitive reference is Gomme, Andrewes, and Dover, *A Historical Commentary on Thucydides* (5 vols.), updated by Simon Hornblower's *A Commentary on Thucydides* (first of two projected vols.). See also Simon Hornblower, *Thucydides*; W.R. Connor, *Thucydides*; J.H. Finley, *Thucydides*, 2d ed.

10. **SUN-TZU**—Tr. Roger Ames, *Sun-tzu: The Art of Warfare* (Ballantine); Ralph Sawyer (Westview); Samuel B. Griffith (Oxford U. Press). The 1910 translation by Lionel Giles remains useful as well.

Further reading: Ralph Sawyer, *The Seven Military Classics of Ancient China*, includes Sun-tzu and other texts, and has an excellent introduction. Both Roger Ames and Ralph Sawyer have also translated *Sun Pin's Art of War*.

11. **ARISTOPHANES**—There is an excellent translation in one volume of *The Birds, The Clouds,* and *The Wasps* by William Arrowsmith (U. Michigan Press). Heinemann has *Plays* in two volumes; Bantam has *Complete Plays* in one. Penguin has *Lysistrata and Other Plays,* tr. Alan H. Sommerstein.

   Further reading: Dana F. Sutton, *Ancient Comedy: The War of the Generations;* Douglas M. MacDowell, *Aristophanes and Athens: An Introduction to the Plays;* Kenneth McLeish, *The Theater of Aristophanes.*

12. **PLATO**—Jowett's translation, though Victorian, is classic. His version of the *Complete Works* may be found in the two-volume Random House edition, introduced by Raphael Demos. *The Portable Plato,* ed. Scott Buchanan (Viking), contains the Jowett translations of *Protagoras, Phaedo, Symposium,* and *The Republic.* Look for the Jowett versions in other paperback editions as well. Other good, more modern translations: *Republic,* tr. Francis M. Cornford (Oxford U. Press); *Protagoras and Meno,* tr. W.K Guthrie (Penguin); *The Last Days of Socrates* (includes *Euthyphro, Apology, Crito, Phaedo*), tr. Hugh Tredennick (Penguin).

   Further reading: Rex Warner, *The Greek Philosophers;* A.E. Taylor, *Plato: The Man and His Work;* G.C. Field, *The Philosophy of Plato;* I.F. Stone's iconoclastic *The Trial of Socrates.*

13. **ARISTOTLE**—*Basic Works,* ed. Richard McKeon (Random); *Aristotle. Selections from Seven Books,* ed. Philip Wheelwright (Odyssey Press); *Introduction to Aristotle,* ed. Richard McKeon (Modern Library); *Ethics, tr.* J.A. Thomson (Penguin); *Nicomachean Ethics,* tr. W.D. Ross (Oxford U. Press); *Politics,* tr. J.A. Sinclair (Penguin); *Poetics,* introd. by G.F. Else (U. of Mich. Press).

   Further reading: Mortimer J. Adler, *Aristotle for Everyone;* Abraham Edel, *Aristotle and His Philosophy.* The Aristotle bibliography is of course enormous; consult your librarian.

14. **MENCIUS**—Translations by D.C. Lau (Penguin; this is the preferred version); W.A.C.H. Dobson (Oxford U. Press); James R. Ware (Mentor); Lionel Giles (abridged; John Murray); James Legge in *The Chinese Classics.*

   Further reading: Fung Yu-lan, *A History of Chinese Philosophy,* tr. Derk Bodde (2 vols); Benjamin I. Schwartz, *The World of Thought in Ancient China.* For translations of Mencius's philosophical rivals: Lao-tzu, *Tao Te Ching,* tr. by Arthur Waley, D.C. Lau, Victor Mair, Moss Roberts, among many others; Chuang-tzu, tr. by A.C. Graham, Burton Watson, Victor Mair; Mo-tzu, tr. Burton Watson, Y.P. Mei.

15. The *Ramayana*—The best translation (of Books I and II) is by Robert P. Goldman, *The Ramayana of Valmiki* (2 vols, Princeton U. Press); also Hari P. Shastri, *The Ramayana of Valmiki* (3 vols., Routledge).

There are good abridged versions by William Buck, *Ramayana: King Rama's Way* (U. California Press); R.K. Narayan (Penguin); Aubrey Menen (Greenwood); C.V. Srinivasa Rao (Bangalore Press); Swami Venkasetenanda (State U. of New York Press).

Further reading: Herbert H. Gowen, *A History of Indian Literature*, has a good chapter on the *Ramayana*. For the culture of ancient India more generally, see the classic work by A.L. Basham, *The Wonder That Was India*.

16. The *Mahabharata*: J.A.B. Van Buitenen's translation of Books I-V is a masterpiece of the translator's art; it also has an excellent introduction to the text (U. Chicago Press). There is a hard-to-find, multivolume complete translation by P. Lal (Writer's Workshop, Calcutta). Also very fine is the performance version by Jean-Claude Carrière, tr. from the French by Peter Brook. There are good abridged versions by R.K. Narayan (Vision) and Chakravarthi V. Narasimhan (Columbia U. Press).

Further reading: The notes and commentary in Van Buitenen's translation are very good. More generally, see Basham, *The Wonder That Was India*.

17. The *Bhagavad Gita*—The most readable translation is by Barbara Stoler Miller, *The Bhagavad Gita: Krishna's Counsel in Time of War* (Columbia U. Press; Penguin); Eliot Deutsch's translation (Holt, Rinehart and Winston) is also good. An excellent scholarly translation is J.A.B. Van Buitenen's *The Bhagavad Gita in the Mahabharata* (U. Chicago Press). Also good are the translations by Franklin Edgerton (Harvard U. Press) and R.C. Zaehner (Everyman).

Further reading: Miller's translation features an excellent introduction; Zaehner's has the best textual commentary.

18. Ssu-ma Ch'ien—There's only one good English translation: Burton Watson's *Records of the Grand Historian* (2 vols., Columbia U. Press; try to get the revised [1993] edition).

Further reading: Burton Watson, *Ssu-ma Ch'ien, Grand Historian of China*; Charles S. Gardner, *Traditional Chinese Historiography*; W.G. Beasley and E.G. Pulleyblank, eds., *Historians of China and Japan*.

19. Lucretius—*Nature of the Universe*, tr. Ronald E. Latham (Penguin); *On Nature*, tr. Russell M. Geer (Bobbs-Merrill); *On the Nature of Things*, ed. S. Palmer Bovie (New American Library); also by Anthony M. Esolen (John Hopkins U. Press); best of all, *The Way Things Are: The De Rerum Natura of Titus Lucretius Carus,* tr. Rolfe Humphries (Indiana U. Press)

Further reading: A fine essay on Lucretius is in George Santayana's *Three Philosophical Poets*, which also contains essays on Dante (31) and Goethe (62). For Rome generally: Michael

Grant, *History of Rome*; R.H. Barrow, *The Romans*; Moses Hadas, A *History of Latin Literature*.

20. **VIRGIL**—*Aeneid*, tr. Rolfe Humphries (Scribner's); tr. Robert Fitzgerald (Random); tr. William F. Knight (Penguin); tr. C. Day Lewis (Anchor); tr. Allen Mandelbaum (Bantam). The Fitzgerald version is highly acclaimed. Note also *Georgics*, tr. S.P. Bovie (U. of Chicago Press); tr. Allen Mandelbaum (U. of Calif. Press).

Further reading: G. Highet, *Poets in a Landscape*; T. R. Glover, *Virgil*.

21. **MARCUS AURELIUS**—Long's translation of the *Meditations* is contained in *The Stoic and Epicurean Philosophers*, ed. Whitney J. Oates (Modern Library Giants). Other versions: tr. G. M. Grube (Bobbs-Merrill); tr. Maxwell Staniforth (Penguin).

Further reading: See Matthew Arnold's famous essay in *The Portable Marcus Aurelius*, ed. Lionel Trilling. A reasonably recent biography is Anthony Birley's *Marcus Aurelius*.

22. **SAINT AUGUSTINE**—The *Confessions* are included in *Basic Writings of St Augustine*, ed. Whitney J. Oates (2 vols., Random). Paperback editions: tr. R.S. Pine-Coffin (Penguin); tr. Edward B. Pusey (Collier); and, especially good, tr. Rex Warner (Mentor). Note also *On the Two Cities: Selections from the City of God*, ed. F. W. Strothmann (Ungar).

Further reading: Martin C. D'Arcy, ed., *St. Augustine: His Age, Life and Thought*; Peter Brown, *Augustine of Hippo*; Rebecca West's brilliant, untraditional *St. Augustine*; Warren T. Smith, *Augustine: His Life and Thought*.

23. **KĀLIDĀSA**—Translations of *The Cloud Messenger* and *Sakuntala* by Arthur W. Ryder (J.M. Dent), old but still beautiful; and by Chandra Rajan, *Kalidasa: The Loom of Time. A Selection of His Plays and Poems* (Penguin). Translations of *Sakuntala* alone by Barbara Stoler Miller in *Theater of Memory: The Plays of Kalidasa* (Columbia U. Press); P. Lal, *Great Sanskrit Plays in Modern Translation* (New Directions); Michael Coulson, *Three Sanskrit Plays* (Penguin). There is a nice verse translation of *The Cloud Messenger* by Franklin and Eleanor Edgerton (U. Michigan Press).

Further reading: Mary B. Harris, *Kalidasa: Poet of Nature*; K. Krishnamoorthy, *Kalidasa*; Henry W. Wells, *The Classical Drama of India*; Arthur B. Keith's great work, *The Sanskrit Drama*, is old but still useful.

24. *The Koran*—There are many English translations; it is important to note that most believers deny that any translation from the original Arabic can be valid. That said, the translations of Marmaduke Pickthall (New American Library), N.J. Dawood (Penguin), and Arthur J. Arberry (Macmillan) are generally satisfactory.

Further reading: Faruq Sharif, *A Guide to the Contents of the*

Qur'an is helpful. See also Karen Armstrong, *Muhammad: A Biography of the Prophet*. More broadly, see Albert Hourani, *A History of the Arab Peoples*; Bernard Lewis, *The Arabs in History* and *Islam in History*.

25. HUI-NENG—Translations of the *Platform Sutra,* by Wing-tsit Chan (St. Johns U. Press); Philip B. Yampolsky (Columbia U. Press).

    Further reading: Kenneth Chen, *Buddhism in China: A Historical Survey* and *The Chinese Transformation of Buddhism*; D.T. Suzuki, *An Introduction to Zen Buddhism*.

26. FIRDAUSI—The only complete English translation of the *Shah Nameh* is by Arthur G. Warner and Edmond Warner; it is unfortunately in antiquated blank verse. Better is Reuben Levy's abridged translation, *The Epic of the Kings* (Routledge and Keegan Paul). There are two very good transations of single episodes from the epic: Jerome Clinton, *The Tragedy of Sohrab and Rostam* (U. Washington Press), and Dick Davis, *The Legend of Seyavash* (Penguin Classics).

    Further reading: Dick Davis, *Epic and Sedition: The Case of Ferdowsi's Shahnameh*; Olga M. Davidson, *Poet and Hero in the Persian Book of Kings).

27. SEI SHŌNAGON—The complete, and excellent, translation of *The Pillow-Book* is by Ivan Morris (2 vols; Columbia U. Press; abridged version, Columbia U. Press; Penguin).

    Further reading: Ivan Morris's highly readable account of Heian court life, *The World of the Shining Prince*, is the best general introduction to both Sei Shōnagon and to *The Tale of Genji*.

28. LADY MURASAKI—Arthur Waley's translation of *The Tale of Genji* (Modern Library) is justly famous; Edward Seidensticker's (Knopf) is nevertheless better overall. See also Richard Bowring's *Murasaki Shikibu: Her Diary and Poetic Memoirs* (Princeton U. Press).

    Further reading: Richard Bowring's *Murasaki Shikibu: The Tale of Genji* gives a useful overview of the novel. See also: Ivan Morris, *The World of the Shining Prince*; Haruo Shirane, *The Bridge of Dreams: A Poetics of the Tale of Genji*; Andrew Pekarik, ed., *Ukifune: Love in the Tale of Genji*, a collection of essays dealing only with the later chapters of *Genji*.

29. OMAR KHAYYAM—Fitzgerald's translation is widely available; the Penguin edition has a good introduction by Dick Davis. The translation by Peter Avery and John Heath-Stubbs is less dramatic as a work of English poetry, but more faithful to the Persian original.

    Further reading: There is surprisingly little; try Ali Dashti's *In Search of Omar Khayyam*, tr. L.P. Elwell-Sutton.

30. DANTE ALIGHIERI—Among many other translations there are good versions of *The Divine Comedy* by John Ciardi (Norton);

Thomas G. Bergin (Harlan Davidson); Dorothy Sayers (Penguin); Allen Mandelbaum (U. of California Press); Robert Pinsky (Farrar, Straus and Giroux). The translation by Charles S. Singleton (Princeton U. Press) inclines to the literal, but this has its value. Note also *La Vita Nuova*, tr. Barbara Reynolds (Penguin); *On World Government (De Monarchia)*, tr. H. S. Schneider (Bobbs-Merrill); and the excellent *Portable Dante* (Viking).

Further reading: Francis Fergusson, *Dante*; Thomas G. Bergin, *Dante*; Jefferson Butler Fletcher, *Dante*; the essay on Dante in George Santayana's *Three Philosophical Poets*; the essay on Dante in T.S. Eliot's *Selected Essays 1917–1932;* Robin Kirkpatrick, *Dante: The Divine Comedy*. Good biography: P.J. Quinones, *Dante Alighieri*.

31. **LUO KUAN-CHUNG**—The best translation is by Moss Roberts, *Three Kingdoms: A Historical Novel* (U. California Press). The older translation by C.H. Brewitt-Taylor, *Romance of the Three Kingdoms* (reprint, Tuttle) is acceptable.

Further reading: C.T. Hsia, *The Classic Chinese Novel: A Critical Introduction* covers all major works of Chinese fiction, as does the briefer work by China's foremost twentieth-century writer, Lu Hsün, *A Brief History of Chinese Fiction*, tr. by Yang Hsien-yi and Gladys Yang.

32. **GEOFFREY CHAUCER**—*Complete Works,* ed. W. W. Skeat (Oxford U. Press). *Canterbury Tales,* tr. Nevill Coghill (Penguin), an excellent translation; also tr. David Wright (Vintage); tr. R. M. Lumiansky (prose, Washington Sq. Press). *Portable Chaucer,* ed. Theodore Morrison (Viking). *Troilus and Crisseyde,* tr. Nevill Coghill (Penguin). *A Choice of Chaucer's Verse*, ed. Nevill Coghill (Merrimack).

Further reading: John Livingston Lowes, *Geoffrey Chaucer*; Marchette Chute, *Geoffrey Chaucer of England*; D.S. Brewer, *Chaucer*, 3d ed.; G.G. Coulton, *Chaucer and His England*; S.S. Hussey, *Chaucer: An Introduction;* Donald R. Howard, *Chaucer*.

33. *The Thousand and One Nights*—The two classic Victorian translations are by Richard Burton (10 vols, 1885, and six supplementary vols., 1886–88), and by John Payne (9 vols, 1882–84, four supplementary vols., 1884–88). There are many reprints and abridgements of both; beware of censorship and of retellings for children.

Further reading: Robert Irving's *The Arabian Nights: A Companion* is an excellent guide to the stories, their historical context, and their translations. See also: Mia I. Gerhardt, *The Art of Story-Telling: A Literary Study of the Thousand and One Nights*, and Peter L. Caracciolo, *The Arabian Nights in English Literature*, a fascinating study of the influence of the tales on a wide range of English authors.

34. **NICCOLO MACHIAVELLI**—*The Prince:* many editions, including Airmont, Mentor, Oxford, Penguin, Everyman.

Further reading: The best biography is R. Ridolfi's *Life of Niccolò Machiavelli.* More recent: Quentin Skinner, *Machiavelli.*

35. **FRANÇOIS RABELAIS**—A good translation of *Gargantua and Pantagruel* is by John M. Cohen (Penguin). See also Penguin's *Portable Rabelais,* ed. Samuel Putnam.

Further reading: The best one-volume life is the translation by Louis P.Roche of Jean Plattard's *The Life of François Rabelais,* but this is hard to come by. Samuel Putnam's *Rabelais: Man of the Renaissance* is good, too. D.B. Wyndham Lewis's *Doctor Rabelais,* by a Catholic and a humorist, offers a sympathetic interpretation of both these aspects of Rabelais. Donald Frame's *François Rabelais: A Study* is a good introductory book, and Mikhail Bakhtin's *Rabelais and His World* a penetrating one.

36. *Journey to the West,* attr. to Wu Ch'eng-en—There are two complete translations, by Anthony C. Yu (4 vols., U. Chicago Press) and by W.J.F. Jenner (3 vols., Foreign Languages Press, Beijing); the most popular version is Arthur Waley's inspired abridgement, *Monkey* (John Day; Grove paperback).

Further Reading: C.T. Hsia, *The Classic Chinese Novel;* even if you only read Waley's abridged *Monkey,* read the introduction to Anthony Yu's complete translation.

37. **MICHEL EYQUEM DE MONTAIGNE**—*Complete Essays,* tr. Donald Frame (Stanford U. Press). Look also for the translation by John M. Cohen in Penguin. A new translation is by M.A. Screech, in two versions: *The Complete Essays* and *The Essays: A Selection* (both in Penguin).

Further reading: The best biography in English is Donald M. Frame's *Montaigne.* Marvin Lowenthal's *The Autobiography of Michel de Montaigne* arranges excerpts from the *Essays* so as to follow the course of Montaigne's life. Frame's *Montaigne's Discovery of Man* is a serious, scholarly work. Two first-class essays: Virginia Woolf's in *The Common Reader* and Ralph Waldo Emerson's in *The Portable Emerson.*

38. **MIGUEL DE CERVANTES SAAVEDRA**—Mentor has an acceptable abridged edition of *Don Quixote.* Penguin has a *Portable Cervantes,* containing the excellent Putnam translation. Also look for the Starkie translation (Signet) or the Cohen version (Penguin).

Further reading: The bibliography is of course enormous. Gerald Brenan's *Literature of the Spanish People* has a fine Cervantes chapter and is well worth reading complete. The old standard biography is still authoritative: F. Fitzmaurice-Kelly, *Miguel de Cervantes Saavedra: A Memoir.* See also: J.W. Krutch, *Five Masters;* Mark Van Doren, *Don Quixote's Profession;* A.F.G. Bell,

Cervantes; Salvador de Madariaga, *Don Quixote: An Introductory Essay in Psychology*; Rudolph Schevill, *Cervantes;* R.L Predmore, *Cervantes;* William Byron, *Cervantes*; M. McKendrick, *Cervantes.*

39. **WILLIAM SHAKESPEARE**—Many publishers offer the individual plays in paperback. A good one-volume complete edition, however, is the thing to buy: S. Wells et al., *William Shakespeare: The Complete Works* (Oxford U. Press); *Complete Plays and Poems,* ed. W.A. Neilson and C.J. Hill; the Hardin Craig edition, revised by Craig and David Bevington; and those published by Riverside, Signet, Penguin, and Scott Foresman. *The Portable Shakespeare* (Viking) offers good selections.

   Further reading: To aid in your reading of Shakespeare, we list several books, each approaching the subject from a different angle, each useful in a different way: M.C. Bradbrook, *Shakespeare: The Poet in His World*; A.C. Bradley, *Shakespearean Tragedy*; Peter Quennell, *Shakespeare*; *Northrop Frye on Shakespeare*; G.B. Harrison, *Introducing Shakespeare*; Marchette Chute, *Shakespeare of London*; Anthony Burgess, *Shakespeare*; A. Nicoll, *Shakespeare in His Own Age*; S. Schoenbaum, *Shakespeare: The Globe and the World*. Jan Kott's *Shakespeare Our Contemporary* is a stimulating modern view, of interest to those involved in production.

40. **JOHN DONNE**—Penguin has *The Complete English Poems*, as does Hendricks House. Modern Library has *Poetry and Prose.*

   Further reading: The definitive biography is R.C. Baid's *John Donne: A Life*. See also: Wilbur Sanders, *John Donne's Poetry*; J.B. Leishman, *The Monarch of Wit: An Analytical and Comparative Study of John Donne*; Edmund Gosse, *Life and Letters of John Donne* (2 vols.); H.I. Faussett, *John Donne, A Study in Discord*; George Williamson, *The Donne Tradition*; Theodore Spencer, ed., *A Garland for John Donne*; T.S. Eliot's influential essay on "The Metaphysical Poets" in his *Selected Essays.*

41. *The Plum in the Golden Vase (Chin P'ing Mei)*—Only the first volume of David Roy's superb translation (Princeton U. Press) has appeared as of early 1997. Meanwhile, Clement Egerton's translation (*The Golden Lotus*; Routledge and Kegan Paul, distributed in the U.S. by Columbia U. Press) is adequate. Arthur Waley's translation (published anonymously by Putnam's), titled *Chin P'ing Mei: The Adventurous History of Hsi Men and His Six Wives*, is abbreviated, bowdlerized, and better avoided.

   Further reading: The introduction, notes and appendices in Roy's translation are the best readily available commentary on the novel. More generally, see also C.T. Hsia, *The Classic Chinese Novel.*

42. **GALILEO GALILEI**—Stillman Drake's translation of the *Dialogue Concerning the Two Chief World Systems* (U. California Press) is

scholarly and complete, and has a foreword by Albert Einstein. Better for the general reader, but hard to find, is the abridged text edition of the older translation by T. Salusbury, edited and with extensive commentary by Giorgio de Santillana. See also *Siderius Nuncius or The Sidereal Messenger*, tr. Albert van Helden (U. Chicago Press).

Further reading: James Reston Jr., *Galileo: A Life*; Giorgio de Santillana, *The Crime of Galileo*; Mario Biagioli, *Galileo, Courtier: The Practice of Science in the Culture of Absolutism*.

43. **THOMAS HOBBES**—*Leviathan:* Bobbs-Merrill; Everyman; Pelican (Penguin); Collier.

Further reading: Richard Peters, *Hobbes*; D.D. Raphael, *Hobbes*. Basil Willey's *The Seventeenth Century Background* discusses, in addition to Hobbes, Descartes (44), Milton (45), and Locke (49).

44. **RENÉ DESCARTES**—*Discourse on Method:* Everyman; Bobbs-Merrill; Penguin. Columbia University Press publishes a full-dress *Philosophical Work* in two volumes.

Further reading: For a full account, see J.R. Vrooman, *René Descartes: A Biography*. See also: Bernard Williams, *Descartes: The Project of Pure Enquiry*, and the relevant chapters in Durant, *Story of Philosophy* and Bertrand Russell, *History of Western Philosophy*.

45. **JOHN MILTON**—Mentor has *Paradise Lost and Other Poems;* Holt offers *Paradise Lost and Selected Poetry and Prose;* and there is a *Portable Milton* (Penguin). Other editions are easily come by.

Further reading: A comprehensive biography is W.R. Parker's *Milton* (2 vols.). Shorter biographical treatments: J.H. Hanford, *John Milton, Englishman*; Rose Macaulay, *Milton*. See also: David Daiches, *Milton*; E.M.W. Tillyard, *Milton* (Macmillan); chapter 10 of Basil Willey, *The Seventeenth Century Background*; and the two interesting Milton essays in T.S. Eliot's *On Poetry and Poets*.

46. **MOLIÈRE**—Signet issues a one-volume edition of Donald Frame's reliable translation of *Tartuffe* and six other important plays; and in another volume his translation of *The Misanthrope* plus other plays. Another good, more unconventional translator is Richard Wilbur. Harcourt Brace issues his *Misanthrope* (with *Tartuffe)* and *The School for Wives* in separate volumes. Penguin has two volumes of John Wood's translations, comprising most of the better-known plays. But the best way to read Molière is to learn French first.

Further reading: W.D. Howarth, *Molière: A Playwright and His Audience*; J.L. Palmer, *Molière: His Life and Works*; Gertrud Mander, *Molière;* D.B.W. Lewis, *Molière: The Comic Mask*.

47. **BLAISE PASCAL**—His *Thoughts* or *Pensées* are in Penguin; *Selections* is published by Harlan Davidson.

Further reading: Jean Mesnard's *Pascal: His Life and Works* and *Pascal* are authoritative. Morris Bishop's *Pascal: The Life of Genius* is a sound biography; also A.G. Krailsheimer's *Pascal*. See also T.S. Eliot's essay on Pascal in his *Selected Essays*.

48. **JOHN BUNYAN**—Paperbacks of *The Pilgrim's Progress* are easily come by: Airmont; Holt, Rinehart; and Signet (with a foreword by the formidable F.R. Leavis) all offer handy volumes.

Further reading: G.B. Harrison, *Bunyan: A Study in Personality*; R. Sharrock, *John Bunyan*, rev. ed.; O.E. Winslow, *John Bunyan,* perhaps the most useful biography.

49. **JOHN LOCKE**—*Second Treatise*: Bobbs-Merrill. *Essay Concerning Human Understanding:* (2 vols., Dover), Meridian; Everyman; Collier.

Further reading: D.J. O'Connor, *John Locke*, a good introduction; R.I. Aaron, *John Locke*; Maurice Cranston, *John Locke: A Biography*, a fine job. See also: *Locke Reader*, ed. J.W. Yolton; *Locke Selections*, ed. S.P. Lamprecht.

50. **MATSUO BASHŌ**—There are many translations; one of the best of *The Narrow Road* is by Nobuyuki Yuasa (Penguin). See also Sam Hamill, *The Narrow Road to the Interior* (Shambala); Lucien Stryk, *On Love and Barley: Haiku of Bashō* (Penguin); Makoto Ueda, *Bashō and His Interpreters: Selected Hokku with Commentaries* (Stanford U. Press).

Further reading: Makoto Ueda, *Matsuo Bashō*; Robert Aitken, *A Zen Wave: Bashō's Haiku and Zen.*

51. **DANIEL DEFOE**—Many paperback editions of *Robinson Crusoe* are available: among others, Signet, Dutton, and Washington Square Press. Dutton and Holt, Rinehart offer *Moll Flanders*; Oxford has *Roxana*, ed. Jane Jack.

Further reading: The fullest biography is J.R. Moore's *Daniel Defoe, Citizen of the Modern World*. See also: James Sutherland, *Defoe*; the essay by Virginia Woolf in *The Common Reader*.

52. **JONATHAN SWIFT**—Dell, Norton, Oxford, and Holt, Rinehart all offer good editions of *Gulliver. The Portable Swift,* ed. Carl Van Doren (Viking), contains a fine selection from Swift's miscellaneous work in both prose and verse.

Further reading: For biography, see I. Ehrenpreis, *Swift: The Man, His Works, and the Age* (2 vols.). See also: Carl Van Doren, *Swift*; R. Quintana, *The Mind and Art of Jonathan Swift*; David Ward, *Jonathan Swift: An Introductory Essay.*

53. **VOLTAIRE**—*Candide* is widely available. Modern Library includes "other writings," as does Signet. Ben Redman's *Portable Voltaire* (Viking) is a good collection. You may be able to find Peter Gay's translation of the *Philosophical Dictionary* (Harvest).

Further reading: The best biography in English is probably Theodore Besterman's *Voltaire*. See also Richard Aldington,

Voltaire; Virgil W. Topazio, *Voltaire: A Critical Study of His Major Works*; W. Andrews, *Voltaire*; H.N. Brailsford, *Voltaire*. A.J. Ayer's *Voltaire* deals brilliantly with his lesser-known works. Peyton E. Richter and Ilona Ricardo's *Voltaire* is a good introductory biography.

54. **DAVID HUME**—*An Enquiry Concerning Human Understanding*: Oxford U. Press, Open Court.

Further reading: E.C. Mossner's *The Life of David Hume* is the definitive biography. J.Y.T. Greig's *David Hume* is shorter. See also: Barry Stroud, *Hume*; *David Hume: Many-Sided Genius*, ed. K.R. Merrill and R.W. Shahan; A.J. Ayer, *Hume*.

55. **HENRY FIELDING**—*Tom Jones* and *Joseph Andrews* are widely available. Signet and Everyman offer *Jonathan Wild*.

Further reading: The standard biography is the two-volume *Henry Fielding: His Life, Work, and Times*, by F. Homes Dudden. Thackeray's estimate of Fielding is good but deeply Victorian: See his *The English Humourists of the Eighteenth Century*. Useful also is Ronald Paulson, ed., *Fielding: A Collection of Critical Essays*; Andrew Wright, *Henry Fielding: Mask and Feast*.

56. **TS'AO HSÜEH-CH'IN**—The best translation of *The Dream of the Red Chamber* is by David Hawkes (with John Minford) under its alternative title, *The Story of the Stone* (5 vols, Penguin). Also good is the version by Yang Hsien-yi and Gladys Yang, *A Dream of Red Mansions* (3 vols., Foreign Languages Press, Beijing). The abridged version by C.C. Wang (Anchor) is not very good, though its introduction, by Mark Van Doren, is interesting. The version by Florence and Isabel McHugh (Pantheon) is translated from Franz Kuhn's very good German translation; it is a nice, readable abridgement, but at two removes from the original.

Further reading: Jeanne Knoerle, *The Dream of the Red Chamber: A Critical Study*, is a good introduction; Andrew H. Plaks, *Archetype and Allegory in The Dream of the Red Chamber* is immensely learned and full of fascinating insights.

57. **JEAN-JACQUES ROUSSEAU**—Penguin has J.M. Cohen's excellent translation of the *Confessions*. Washington Square Press issues in one volume *The Social Contract* and *Discourse on the Origin of Inequality*.

Further reading: The recommended biography is Jean Guéhenno's *Jean-Jacques Rousseau*. See also: Peter France, *Rousseau: Confessions*; Maurice Cranston, *Jean-Jacques: The Early Life and Work of Jean-Jacques Rousseau, 1712–1754*. For a classic attack on Rousseau, see Irving Babbitt's *Rousseau and Romanticism*.

58. **LAURENCE STERNE**—Editions of *Tristram Shandy*: Oxford, Penguin, Riverside, Airmont, Signet, Norton, Evergreen. The Harvard University Press edition also contains A *Sentimental*

Journey and *Selected Sermons and Letters. A Sentimental Journey* is available in Everyman and Penguin.

Further reading: Arthur H. Cash, *Laurence Sterne* (2 vols.). See also Virginia Woolf's essay "The Sentimental Journey" in her *Second Common Reader*. This also discusses, among other topics, *Robinson Crusoe*, Swift's *Journal to Stella*, and the novels of Thomas Hardy.

59. **JAMES BOSWELL**—Penguin, Modern Library, and Signet (abridged) offer the *Life*. McGraw-Hill publishes the Boswell *Private Papers* in many hardbound volumes. Oxford publishes in paperback Boswell's interesting *Journal of a Tour to the Hebrides.*

Further reading: The multivolume Yale Editions of the *Private Papers of James Boswell* is published by McGraw-Hill, edited in the main by Frederick Pottle; some volumes have collaborative editors. On these papers Pottle based his important *James Boswell: The Earlier Years, 1740–1769.* The first volume of the Yale series, the fascinating *Boswell's London Journal 1762–1763,* is available in paperback. Other studies of this curiously flawed genius: Hesketh Pearson, *Johnson and Boswell*; Wyndham Lewis, *James Boswell: A Short Life*; C.B. Tinker, *Young Boswell.*

60. *Basic Documents in American History*, edited by Richard B. Morris, is published by both Krieger and Van Nostrand (Anvil Books).

Further reading: For a wider sampling and discussion of American historical records, see Richard Hofstadter's *Great Issues in American History* (2 vols.). For the Declaration, see Carl Becker's *The Declaration of Independence.* For the making of the Constitution, see Carl Van Doren, *The Great Rehearsal*; C.D. Bowen, *Miracle at Philadelpia.* See also Garry Wills, *Inventing America*, and Pauline Maier, *American Scripture.*

61. *The Federalist Papers*—Rossiter's *Federalist Papers* is in New American Library. Bantam, Harvard University Press, and Modern Library also have good editions. AHM Publications offers *Selections from the Federalist*, ed. Henry S. Commager.

Further reading: An excellent compendium is Bernard Bailyn, ed., *The Debate on the Constitution: Federalist and Antifederalist Speeches, Articles and Letters during the Struggle over Ratification* (Library of America/Viking).

62. **JOHANN WOLFGANG VON GOETHE**—Oxford University Press issues an abridged version of both parts of *Faust* by the fine poet Louis MacNeice. Also recommended: the two parts, tr. Walter Kaufmann (Anchor); Part 1, tr. C.F. MacIntyre (New Directions); Part 1, tr. Randall Jarrell (Farrar, Straus); Part 1, tr. David Luke (World's Classics). Avoid the antiquated Bayard Taylor version. *Great Writings of Goethe*, ed. by Stephen Spender (New

American Library), contains MacNeice's version of *Faust*, Part 1, and many other works worth reading.

Further reading: G.W. Lewes, *The Life and Works of Goethe*; the essay on Goethe in Santayana's *Three Philosophical Poets*; various essays on Goethe in Thomas Mann's *Essays of Three Decades*; Nicholas Boyle, *Faust, Part 1*. Emil Ludwig's *Goethe: The History of a Man, 1749–1832* is a readable, popularized biography.

63. **WILLIAM BLAKE**—A very good edition is Oxford's *Complete Writings of William Blake*. Penguin has the *Complete Poems* as well as a good *Portable Blake*, ed. Alfred Kazin.

Further reading: Mona Wilson, *The Life of William Blake*; S. Foster Damon, *William Blake: His Philosophy and Symbols*; Mark Schorer, *William Blake*; essay on Blake in T.S. Eliot's *Selected Essays*; Jacob Bronowski, *William Blake and the Age of Revolution*; Northrop Frye, *Fearful Symmetry: A Study of William Blake*. An investigation in depth by a fine Blake scholar is Kathleen J. Raine's *Blake and Tradition* (2 vols.). See also her *William Blake*. The latest study is *Blake* by Peter Ackroyd.

64. **WILLIAM WORDSWORTH**—The best moderately priced edition is Oxford's *Poetical Works with Introduction and Notes*. Less comprehensive but good: Riverside's *Selected Poems and Prefaces;* Modern Library's *Selected Poetry*, ed. Mark Van Doren.

Further reading: For a standard biography, see G. McL. Harper, *William Wordsworth, His Life, Works, and Influence* (2 vols.). See also Mary Moorman's *William Wordsworth: A Biography* (2 vols.), and Hunter Davies, *William Wordsworth*. For diverse critical appraisals, see H.I. Faussett, *The Lost Leader: A Study of Wordsworth*; H.W. Garrod, *Wordsworth: Lectures and Essays*; Coleridge's *Biographia Literatia*; J. Wordsworth, *The Music of Humanity*; Matthew Arnold's essay in *Essays in Criticism,* 2nd series.

65. **SAMUEL TAYLOR COLERIDGE**—Modern Library has *Selected Poetry and Prose;* Oxford has *Complete Poems*; Penguin has a *Portable Coleridge;* Everyman has the *Biographia Literaria*.

Further reading: Oswald Doughty, *Perturbed Spirit: The Life and Personality of Samuel Taylor Coleridge*. Another good modern brief biography is W.J. Bate's *Coleridge*. E.K. Chambers's *Samuel Taylor Coleridge* is fuller, but dated. See also Lawrence Hanson's *The Life of Samuel Taylor Coleridge*. The finest book on Coleridge's genius and a masterpiece in its own right is John Livingston Lowes's *The Road to Xanadu*. See also: Thomas De Quincey, *Reminiscences of the English Lake Poets*, for a firsthand glimpse; I.A. Richards, *Coleridge on Imagination*; Basil Willey, *Samuel Taylor Coleridge*; S. Prickett, *Coleridge and Wordsworth: The Poetry of Growth*.

66. **JANE AUSTEN**—*Pride and Prejudice* can be found everywhere: among others, Riverside (ed. Mark Schorer, a fine scholar). Modern Library binds it with *Sense and Sensibility*, introd. by David Daiches. Riverside's *Emma* is introduced by the brilliant critic Lionel Trilling. The magisterial R.W. Chapman edition (Oxford) comes in six volumes and includes the minor works.

    Further reading: The standard life is *Jane Austen, Her Life and Letters*, by W. and R.A. Austen-Leigh. See also Elizabeth Jenkins, *Jane Austen*; essay by Virginia Woolf in *The Common Reader*; Marghanita Laski, *Jane Austen and Her World*; John Halperin, *The Life of Jane Austen*; Tony Tanner, *Jane Austen*; Mary Lascelles, *Jane Austen*; David Cecil, *A Portrait of Jane Austen*; and two new biographies, *Jane Austen: Obstinate Heart*, by Valerie Grosvenor Myer and *Jane Austen: A Life* by David Nokes.

67. **STENDHAL**—Signet's edition of *The Red and the Black* is good; so is the Bantam edition, tr. Lowell Bair. *Charterhouse* is in Penguin and Signet—the latter, tr. C. K Scott-Moncrieff, is better. University of Chicago Press publishes *The Life of Henry Brulard: The Autobiography of Stendhal.*

    Further reading: For a sound biography in English see Matthew Josephson's *Stendhal*. Martin Turnell's brilliant *The Novel in France* offers penetrating analyses of Stendhal along with Balzac (68), Flaubert (86), and Proust (105). The excellent Lowell Bair translation of *The Red and the Black* contains a longish introduction by Clifton Fadiman. See also: Harry Levin, *The Gates of Horn: A Study of Five French Realists*; Storm Jameson, *Speaking of Stendhal*.

68. **HONORÉ DE BALZAC**—*Père Goriot* is in Airmont, Signet, and Penguin (under the title *Old Goriot*). *Eugénie Grandet* is in Penguin and Everyman. *Cousin Bette* is in Penguin.

    Further reading: Some good biographies and studies are V.S. Pritchett, *Balzac*; André Maurois, *Prometheus: The Life of Balzac*; Herbert J. Hunt, *Honoré de Balzac*; Stefan Zweig, *Balzac*. Shorter studies are to be found in Harry Levin's *Toward Balzac* and particularly Henry James's "The Lesson of Balzac" in *The Future of the Novel*, ed. Leon Edel. The latter also contains estimates of Flaubert (86), Turgenev (81), Tolstoy (88), and Conrad (100).

69. **RALPH WALDO EMERSON**—Good collections of the *Essays* are to be found in Penguin, Everyman, Modern Library, Signet, Riverside. The Library of America has an omnibus volume of *Essays and Lectures*.

    Further reading: A standard biography is R.L. Rusk's *The Life of Ralph Waldo Emerson*. See also: Lewis Leary, *Ralph Waldo Emerson: An Interpretive Essay*; Van Wyck Brooks, *The Flowering of New England*; F.O. Matthiessen, *American Renaissance*; Bliss

Perry, ed., *The Heart of Emerson's Journals*; George Santayana's essay on Emerson in *Interpretations of Poetry and Religion*; Kenneth Walter Cameron, *Emerson the Essayist;* Stephen E. Whicher, *Freedom and Fate: An Inner Life of Ralph Waldo Emerson*. On the transcendentalists as a group, see Carlos Baker, *Emerson among the Eccentrics*. See also the recent book by Robert D. Richardson, Jr. and Barry Moser, *Emerson: The Mind on Fire*.

70. **NATHANIEL HAWTHORNE**—Too many editions available to warrant listing. Penguin issues a *Portable Hawthorne,* and Vintage his *Short Stories.* The Library of America has a volume of *Collected Novels,* and another of *Tales and Sketches.*

Further reading: One of the finest critical works (but it requires close attention) on the major American writers of the mid-nineteenth century is F.O. Matthiessen's *American Renaissance.* The major emphasis is on Hawthorne, Thoreau (80), Melville (83), and Whitman (85), with good material also on Poe (75); it may be consulted in connection with all of these writers. Two excellent short treatments: Mark Van Doren's *Nathaniel Hawthorne: A Critical Biography*; Randall Stewart's *Nathaniel Hawthorne: A Biography*. See also: Henry James's pioneering study, *Hawthorne* (1879); Hyatt H. Waggoner, *Hawthorne: A Critical Study*; J.R. Mellow, *Nathaniel Hawthorne and His Times*; Arlin Turner, *Nathaniel Hawthorne: A Biography.*

71. **ALEXIS DE TOCQUEVILLE**—The best edition of *Democracy in America* is that edited by Phillips Bradley. Vintage has it in two volumes, Anchor in one. Mentor offers an abridged edition.

Further reading: A good standard biography is J.P. Mayer's *Alexis de Tocqueville: A Biographical Essay in Political Science.* Recommended: a careful reading of Phillips Bradley's long and thoughtful introduction to his monumental two-volume edition of *Democracy in America.* See also: G. W. Pierson, *Tocqueville in America,* abridged by Dudley C. Lunt; J.P. Mayer, *Alexis de Tocqueville: Journey to America.*

72. **JOHN STUART MILL**—*On Liberty:* Bobbs-Merrill, Norton. Oxford has *Three Essays (On Liberty, Representative Government, Subjection of Women).* Columbia U. Press and Riverside publish the *Autobiography.*

Further reading: Maurice Cranston, *J.S. Mill*; Michael St. John Packe, *The Life of John Stuart Mill,* the fullest account; E.R. August, *John Stuart Mill;* J. Plamenatz, *The English Utilitarians.*

73. **CHARLES DARWIN**—*On the Origin of Species* (Harvard U. Press, Penguin); *The Descent of Man* (Princeton U. Press, Penguin); *Charles Darwin's Beagle Diary,* ed. R.D. Keynes (Cambridge U. Press); *Journal of Researches. . . during the Voyage of H.M.S.*

Beagle... [more commonly known by its short title, *The Voyage of the Beagle*] (John Murray); *The Autobiography of Charles Darwin*, ed. Nora Barlow (Collins). Cambridge University Press publishes the *Complete Correspondence* and the *Scientific Journals* in multiple volumes, edited by Frederick Burkhardt.

Further reading: Gertrude Himmelfarb, *Darwin and the Darwinian Revolution*; Janet Browne, *Charles Darwin: A Biography* (2 vols); Adrian Desmond and James Moore, *Darwin: The Life of a Tormented Evolutionist*; John Bowlby, *Charles Darwin: A New Life*; Peter J. Bowler, *Charles Darwin: The Man and His Influence*. On Darwinian evolution, see Richard Dawkins, *The Blind Watchmaker*.

74. **NIKOLAI VASILIEVICH GOGOL**—*Dead Souls*, tr. B. G. Guerney (Holt, Rinehart), may be hard to find. Other good versions are issued by Norton, Airmont, Signet, and Penguin. Signet has *Diary of a Madman and Other Stories;* Norton offers *The Overcoat and Other Tales of Good and Evil;* University of Chicago Press issues *The Complete Tales of Nikolai Gogol* in two volumes.

Further reading: As you read Gogol, Turgenev (81), Tolstoy (88), Dostoyevsky (87), and Chekhov (101), you may find useful Mark Slonim's *Outline of Russian Literature*. Fuller treatments of Gogol: Vladimir Nabokov's somewhat eccentric but interesting *Nikolai Gogol*; J. Lavrin, *Gogol;* V. Erlich, *Gogol*; Jesse Zeldin, *Nicolai Gogol's Quest for Beauty: An Exploration into His Works;* V. Setchkarev, *Gogol: His Life and Works*; D. Magarshack, *Gogol: A Life.*

75. **EDGAR ALLEN POE**—Vintage (Giant) has *Complete Tales and Poems*. Other convenient editions: Meridian, Signet, Everyman. Viking issues a good *Portable Poe*. The Library of America has a volume of *Poetry and Tales,* and one of *Essays and Reviews.*

Further reading: The standard authority is Arthur H. Quinn's *Edgar Allan Poe: A Critical Biography*. See also Joseph Wood Krutch's excellent *Edgar Allan Poe: A Study in Genius*; Edward Wagenknecht, *Edgar Allan Poe: The Man Behind the Legend*; Constance Pope-Hennessy, *Edgar Allan Poe, 1809–1849: A Critical Biography;* Perry Miller, *The Raven and the Whale*; William L. Howarth, ed., *Twentieth Century Interpretations of Poe's Tales*; Roger Asselineau, *Edgar Allan Poe.*

76. **WILLIAM MAKEPEACE THACKERAY**—*Vanity Fair* is available generally. Good editions: Modern Library, Oxford U. Press, Penguin, Riverside. Penguin has a good *Henry Esmond*. His *English Humourists of the Eighteenth Century* (Dutton) contains interesting assessments of some of his predecessors.

Further reading: The standard life is Gordon N. Ray's *Thackeray: The Uses of Adversity (1811–1846)* and *Thackeray: The Age of*

Wisdom (1847–1863). A good one-volume biography: Ann Monsarrat, *An Uneasy Victorian.* A fine critical study is Geoffrey Tillotson, *Thackeray the Novelist.* See also John Carey's *Thackeray: Prodigal Genius.*

77. **CHARLES DICKENS**—All of the major novels are available in multiple paperback editions. Oxford offers a handsome complete set of Dickens's novels in hardcover.

Further reading: The comprehensive biography is Edgar Johnson, *Charles Dickens: His Tragedy and Triumph.* The Dickens literature is formidable. Here are some interesting treatments: F.R. and Q.D. Leavis, *Dickens the Novelist*; Humphry House, *The Dickens World*; Angus Wilson, *The World of Charles Dickens*; Edmund Wilson's pathbreaking essay "Dickens: The Two Scrooges" in *The Wound and the Bow*; J. Hillis Miller, *Charles Dickens: The World of His Novels*; G.K Chesterton, *Charles Dickens: A Critical Study*, a brilliant study; George Orwell, "Dickens" in *Dickens, Dali & Others.*

78. **ANTHONY TROLLOPE**—Virtually all of the novels are available in Penguin; also most from Oxford U. Press, Everyman, and Ayer.

Further reading: Victoria Glendenning, *Anthony Trollope*; Robert H. Soper, *The Chronicler of Barsetshire: A Life of Anthony Trollope*; N. John Hall, *Trollope: A Biography.* Old but still interesting is Elizabeth Bowen's *Anthony Trollope: A New Judgement.* See also James R. Kincaid, *The Novels of Anthony Trollope.*

79. **THE BRONTË SISTERS**—Among the many available editions of Emily's *Wuthering Heights* note especially: Riverside, ed. V.S. Pritchett; Penguin, ed. David Daiches. Penguin publishes a large paperback that also contains Charlotte's *Jane Eyre* and Anne's *The Tenant of Wildfell Hall.* Separate editions of *Jane Eyre* are widely available.

Further reading: Though of course somewhat outmoded by subsequent scholarship, Elizabeth Gaskell's *Life of Charlotte Brontë* still offers an interesting picture of the whole family. See also Muriel Spark's *Emily Brontë: Her Life and Work.* Other informative books: Irene Cooper Willis, *The Brontës*; Thomas Winnifirith, *The Brontës*; Winifred Gerin, *Emily Brontë: A Biography*; Juliet Barker, *The Brontës.*

80. **HENRY DAVID THOREAU**—*Walden* is readily available. Most editions include *Civil Disobedience.* Penguin has a *Portable Thoreau* and *A Week on the Concord and Merimack Rivers;* Bantam has *Walden and Other Writings*, ed. J.W. Krutch. The Library of America has all of Thoreau's major works in a single large volume. A newly published Thoreau work is of interest: *Faith in a Seed: The Dispersion of Seeds and Other Late Natural History Writings* (Island Press).

Further reading: A good biography is Walter Harding's *The Days of Henry Thoreau*. See also Richard Lebeaux, *Young Man Thoreau;* R.T. Richardson Jr., *Henry Thoreau: A Life of the Mind;* Sherman Paul, *The Shores of America: Thoreau's Inward Exploration;* H.S. Canby, *Thoreau*.

81. **IVAN SERGEYEVICH TURGENEV**—*Fathers and Sons* is available in Modern Library (Guerney's translation), Bantam, Norton, Signet, Penguin. Penguin has *Sketches from a Hunter's Album* (another rendering of A *Sportsman's Sketches*).

Further reading: Three reliable biographies are A. Yarmolinsky's *Turgenev: The Man, His Art, and His Age;* L.B. Shapiro's *Turgenev: His Life and Times;* and D. Magarshack's *Turgenev: A Life*. Edmund Wilson contributes an interesting, lengthy introduction to a Turgenev collection, *Literary Reminiscences and Autobiographical Fragments* (Evergreen). A fine study is V.S. Pritchett's *The Gentle Barbarian: The Life and Work of Turgenev*.

82. **KARL MARX** and **FRIEDRICH ENGELS**: There are many editions of the *Communist Manifesto;* Penguin has a handy volume. International Publishing has *Selected Works of Marx & Engels;* you might want to try reading their greatest work, *Capital (Das Kapital)*.

Further reading: A standard life is Franz Mehring's *Karl Marx: The Story of His Life*. See also: S.K. Padover, *Karl Marx: An Intimate Biography;* Isaiah Berlin, *Karl Marx. His Life and Environment*, a brilliant short account; Sidney Hook, *Marx and the Marxists*. For insight into Marx and his connection with thought in general, see R.H. Heilbroner, *The Worldly Philosophers;* Jacques Barzun, *Darwin, Marx, Wagner;* J.K. Galbraith, *The Evolution of Economics*. An excellent psychological study is Bruce Mazlish, *The Meaning of Karl Marx*.

83. **HERMAN MELVILLE**—*Moby Dick* is generally available in many editions. Riverside has a good one edited by the distinguished scholar Alfred Kazin. Penguin issues a *Portable Melville* and Perennial has *Great Short Works,* including *Bartleby*. Signet and Phoenix, among other imprints, offer *Billy Budd*. The Library of America has a three volume Melville set containing all the major works.

Further reading: The literature is vast and various. Some interesting treatments: Leon Howard's *Herman Melville: A Biography;* Newton Arvin's *Herman Melville;* Richard Chase's *Herman Melville: A Critical Study;* W.E. Sedgwick, *Herman Melville: The Tragedy of Mind;* Lewis Muniford, *Herman Melville;* A.R. Humphreys, *Melville;* Van Wyck Brooks, *The Times of Melville and Whitman;* Jay Leyda's *The Melville Log: A Documentary Life of Herman Melville* is just what the title suggests. Two recent biographies are Laurie Robertson-Lorant's *Melville: A Biography,* and the authoritative *Herman Melville: A Biography* by Herschel Parker (the first of two volumes).

84. **GEORGE ELIOT**—*Mill on the Floss, Middlemarch,* and *Adam Bede* are widely available. The Riverside editions are edited by the great Eliot scholar G.S. Haight. *Daniel Deronda:* Penguin, Signet.

Further reading: The definitive life is Gordon S. Haight's *George Eliot: A Biography.* Also excellent is Rosemary Ashton's recent *George Eliot.* For acute criticism, see Joan Bennett, *George Eliot: Her Mind and Her Art;* Barbara Hardy, *The Novels of George Eliot: A Study in Form.* See also: R.T. Jones, *George Eliot;* Marghanita Laski, *George Eliot and Her World;* Lawrence and Elizabeth Hanson, *Marian Evans and George Eliot.* Other views of George Eliot may be found in Virginia Woolf's *The Common Reader,* F.R. Leavis's *The Great Tradition,* David Cecil's *Victorian Novelists,* and Henry James's *Partial Portraits.* Gillian Beer, *George Eliot,* offers an interesting feminist approach.

85. **WALT WHITMAN**—Riverside gives you the *Complete Poetry and Selected Prose.* Penguin has a good *Portable Whitman. Leaves of Grass* is available from many publishers. The Library of America has a *Poetry and Prose* volume.

Further reading: David S. Reynolds, *Walt Whitman's America;* Gay Wilson Allen, *The Solitary Singer,* a good standard biography. Other good book-length treatments: Justin Kaplan, *Walt Whitman: A Life;* H.S. Canby, *Walt Whitman: An American;* Emory Holloway, *Whitman: An Interpretation in Narrative.* See also: Richard Chase, *Walt Whitman;* D.H. Lawrence, "Whitman," in *Studies in Classic American Literature;* Paul Zweig, *Walt Whitman: The Making of the Poet.*

86. **GUSTAVE FLAUBERT**—The Modern Library edition of *Madame Bovary,* tr. Francis Steegmuller, is preferred. Other acceptable versions: Bantam, Airmont, Riverside, Signet, Penguin. There is also a Penguin edition of *Three Tales,* tr. Robert Baldick. See also *Sallambo* and *Flaubert in Egypt,* both tr. Steegmuller, both Penguin.

Further reading: An adequate biography in English is P. Spencer's *Flaubert. A Biography.* Enid Starkie's *Flaubert: The Making of the Master* and Francis Steegmuller's *Flaubert and Madame Bovary* are good studies. See also B.F. Bart's *Flaubert.* University of Chicago Press has published Jean-Paul Sartre's brilliant but idiosyncratic and unfinished *The Family Idiot: Gustave Flaubert, 1821–1857.*

87. **FEODOR MIKHAILOVICH DOSTOYEVSKY**—*Crime and Punishment:* Oxford, Norton, Bantam, Everyman, Modern Library (Garnett tr.), Signet, Vintage, Airmont, Penguin (Magarshack tr.), Viking (McDuff tr.). *The Brothers Karamozov:* Penguin (2 vols.), Airmont, Vintage, Bantam, Modern Library (Garnett tr.). Try also *The Idiot:* Signet, Penguin.

Further reading: R. Hingley, *Dostoyevsky: His Life and Work;* Henri Troyat, *Firebrand: The Life of Dostoevsky;* E.H. Carr, *Dostoevsky;* Avrahm Yarmolinsky, *Dostoevsky, His Life and Art.* Perhaps the best treatment: Janko Lavrin, *Dostoevsky.*

88. **LEO NIKOLAYEVICH TOLSTOY**—*War and Peace:* Penguin (2 vols.), Norton (annotated), Signet, Washington Sq. Press (abridged). *Anna Karenina,* some good editions: Penguin, Norton, Modern Library, Oxford U. Press. Perennial has *Great Short Works* and Penguin *The Portable Tolstoy.*

Further reading: Perhaps the most readable life is Henri Troyat's *Tolstoy.* The standard biography is Aylmer Maude's *The Life of Tolstoy* (2 vols.). For shorter biographies, see Janko Lavrin, *Tolstoy: An Approach;* Ernest Simmons, *Leo Tolstoy;* and Martine de Courcel, *Tolstoy: The Ultimate Reconciliation.* Special interpretations of high interest: D.S. Merezhkovski, *Tolstoi as Man and Artist;* Isaiah Berlin, *The Hedgehog and the Fox: An Essay on Tolstoy's View of History;* George Steiner, *Tolstoy or Dostoevsky: An Essay in the Old Criticism;* Edward Crankshaw, *Tolstoy: The Making of a Novelist;* Alexandra Tolstoy, *Tolstoy: A Life of My Father.*

89. **HENRICK IBSEN**—Virtually all the plays have been translated by Michael Meyer and are published in five paperback volumes by Methuen. Anchor publishes his *When We Dead Awaken and Three Other Plays.* Another reputable translator is James W. MacFarlane; see his *Henrik Ibsen: Penguin Critical Anthology* (Penguin). Oxford offers three volumes comprising Ibsen's best work. Modern Library has Eva Le Gailienne's translation of six well-known plays. New American Library offers complete *Major Prose and Plays;* tr. Rolf Fjelde.

Further reading: M.J. Valency, *The Flower and the Castle.* A slanted but brilliant essay is Shaw's *The Quintessence of Ibsenism.* See also: H. Clurman, *Ibsen;* J. Northam, *Ibsen: A Critical Study.* For biography, see M.C. Bradbrook, *Ibsen the Norwegian;* H. Meyer, *Ibsen: A Biography.* For Ibsen's influence on Asian literature, see Lu Hsün's famous essay, "What Happens After Nora Leaves Home," in his *Selected Works,* tr. Yang and Yang.

90. **EMILY DICKINSON**—Little, Brown publishes the *Complete Poems;* there are various editions of selected poems. Her *Letters,* in three volumes (Belknap), are very interesting.

Further reading: Biographies by Cynthia G. Wolff; Helen McNeil; John E. Walsh, *The Hidden Life of Emily Dickinson;* R.B. Sewell, *The Life of Emily Dickinson.*

91. **LEWIS CARROLL**—The two Alice books are so readily available that editions need not be cited. Try, of course, to get one containing the Tenniel illustrations. Dover has *Humorous Verse of Lewis*

Carroll and also *Pillow Problems* (bound with A *Tangled Tale*).

Further reading: Official, dull, and reticent is S. Dodgson Collingwood's *Life and Letters of Lewis Carroll*. It's rather hard to find, which may be a good thing. Derek Hudson's *Lewis Carroll* takes advantage of the diaries and many hitherto unpublished letters. Anne Clark's *Lewis Carroll* is also a good short biography. See also Morton N. Cohen, *Lewis Carroll: A Biography*. Florence Becker Lennon's *The Life of Lewis Carroll* offers an interesting analysis of Carroll's peculiar temperament, as refracted through his work. Shorter studies are legion, one of the best being Edmund Wilson's "C. L. Dodgson: The Poet-Logician" in his *The Shores of Light*. Highly amusing and instructive is *The Annotated Alice*, edited by Martin Gardner. For an interesting collection of mainly modern viewpoints, some profound, some mildly lunatic, see Robert Phillips, ed., *Aspects of Alice*.

92. **MARK TWAIN**—*Huckleberry Finn* is available in many editions. A good one, ed. by Lionel Trilling, is the Holt, Rinehart issue. Perennial has *Great Short Works*, and there are many editions of *Life on the Mississippi*—well worth reading. The Library of America publishes the complete novels in three volumes, and *Collected Tales, Sketches, Speeches & Essays* in two volumes. Oxford U. Press publishes the *Complete Works* in 29 volumes.

Further reading: The (highly) official biography is Albert B. Paine, *Mark Twain, A Biography: The Personal and Literary Life of Samuel Langhorne Clemens* (3 vols.). Two quite different interpretations: Van Wyck Brooks, *The Ordeal of Mark Twain*; Bernard De Voto, *Mark Twain's America*. See also: H.N. Smith, *Mark Twain: The Development of a Writer*; Charles Neider's remarkable edition of *The Autobiography of Mark Twain*; Justin Kaplan, *Mister Clemens and Mark Twain*; Walter Blair, *Mark Twain and Huck Finn*; Andrew Jay Hoffman, *Inventing Mark Twain*.

93. **HENRY ADAMS**—Riverside has a fine edition of *The Education*; also Houghton Mifflin (Sentry edition). Penguin offers *Mont-Saint-Michel and Chartres* in paperback. The Library of America has *The Education* and *Mont-Saint-Michel* together with Adams's complete novels in a single volume.

Further reading: The letters are important, if you find yourself interested in Adams. Worthington Chauncey Ford has edited three volumes of them: A *Cycle of Adams Letters, 1861–1865; Letters of Henry Adams 1858–1891; Letters of Henry Adams 1892–1918*. The definitive biography (a fine one) is Ernest Samuels's three-volume life: *The Young Henry Adams; Henry Adams: The Middle Years; Henry Adams: The Major Phase*. Other admirable studies: J.C. Levenson, *The Mind and Art of Henry Adams*; Elizabeth Stevenson, *Henry Adams: A Biography*; R.A.

Hume, *Runaway Star: An Appreciation of Henry Adams*; William
Dusinberre, *Henry Adams: The Myth of Failure.*

94. **THOMAS HARDY**—Various editions of the most famous novels—
*Mayor of Casterbridge, Jude the Obscure, Return of the Native,
Tess of the D'Urbervilles*—are widely available. *Complete Poems:*
Macmillan. *The Dynasts* (3 vols. hardbound; St. Martin's); *Wessex
Tales* (St. Martin's).

Further reading: The official life is by Florence E. Hardy, now
in one volume: *The Early Life of Hardy, 1840–1891* and *The Later
Years; 1892–1928.* Professor Guerard's introduction to *The Mayor
of Casterbridge* is excellent. See also Lord David Cecil, *Hardy, the
Novelist*; Douglas Brown, *Thomas Hardy*; Virginia Woolf's essay in
The Second Common Reader; Robert Gittings, *Young Thomas
Hardy* and *Thomas Hardy's Later Years;* Irving Howe, *Thomas
Hardy.*

95. **WILLIAM JAMES**—Dover publishes *The Principles of Psychology*
(2 vols.); *Pragmatism* is issued by Meridian and Harvard University
Press; *The Varieties of Religious Experience* by Collier and
Mentor. The Library of America's two-volume set contains all of
the major works.

Further reading: The basic account is Ralph Barton Perry's
The Thought and Character of William James (2 vols., Harvard U.
Press), of which there is a good one-volume abridgement
(Braziller). See also: Jacques Barzun, A *Stroll with William James*;
C.H. Grattan, *The Three Jameses*; Gay Wilson Allen, *William
James*; G. Santayana's chapter on James in *Character and Opinion
in the United States*; R.B. Perry, *In the Spirit of William James.*
The Letters of William James have been edited by his son Henry in
two volumes; and his brother, Henry, offers *Notes of a Son and
Brother.* For the family life of William and Henry, see Alfred
Habegger, *The Father: A Life of Henry James Sr.*, and R.W.B.
Lewis, *The James, A Family Narrative.*

96. **HENRY JAMES**—*The Ambassadors*: Many editions; the Riverside is
edited by Leon Edel, the master of James scholarship. Penguin has
a *Portable Henry James.* Perennial offers *Great Short Works.* The
Library of America publishes nearly all of the important novels,
travel writings, criticism, and stories in nine big volumes. If you're
hooked on Henry James, try *The Complete Notebooks of Henry
James,* ed. Leon Edel and Lyall H. Powers (Oxford U. Press). U. of
Nebraska Press is about to begin publishing the *Complete Letters.*

Further reading: One of the great biographies of our time is Leon
Edel's *The Life of Henry James* (5 vols.). For the best commentator
on Henry James, see his own *The Art of the Novel.* Other excellent
studies: F.W. Dupee, *Henry James*; F.O. Matthiessen, *Henry James:
The Major Phase* and *The James Family: A Group Biography*;

Edmund Wilson in *The Triple Thinkers*; Gordon Pirie, *Henry James;* F.R. Leavis, *The Great Tradition*; Fred Kaplan, *Henry James: The Imagination of Genius*. Sheldon M. Novick, in *Henry James: The Young Master*, makes the controversial claim that James was actively homosexual. See also a study of *The Princess Casamassima* in Lionel Trilling's highly recommended *The Liberal Imagination*.

97. **FRIEDRICH WILHELM NIETZSCHE**—*Thus Spake Zarathustra* is in Penguin, and you may find other editions. *Beyond Good and Evil:* Gateway, Penguin, Random. *The Birth of Tragedy* (with *The Genealogy of Morals):* Anchor. Penguin has a *Portable Nietzsche* and also a *Nietzsche Reader.*

Further reading: Walter Kaufmann's *Nietzsche: Philosopher Psychologist, Antichrist* is a learned work defending Nietzsche against the kind of charges made by such critics as Bertrand Russell. See also: Ronald Hayman, *Nietzsche: A Critical Life;* Richard Schacht, *Nietzsche;* Karl Jaspers, *Nietzsche;* Janko Lavrin, *Nietzsche: A Biographical Introduction; Nietzsche Reader;* Alexander Nehamas, *Nietzsche: Life as Literature;* Robert C. Holub, *Friedrich Nietzsche;* Heinz F. Peters, *Zarathustra's Sister: The Case of Elizabeth and Friedrich Nietzsche.*

98. **SIGMUND FREUD**—The Freud bibliography, for he was a prolific writer, is a bit intimidating. Some important works are available only hardbound; Norton publishes the multivolume *Standard Edition* of the complete works. Here are some recommended paperbacks: *General Selection from the Works of Sigmund Freud* (Anchor); *Civilization and Its Discontents* (Norton); *General Psychological Theory* (Collier); *Interpretation of Dreams* (Avon); *New Introductory Lectures on Psychoanalysis* (Norton); *Psychopathology of Everyday Life* (Norton, Mentor); *Three Essays on the Theory of Sexuality* (Dutton).

Further reading: The standard biography, a classic, is Ernest Jones's *Life and Works of Sigmund Freud* (3 vols.). Basic Books also has this in an abridged edition edited by Lionel Trilling and Steven Marcus. In *An Autobiographical Study* Freud himself offers a brief account. See also: Peter Gay, *Freud: A Life for Our Time;* Philip Rieff, *Freud: The Mind of the Moralist;* Ralph Steadman, *Sigmund Freud;* Lionel Trilling, *Freud and the Crisis of Our Time;* R.W. Clark, *Freud: The Man and the Cause.* A trenchant critique of the Freudian position is Jeffrey Masson, *Final Analysis: The Making and Unmaking of a Psychoanalyst.*

99. **GEORGE BERNARD SHAW**—*Bernard Shaw's Plays* (Norton), *Four Plays by Shaw* (Dell), and *Plays Unpleasant* (Penguin) will collectively provide you with eleven of the best plays. In separate volumes Penguin offers *Androcles, The Apple Cart, Arms and the Man, Caesar and Cleopatra, Candida, The Devil's Disciple,*

Heartbreak House, Major Barbara, Man and Superman, The Millionairess, Pygmalion, Saint Joan, and *Selected One-Act Plays.* Oxford offers *Back to Methusaleh* in hardcover, as Hill and Wang does for *The Quintessence of Ibsenism.* There are many other easily procurable editions.

Further reading: For an interesting collection of essays by various hands try Louis Kronenberger, ed., *G.B. Shaw: A Critical Survey.* Other perspectives: Eric Bentley's *Bernard Shaw*; G.K. Chesterton's *George Bernard Shaw*; and Hesketh Pearson, *George Bernard Shaw: His Life and Personality.* See also: Michael Holroyd, *The Genius of Shaw*; J.F. Matthews, *George Bernard Shaw.*

100. **JOSEPH CONRAD**—*Nostromo*: Signet, Penguin, Everyman, and Modern Library offer good editions. Many critics rate *Lord Jim* above *Nostromo.* It's available in Penguin, Airmont, Riverside, and other editions. Try also *The Secret Agent* (Anchor); *Heart of Darkness* (with *The Secret Sharer*) (Signet); *Nigger of the Narcissus, Typhoon, and Other Stories* (Penguin).

Further reading: Two standard lives are Jocelyn Baines's *Joseph Conrad: A Critical Biography*; and F.R. Karl's *Joseph Conrad. The Three Lives.* See also: B.C. Meyer, *Joseph Conrad: A Psychoanalytical Biography*; Leo Gurko, *Joseph Conrad: Giant in Exile*; Zdzislaw Najder, *Joseph Conrad: A Chronicle*; G. Jean-Aubry, *Sea-Dreamer, A Definitive Biography of Joseph Conrad*; A.J. Guérard, *Conrad the Novelist*; F.R. Leavis, *The Great Tradition*; E.M. Forster, "Joseph Conrad: A Note" in *Abinger Harvest.*

101. **ANTON CHEKHOV**—The handiest edition of the complete plays is in the Penguin Classics series, translated and introduced by Elisaveta Fen. Another good paperback is *Plays and Letters, 1884–1904* (Norton). His short stories have appeared in a bewildering profusion of editions. See representative volumes: *Anton Chekhov: Selected Stories,* tr. Ann Dunnigan (Signet Classics); *Ward Six and Other Stories,* tr. Ann Dunnigan (Signet Classics); *Peasants and Other Stories,* selected and with a preface by Edmund Wilson (Doubleday Anchor). Ecco Press has issued in paperback twelve volumes of *The Tales of Anton Chekhov,* using the classic version by Constance Garnett.

Further reading: Good biographies are David Magarshack, *Chekhov: A Life;* Ernest J. Simmons, *Chekhov: A Biography;* Ronald A. Hingley, *A New Life of Anton Chekhov;* Henri Troyat, *Chekhov,* which is both recent and highly readable. See also M.J. Valency, *The Breaking String.*

102. **EDITH WHARTON**—All of her major novels are in print from Scribner's; there are also Penguin editions of most. The Library of America's volume of selected novels includes the three that we

recommend, plus *The Reef*. See also *The Collected Short Stories of Edith Wharton*, ed. R.W.B. Lewis (Scribner's), and *Edith Wharton Novellas and Other Writings*, ed. Cynthia Griffin Wolff (Library of America).

Further reading: The standard life is R.W.B. Lewis, *Edith Wharton: A Biography*. See also Millicent Bell, *Edith Wharton and Henry James*, and the same author's *The Cambridge Companion to Edith Wharton*; Louis Auchincloss, *Edith Wharton: A Woman in Her Time*; Gloria Erlich, *The Sexual Education of Edith Wharton*; Katharine Joslin, *Edith Wharton*; Cynthia Griffin Wolff, *A Feast of Words: The Triumph of Edith Wharton*; and a pictorial biography by Eleanor Dwight, *Edith Wharton: An Extraordinary Life*.

103. **WILLIAM BUTLER YEATS**—The best edition (hardbound): *The Poems of W.B. Yeats*, ed. Richard Finneran (Macmillan). Through Collier, Macmillan also issues *Eleven Plays, The Autobiography*, and *Essays and Introductions. Last Poems* (Aurora); *Selected Poems* (Macmillan).

Further reading: A standard biography is J.M. Hone's *William Butler Yeats (1865–1939)*. See also: T.R. Henn, *The Lonely Tower*; Richard Ellmann, *Yeats: The Man and the Masks*; Douglas Archibald, *Yeats*; Denis Donoghue, *Yeats*; Harold Bloom, *Yeats* and R.F. Foster, *W.B. Yeats: A Life*; essays on Yeats in Arland Ussher's *Three Great Irishmen*; Edmund Wilson, *Axel's Castle*; T.S. Eliot's essay in *On Poetry and Poets*; Keith Alldritt, *W.B. Yeats: Man and Milieu*.

104. **NATSUME SOSEKI**—*Kokoro*, tr. Edwin McClellan (Regnery); *Botchan*, tr. Umeji Sasaki (Charles E. Tuttle).

Further reading: Takeo Doi, *The Psychological World of Natsume Soseki*; Edwin McClellan, *Two Japanese Novelists: Soseki and Toson*; Beongcheon Yu, *Natsume Soseki*; Van C. Gessel, *Three Modern Novelists: Soseki, Tanizaki, Kawabata*.

105. **MARCEL PROUST**—The complete "definite Pléiade edition" of *Remembrance of Things Past*, tr. C.K Scott-Moncrieff, Terence Kilmartin, and Andreas Mayor, is published by Random House in three volumes. The seven parts are also available separately.

Further reading: An excellent brief biography is André Maurois's *Proust*. Another is Richard H. Barker's *Marcel Proust*. George D. Painter's *Marcel Proust* (2 vols.) is a detailed, comprehensive, well-researched classic biography. For a brief but masterly appreciation, see Edmund Wilson's *Axel's Castle*. See also: Germaine Brée, *Marcel Proust and Deliverance from Time*; and the same author's *The World of Marcel Proust*; Roger Shattuck, *Proust's Binoculars: A Study of Memory, Time, and Recognition in A la récherche du temps perdu*; Samuel Beckett, *Proust*; Julia

Kristeva, *Time and Sense: Proust and the Experience of Literature*, difficult but full of penetrating insights.

106. **ROBERT FROST**—Holt, Rinehart publishes *Collected Poems* in hardback and *Selected Poems* in paperback. Washington Square Press has Untermeyer's edition, the *New Enlarged Anthology of Robert Frost's Poems*. You may come upon other paperback editions. The Library of America has a one-volume *Collected Poems, Prose & Plays*.

　　Further reading: Lawrence Thompson's *Robert Frost* (3 vols.) is official but not reverent. Qualifying Thompson's interpretation of Frost's character is W.H. Pritchard's *Frost: A Literary Life Reconsidered*. See also: E.S. Sergeant, *Robert Frost: The Trial by Existence;* Sidney Cox, *A Swinger of Birches: A Portrait of Robert Frost;* R.L. Cook, *The Dimensions of Robert Frost;* R.A. Brower, *The Poetry of Robert Frost;* Richard Poirier, *Robert Frost: The Work of Knowing*.

107. **THOMAS MANN**—Modern Library and Vintage offer *The Magic Mountain* in the standard translation by H.T. Lowe-Poreter. Knopf has a new translation by John E. Woods. Vintage also has *Buddenbrooks* and *Doctor Faustus*, both well worth reading, as is *Death in Venice and Seven Other Stories* (Vintage).

　　Further reading: Hans Buergin and Hans-Otto Mayer, *Thomas Mann: A Chronicle of His Life;* Richard Winston, *Thomas Mann: The Making of an Artist, 1875–1911*. The reader may find useful commentary in *The Stature of Thomas Mann*, ed. by Charles Neider; J.G. Brennan's *Thomas Mann's World;* Clifton Fadiman, *Reading I've Liked*.

108. **E.M. FORSTER**—*A Passage to India*: Harvest. *Howards End, The Longest Journey, A Room with a View,* and *Where Angels Fear to Tread* are all in Vintage. The interesting *Aspects of the Novel* is in Harvest. His memoir of youthful employment as a secretary in India, *The Hill of Devi*, is out of print and hard to find, but worth looking for.

　　Further reading: Lionel Trilling's *E.M. Forster* is the best study. The authorized biography is by P.N. Furbank. See also: Rose Macaulay, *The Writings of E.M. Forster;* Virginia Woolf, *The Death of the Moth and Other Essays;* F.C. Crews, *E.M. Forster: The Perils of Humanism;* Wilfred Stone, *The Cave and the Mountain*.

109. **LU HSÜN**—There are many translations; three good editions are William Lyell, tr., *Diary of a Madman and Other Stories* (U. Hawaii Press); *Ah Q and Others: Selected Stories of Lu Hsün*, tr. by Chi-chen Wang (Greenwood); and Yang Hsien-yi and Gladys Yang, tr., *Lu Xun: Selected Works* (Foreign Languages Press, Beijing).

Further reading: Leo Ou-fan Lee, *Voices from the Iron House: A Study of Lu Xun*; William Lyell, *Lu Hsün's Vision of Reality*.

110. **JAMES JOYCE**—The *Ulysses* to own is the Vintage "corrected text" edition. If you're determined to try the difficult *Finnegans Wake,* it's in Penguin, which also publishes *The Portable James Joyce, Portrait of the Artist as a Young Man*, and *Dubliners.*

Further reading: The definitive biography is Richard Ellmann's *James Joyce*. Excellent general studies: Harry Levin, *James Joyce: A Critical Introduction*; W.Y. Tindall, A *Reader's Guide to James Joyce*; Anthony Burgess, *Re Joyce*. Edmund Wilson's brilliant estimate is in his *Axel's Castle*. A good recent study is John Bishop, *Joyce's Book of the Dead.* On *Ulysses* see Stuart Gilbert, *James Joyce's Ulysses*; H. Blamires, *The Bloomsday Book*; Frank Budgen, *James Joyce and the Making of Ulysses*; Hugh Kenner, *Ulysses*. If you attempt *Finnegans Wake,* take along Campbell and Robinson, A *Skeleton Key to Finnegans Wake.*

111. **VIRGINIA WOOLF**—All four recommended titles as well as *The Common Reader, First Series* are in Harvest. Several volumes of the *Essays* and the *Letters* are published by Harcourt.

Further reading: Quentin Bell, *Virginia Woolf* (2 vols.) is the fullest biography. See also P. Rose, *Woman of Letters: A Life of Virginia Woolf* and Hermione Lee, *Virginia Woolf.* There is a large and increasing corpus of literature about Virginia Woolf and the Bloomsbury group of which she was the center. In connection with the latter, see Michael Holroyd's life of Lytton Strachey (2 vols.); Leon Edel, *Bloomsbury: A House of Lions*.

112. **FRANZ KAFKA**—Modern Library and Vintage offer *The Castle*; Schocken has a "definitive edition" with commentary by Thomas Mann. Vintage has *The Trial;* Schocken publishes a "definitive edition" with Kafka's own drawings. Schocken also has the *Complete Stories.*

Further reading: The Kafka literature is approaching industrial proportions. For biographies, see Max Brod, *Franz Kafka: A Biography*; Ronald Hayman, *Kafka: A Biography*; Ernst Pawel, *The Nightmare of Reason*, a remarkable book. Critical studies: Erich Heller, *Franz Kafka*; Heinz Politzer, *Franz Kafka: Parable and Paradox*; Ronald D. Gray, ed., *Kafka: A Collection of Critical Essays*; Angel Flores, ed., *The Kafka Problem*.

113. **D.H. LAWRENCE**—*Sons and Lovers* and *Women in Love* are in Penguin, as are *The Rainbow, Complete Poems*, and *Complete Short Stories* (3 vols.). The once shocking *Lady Chatterly's Lover:* Grove, Signet, Bantam. Viking publishes the *Portable D.H. Lawrence,* ed. Diana Trilling.

Further reading: *D.H. Lawrence: A Composite Biography*, ed. Edward Nehis; H.T. Moore, *The Intelligent Heart*; Keith Sagar, *The*

Life of D. H. Lawrence; George J. Becker, *D.H. Lawrence;* Richard Aidington, *Portrait of a Genius, But. . .* ; John Worthen, *D.H. Lawrence. Vol. I: The Early Years;* and an illuminating study of Lawrence's wife: Janet Byrne, *A Genius for Living: The Life of Frieda Lawrence.* Critical studies: F.R. Leavis, *D.H. Lawrence, Novelist;* Aldous Huxley, *Collected Essays;* Graham Hough, *The Dark Sun: D.H. Lawrence: A Centenary Celebration,* ed. Peter Balbert and P.L. Marcus. Lawrence's *Letters* have been edited by both Aldous Huxley and (in two volumes) by H.T. Moore. See also Frieda Lawrence, *Not I But the Wind and Other Autobiographical Writings,* ed. Rosemary Jackson.

114. **TANIZAKI JUNICHIRO**—Edward Seidensticker has had a virtual monopoly on Tanizaki translations; *The Makioka Sisters, Some Prefer Nettles,* and several others (all Knopf).

Further reading: Donald Keene, *Dawn to the West: Japanese Literature of the Modern Era* (2 vols.); Ken K. Ito, *Visions of Desire: Tanizaki's Fictional Worlds;* Van C. Gessel, *Three Modern Novelists: Soseki, Tanizaki, Kawabata;* Gwenn Boardman Peterson, *The Moon in the Water: Understanding Tanizaki, Kawabata, and Mishima;* also two autobiographical/critical works by Tanizaki himself, *Childhood Years* and *In Praise of Shadows.*

115. **EUGENE O'NEILL**—Vintage has *Three Plays* (*Mourning Becomes Electra, Desire Under the Elms, Strange Interlude*); Vintage has *The Iceman Cometh;* and Yale University Press has *Long Day's Journey into Night.* For other O'Neill plays, see *Six Short Plays of Eugene O'Neill* (Vintage); *Seven Plays of the Sea* (Vintage); *Anna Christie* (bound with *The Emperor Jones* and *The Hairy Ape* [Vintage]); *Touch of the Poet* (Yale U. Press); *More Stately Mansions* (Yale U. Press). The Library of America has the *Complete Plays* (3 vols.).

Further reading: The standard biography is Arthur and Barbara Gelb, *O'Neill.* See also Barrett H. Clark, *Eugene O'Neill: The Man and His Plays* rev. ed.; Doris Alexander, *The Tempering of Eugene O'Neill;* F.I. Carpenter, *Eugene O'Neill.*

116. **T.S. ELIOT**—Harcourt issues hardbound volumes of the *Collected Poems* and *Collected Plays.* Some useful paperbacks: *The Waste Land and Other Poems* (Harcourt); *Four Quartets* (Harvest); *The Sacred Wood* (Methuen). Harvest also has Eliot's plays in separate volumes.

Further reading: A good biography is Peter Ackroyd's *T.S. Eliot: A Life.* See also: F.O. Matthiessen, *The Achievement of T.S. Eliot;* George Williamson, *A Reader's Guide to T.S. Eliot;* Hugh Kenner, *The Invisible Poet: T.S. Eliot;* Helen Gardner, *The Art of T.S. Eliot;* essay on Eliot in Edmund Wilson's *Axel's Castle;* Elizabeth Drew, *T.S. Eliot: The Design of His Poetry;* E. Martin

Browne, *The Making of T.S. Eliot's Plays*. A good essay collection is Allen Tate, ed., *T.S. Eliot: The Man and His Work*. A sympathetic interpretation of Eliot as conservative is Russell Kirk's excellent *Eliot and His Age*.

117. **ALDOUS HUXLEY**—Perennial Library (HarperCollins) issues *Brave New World* separately and also bound with *Brave New World Revisited*. The same imprint also at one time published many of Huxley's other novels, such as *After Many a Summer Dies the Swan, Antic Hay, Crome Yellow, Point Counter Point, Eyeless in Gaza*, as well as *Great Short Works*. Consult your bookseller or library for collections of his essays.

    Further reading: For the formidable Huxley family, see Ronald W. Clark, *The Huxleys*. Biographies: Sybille Bedford, *Aldous Huxley: A Biography*, (2 vols.); Jocelyn Brooke, *Aldous Huxley*. A good academic study: Robert S. Baker, *The Dark Historic Pages: Social Satire and Historicism in the Novels of Aldous Huxley, 1921–1939*.

118. **WILLIAM FAULKNER**—*The Sound and the Fury:* Vintage and Modern Library. *As I Lay Dying:* Vintage. Viking has *The Portable Faulkner*, splendidly edited by Malcolm Cowley. Vintage issues *Collected Stories. Absalom, Absalom!:* Penguin, Vintage. The Library of America's three-volume set includes all of the major novels.

    Further reading: The authorized life is J. L. Blotner's *William Faulkner: A Biography* (2 vols.). Faulkner may end by having more commentators than readers. Here are a few excellent studies: Michael Millgate, *The Achievement of William Faulkner*; Cleanth Brooks's three-volume work: *William Faulkner: First Encounters*; *William Faulkner: The Yoknapatawpha Country* and *William Faulkner: Toward Yoknapatawpha and Beyond*; F.J. Hoffman, *William Faulkner*; Irving Howe, *William Faulkner: A Critical Study*. Perhaps the finest short estimate remains Malcolm Cowley's classic introduction to *The Portable Faulkner*.

119. **ERNEST HEMINGWAY**—All of Hemingway is published by Scribner's; they offer an omnibus *Short Stories* and also a *Hemingway Reader*. The recent *Complete Stories of Ernest Hemingway* (the so-called Finca Vigia edition) includes stories previously uncollected and is the one to read.

    Further reading: The standard biography is Carlos Baker's *Ernest Hemingway: A Life Story*. See also: Philip Young, *Ernest Hemingway: A Reconsideration*; Carlos Baker, *Hemingway: The Writer as Artist*; Scott Donaldson, *By Force of Will;* Peter Griffin, *Along with Youth: Hemingway, The Early Years*; Jeffrey Meyer, *Hemingway*; Michael Reynolds. *The Young Hemingway* and *Hemingway: The 1930s*; K.S. Lynn, *Hemingway: The Life and Work*. This last stresses his early years, and treats Hemingway's darker side. For other insights, see Alfred Kazin, *On Native Grounds*; F.J. Hoffman, *The Modern Novel in America*; Edmund Wilson's essay in *Eight Essays*; Denis Brian, *The True Gen: An Intimate Portrait of Hemingway by Those Who Knew Him*.

120. **KAWABATA YASUNARI**—*Beauty and Sadness, Snow Country, The House of the Sleeping Beauties, A Thousand Cranes, The Master of Gō*, and other works, mostly translated by Edward Seidensticker, are available from Knopf.

Further reading: Kawabata reflects on his own work in his Nobel Prize acceptance speech, *Japan, The Beautiful, and Myself*, tr. by Edward Seidensticker. See also Van C. Gessel, *Three Modern Novelists: Soseki, Tanizaki, Kawabata*; Gwenn Boardman Peterson's essay in *The Moon in the Water: Understanding Tanizaki, Kawabata, and Mishima*.

121. **JORGE LUIS BORGES**—*Labyrinths*: New Directions; *Dreamtigers*: U. of Texas Press. Dutton issues *The Aleph & Other Stories, The Book of Imaginary Beings*, and *The Book of Sand*. Evergreen has *A Personal Anthology*. The University of Texas Press offers *Other Inquisitions*. For his poetry, see *Jorge Luis Borges: Selected Poems*, tr. Di Giovanni (Dell).

Ana Maria Barrenechea, *Borges: The Labyrinth Maker*; Ronald Christ, *The Narrow Act: Borges' Art of Illusion*; Emir Rodriguez Monegal, *Jorge Luis Borges: A Literary Biography*; G.H. Bell-Villada, *Borges and His Fiction: A Guide to His Mind and Art*; M.S. Stabb, *Jorge Luis Borges*.

122. **VLADIMIR NABOKOV**—*Lolita* is in Medallion Books, and you may find it in the Capricorn series. McGraw-Hill has an annotated *Lolita*. Medallion Books offers *Pale Fire*. *Speak, Memory* is published by Pyramid. Penguin issues a useful *Portable Nabokov*. The Library of America has the major prose works in three volumes.

Further reading: Two interesting works by Andrew Field supplement each other: *Nabokov: His Life in Art* and *Nabokov: His Life in Part*. See also: Peter Quennell, ed., *Nabokov: A Tribute*; D.E. Morton, *Vladimir Nabokov*; J. Moynihan, *Vladimir Nabokov*.

123. **GEORGE ORWELL**—*Animal Farm* and *Nineteen Eighty-Four* are both in New American Library, among others. *Burmese Days* is published by Harvest, which also offers five volumes of his *Collected Essays, Journalism & Letters*, as well as an *Orwell Reader* with an introduction by R.H. Rovere.

Further reading: A good authorized biography is Bernard Crick's *George Orwell: A Life*. Perhaps the most penetrating short study is Lionel Trilling's "George Orwell and the Politics of Truth," in his *The Opposing Self: Nine Essays in Criticism*. An excellent two-volume treatment is by Peter Stansky and William Abrahams: *The Unknown Orwell* and *Orwell: The Transformation*. Various points of view are represented in *George Orwell: A Collection of Critical Essays*, ed. Raymond Williams.

124. **R.K. NARAYAN**—*The English Teacher* is published by U. Chicago Press. Most of his other Malgudi novels and stories are available singly in Penguin.

Further reading: Narayan's autobiography, *My Days*; and his essays, *Critical Perspectives*, ed. A. L. McLeod. See also Mary Beatina, *Narayan: A Study in Transcendence*.

125. **SAMUEL BECKETT**—Grove publishes all of Beckett. His *Collected Works* so far extend to more than twenty-five volumes, which include of course the three recommended plays. *Endgame* also includes *Act Without Words,* and *Krapp's Last Tape* includes four shorter plays and "mimes." Three of Beckett's best-known novels (*Molloy, Malone Dies, The Unnamable)* are assembled in one volume.

Further reading: The recent authorized biography by James Knowlson, *Damned to Fame: The Life of Samuel Beckett* contains a great deal of genuinely new material. See also: *On Beckett: Essays and Criticism*, edited and introduced by S.E. Gontarski; Hugh Kenner, *Samuel Beckett. A Critical Study*; Charles Lyons, *Samuel Beckett*; J. Fletcher and J. Spurling, *Beckett: A Study of His Plays*; Vivian Mercier, *Beckett/Beckett*. For a more general approach, see Martin Esslin's excellent *The Theatre of the Absurd*.

126. **W.H. AUDEN**—The *Complete Poetry* is published by Random House, which also has a *Selected Poems*. See also Auden's *Forewords and Afterwords* from Random; Edward Mendelson, ed., *The English Auden: Poems, Essays, and Dramatic Writings, 1927–39* (Faber and Faber).

Further reading: A.L. Rowse, *The Poet Auden: A Personal Memoir*; Humphrey Carpenter, *W.H. Auden: A Biography*; Richard Davenport-Hines, *Auden*; Anthony Hecht, *The Hidden Law: The Poetry of W.H. Auden*.

127. **ALBERT CAMUS**—*The Plague* is in Modern Library and Vintage; *The Stranger* in Vintage. Other Camus titles of interest: *The Fall, The Rebel, Exile and the Kingdom* (all Vintage); and *The First Man*, the manuscript of which was in Camus's car when he died, now newly published by Random House.

Further reading: Herbert Lottman, *Albert Camus: A Biography*; Germaine Brée, *Camus*; Philip Thody, *Albert Camus 1913–1960*; Adele King, *Camus*; P.H. Rhein, *Albert Camus;* R. Quilliot, *The Sea and Prisons;* Patrick McCarthy, *Camus: A Critical Study of His Life and Work*; Oliver Todd, *Albert Camus: A Life*.

128. **SAUL BELLOW**—*Adventures of Augie March*: Avon. *Herzog*: Avon, Penguin. *Humboldt's Gift*: Avon. *Portable Saul Bellow*: Penguin. *More Die of Heartbreak*: Morrow (hardbound).

Further reading: J.J. Clayton, *Saul Bellow: In Defense of Man*; Malcolm Bradbury, *Saul Bellow*; Earl Rovit, *Saul Bellow*; Earl Rovit, ed., *Saul Bellow: A Collection of Critical Essays*.

129. **ALEKSANDER ISAYEVICH SOLZHENITSYN**—*The First Circle* (Bantam); *Cancer Ward* (Bantam, Dell); *Gulag Archipelago* (3 vols., Harper & Row); *One Day in the Life of Ivan Denisovich* (Signet).

Further reading: Hans Björkgren, *Aleksandr Solzhenitsyn: A Biography*, tr. Kaa Eneberg; John B. Dunlop et al., *Aleksandr Solzhenitsyn: Critical Essays and Documentary Materials*; Györgi Lukács, *Solzhenitsyn*, tr. William D. Graf; Abraham Rothberg, *Aleksandr Solzhenitsyn: The Major Novels*; Michael Scammell, *Solzhenitsyn*; *Solzhenitsyn: A Pictorial Autobiography*; D. Burg and G. Feifer, *Solzhenitsyn*.

130. **THOMAS KUHN**—*The Structure of Scientific Revolutions* (U. Chicago Press).

Further reading: Howard Margolis, *Paradigms and Barriers: How Habits of Mind Govern Scientific Belief*; Barry Barnes, *Thomas Kuhn and Social Science*; Paul Harwich, ed., *World Changes: Thomas Kuhn and the Nature of Science*; Paul Hoyningan-Huene, *Reconstructing Scientific Revolutions: Thomas S. Kuhn's Philosophy of Science*.

131. **MISHIMA YUKIO**—*The Temple of the Golden Pavilion*, tr. Ivan Morris; *The Sailor Who Fell from Grace with the Sea* and *The Sea of Fertility*, tr. John Nathan; *Confessions of a Mask*, tr. Meredith Weatherby; all published by Knopf, with various paperback reprints.

Further reading: Henry Scott-Stokes, *The Life and Death of Yukio Mishima*; John Nathan, *Mishima: A Biography*; Henry Miller, *Reflections on the Death of Mishima*; Marguerite Yourcenar, *Mishima: A Vision of the Void*; Gwenn Boardman Peterson, *The Moon in the Water: Understanding Tanizaki, Kawabata, and Mishima*.

132. **GABRIEL GARCIA MARQUEZ**—*One Hundred Years of Solitude* is in Avon. HarperCollins offers three volumes of his short stories: *Innocent Indira and Other Stories; Leaf Storm and Other Stories; No One Writes to the Colonel and Other Stories*. An interesting recent novel is *Love in the Time of Cholera* (Knopf).

Further reading: G.H. McMurray, *Gabriel Garcia Marquez*.

133. **CHINUA ACHEBE**—*Things Fall Apart* from Doubleday and Heinemann; *A Man of the People*, *No Longer at Ease*, and *Hopes and Impediments: Selected Essays* all from Doubleday.

Further reading: Catherine L. Innes, *Chinua Achebe* ; Robert M. Wren, *Achebe's World: The Historical and Cultural Context of the Novels of Chinua Achebe*; R.O. Muoneke, *Art, Rebellion, and Redemption: A Reading of the Novels of Chinua Achebe*.

Some Important General Works

Fiction: Though hardly new, perhaps the most penetrating studies of the novel still remain: E.M. Forster's *Aspects of the Novel*; Henry James's *The Art of Fiction and Other Essays* and *The Art of the Novel*; Percy Lubbock's *The Craft of Fiction*.

For a good general survey of English fiction see Walter Allen, *The English Novel*; also I.P. Watt, *The Rise of the Novel*. F.R. Leavis's influential *The Great Tradition* has long chapters on George Eliot, Henry James, and Joseph Conrad, as well as a general discussion of English fiction. For Dickens, Thackeray, the Brontës, and George Eliot, see David Cecil's *Victorian Novelists*.

Poetry: There are dozens of good general anthologies of English and American verse. The anthology edited by W.H. Auden and Norman Holmes Pearson, *Poets of the English Language* (5 vols., paperback) seems as good as any, but you may also wish to consult Richard Aldington, ed., *The Viking Book of Poetry of the English Speaking World* (2 vols.); *The Oxford Book of English Verse*; J.F. Nims, *The Harper Anthology of Poetry* and the Library of America's *American Poetry: The Nineteenth Century* (2 vols.). Louis Untermeyer's *Lives of the Poets* is a good, readable compendium of biography plus critical summary. It deals with English and American poets from Beowulf to Dylan Thomas.

Obviously the bulk of the world's great poetry is in languages other than English. See D. Weissbort and Ted Hughes, eds., *Modern Poetry in Translation*. If you can search out a copy of Mark Van Doren's out-of-print *An Anthology of World Poetry*, you will find it worthwhile. Hubert Creekmore's *A Little Treasury of World Poetry*, though built on a smaller scale, is also good. Both of these are now rendered obsolete by our own *World Poetry: An Anthology of Verse from Antiquity to Our Time*, edited by Katharine Washburn and John S. Major under the general editorship of Clifton Fadiman.

For modern poetry in English: Richard Ellmann and Robert O'Clair, eds., *The Norton Anthology of Modern Poetry* is an entirely serviceable collection of modern verse. But others may do as well. A first-rate collection is *Modern Verse in English, 1900–1950*, ed. David Cecil and Allen Tate. It contains splendid introductions by the distinguished editors. A few inexpensive small anthologies of modern verse: *New Poets of England and America*, ed. Hall, Pack, and Simpson; *The Pocket Book of Modern Verse*, ed. Oscar Williams; *100 Modern Poets*, ed. Selden Rodman; *Faber Book of 20th Century Verse*, ed. Heath-Stubbs and Wright. For a comprehensive history of British and American poetry, see *A History of Modern Poetry*, ed. David Perkins.

For translations from the Greek: Dudley Fitts, *Poems from the Greek Anthology*; Higham and Bowra, *The Oxford Book of Greek Verse in Translation*; *Greek Lyrics*, tr. Richmond Lattimore; *Poems from the*

Greek Anthology, tr. Kenneth Rexroth; Constantine A. Trypanis, ed., *The Penguin Book of Greek Verse.*

From the Latin: L.R. Lind, *Latin Poetry in Verse Translation.* A delightful book on the Latin poets, containing some superb translations, is Gilbert Highet's *Poets in a Landscape.*

From the Middle Ages (fourteen languages): Hubert Creekmore's *Lyrics of the Middle Ages.*

From the French: Broome and Chesters, eds., *Anthology of Modern French Poetry*; B. Woledge et al., eds., *The Penguin Book of French Verse*; C.F. MacIntyre, *French Symbolist Poetry*; Wallace Fowlie, *Mid-Century French Poets*; Angel Flores, An *Anthology of French Poetry from Nerval to Valéry in English Translation.*

From the Spanish: J.A. Crow, ed., *Anthology of Spanish Poetry from the Beginnings to the Present Day, Including Both Spain and Spanish America*; J.M. Cohen, ed., *The Penguin Book of Spanish Verse.*

From the Italian: George Kay, ed., *The Penguin Book of Italian Verse.*

From the German: Angel Flores, ed., An *Anthology of German Poetry from Hölderlin to Rilke; The Penguin Book of German Verse*, ed. Leonard Forster; *Anthology of German Poetry through the 19th Century*, ed. Gode and Ungar.

From the Irish: *Penguin Book of Irish Verse*, ed. Brendan Kennelly; *Kings, Lords, and Commoners*, ed. and tr. by Frank O'Connor.

From the Russian: *New Russian Poets*, ed. and tr. by George Reavey.

From the Arabic: *Modern Poetry of the Arab World*, ed. and tr. by Abdullah al-Udhari.

From the Chinese: Burton Watson, *The Columbia Book of Chinese Poetry*, and Jonathan Chaves, *The Columbia Book of Later Chinese Poetry*; Victor Mair, ed., *The Columbia Anthology of Traditional Chinese Literature*; Stephen Owen, *An Anthology of Chinese Literature*; Wu-chi Liu and Irving Lo, eds., *Sunflower Splendor: Three Thousand Years of Chinese Poetry.*

From the Japanese: Stephen D. Carter, *Traditional Japanese Poetry*; Hiroaki Sato and Burton Watson, *From the Country of Eight Islands*; Donald Keene, *An Anthology of Japanese Literature.*

From Indian languages: A.K. Ramanujan et al., eds., *The Oxford Book of Modern Indian Poetry.*

From African languages: Gerald Moore and Ulli Beier, eds., *The Penguin Book of Modern African Poetry*; Stella and Frank Chipasula, eds., *The Heinemann Book of African Women's Poetry.*

Caribbean Poetry: Paula Burnett, ed., *The Penguin Book of Caribbean Verse in English*; Ian McDonald and Stewart Brown, eds., *The Heinemann Book of Caribbean Poetry.*

African-American Poetry: The new *Norton Anthology of African-American Literature*, ed. Henry Lewis Gates *et al.*, includes both poetry and prose.

Native American Poetry: Margot Astrov, ed., *The Winged Serpent*; Paula G. Allen, ed., *Voice of the Turtle: American Indian Literature 1900–1970.*

Poetry from Oral Traditions: Jerome Rothenberg, ed., *Technicians of the Sacred.*

Books *about* poetry are not generally very helpful. There are exceptions. One is Mark Van Doren's *Introduction to Poetry.* This precedes a good general anthology with 135 pages of sharp, intelligible, no-nonsense commentaries on thirty varied examples of first-rate verse. See also the excellent *How Does a Poem Mean* by Ciardi and Williams.

Philosophy: Bertrand Russell's *History of Western Philosophy* covers the entire period from the Greeks to our own day, not always to the satisfaction of academic minds. Will Durant's *Story of Philosophy* remains a highly readable account, particularly strong on the biographical side. Mentor publishes five useful little books: Giorgio De Santillana's *The Age of Adventure* (Renaissance philosophers); Stuart Hampshire's *The Age of Reason* (seventeenth century); Isaiah Berlin's *The Age of Enlightenment* (eighteenth century); Henry D. Aiken's *The Age of Ideology* (nineteenth century); Morton White's *The Age of Analysis* (twentieth century).

INDEX